Kim Il Sung

On Juche in Our Revolution

Volume II

**Dedicated to the Great Leader
President Kim Il Sung
on his 65th Birthday**

**Weekly Guardian Associates, Inc.
New York, N.Y.**

Copyright ©1977 by Guardian Associates, Inc.

Printed in the United States of America by Faculty Press, Inc.,
    Brooklyn, N.Y.

Library of Congress Cataloging in Publication Data

Kim Il Sung, 1912-
On Juche in our Revolution

Selection from the author's writings, speeches and reports,
    1967-1974
Library of Congress catalogue number 77-72756

ISBN 0-917654-32-3 (paperback)
ISBN 0-917654-33-1 (hardcover)

CONTENTS

ON SOME THEORETICAL PROBLEMS OF THE SOCIALIST ECONOMY

ANSWERS TO THE QUESTIONS RAISED BY ALI BALOUT, CORRESPONDENT OF THE LEBANESE NEWSPAPER, *AL ANWAR*

REPORT TO THE FIFTH CONGRESS OF THE WORKERS' PARTY OF KOREA ON THE WORK OF THE CENTRAL COMMITTEE (Excerpt)

ANSWERS TO THE QUESTIONS RAISED BY THE IRAQI
JOURNALISTS' DELEGATION (Excerpt)

ON THE CHARACTER AND TASKS OF THE TRADE UNIONS
IN SOCIALIST SOCIETY

ON THE THOROUGH IMPLEMENTATION OF THE PRIN-
CIPLES OF SOCIALIST PEDAGOGY IN EDUCATION

ON PRESENT POLITICAL AND ECONOMIC POLICIES OF
THE DEMOCRATIC PEOPLE'S REPUBLIC OF KOREA AND
SOME INTERNATIONAL PROBLEMS

ON SOME PROBLEMS OF OUR PARTY'S JUCHE IDEA AND
THE GOVERNMENT OF THE REPUBLIC'S INTERNAL AND
EXTERNAL POLICIES (Excerpt)

*Answers to the Questions Raised by Journalists
of the Japanese Newspaper* Mainichi Shimbun,

TALK WITH THE MANAGING EDITOR OF THE JAPANESE
POLITICO-THEORETICAL MAGAZINE *SEKAI* (Excerpt)

LET US FURTHER STRENGTHEN THE SOCIALIST SYSTEM
OF OUR COUNTRY

*Speech at the First Session of the Fifth Supreme
People's Assembly of the Democratic People's Republic
of Korea,* December 25, 1972

PREFACE

President Kim Il Sung's writings on Juche, based on the experiences of the Korean revolution and the building of socialism in the Democratic People's Republic of Korea (DPRK), are among the most important theoretical contributions to Marxism-Leninism in the modern era.

The idea of Juche, reduced to a few words, means independence in politics, self-reliance in the economy and self-defense against aggression.

Juche, which has guided the Korean people through the struggle against Japanese colonialism and U.S. imperialism and has been the basis of the DPRK's phenomenal development from the ashes of World War 2 and the Korean War, is predicated on the theory that the masses of people are the true makers of history; that the people alone are responsible for their own destiny.

In order for the masses to fulfill their destiny as a nation, President Kim Il Sung has emphasized, a people must have genuinely independent government and practice absolute independence in politics. In this regard, the great leader of the Korean people has said:

"The government that acts under pressure from or instructions of others cannot be called a genuine people's government responsible for the destiny of the people. A country with this sort of government cannot be regarded as an independent, sovereign state. The principle of independence in politics demands complete equality and mutual respect among all nations. It opposes both subjugating others and being subjugated by others. A nation that subjugates others can never be free itself."

In order for a people to practice genuine political independence, it is essential that they achieve economic independence, according to the Juche idea. President Kim Il Sung has said:

"Without self-reliance in the economy, it is impossible to meet the people's growing material demands and materially guarantee them a real role as masters of the state and society. Economic dependence on others cannot guarantee political independence and without independent economic power, it is impossible to carry through the line of self-defense in national defense."

The ability of a people and nation to be able to adequately defend itself is a key element in Juche. "Self-defense in national defense is an essential requirement of an independent and sovereign state," President Kim Il Sung has said. "While there are still imperialist aggressors, the state that has no defense power of its own to protect its sovereignty against the internal and external enemies is, in fact, not a fully independent and sovereign state."

This book, Volume 2 of "On Juche In Our Revolution," is a continuation of President Kim Il Sung's writings on the subject of political independence, economic self-reliance and self-defense covering the period from 1967 to 1974.

During this period, the people of the DPRK led by their vanguard, the Workers' Party commanded by President Kim Il Sung, demonstrated time and again the great vitality of Juche in day-to-day practice. Politically, the DPRK showed that it was a model of principled independence during a time when the world socialist movement was experiencing a number of stresses and strains due to conflicting points of view. Economically, the DPRK assumed its role as an advanced socialist industrial state in the years covered in this volume, despite great difficulties imposed by world imperialism. Militarily, relying strictly on itself and its self-defense capabilities, the DPRK repeatedly stood up to provocations by U.S. imperialism and the puppet fascist regime in south Korea.

Thus, each one of President Kim Il Sung's theoretical articles in this book parallels the actual practical experiences of the Korean people in their struggle for national independence, peace and prosperity and against all forms of imperialism.

Today, having provided an example for the world in achieving political independence, economic self-reliance and defense preparedness, the peaceful reunification of all Korea remains one of the most important tasks for the Korean people in line with the Juche idea. While struggling to further enhance the development of the north, the DPRK is devoted to creating the conditions necessary for both halves of the Korean peninsula to reunite once again. Such conditions include the removal of all foreign troops from south Korea and the establishment of a single confederated republic eventually leading toward a fully integrated state of all the people of Korea.

We publish this volume with great pride and in the expectation that by making President Kim Il Sung's writings on Juche available to the American people, the struggle will be advanced both for socialist unity, enlightenment and understanding and for the peaceful reunification of Korea as well.

Jack A. Smith
Guardian Publications
New York,
September 1977

ON THE QUESTION OF THE PERIOD OF TRANSITION FROM CAPITALISM TO SOCIALISM AND THE DICTATORSHIP OF THE PROLETARIAT

Speech Delivered to Party Ideological Workers, *May 25, 1967*

Recently, while studying documents of the Party Conference some scholars and others responsible for ideological work have put forward diverse opinions on the questions of the transition period and the dictatorship of the proletariat. Particularly, following the publication of an essay on these questions, opinion was all the more divided. So, I studied the data on the subject, exchanged views with scholars, and gave a short summary. But those who heard my views interpreted and conveyed them to others in their own way, with the result that they were distorted in many points. Since the subject under discussion relates to the documents of the Party Conference, it is a very important matter and can in no way be neglected. I will therefore discuss it in some detail.

Like all other scientific and theoretical problems, the questions of the transition period and the dictatorship of the proletariat, too, must be solved from our Party's Juche viewpoint. You should neither cling to propositions of the classics and try to settle the questions dogmatically nor be enthralled by the ideas of flunkeyism and try to interpret the issues as others do. Judging from the written opinions of several scholars and from other essays, almost all comrades either interpret the propositions dogmatically or tend to flunkeyism and attempt to follow the thinking of other countries. Consequently, they advance the questions in a direction which is entirely different from that of our Party. You can never study and solve problems correctly in such a way. You can only arrive at a correct conclusion if you use your own faculties to solve the problems, free from flunkeyism and dogmatism.

Let us deal first with the problem of the transition period.

To explain the issue correctly, it is necessary first of all to consider in what historical circumstances and on what premises the classics, particularly Marx, advanced this question.

Firstly, as we see it, Marx obviously had in mind the developed capitalist countries when he laid down his definition of socialism and formulated the question of the period of transition from capitalism to communism or to socialism. I think we must be fully aware of this fact at the outset if we want to find a correct solution to this question.

What, then, are the developed capitalist countries we have referred to? They consist of those countries where both rural and urban areas have become completely capitalistic and the capitalist relations predominate in the whole society, with the result that peasants no longer exist but there are agricultural laborers, side by side with the industrial laborers. Marx had this kind of developed capitalist country in mind when he put forward his theory, and England, which he had visited and where he had lived and worked, was precisely such a country. In formulating the question of the period of transition from capitalism to socialism, therefore, Marx assumed first of all a condition in which there existed no class distinction between the working class and the peasantry, and he proceeded from it.

Now, to cite the instance of the most developed capitalist countries of modern times, their productive forces have become so highly developed as to make even the countryside fully capitalistic and, as a result, the working class is the only laboring class both in town and country. In a certain capitalist country there are tens of thousands of farms, all of which are very highly mechanized. Not only that, the electrification, chemicalization and irrigation of the countryside, too, is on a very high level. Thus, it is said, one agricultural laborer can take care of thirty *chongbo* of land in that country. What does this mean? It means not only that there exists actually no class distinction between the working class and the peasantry but also that the agricultural and industrial productive forces are almost on the same level. The only difference, if any, lies in the working conditions of the industrial laborer in the factory and the agricultural laborer on the farm.

That is why Marx thought that the stage of transition to socialism following the seizure of power by the proletariat in those developed capitalist countries would cover a comparatively short period. In other words, he believed that because there were only two classes in society, the capitalists and the workers, the tasks of the transition period could be carried out in a relatively brief period of time and it would be possible to pass quickly to the higher phase of communism, once the capitalist class was crushed and expropriated and its property turned over to ownership of the whole people in the course of the socialist revolution. Yet Marx did not say that it would be possible to progress to communism directly from capitalism, without going through the stage of socialism. No matter how highly the productive forces may have developed and how completely the class distinction between the working class and the peasantry may have disappeared, it is essential to solve the tasks of the transition period before advancing farther. These tasks include liquidating the remnant forces of the exploiter classes and eliminating the survivals of the old ideologies in the minds of people. We must first of all take account of this point.

The second point is the Marxist view of the uninterrupted revolution, which we must take into consideration in studying Marx's theory on the transition period and in expounding this question correctly.

As you all know, Marx lived in the era of premonopoly capitalism, so that he could not clearly see the imbalance in the political and economic development of capitalism. Therefore, he believed that the proletarian revolution would break out almost simultaneously in the major capitalist countries of Europe and that the world revolution would triumph relatively soon. Proceeding from such premises, Marx presumed that the period of transition from capitalism to socialism would be a comparatively short historical epoch, and defined that the dictatorship of the proletariat would exist only during the time of the transition period, that is, these two could never be divorced. We must also take account of this point.

Lenin, too, we can say, followed in the main the Marxist standpoint when he raised the questions of the transition period and the dictatorship of the proletariat. Unlike England or Germany where Marx had lived and worked, Lenin's Russia was of course not advanced at all but was a backward though nevertheless capitalist country. Consequently, Lenin considered the stage of socialism, the transitional stage, to be relatively long and not short as Marx had theorized.

But Lenin, too, following the Marxist view, said that a society where the working class had overthrown the capitalist system and seized power but where class distinction still remained between the workers and the peasants, was a transitional society being as yet not communist and neither fully socialist. He further said that in order to implement total socialism, it would not be enough to merely smash the capitalists as a class; the distinction between the workers and the peasants would also have to be eliminated. Thus it was that Lenin finally considered the period up to the materialization of a classless society—where there would be no distinction between the working class and the peasantry following the overthrow of the capitalist class by the working class—to be the period of transition from capitalism to socialism or the period of transition to communism. I think such a definition of the transition period is fundamentally correct.

But the problem is that our comrades interpret the propositions of Marx and Lenin dogmatically, without taking into consideration the times and historical circumstances in which they were formulated and, above all, they think the transition period and the dictatorship of the proletariat coincide with and are inseparable from each other.

It is true that the period of transition from capitalism to socialism or communism will only end when a classless society with no distinction between the working class and the peasantry is realized following the overthrow of the capitalist class. It can also be taken for granted that should the socialist revolution take place consecutively in all countries and the revolution emerge victorious on a worldwide scale, the transition period and the dictatorship of the proletariat would coincide with each other, and with the termination of the transition period, the dictatorship of the proletariat would also cease to exist and the withering away of the state would follow.

And yet, if socialism has been founded and a classless society materialized in one country or certain areas, the transition period should be regarded as terminated there even though the revolution has not brought victory on a worldwide scale. As long as capitalism remains in the world, however, the dictatorship of the proletariat will not vanish, and we cannot even talk about the withering away of the state. Therefore, in order to find a correct solution to the questions of the transition period and the dictatorship of the proletariat, we should not cling dogmatically to the propositions of Marx or Lenin, but proceed from the practical experiences in socialist construction in our country to consider the questions.

At present, certain people accept the period of transition from capitalism to socialism, but do not appreciate, in any sense, the concept of the period of transition from capitalism to communism, that is to say, the period of transition to the higher phase of communism. They use, however, the expression: gradual transition from socialism to communism.

It is the deviation of the Right opportunists to regard the transition period as the period from the seizure of power by the working class to the victory of the socialist system, and to suppose that the historical mission of the proletarian dictatorship will end with the termination of the transition period, conforming the transition period and the period of the dictatorship of the proletariat to each other. Therefore, people with such a viewpoint say that following the attainment of the complete and final victory of socialism, which is the first phase of communism, and with the transition to the all-out construction of communism, the dictatorship of the proletariat has fulfilled its historical mission and is thus no longer necessary. This is a Right opportunist view, which is entirely contradictory to Marxism-Leninism.

What, then, is the "Left" opportunist view? Those who have the "Left" view used to regard the question of the transition period exactly in the same light as those with the Right opportunist view, but proceeding from their standpoint that communism can be realized some generations later, contend that the transition period should be regarded as the period of transition from capitalism to the higher phase of communism. By so doing they apparently mean to criticize Right opportunism. It is all very well to criticize the Right deviations; yet we cannot consider such views on the question of the transition period to be correct.

As mentioned above, it is clear that these people have all fallen alike into deviations in viewing the questions of the transition period and the dictatorship of the proletariat.

We think the transition period can either be called the period of transition from capitalism to socialism, or the period of transition from capitalism to communism, because socialism is the first phase of communism. But the trouble is that some of our comrades, enthralled with flunkeyism, either regard the transition period as the period from capitalism to the higher phase of communism in the wake of the "Left" opportunist view or regard it as the period up to the victory of socialism in the wake of the Right opportunist view.

Therefore, the point at issue concerning the transition period is not a terminological matter of whether it is the transition to socialism or to communism, but rather the question of where to draw the demarcation line of the transition period. Many people, having made a bungle of determining this demarcation line, are presently confused and have given rise to various problems. Both of the demarcation lines, drawn by those with either the Right or the "Left" view, are problematical.

By the higher phase of communism is meant not only a classless society where there is no distinction between the workers and the peasants, but also a highly advanced society where there is no distinction between mental and physical labor and each member of society works according to his ability and receives according to his needs. So it is, in fact, tantamount to drawing no demarcation line at all to regard the transition period as the period up to such a higher phase of communism. Some people not only regard the transition period as a period right up to the higher phase of communism, but also say that it is impossible to bring about communism in a single country. They say, we will enter communism only when the world revolution is consummated. According to this view, the transition period cannot end before the world revolution is completed. These people interpret the transition period and the dictatorship of the proletariat as corresponding to each other, regarding the former as the period up to the higher phase of communism, while the people from the Rightist standpoint consider the transition period and the dictatorship of the proletariat as coinciding with each other, regarding the former as the period up to the point of victory of socialism. In our opinion, this is an extreme viewpoint.

It is also questionable that people holding Rightist views regard the transition period as the period up to the victory of the socialist revolution. This viewpoint stems from the ideological view of abandoning domestically the class struggle against survivors of the overthrown exploiter classes, and internationally refraining from the world revolution, by opting to live at peace with imperialism. Moreover, they claim that the dictatorship of the proletariat will disappear when the transition period comes to an end. But how can this be? They are fundamentally wrong.

It will not do, therefore, to follow mechanically what is set by those who hold the Rightist views, or to take as a model what is set by those holding the "Leftist" views.

We must firmly establish Juche and settle problems from the practical experiences we have gained in the revolution and construction of our country.

As already mentioned, the questions of the transition period and the dictatorship of the proletariat as defined by the classics were perfectly correct under the historical circumstances of their times and the premises they had developed from.

Our present reality, however, demands that we develop them creatively and not simply apply them without full consideration. We carried out the socialist revolution under the conditions where we had taken over the very backward productive forces of a colonial agrarian country, and are building socialism under circumstances where capitalism still exists as a considerable force in the world.

We must take into account these specific realities in order to give correct solutions to the questions of the transition period and the dictatorship of the proletariat. Bearing this point in mind, I consider it to be incorrect to regard the transition period in our country as the period up to the higher phase of communism, and deem it right to regard it rather as the period up to socialism. But it is wrong to believe that the transition period will come to a close as soon as the socialist revolution has triumphed and the socialist system is established. Considering the issue either on the basis of what the founders of Marxism-Leninism said or in the light of the experiences we have gained in our actual struggles, we cannot say that a complete socialist society is already built just because the capitalist class has been overthrown and socialist revolution carried through after the working class seized power. We, therefore, have never said that the establishment of the socialist system means the complete victory of socialism.

When will the complete socialist society ever come into being? Complete victory of socialism will come only when the class distinction between the working class and the peasantry has disappeared and the middle classes, particularly the peasant masses, actively support us. As long as the peasants are not working-classized, the support they may give us cannot be firm and is bound to be rather unstable.

The seizure of power by the working class is but the beginning of socialist revolution. To build a complete socialist society the revolution must be steadily advanced and a firm material basis of socialism laid. I have already emphasized this time and again in my reports and speeches. Nevertheless, some of our comrades, because of their flunkeyist mentality, have not properly studied the documents of our Party but have shown much interest in what others had said. They are very wrong.

We must base ourselves on today's realities and take a correct perspective of all the questions from there. Since our country did not go through a capitalist revolution, its productive forces are very backward, and the distinction between the working class and the peasantry will have to remain for a very long time even after the socialist revolution. In fact, there are only a few highly developed capitalist countries in the world today. Most countries are backward, and were formerly colonies or semi-colonies like our country, or are still dependent on others. In such countries the construction of a classless society and the consolidation of socialism are possible only by developing the productive forces for a comparatively longer period even after the socialist revolution.

As we did not go through the normal course of capitalist development, we have the task of developing the productive forces in our socialist era—a task which we should have tackled under capitalism. There is no need to make society capitalistic and go to the trouble of fostering the capitalists just to smash them and then build socialism, on the basis that we could not discharge the task which we should have completed in the capitalist stage. The working class in power should not revive capitalist society, but should carry out this task under the socialist system which it could not tackle in the stage of capitalist revolution, in order to build a classless society.

We must keep consolidating the material basis of socialism and boost the productive forces at least to the level of developed capitalist countries, and completely get rid of the distinction between the working class and the peasantry. To this end, the technical revolution should be carried out to the extent that the developed capitalist countries have turned their countryside capitalistic, so that farming may be mechanized, chemicalization and irrigation be introduced and the eight-hour day adopted.

It was precisely for this purpose that we published the theses on the socialist rural question. Yet, our comrades do not properly study even the theses. We must always solve problems with our own brains, drawing on our Party documents. What is the central idea of the *Theses on the Socialist Rural Question in Our Country*? The basic idea of the theses is to carry out the technical revolution in the rural areas and develop the agricultural productive forces to a high level. At the same time, it seeks to promote the ideological and the cultural revolution and gradually abolish the distinction between the working class and the peasantry in the spheres of technology, ideology and culture, and bring cooperative property up to the level of property of all the people.

And these tasks cannot be realized unless the working class gives guidance and assistance to the peasantry. It is our Party's line to give material and technical assistance to the peasants and carry out the technical revolution in the rural areas by relying on the solid basis of industry. To this end, large numbers of tractors should be supplied to the countryside, fertilizers and agricultural chemicals should be furnished in quantities for chemicalization, and irrigation should also be carried out. Along with this, the working class must help the peasantry in their ideological remolding and exert also a cultural influence on them. Only in this way can the peasantry be completely working-classized.

It is in fact one of the most important questions in building socialism and communism to turn the peasantry into the working class. In this way we will working-classize the peasants and abolish the distinction between the working class and the peasantry.

We should not take to flunkeyism but should hold fast to our Party's stand of Juche in solving the question of working-classizing the peasantry. We must develop the productive forces to a higher plane, get rid of the disparity between town and country and raise the people's living standards by putting into effect the spirit of the theses and laying a firm material basis of socialism.

Only by so doing can we completely win over the former middle classes. We cannot say socialism has been consolidated or consider it has won complete victory before the middle classes stop wavering and fully support us. Only when they actively support us, can we say socialism has been completely realized. When we advance socialist construction and thoroughly win over the middle classes to our side, when we eliminate the distinction between the working class and the peasantry and build a classless society, we shall be able to say that the tasks of the period of transition from capitalism to socialism have been accomplished.

I deem it right to draw the demarcation line for the transition period at the border of the classless society, unlike those who are biased to the Right or to the "Left."

What, then, shall we say is the society that will exist, after the triumph of the socialist revolution and the accomplishment of socialist transformation, until the disappearance of the class distinction between the working class and the peasantry? It can be called nothing other than a socialist society, since it is a society free from exploitation even though it undoubtedly belongs to the transition period.

Needless to say, the end of the transition period will not immediately be followed by the higher phase of communism. Even after the close of the transition period, the revolution and construction must be continued and the productive forces developed to such a level that each individual works according to his ability and each receives according to his needs, in order to enter the higher phase of communism.

In my opinion, this approach to the question of the transition period accords with the definitions laid down by Marx and Lenin, and it proceeds from the new historical conditions as well as the practical experiences of the revolution and construction in our country. This is a preliminary and not final conclusion reached by us. It is desirable that you make further studies in this direction.

Having given such a definition of the period of transition, how should we view the question of the dictatorship of the proletariat? The classics, as already mentioned, understood that the transition period and the dictatorship of the proletariat would coincide with each other. Then, if a classless society materializes and the complete victory of socialism is achieved in our country, i.e., if the tasks of the transition period are accomplished, will the dictatorship of the proletariat become no longer necessary? The answer to this is no. Even when the transition period is over, the dictatorship of the proletariat must be continued up to the higher phase of communism, to say nothing of its necessity during the entire period of transition.

Even after we have carried out the technical revolution in the rural areas, elevated cooperative property to the level of property of the whole people, working-classized the peasantry and done away with the distinction between the working class and the peasantry by solidifying the material and technical basis of socialism and carrying into effect the theses on the socialist rural question, the level of our productive forces will not yet be high enough to apply the principle of communism that each works according to his ability and receives according to his needs. Therefore, it will be necessary to continue to build socialism and strive to realize communism. It is quite clear that these tasks cannot be fulfilled without the dictatorship of the proletariat. In other words, even when the transition period is over, the dictatorship of the proletariat should still exist until the higher phase of communism is attained.

But here is another question. What will become of the proletarian dictatorship once communism is realized in one country or certain areas while capitalism still exists in parts of the world? Even if communism materialized in one country or certain areas, that society would not be free from the menace of imperialism and the resistance of internal enemies who conspire with external enemies, because the world revolution has not yet been accomplished and capitalism and imperialism remain in existence. Under such circumstances, the state cannot wither away and the dictatorship of the proletariat must therefore remain in existence in the higher phase of communism. Should the revolution successively sweep all countries eliminating capitalism and allowing the socialist revolution to emerge victorious on a global scale, the transition period and the dictatorship of the proletariat would correspond to each other. With the end of the one, the other would no longer be necessary and the functions of the state would wither away. But inasmuch as we accept the theory that it is possible to build communism in a particular country or certain areas, it is entirely correct to view the transition period and the dictatorship of the proletariat separately in this way.

It is no revision on our part of Marxism-Leninism to consider the questions of the transition period and the dictatorship of the proletariat in this manner. It is our standpoint to creatively apply the propositions of Marx and Lenin to the new historical circumstances and the specific practices of our country. I think this is the way of safeguarding the purity of Marxism-Leninism against dogmatism and flunkeyism.

I am now going to say a few words about the question of class struggle in connection with the dictatorship of the proletariat. As long as the class struggle exists, there will exist the dictatorship of the proletariat, and this dictatorship is essential to class struggle. The class struggle has, however, various forms. At the stage of overthrowing capitalism this struggle differs in form from that after its overthrow. This has already been expressly detailed in the documents of our Party. Many people, however, commit Right or "Left" errors simply because they don't have a clear idea of this.

The class struggle at the stage of the socialist revolution is a struggle to liquidate the capitalists as a class, and the class struggle in socialist society is a struggle aimed at achieving unity and solidarity, and is by no means a class struggle waged between the members of that society at feud. In socialist society the class struggle certainly exists, but its existence is by way of cooperation for the purpose of achieving unity and solidarity. It goes without saying that our present ideological revolution is a class struggle; and it is also a form of class struggle to render assistance to the countryside to working-classize the peasantry. Because the state of the working class aims, after all, at eliminating the peasants as a class and completing their working-classization through the supply of machines and chemical fertilizers and through providing them with irrigation works. Our class struggle is designed not only to working-classize the peasantry and terminate its existence as a class, but also to revolutionize previous middle classes including the intelligentsia and urban petty bourgeoisie and remold them on the pattern of the working class. This is the principal form of the class struggle we are now waging.

Also, within our social system subversive counterrevolutionary influences infiltrate from without and the survivors of the overthrown exploiter classes agitate within; so, the class struggle is necessary to suppress these counterrevolutionary activities.

In this way, there is in socialist society a form of class struggle exercising dictatorship over both external and internal enemies, along with the basic form of class struggle which aims through cooperation to revolutionize and remold the workers, peasants and working intellectuals to achieve unity and solidarity.

In socialist society, therefore, the class struggle does not disappear but continues in different forms. It is perfectly correct to consider the question of the class struggle in socialist society in this way.

In connection with this question, I should like to direct a few more words to the issue of revolutionizing the intellectuals. We cannot as yet say that we have fully worked out the correct approach to this question. We once sent our intellectuals into factories to labor among the workers with a view to revolutionizing them. But it is doubtful if that is really a good way. We have cultivated the intellectuals because we want them to write, study science and technology or serve as teachers. If they were intended to labor in the factories, we should obviously have made them workers from the outset, instead of providing them with expensive training. So, this way, too, is not quite appropriate.

Of course, it is a good thing to bring the intellectuals close to the workers to learn from them their organization and fortitude as well as their devotion to the people they serve with their physical labor. But this is still far from being an adequate answer to the question of revolutionizing the intellectuals. Many of our writers have been to the factories, and yet some of them made little progress in spite of all their work there. So, we cannot revolutionize the intellectuals merely by sending them to the factories to work.

What is important here is to make them strengthen their organizational life, including their participation in Party activities. At present, some of our intellectuals do not like the strengthening of Party and other organizational activities, and do not conscientiously take part in organizational life. They think that by strengthening their Party life and by taking part in organizational life they are losing their freedom.

Those cadres who neglect both their Party activities and Party study, also go against the Party's policies. Even the Central Party School does not strengthen the Party life of its students, so that, after graduation, they cannot make the most of what they have learned and fail to work and live in a revolutionary way.

It is therefore of paramount importance in revolutionizing the intellectuals to make them take an active part in revolutionary organizational life. Above all, it is essential for them to strengthen the Party-cell life, refrain from displaying their knowledge and conduct the Party study well to arm themselves with revolutionary ideas. Further, they should neither be afraid of being criticized nor be unwilling to criticize others; they should intensify criticism and self-criticism and strictly observe organizational discipline. This alone will help them revolutionize themselves. People should cultivate collectivist ideas in the course of their organizational life in the Party or any social organizations, and acquire the revolutionary spirit of receiving definite revolutionary assignments from their organizations and carrying them out without fail. The members of the Party and social organizations should positively equip themselves with the Party's policies and propagandize them, and should become the kind of revolutionaries that carry out their revolutionary tasks to the letter and in accordance with the Party's policies. A revolutionary is a genuine Communist. The Communist has nothing to do with selfishness, which means seeking one's own interests alone. Revolutionaries must have the communist traits of working and living under the motto: "One for all and all for one." They must temper themselves with the Party, class and popular spirit of serving the working class and the entire people.

The intellectuals will become spoiled in the end, if they do not take an active part in all organizational life including that of the Party. There are many such instances. I should like to emphasize once again that both the old and new intellectuals should strengthen their activities in the Party and other institutions, to do away with their liberalistic and petty-bourgeois mentalities and train themselves into revolutionaries.

Today I have dwelt on the questions of the transition period and the dictatorship of the proletariat in considerable detail. I think this should be enough to give you a general idea of the questions raised in the course of studying the documents of the Party Conference.

STUDENTS MUST ACQUIRE A COMMUNIST ATTITUDE TOWARD LABOR AND LEARN SCIENCE AND KNOWLEDGE TO SERVE THE INTERESTS OF THE KOREAN REVOLUTION

Speech at a Meeting with the Students of Universities and Higher Technical Schools—Participants in the Rebuilding of the Capital, *November 15, 1967*

On behalf of the Party Central Committee and the Government of the Republic, I would like first to extend warm congratulations to you, comrade students, who have displayed great revolutionary enthusiasm and achieved brilliant labor successes in rebuilding Pyongyang after the flood damage and, through you, to all the students who took part in the reconstruction of the capital.

This year our students not only participated in rebuilding Pyongyang. In order to assist all our working people in their efforts to implement the Party's revolutionary line on simultaneously building the economy and defenses, our students volunteered to work instead of taking their summer vacation and accomplished great feats in every nook and corner of the land. We highly estimate this patriotic initiative.

All these facts have clearly shown that our Party trusts our students and the latter the former and that under the Party's care, our students are growing to be the nation's excellent, dependable cadres.

I think your participation in the rebuilding of the capital greatly contributed to your working-classization and revolutionization. Students study at schools in order to serve the interests and well-being of the working class and the entire people. Therefore, if you are to become good Korean cadres as required by the Party, you must revolutionize and working-classize yourselves. For students and teachers who are engaged in mental labor, physical labor affords them an excellent opportunity to revolutionize and working-classize themselves.

At present the south Korean reactionaries are slandering the voluntary labor of our working people and students as "forced labor." This is really preposterous. I am sure none of you regard your participation in the recent reconstruction of the capital as "forced labor."

One of the most important aspects in building socialism and communism is to educate the working people to love labor and voluntarily take part in it.

Labor is the source of all wealth and happiness. Only through men's purposeful and conscious labor, can wealth be created and tools constantly improved, and do the productive forces as well as society develop. Without labor we can never consolidate the country's economic foundations and build a good society to live in. Even when our economic foundations are incomparably stronger and our people much better off than now, the working people will continue to enjoy happy lives only through their labor. Even in a communist society people will have to work. Communist society is a society where everybody works and leads a bountiful life. It is true that in communist society labor will become much easier and pleasanter because in that society techniques will be highly developed. Even in that society, however, people will not be able to live without doing work. Therefore, one of the most important tasks in educating the working people along communist lines is that of cultivating a correct attitude toward labor. Loving labor and taking an active part in it is a most sacred task devolving upon all the working people.

We should, all of us, have a correct attitude toward labor and must not hate it or seek an idle life. Seeking an idle life without working is precisely the expression of the obsolete ideology of the exploiter class, which we must combat firmly.

Love of labor is one of the most important qualities of a Communist. Accordingly, we can say, a correct attitude toward labor is a major criterion of a revolutionary. Only one who loves labor and voluntarily participates in it can be a genuine revolutionary who serves the working class and the people; a lazy man who dislikes labor can never be a revolutionary. A person who hates labor is a laggard; in the long run, he will turn into a good-for-nothing in our society. Our students must tirelessly strive to acquire a communist attitude toward labor; they must always love labor and work earnestly.

You should not only voluntarily engage in labor but also strive to liberate the working people from hard, backbreaking work and obliterate the distinctions between mental and physical labor, light and heavy labor, as well as between industrial and agricultural labor.

After the establishment of a socialist system free from exploitation and oppression, an important task confronting us Communists is to liberate the working people from arduous and backbreaking work and eliminate the distinctions in labor thus enabling all of them to increase production while working with much more ease. In order to carry out this task, we should vigorously push ahead with the technical revolution and turn our country into a highly developed industrial state. In accordance with the line set forth by the Fourth Congress of our Party, we should effect the nation's industrialization by forcefully stepping up the technical revolution. Thus we will emancipate the working people from arduous labor and eliminate the differences between heavy and light labor and, further, gradually obliterate the distinctions between mental and physical labor through the mechanization and automation of all production processes. Your study of sciences such as physics, chemistry, mechanical and electrical engineering as well as technology is chiefly aimed at carrying out this very task successfully.

If you are to fulfill this task satisfactorily, you should also engage in physical labor. Only when you take part in it yourselves and experience its difficulty, will you study more assiduously and strive still more to make a lot of good machines and develop technology in order to relieve the working people from onerous toil. The teachers should also perform physical labor themselves. Then they will teach their students better and carry out their research work more actively for scientific and technological advancement in order to free the working people from backbreaking work as the Party intends. So your participation in the recent undertaking is quite useful to you, I think.

Twenty-two years have already passed since our country was liberated from the colonial rule of Japanese imperialism and it is more than twenty years after we established our universities and colleges. Before liberation there was not a single institute of higher learning in the northern half of the Republic. After liberation we started to set up a university in a difficult situation. When we were building the university for the first time immediately after liberation, there was a great deal of fuss about the feasibility of the project. But this is a thing of the past now. At present our country has scores of institutes of higher learning, not counting the factory colleges. Tens of thousands of students are enrolled in them and the teaching staff alone runs to thousands. This is our great pride and priceless asset.

We must turn all the universities and colleges into centers of training communist revolutionaries, communist builders. To do this, we must revolutionize and working-classize them. In other words, we must prepare all the teachers and students to be staunch revolutionaries, excellent builders of communism, who will faithfully serve the revolution.

What is most important here is to thoroughly arm all of them with communist ideology, with our Party's revolutionary ideas. Thus we will see to it that everyone becomes a Korean revolutionary, a Korean communist builder. Our universities and colleges must never turn out even a single alien element or a person who dislikes labor or neglects the implementation of the Party's policies or is behindhand in carrying out revolutionary tasks.

As I stressed at the Party Conference, in order to build socialism and communism everyone should make continued efforts to revolutionize himself. At the Hwanghae Iron Works some time ago, I said the members of the working class must also endeavor tirelessly to revolutionize themselves. Not all of them are fully armed with communist ideology. Many of the workers were not exploited and oppressed by the landlords and capitalists before, and most of them were not engaged in revolutionary struggle. Moreover, many of the former petty bourgeoisie—peasants, handicraftsmen or small traders—joined the ranks of the working class not long ago. All these people cannot be revolutionized so easily. In addition, among old workers, too, there may be some who have not abandoned obsolete ideas. Therefore, the working class should also strive to revolutionize themselves.

The struggle for revolutionization should be intensified especially at educational institutes which have old intellectuals. Our Party's policy is not to leave out the old intellectuals but to revolutionize all of them through education and remolding. Our Party trusts all the intellectuals, it is not particular about their family origin. Therefore, they should firmly arm themselves with our Party's ideology by redoubling their efforts to revolutionize themselves; with profound fidelity to the Party, the class, and the people, they should also strive to equip the students with communist ideology, with our Party's revolutionary ideas.

We must make sure that the teachers strengthen their organizational life in the Party, the League of Socialist Working Youth or other organizations and actively help them to speed up their working-classization and revolutionization.

The students should also tirelessly strive during their school days to thoroughly revolutionize and working-classize themselves. There may be some whose parents were small tradesmen or handicraftsmen or led affluent lives in the past. We should not fear or leave out these students, but should revolutionize and working-classize them by educating and remolding all of them while at school.

The revolutionization of the intellectuals does not mean that we oppose the intellectuals themselves; it means that we oppose the obsolete ideas remaining in their minds. The biggest obstacle to their revolutionization and working-classization is the ideologies of the petty bourgeoisie, capitalism, feudalism and flunkeyism still persisting in their minds. Our intellectuals must root out all survivals of these outworn ideas and thoroughly equip themselves with our Party's monolithic ideology.

At present many intellectuals are endeavoring to revolutionize and working-classize themselves. According to a recent report from the chief secretary of the South Hamgyong Provincial Party Committee, since we assigned the teachers to the task of revolutionizing themselves during our visit to Hamhung, the faculty members of the Hamhung College of Chemical Industry and the Hamhung Medical College have been taking an active part in their organizational life and striving to remold their ideology. This is very good. All our intellectuals should do so.

Our Party trusts the intellectuals, and has left to their care the students, research institutes and factories. The Party trusts them so that it has not only given schooling to the intellectuals but also charged them with such important revolutionary tasks. Therefore, they should trust the Party and work devotedly to come up to its expectations.

As we always say, educational work is a very honorable revolutionary task. That is why the teacher is not one who is simply engaged in an occupation, but one who carries out an important revolutionary task. If the teachers are to fulfill their task successfully at this important post to which the Party has assigned them, they must become out-and-out revolutionaries by tempering themselves ceaselessly.

It is only through their revolutionization that the intellectuals can be one of our Party's major components. As you all know, our Party's emblem symbolizes the intellectuals along with the workers and farmers. But how can they be one of our Party's components if they fail to revolutionize themselves? Our intellectuals must constantly endeavor to revolutionize and working-classize themselves.

We should revolutionize and working-classize all our intellectuals and, further, revolutionize the whole of society and also intellectualize it.

If we are to build a rich and powerful country, promote social progress and, further, build communism, all people must have broad and profound knowledge. Then, we will be able to rapidly develop technology and culture and, consequently, bring about complete equality in labor by obliterating the distinctions and build a happy society where all people work and lead affluent lives.

The entire people's level of knowledge will be raised rapidly if we intensify the struggle to revolutionize and working-classize the intellectuals and all the other members of society at the same time as strengthening cultural education and carrying out the cultural revolution through a mass movement. We will have a large army of intellectuals in the future when all people have received compulsory technical education and graduated from institutes of higher learning. By that time the working class will also have acquired a great store of knowledge. When all people have attained a high level of knowledge, it will be impossible to differentiate the intelligentsia from others. Because there are not so many intellectuals at present, they are called the intelligentsia. But when all people have acquired broad and deep knowledge, there will not be such a category of people any more. Thus, when all the members of society have obtained wide and profound knowledge, we will be able to say that the whole of society has been intellectualized.

Now, let me reemphasize the necessity to thoroughly establish Juche in the spheres of science.

What is most important in all spheres of sciences, natural or social, is to thoroughly establish Juche. Our students should always study science and acquire knowledge so as to serve the Korean people and carry out the Korean revolution.

When singing a song, too, we must sing the one which the Koreans like. Only such a song is worth hearing. The songs which the Koreans do not like and which they cannot understand are of no use. They say some people claim that the Koreans are so uncultured and ignorant that they cannot sing Italian or other foreign songs. This is really deplorable. Italian songs are loved by the Italians. Why should the Koreans like such songs? We must not praise foreign songs. We must sing songs suited to Korean sentiments; we must develop our own songs.

Not only music but also all realms of social sciences must be firmly based on our country's reality and our Party's ideas.

This also applies to natural sciences. As we always say, even when communist society is materialized, the Koreans should live in Korea, the beautiful land of three thousand *ri*. Even when the whole world turns into communist society, the Koreans could never live in an alien land. In order to lead a happy life in Korea, they should be familiar with its natural resources and actively develop them. They should industrialize the country and produce many things with domestic raw materials. Therefore, we should develop our science from the standpoint of Juche.

Only when we reject flunkeyism and firmly establish Juche in science, can we rapidly develop our country, make it richer, more powerful and civilized and reunify it quickly. If we develop our science on the basis of Juche and properly use our own resources, our people will be as well-off as can be, though our country covers an area of a little more than 220,000 square kilometers.

Our country has almost all kinds of natural resources in great abundance. However, because our scientists and technicians have not thoroughly studied their country, they cannot opportunely find even the resources we have. If they vigorously carry out scientific research work, solidly basing themselves on Juche, they will discover lots of new resources.

In the past our scholars only read books written by foreigners and claimed that our country had no nickel necessary for the production of stainless steel. It is very difficult to import. We needed plenty of stainless steel to develop the national economy and build new chemical factories. So we were resolved to make it by our own efforts and started to find nickel. In this way, we struck a vein of nickel and could produce stainless steel for ourselves.

Let me cite another example. In former days our personnel engaged in geological prospecting had not tried to find iron ore at Unryul because their foreign counterparts claimed that there could be no iron ore in such a low land. Later, however, our geological prospectors found a huge iron ore deposit at the Unryul area.

We also found apatite which had been claimed to be nonexistent in our country. We have it in Sakju, too. Songhwa abounds in high-grade apatite. There is plenty of apatite in Pyongwon, Chungsan and Songchon in South Pyongan Province as well as in South and North Hamgyong Provinces. Therefore, we are able to produce large quantities of phosphatic fertilizer with our own raw materials.

We also found raw materials for potash fertilizer.

Our geological prospecting personnel found bauxite, too. This enabled us to have our own raw material center for creating the light metal industry.

These examples eloquently tell how important it is to root out flunkeyism and thoroughly establish Juche in developing science and technology.

Some of our scholars are still obsessed by flunkeyism. It is very detrimental. If a people fall into flunkeyism, their country is bound to perish. Therefore, it is very important to oppose it and establish Juche firmly.

First of all, we must firmly establish Juche in ideology, so that all of us arm ourselves closely with our Party's ideas and have a strong viewpoint that we never accept any ideology but our Party's ideology. This is not enough, however. We must firmly establish Juche in science as well.

We have long stressed the necessity to establish Juche in science. We cannot say, however, that Juche has been firmly established in the institutions of scientific research and education. We must continue to wage a dynamic struggle to establish Juche in the spheres of science.

We need the science that is necessary for our country's development and that serves our revolution and our people. Both natural and social sciences should serve our working class and people and contribute to the Korean revolution and to the building of socialism and communism in Korea. Such science which does not serve our people and contribute to our revolution is of no use.

If we advance science along Juche lines, we can fully develop our national economy with our domestic resources. Of course, we do not mean that we have all natural resources. But, if we develop science to suit our country's reality, we can obtain more new resources and exchange what we have for what we do not have.

We have not yet found petroleum in our country, but we can find it if we work well. We cannot say that there is not petroleum in our country. Now scholars are saying that we can find petroleum anywhere, if we go deep underground. So I think we can find it if we try.

Even if petroleum is not produced in our country, we need not worry; we can actively develop our abundant resources and exchange them for petroleum. As we always say, if we develop the cement industry by using anthracite and limestone plentiful in our country and produce and export cement in large quantities, we can import as much petroleum as we want. Then, we can also develop the petroleum chemical industry.

Together with the cement industry, we must develop the machine-building industry. Our country has very favorable conditions for its development. Our country abounds in iron ore and has solid centers of the steel industry; we also have plenty of nonferrous and rare metals. We can say our machine-building industry has broad prospects. At present, even countries which are not endowed with iron or rare metals are producing and exporting machinery. Why, then, should we not develop the machine-building industry in our country which is rich in mineral resources? We should develop this industry and make many machines and exchange them for what we have not.

Even in the future, when the whole world has gone over to communism, everything will not be produced at one place; we will give others what we produce in large quantities where we live, and get what we have not from them; that is to say, the method of filling each other's needs will be applied.

We must resolutely oppose flunkeyism, establish Juche in education and develop our science from the standpoint of Juche. Opposing flunkeyism and establishing Juche is the most important aspect in revolutionizing our students and teachers.

I again emphasize that the students must study hard and make strenuous efforts to revolutionize themselves and that the teachers must tirelessly endeavor to establish Juche in science and revolutionize and working-classize themselves, at the same time fully educating the students in our Party's Juche idea.

In conclusion, I am firmly convinced that you will fulfill the Party's expectations by striving to revolutionize your schools and to become dependable builders of communism and excellent revolutionaries.

LET US EMBODY THE REVOLUTIONARY SPIRIT OF INDEPENDENCE, SELF-SUSTENANCE AND SELF-DEFENSE MORE THOROUGHLY IN ALL FIELDS OF STATE ACTIVITY

Political Program of the Government of the Democratic People's Republic of Korea Announced at the First Session of the Fourth Supreme People's Assembly of the DPRK, *December 16, 1967*

Comrade Deputies,

The elections of deputies to the Fourth Supreme People's Assembly of the Democratic People's Republic of Korea have been held successfully with a great, new revolutionary upsurge being made and the political and labor enthusiasm of the entire people running exceptionally high in all fields of socialist economic construction and defense upbuilding to carry through the decisions of the historic Conference of the Workers' Party of Korea.

All the citizens of our country took part in the elections, as one man, with high patriotic zeal, thereby manifesting their firm determination to resolutely defend the people's power and the revolutionary gains and further consolidate and develop them, successfully carry out the building of socialism in the northern half of the Republic and accomplish the revolutionary cause of reunification of the country whatever the costs.

The results of the elections clearly demonstrated our people's unreserved support for and profound trust in our Party and the Government of the Republic and again showed the world the monolithic political and ideological unity of all our people.

On behalf of the Central Committee of the Workers' Party of Korea and the Government of the Democratic People's Republic of Korea, I want to warmly thank you deputies elected to this Supreme People's Assembly and all the people of our country for trusting and authorizing us once again to form the Cabinet of the Republic.

Comrades,

The elections of deputies to the Supreme People's Assembly have been held on four occasions in our country in the last 19 years since the founding of the Democratic People's Republic of Korea, a genuine people's state, in accord with the unanimous will of the entire Korean people, and the Cabinet of the Republic has been formed today for the fourth time.

During this period a great stride forward along the road of social progress and civilization has been made in our country, thanks to the correct policies of the Workers' Party of Korea and the invincible vitality of the people's power and to the heroic struggle of our people, who, as masters of the state, have taken their destiny into their own hands. In this land, where harsh exploitation and oppression, centuries-old underdevelopment and poverty once prevailed, an advanced, socialist system has now been established under which all of us help each other, work together and live happily; and our country has become a socialist state with a firm independent national economy and brilliant national culture.

Since the elections of deputies to the Third Supreme People's Assembly held in 1962, the Cabinet of the Republic has exerted all its efforts to carry through the decisions of the Fourth Congress of the Workers' Party of Korea, and has, especially, concentrated its efforts on the implementation of our Party's new revolutionary line of carrying out economic construction in parallel with defense upbuilding, which was set forth at the Conference of the Workers' Party of Korea held in October 1966. As a result, tremendous successes have been made in all the political, economic, cultural and military fields and the might of our country has been further increased.

On a socialist basis the alliance of the workers and peasants has been further cemented, and the political and ideological unity of the entire people has become firmer than ever. Our people have been more tempered in the hard-fought struggle for revolution and construction; through practical experience they have acquired boundless confidence in the Workers' Party of Korea and the Government of the Republic, around which they are united rock-firm. Our people accept the policies and lines of our Party and the Government of the Republic as their vital cause and devote all their talents and energies to the struggle for the cause of the revolution and for the prosperity and progress of the Republic. This rock-firm unity and cohesion of our people is precisely the solid foundation of our state and social system and the source of our invincible might.

Our people are now in a position to enter the international arena under the glorious banner of the Democratic People's Republic of Korea, equal in rights to the peoples of both the large and small countries of the world, and the international position of the Republic is ever on the rise.

The correct economic policy of our Party and the Government of the Republic has brought about giant strides forward in all fields of the national economy.

In 1966, industrial production was 1.4 times greater than in 1962 and 41 times that of 1946, the year immediately after liberation.

The foundations of the independent national economy of the country have been further consolidated as a result of the vigorous struggle organized and carried forward by the Government of the Republic to implement the decisions of the Fourth Congress of the Workers' Party of Korea on the realization of socialist industrialization and the all-round promotion of the technical revolution in every field of the national economy.

The foundations of our heavy industry, with the machine-building industry as its core, have been further improved and reinforced, and the production of diverse heavy industrial goods has grown conspicuously. Our heavy industry is now displaying still greater strength and making a better contribution to the advancement of light industry and agriculture, as a solid base for strengthening the economic independence of the country and for accelerating the technical reconstruction of our national economy.

Great progress has also been made in the field of light industry. In our country the people's consumer demands are met with domestically produced goods, though these are not abundant yet, and the firm foundations of light industry have been laid for turning out diverse high-quality consumer goods in larger quantities in the future.

Our socialist agriculture, too, has made big headway. The technical, cultural and ideological revolutions have been promoted successfully in the countryside, the direction and management of cooperative farms improved and assistance to the countryside further intensified; the farmers' political and work enthusiasm has increased greatly. Our country was hit hard by repeated natural disasters in recent years, but their effects were completely overcome in all sectors of our agricultural production.

With the successful acceleration of socialist economic construction and the rapid growth of production, the people's material and cultural standards of living have risen markedly.

Per capita national income was 500 *won* in 1966, or a 1.2-fold increase as against 1962, and it is expected to rise to 580 *won* this year.

The Government of the Republic upped the real incomes of the workers, office employees and farmers considerably, while also steadily increasing accumulation for expanded production and allocating a large part of the national income to defense upbuilding to meet the prevailing situation. In particular, the Government of the Republic, in keeping with the line set forth in the *Theses on the Socialist Rural Question in Our Country*, took a series of radical measures for increasing the farmers' income: total elimination of agricultural tax in kind, capital construction in the rural areas with state investment, construction of farmers' homes at state expense, etc.

Housing conditions for the working people improved considerably as a result of extensive dwelling construction. During the period from 1963 to 1966, homes with a total floor space of 10,210,000 square meters were newly built in towns and the countryside for the working people.

Not only were the basic problems of food, clothing and housing solved, but the supply of commodities to the working people was generally improved. In our country today the working people can buy any goods as needed at uniform prices everywhere, not merely in towns but even in remote mountain areas where merchandise was seldom seen before.

Further progress has also been made in education, culture and public health.

In our country, thanks to the correct educational policy of our Party and the Government of the Republic, 2,600,000 pupils and students, or one-fourth of the population, are now studying free of charge at more than 9260 schools at all levels, including 98 institutes of higher learning. Particularly, universal compulsory nine-year technical education which has been introduced this year, combining general education with polytechnic training, will make it possible for us to bring up all the coming generation as a reserve of versatile builders of socialism and communism, reliable heirs to our revolutionary cause, and further raise the technical and cultural levels of all the working people. This will contribute greatly to the further development of public education and the acceleration of the technical and cultural revolutions in our country.

In 1966 the number of university and college graduates was 1.2 times that of 1962, and that of the graduates from higher technical schools and specialized secondary schools, 3.2 times the 1962 figure. At present, over 425,700 engineers, assistant engineers and specialists—2.3 times as many as in 1962—are working in all fields of the national economy. Thanks to the intelligence and energy of our technicians and specialists, all branches of our national economy are managed and operated efficiently, and new, up-to-date factories and enterprises are going up one after another in our country today. This is one of the biggest successes achieved by our Party and the Government of the Republic in the building of a new country.

The correct policy of our Party and the Government of the Republic with regard to health services has enabled the working people of our country to enjoy greater benefits from the system of universal free medical care. In the field of health services, the number of medical workers has increased considerably, medical facilities have been expanded and medical service for the working people has been further improved over the past four years. As a result of these improved public health services and the raising of the people's living standard as a whole, the mortality of the population dropped in 1966 to half that of the preliberation years, and the people's average life span has been lengthened by 20 years. This is possible only under the socialist system, where the masses of people are the true masters of the country.

Large numbers of nurseries and kindergartens, run at state and community expense, have been established in our country to bring up and educate our children well and to provide women with adequate conditions for social labor.

All this is an unequivocal manifestation of the popular policies of our Party and the Government of the Republic, which have as the supreme principle of their activities the promotion of the well-being of the working people.

Our Party and the Government of the Republic have in recent years directed special attention to strengthening the country's defense capabilities to counter the intensified aggressive maneuvers of the imperialists. The U.S. imperialists created the Caribbean crisis against the Republic of Cuba in 1962 and later provoked the Gulf of Bac Bo incident against the Democratic Republic of Vietnam and embarked on a course of intensifying the war of aggression in South Vietnam on a large scale. In the face of this situation, our Party and Government put forward the line of carrying out economic construction and defense upbuilding in parallel and took a number of important measures to further increase our defense capabilities while reorganizing the national economy. We are thus fully able to repulse any hostile armed invasions and defend the security of our country more reliably.

All these successes scored in the revolutionary struggle and work of construction in recent years signify the shining victory of the lines and policies of our Party and the Government of the Republic which have creatively applied and developed the universal truth of Marxism-Leninism in line with the actual conditions in our country, the vivid manifestation of the indomitable vitality and great superiority of the state and social system of our Republic, and the great fruition of the patriotic struggle and creative labor of our people, closely united around our Party and Government.

We cannot rest content with the successes already achieved; our revolutionary cause has not yet been completed. To advance the revolution and construction of the country further, we still have much to do and must keep struggling to overcome difficulties and hardships.

Basing itself strictly on the lines and policies of the Workers' Party of Korea, the General Staff of our revolution and organizer of all the victories of the Korean people, the newly formed Cabinet of the Republic will, in the future, as in the past, organize and carry out all its work in the interests of the entire Korean people, and it will fight persistently to accelerate socialist construction in the northern half of the Republic and the accomplishment of the sacred cause of liberating the south Korean people and reunifying the country.

The Government of the Republic, proceeding from the general tasks of our revolution, will concentrate all its efforts on carrying out the following immediate political, economic, cultural and military tasks:

First. The Government of the Republic will thoroughly implement the line of independence, self-sustenance and self-defense to consolidate the political independence of the country, further strengthen the foundations of an independent national economy capable of ensuring the complete reunification, independence and prosperity of our nation, and increase the defense capabilities of the country so as to reliably safeguard its security on the basis of our own forces, by excellently materializing our Party's idea of Juche in all fields.

Our Party's idea of Juche represents the most correct Marxist-Leninist idea of leadership for the successful accomplishment of our revolution and construction and is the invariable guiding principle of the Government of the Republic in all its policies and activities.

Only by firmly establishing Juche can each country repudiate flunkeyism to great powers and dogmatism and creatively apply the universal truth of Marxism-Leninism and the experience of other countries in line with its historical conditions and national characteristics; always solve its own problems by itself on its own responsibility, eliminating reliance on others while displaying the spirit of self-reliance; and accordingly, carry on its revolutionary cause and construction work successfully.

Establishing Juche is a question of special importance for us in the light of our country's geographical situation and environment, the specifics of its historical development and the complex and arduous character of our revolution. The establishment of Juche is a question of key importance on which the success of our revolution depends, a vital question which will determine the future of our nation.

The Government of the Republic has been able to score great victories and successes in the revolutionary struggle and construction work, as it has persistently endeavored to solve all problems independently, in conformity with the specific realities of our country and mainly through its own efforts, guided consistently by the Juche idea of the Workers' Party of Korea in its activities and strictly adhering to the principles of Marxism-Leninism.

As a result of our efforts to establish Juche in the ideological field, the national pride of our workers and their sense of independence have grown tremendously, and they have acquired the revolutionary characteristics: not following others blindly, approaching foreign things critically instead of mechanically copying or swallowing them whole; and striving to solve all problems according to the actual conditions of our country and on the basis of their own wisdom and strength.

Thanks to the fact that our Party's spirit of independence, self-sustenance and self-defense is finding full expression in all fields of national construction, the political independence of the Republic has been consolidated and the economic independence and military power of our country have grown even more.

As a full-fledged, independent state, our country now sets its own lines and policies independently and exercises complete equality and sovereignty in its foreign relations.

Under the leadership of our Party and the Government of the Republic, our people have laid firm foundations for an independent national economy in accord with the revolutionary principle of self-reliance and thus eliminated the centuries-old backwardness and poverty, further increased the economic might of the Republic and radically improved their standard of living. The establishment of Juche in science and culture has accelerated scientific and technological progress, brought about a great qualitative change in education and in the work of training cadres, and led to the blossoming and advancement of a new, socialist national culture congenial to the life and sentiments of our people.

In the field of defense construction, too, we have strengthened our defense capabilities to such an extent that we are in a position to firmly defend the security of our country and our socialist gains even in the complex situation existing today on the basis of our own strength.

The great victories and successes we have attained in our socialist revolution and socialist construction over the past years are, indeed, the brilliant fruition of the great vitality of our Party's idea of Juche and of our line of independence, self-sustenance and self-defense—the embodiment of that idea in all fields. We formulated our policies independently by creatively applying the principles of Marxism-Leninism to the specific realities of Korea and enlisted the inexhaustible creative potential of our industrious and talented people and our rich national resources to carry out these policies. This has enabled us to build a socialist state in a short time, which has political independence, economic self-sustenance and national self-defense.

Our Party's line of strengthening the political, economic and military might of the country in every way with all our efforts is the most correct way of expediting the victory of the Korean revolution.

The Government of the Republic will continue to adhere firmly to the principle of settling independently all the problems that arise in revolution and construction, studying and analyzing the realities of Korea in strict accordance with the Juche idea of the Workers' Party of Korea.

All nations are equal and have the solemn right of national self-determination of deciding their own destinies for themselves. A nation can secure independence and freedom and attain welfare and prosperity only if it achieves complete political self-determination and exercises its rights taking them firmly into its hands.

Under the leadership of our Party, the Government of the Republic will use its own head in formulating all our policies for socialist construction in the fields of industry, agriculture, education, literature and art, judicial adminsitration, etc., in conformity with our realities, and carry them out with its own efforts. We must not act on orders and instructions of others but, on the basis of the interests of our revolution and construction, settle all problems from the standpoint of Juche, using our own judgment and making our own decisions. It is true that we should unite with friends who are fighting for a common goal and learn from their experience if it accords with the principles of Marxism-Leninism and it is worth learning. But, even so, we must always approach such experience critically, vehemently opposing the tendency to swallow foreign things whole or imitate them mechanically; we must not blindly copy what does not fit our actual conditions.

In the struggle for our country's reunification, too, the Government of the Republic will always hold fast to its independent position. We regard all attempts to effect the country's reunification by relying on outside forces as treacheries against the country and the nation aimed at placing the whole of Korea in the hands of foreign aggressors. The question of Korean reunification is an internal affair of the Korean people, one which cannot be settled by any outside forces. Ours is a wise and civilized nation, fully capable of settling its national problems for itself. We consistently hold that the question of reunifying our country must be settled through the efforts of our people themselves, without interference from any outside forces, under the condition that the aggressive army of U.S. imperialism is withdrawn from south Korea.

In the sphere of foreign policy, too, we should continue to work to establish political and economic relations with other countries on the principles of complete equality and mutual respect. We must always rely on our own judgment and conviction in struggling against imperialism and Right and "Left" opportunism, in conformity with our actual conditions and let no one violate and affront the rights and dignity of our nation.

The Government of the Republic will continue to faithfully carry out our Party's line of building an independent national economy by fully applying the principle of self-reliance in the economic sphere, while, at the same time, consolidating political independence.

Today we are confronted with the weighty task of carrying on economic construction and defense upbuilding in parallel to lay a firm material foundation for the prosperity of all the generations to come and establish a sound economic base which will enable us to readily cope with the great revolutionary event of the reunification of our country. All this can be achieved successfully only if the principle of self-reliance, the line of building an independent national economy is adhered to consistently and implemented more thoroughly.

Self-reliance is a thoroughly revolutionary stand for a people to accomplish the revolution in their country mainly relying on their own forces; it is an independent stand of building up their country through their own labor and with their own national resources.

Only by firmly maintaining such a revolutionary stand and revolutionary principle can we carry on the struggle without forsaking revolutionary constancy, no matter what complex and difficult situation may confront us, and assure victory in the revolutionary struggle and success in our work of construction, bravely overcoming difficulties and hardships that stand in the way of our advance. If you lack the revolutionary spirit of self-reliance, you may lose faith in your own strength, neglect efforts to tap the inner resources of your country, grow indolent and loose, and fall into a state of passivity and conservatism.

Only when a nation builds an independent national economy can it secure political independence, make its country rich, strong and advanced, and achieve national prosperity.

Economic independence is the material foundation for political independence. A country which is economically dependent on outside forces becomes a political satellite of other countries; an economically subjected nation cannot free itself from colonial slavery politically.

Without building an independent national economy it is impossible to establish material and technological foundations for socialism and build socialism and communism successfully.

To build socialism, it is essential to create a powerful base of heavy industry with the machine-building industry as its core, and on this basis, equip light industry, agriculture, transport and all other branches of the national economy with up-to-date techniques, thus laying the powerful material and technological foundations for socialism—needed to improve the welfare of the working people as a whole—as the laws of socialism require.

As long as national distinctions remain and states exist, these material and technological foundations of socialism must be built by each national state as a unit. Therefore, it can be said that firm material and technological foundations of socialism have been laid in each country only when it has built a comprehensive, independent national economy diversified in its development, equipped with the latest technology and run by its own national cadres, using its own natural resources, raw materials and other supplies so that its domestic products can fully meet the varied and ever-growing requirements of economic and defense construction and the people's consumption for heavy and light industrial goods and farm produce.

Only if the material and technological foundations of socialism are established in this way within the bounds of each national state as a comprehensive, independent economic unit, can the country's natural resources be tapped and utilized to the fullest and a high rate of growth in production be maintained together with a correct and flexible balance among all branches of the national economy. Moreover, only in this way is it possible to develop science, technology and culture rapidly, steadily raise the technological and cultural standards of the working people, and turn them into people of a new type, developed in an all-round way.

The building of an independent national economy is also the basic guarantee that nations can eliminate the economic backwardness which constitutes the real basis of inequalities between them, achieve national prosperity and build a socialist and communist society successfully.

The building of socialism and communism, as you know, requires the eradication of inequalities between nations as well as of class distinctions.

Such inequalities, however, do not disappear immediately when the socialist revolution triumphs in each country, nor do they vanish through the amalgamation of nations in one way or another.

The era of capitalism is an era in which national oppression prevails side by side with class exploitation, an era in which the free development of the great majority of nations is held back by a few nations and inequalities between nations exist. It is, therefore, necessary for the nations liberated from capitalist exploitation and oppression not only to become laboring socialist nations but also to build highly developed, independent national economies for their fullest free development and all-round efflorescence. Only by so doing can all inequalities among nations be done away with and can all nations build socialism with success and gradually go on to communism.

All this testifies to the fact that the line of building an independent national economy, consistently followed by our Party and the Government of the Republic, is a thoroughly revolutionary line of economic construction that conforms with the laws which govern the building of socialism and communism.

We will apply the revolutionary principle of self-reliance in building up our national defenses as well and thus further increase our country's capabilities for self-defense.

Needless to say, the international unity of the proletariat of all countries and the friendly alliance of the socialist countries in the revolutionary struggle against imperialist aggression and against the pressures of international capital are an important guarantee for safeguarding the revolutionary gains already obtained and winning new victories. It is the sacred internationalist duty of Communists to do all they can to help and give support and encouragement to each other in the battle against imperialism, their common enemy, and each country should strive to strengthen this international solidarity in the struggle against imperialist forces of aggression from without.

The decisive factor for victory in the struggle against imperialist reaction, however, is the internal forces of the country concerned. Although foreign support is important in a war against foreign aggressors, to all intents and purposes it plays no more than a secondary role. When the internal forces in a country are not prepared, its revolutionary struggle cannot emerge victorious, no matter how great its foreign support may be. If the Communists only pin their hopes on foreign support and aid, without developing their own revolutionary forces, they cannot be sure of defending the security of their country and their revolutionary gains against imperialist aggression.

The Government of the Republic will materialize our Party's spirit of self-defense, thoroughly preparing our people and soldiers politically and ideologically for war; it will make full material preparations to defend our country, relying on the solid foundations of the independent national economy we have already established and, at the same time, further increase our military might.

Particularly, by carrying out the decisions of the Conference of the Workers' Party of Korea in full, we will concentrate all our efforts on reorganizing the whole work of building our socialist economy to fit the requirements of the present situation and on reinforcing our defense capabilities to meet the undisguised aggressive maneuvers by the enemy. Thus, we will make ours an ever more solid and viable, independent economy to fully meet the material needs of both the front lines and the rear in case of emergency, and we will make our country's military power impregnable to repel the enemy on our own no matter when he may launch a surprise attack against us.

Materializing the Juche idea of the Workers' Party of Korea successfully in all fields, we will build an ever richer, stronger and mightier socialist state—independent in politics, self-sustaining in the economy and self-defensive in national defense.

Second. In order to end the present misfortunes of our people caused by the artificial split of our territory and nation as soon as possible, liberate the people in south Korea and reunify our country, the Government of the Republic will firmly equip the people in the northern half morally and materially to always support the south Korean people in their sacred anti-U.S. struggle for national salvation and to readily cope with the great revolutionary event.

Owing to the occupation of south Korea by the U. S. imperialists, our country is still divided into north and south, and the reunification of the country, the heartfelt desire of the nation, has not yet been achieved when a new generation has grown up; and our people have been suffering from the national split for more than 20 years. As the days go by, the gulf between north and south Korea is widening in all spheres—political, economic and cultural—and the national community of our people, formed through a long history, is gradually melting away. Territorial partition and national split make it impossible to coordinate our efforts to enlist and utilize our country's wealth, national wisdom and talents to promote the prosperity of the country and the welfare of the people.

The division of Korea into north and south has caused immeasurable misery and distress particularly to the south Korean people. South Korea today has been completely turned into a colony of the U. S. imperialists, into their military base of aggression. The national industry of south Korea has been reduced to dependency on foreign capital, and its agriculture, too, is in serious crisis. The national culture and the beautiful customs inherent in the Korean people have been utterly trampled underfoot, and all kinds of immorality and depravity prevail everywhere in south Korea. The south Korean people are going hungry in rags, doubly and triply exploited and oppressed, many of them roaming the streets in quest of work and living in a state of constant anxiety with all hopes blighted. They are subjected to unbearable racial insults and contempt, and even their right to existence is constantly threatened by the U.S. imperialist aggressors.

Where there are exploitation and oppression, there will always be revolutionary struggle on the part of the people. Ever since the first days of the occupation of the southern half by the U. S. imperialist aggressors, the south Korean people have been fighting tenaciously against their policies of colonial enslavement and military aggression. The October Popular Resistance Struggle in 1946, the April Uprising in 1960 which toppled the puppet regime of Syngman Rhee, and many struggles waged successively by the south Korean people against the "ROK-Japan talks" and for the abrogation of the "ROK-Japan agreements," dealt telling blows to the colonial rule of U.S. imperialism.

Each time, the U.S. imperialists and their stooges harshly repressed the people's righteous patriotic struggle at the point of the bayonet. The policy of military fascist dictatorship pursued in south Korea today has assumed unprecedented ferocity and barbarity and has become a prototype of vicious fascist rule by the imperialists over their colonies. The U.S. imperialist aggressors and their puppets, while manufacturing numerous wicked fascist laws, greatly increased their repressive apparatuses, and covered the whole of south Korea with military, police, intelligence and special agent networks, thereby turning it into a living hell of terrorism and murder.

In south Korea today the U. S. imperialists and the Pak Jung Hi clique are intensifying their fascist repression to the limit. Everywhere they are making all sorts of frenzied attempts to repress the south Korean people, who are fighting harder than ever for the right to live, for democratic liberties and for the reunification of their country. According to south Korean press reports, this year alone ten or more divisions including U. S.

imperialist troops, south Korean puppet army, police forces and reserve divisions, were mobilized to crush the armed groups of south Korean revolutionaries in action and the mass revolutionary struggle, breaking out one after another all over south Korea. A total of more than six million U. S. imperialist troops, south Korean puppet troops and police took part directly in the so-called "mopping-up operations." The U.S. imperialists and the Pak Jung Hi clique cruelly suppressed the revolutionary organization formed around Dr. Kim Dae Su, professor at Kyongbuk University, arresting and imprisoning more than ten patriotic intellectuals, and last autumn arrested many young people in and around Pusan on the charge of involvement in the alleged "case of the People's Revolutionary Party." Again, they recently used trumped-up charges in what they called the "Case of the Operative Group for the Communization of South Korea" in Seoul and, on the other hand, arrested and imprisoned many university professors, other intellectuals and patriotic figures, branding the Society for Comparative Studies on Nationalism—an academic organization—as a "seditious organization," and tried the victims in a kangaroo court. They have thus committed the heinous crime of "demanding" the death penalty or life imprisonment for many innocent persons.

They are raising an ever-louder "anti-communist" hue and cry under the nonsensical allegation that all the fierce revolutionary struggles of the patriotic people which are breaking out all over south Korea today are the work of "spies" sent down from north Korea, and they are trying hard to take the minds of the south Korean people off their troubles and to deceive the peoples of the world.

But no amount of brutal repression and "anti-communist" campaign by the U.S. imperialists and the Pak Jung Hi puppet clique can ever dampen the indomitable revolutionary fighting spirit of the south Korean people or block their sweeping revolutionary advance. Today broad sections of the south Korean people are waging a vigorous struggle in all fields, holding still higher the banner of anti-U.S. resistance struggle for national salvation. A people can win freedom and liberation only through its own struggle. When the broad masses of the people rise as one in a struggle against their oppressors, they can destroy any imperialist bulwark. If the workers and peasants, youth and students, intellectuals and other broad sectors of the people in south Korea unite firmly and come out courageously in revolutionary struggle, they will be able to deal a crushing defeat to the U. S. imperialists and the Pak Jung Hi clique and accomplish the cause of the south Korean revolution.

On behalf of the entire people in the northern half of the Republic, I send warm revolutionary greetings to the revolutionaries and democratic figures, to all the patriotic people who are putting up a valiant struggle in various parts of south Korea, underground, in mountains and even in prison.

All the people in the northern half of the Republic bear the great responsibility of carrying the south Korean revolution to a conclusion, giving active support to the struggle of the south Korean people, keeping up with their exalted fighting spirit.

As long as the U. S. imperialists continue to occupy south Korea and our country remains partitioned, the Korean people cannot live in peace even for a moment and the people in south Korea cannot extricate themselves from their present misery and pain. The occupation of south Korea by U. S. imperialism and its policy of aggression are the source of all the misfortunes of our nation and the main obstacle to the reunification of our country.

We cannot simply contemplate the miserable plight of our south Korean compatriots with folded arms and we can never bequeath a divided country to our descendants. As long as this wretched situation continues in which the country and the nation are divided and our compatriots, blood brothers and sisters, are subjected to all sorts of racial insults and ill-treatment by the foreign aggressors, no Korean Communist or conscientious Korean nationalist can say that he has fulfilled his duty.

We must accomplish the south Korean revolution and reunify the country in our generation and bequeath a unified country to the new generations. We must prepare all necessary conditions for the reunification of our country as soon as possible.

The accomplishment of the great cause of liberating south Korea and reunifying the country at the earliest possible date depends not only on how the revolutionary organizations and revolutionaries in south Korea expand and strengthen the revolutionary forces and how they fight the enemy but also, to a large extent, on how the people in the northern half of the

Republic prepare themselves to cope with the great revolutionary event.

The most important thing in completing the south Korean revolution and hastening the reunification of the country is to well prepare all our people politically and ideologically and, at the same time, create all the necessary material conditions.

We should always give active material and moral support and encouragement to the south Korean people in their anti-U. S., national-salvation struggle and consider the south Korean revolution and the reunification of the country our first and foremost revolutionary task. We can never allow ourselves to become self-complacent with the achievements wrought in the northern half and become lax and indolent. How can we sit idly by at a time when the south Korean people, suffering from hunger, are waging a struggle at the cost of their blood? It is our lofty national duty and the supreme task of the nation to force the U. S. imperialist aggressors out of our territory, liberate south Korea and reunify our country by pooling our strength with that of the south Korean people.

The people in the northern half of the Republic should always remember their brothers in the south and have revolutionary determination to liberate them at all costs; they should be firmly prepared ideologically to be mobilized for a decisive struggle to accomplish the cause of the reunification of the country by joining forces with the south Korean people whenever called upon to go to their aid as the struggle of the people surges forward and the revolutionary situation ripens in south Korea.

Meanwhile, socialist economic construction, the principal guarantee for strengthening the material forces of our revolutionary base, should be successfully carried on to further consolidate the economic foundations of our country so that adequate material preparations can be made to support the revolutionary struggle of the south Korean people and to readily cope with the great revolutionary event of realizing the reunification of our country.

The present situation requires us to conduct all our work in a more active, more revolutionary manner and subordinate everything to the struggle to accomplish the south Korean revolution by giving support to the south Korean people in their struggle and to reunify our country.

The northern half of the Republic is the revolutionary base for accomplishing the great cause of national liberation throughout the country, and its revolutionary forces are the most important motive power for the Korean revolution as a whole. All the working people should fully realize that, unless the revolutionary base of the northern half of the Republic is fortified and its revolutionary forces are strengthened still more, it will be impossible to give positive support to the south Korean revolution and achieve the reunification of our country; they must continue to wage a tenacious struggle on all fronts of socialist economic construction and produce and build more, better and cheaper with our existing manpower, equipment and materials by discovering and activating reserves and potentialities to the utmost. All functionaries and working people, as masters in their country, should assiduously manage all aspects of economic life, both national and individual, and make every effort not to waste a single grain of rice, a single gram of iron or a single drop of gasoline.

Only when our country's economic foundations are more consolidated and the necessary material conditions are sufficiently created can we cope with the great event with full preparations, bring the superiority of the socialist system home to the fighting people of south Korea and give powerful support to their revolutionary struggle. Only then will it be possible to create assets with which to put the devastated south Korean economy back on its feet and rapidly improve the deteriorated living conditions of the people in the southern half, after the reunification of the country.

All our functionaries and working people should work like masters and live frugally with great revolutionary zeal, in the lofty spirit of supporting the south Korean people more actively in their anti-U. S., national-salvation struggle and of expediting the revolutionary cause of the reunification of the country. We can never get complacent and lax nor countenance the slightest laziness, immorality or luxury. We are making a revolution and we should work and live in a revolutionary way, ready and alert at all times.

All our people will, in this way, be made ready to cope with the great revolutionary event of national reunification. We should all be ready and willing to take part in the revolutionary struggle whenever called upon to do so by the Party.

Third. The Government of the Republic, under the leadership of the Workers' Party of Korea, will wage a vigorous struggle to revolutionize and working-classize the peasants, intellectuals and all other members of society by further stepping up the ideological and cultural revolutions and enhancing the leading role of the working class.

By strengthening the state's functions of proletarian dictatorship steadily, we should not only crush the hostile elements that are worming their way in from without with the aim of disorganizing our revolutionary base and put down the resistance offered by the remnants of the overthrown exploiter classes, but also revolutionize and working-classize all members of society by pushing ahead vigorously with the ideological and cultural revolutions.

To educate and remold the entire people and thereby revolutionize and working-classize the whole society is an important task of the dictatorship of the proletariat in our society, in which the exploiter classes have been liquidated and the socialist system has triumphed. The process of building socialism and communism is one of revolutionizing all the members of society—workers, peasants and intellectuals—a process of doing away with all class distinctions by transforming the whole of society on the working-class pattern.

In order to build socialism and communism, we must develop our productive forces and do away with the distinctions between the working class and the peasantry in working conditions and forms of ownership of the means of production, and we must also eliminate step by step disparities among all members of society in the ideological, moral, cultural and technical standards. To this end, the ideological revolution should be intensified so as to root out all the hangovers of outmoded bourgeois ideology that still remain in the minds of the people, and firmly arm all our working people with the revolutionary ideas of the working class, with the Marxist-Leninist world outlook, so that they can fight devotedly through thick and thin, in the interests of the collective and the whole society, for our country and people; moreover, the cultural revolution should be carried out at the same time, so as to bring them to attain high cultural and technical levels.

Today, more than ever before, the task of further

revolutionizing and working-classizing all members of society —
workers, peasants and intellectuals — is urgently confronting
us. We should further accelerate socialist construction through
our own efforts under the difficult conditions facing the
country, now divided into north and south, and should force the
U. S. imperialist aggressors, the chief of world reaction, out of
our territory, liberate south Korea and accomplish the
revolutionary cause of reunifying the country. This is a
revolutionary task which requires a very arduous and difficult,
protracted and intense struggle. Only when all the working
people are revolutionized and working-classized through the
promotion of the ideological and cultural revolutions will it be
possible to bring their revolutionary enthusiasm and creative
initiative into full play and raise their technical and cultural
levels, and thus bravely overcome the difficulties that crop up
in the course of progress, solve economic and technical
problems with credit and also successfully expedite the
building of socialism in the northern half of the Republic,
complete the revolution in south Korea and accomplish the
revolutionary cause of reunifying the country.

We must wage a powerful struggle to revolutionize and
working-classize all members of society by further elevating the
leading role of the working class.

Our working class is young, and it needs much revolutionary
training. The ranks of the working class swelled suddenly in our
country as industry was given a big boost in a short time
following liberation. Our working class includes many people
who have never personally experienced exploitation and
oppression by the capitalists, as well as a considerable number
of former small traders and handicraftsmen who became
workers after the socialist transformation of production
relations.

We should further enhance the ideology, organization and
culture of the working class so as to turn it into a still more
revolutionary, progressive and cultured class and to enable it to
better perform its historical mission of transforming the whole
of society and educating and remolding all the working people.

Revolutionizing and working-classizing the peasantry, the
most reliable ally of the working class in the building of
socialism and communism, is an important guarantee of victory
for our revolution. The Government of the Republic, in keeping

with the line set forth in the *Theses on the Socialist Rural Question in Our Country,* should carry forward the ideological and cultural revolutions in the countryside energetically and continue to strengthen the working class's political leadership and cultural influence among the peasantry. The peasants should thus be thoroughly equipped with the revolutionary ideas of the working class and their cultural level should be brought up to that of the working class.

The revolutionization of the intellectuals holds the most important place in the working-classization of the whole society. We should eradicate all remnants of obsolete ideologies from the minds of our intellectuals, arm them with communist ideas and thus lead them to become revolutionaries loyal to the Party, to the working class, to the country and to the people.

The most important thing in revolutionizing and working-classizing all the members of society through the ideological revolution is to firmly arm the working people with the policies of the Workers' Party of Korea and thoroughly establish the Party's unitary ideological system among them. We should fully explain and bring the Party's lines and policies home to the working people and make sure that they acquire a clear grasp of their essentials and correctness. In this way, we should see to it that they combat all unsound, counterrevolutionary ideological elements vehemently—such as revisionism, "Left" opportunism, flunkeyism to great powers, bourgeois ideas, feudal-Confucian ideas, factionalism, parochialism and nepotism—that they think and act in accord with the ideas of the Workers' Party of Korea at all times and places and advance confidently along the only path indicated by the Party, without the slightest vacillation in any storm and stress.

We should step up our political and ideological work among the masses so as to further stimulate the class awakening of the working people and lead them to fight uncompromisingly against their class enemies.

The primary targets of our struggle in revolutionizing people are individualism and egoism, the hangovers from the exploiter classes. We should tirelessly strive to cultivate among the working people the collectivist spirit of placing the interests of the organization and the collective above personal interests and helping and leading each other forward and the lofty revolutionary spirit of valuing political life, and educate all the people to acquire a communist way of life, living and working in a revolutionary way.

The great vitality of the socialist system lies, above all, in the fact that the working people, freed from exploitation and oppression, display conscious enthusiasm and creative initiative and work devotedly for their homeland, for the people and for their own happiness as masters of their country and their future. In order to bring this superiority into play and demonstrate the might of the socialist system to the full, education in socialist patriotism should be stepped up decisively among the working people.

We should acquaint our working people clearly with the essential nature and superiority of the socialist system and lead them to fight resolutely in defense of this system and struggle actively for the prosperity and development of their homeland and for the well-being of our people. In particular, serious attention should be directed to educating the working people to take loving care of everything we have already created and to make more effective use of the valuable assets we have already obtained. The entire working people should clearly understand that all our wealth is for the prosperity and progress of our country, for the happiness of our people and for their own good and should take the attitude proper to masters as respects the economic life of the country, carry out their revolutionary tasks in an efficient, responsible way, and do their best to benefit the country and the people. Everyone should sincerely take part in collective labor to increase the wealth of the country and the people and to manage it with care; system and order should be established and revolutionary work discipline voluntarily observed in all branches, in all units of work.

Education in the revolutionary traditions is one of the most powerful means of revolutionizing people. Experience has shown that education in the revolutionary traditions has an incomparably great influence in revolutionizing those who have never personally undergone the ordeals of revolutionary struggle and the younger generation which has never experienced exploitation and oppression by landlords and capitalists. We should step up education in the revolutionary traditions among the working people so that everyone may model himself after the indomitable lofty revolutionary spirit of the forerunners of our revolution and their noble revolutionary characteristics.

Parallel with the ideological revolution, the cultural revolution should also be actively pushed forward.

Without carrying out the cultural revolution the cultural and technical levels of our working people cannot be raised, nor can the ideological revolution be carried out successfully.

The habit of studying should be firmly established among the working people so that everyone may make all his efforts to raise his level of general knowledge, and that all people may master more than one skill. Moreover, we must work hard to form a large contingent of steadfast, competent working-class intellectuals, capable of skillfully solving the problems which arise in all fields of our revolution and construction.

We should step up the ideological and cultural revolutions and thus further revolutionize and working-classize people so as to build up the entire country into one big Red family, make the whole society seethe with revolutionary enthusiasm and see that all our working people make continuous innovations and continuous advance at the speed of Chollima, always ready and alert, working new miracles and bringing about a great upsurge in revolutionary struggle and the work of construction.

Fourth. The Government of the Republic will see to it that the functionaries of the state and economic bodies eliminate bureaucracy and establish a revolutionary mass viewpoint so as to enhance the functions and role of the people's power and actively organize and mobilize the broad masses of the people for revolution and construction.

In order to successfully carry out the huge tasks confronting us at present, we should further enhance the functions and role of the people's power as the executor of the lines and policies of the Workers' Party of Korea and as a powerful weapon for socialist construction; we should also further improve the guidance of the revolution and construction. This requires that the functionaries of state and economic bodies maintain closer ties with the popular masses, rid themselves of the bureacratic style of work and adopt the revolutionary mass viewpoint.

When the Party's lines and policies are correct and proper ways and means are adopted for their execution, success in carrying forward the revolutionary tasks depends entirely on the method and style of work of those who directly organize and carry them out, on how they organize and mobilize the broad masses for the work.

Our Party and the Government of the Republic have constantly paid close attention to reorganizing the system of work in the state and economic bodies and improving the method and syle of work of their functionaries, in accord with new circumstances and conditions. As a result, no small success has been achieved in this respect. Particularly, a great change has taken place in the activities of state and economic bodies in the course of generalizing the experience of the guidance given at Chongsan-ri in February 1960.

Our functionaries, however, still fall short of the standards required by our Party in their method and style of work, failing to skillfully organize and mobilize the broad masses of the people so as to give full play to their exalted revolutionary spirit in the fulfillment of revolutionary tasks.

For our people's power to solidly defend the interests of people from all walks of life, rally the broad masses of the people around itself and bring their enthusiasm and activity into full play, the functionaries of state and economic bodies should make drastic changes in their method and style of work.

All the functionaries of our state and economic bodies are workers selected by the people; they are the servants of the people. They should never forget that their job is to protect the interests of the workers, peasants and the rest of the working people and serve them; they should work heart and soul for the Party, the working class and the people.

In order to be faithful to the Party and the revolution and be true servants of the people, our functionaries must have Party spirit, working-class spirit and popular spirit, which should be manifested in their practical struggle to implement our Party's lines and policies and in their practical activities on behalf of the workers, peasants and other working people. Only those who carry our Party's policies through to completion can be considered revolutionaries faithful to our Party and revolution, faithful to the working class and the people. All our functionaries must become ardent defenders, active propagandists and staunch executors of our Party's policies. They should study our Party's policies in depth, and grasp their essential nature, adhere to them strictly in their work, weigh all problems in terms of our Party's policies and wage a timely and uncompromising struggle against practices which run counter to the Party's intentions. Our functionaries should be active in explaining and spreading our Party's policies among the masses and strive persistently to carry them through correctly. The functionaries of our state and economic bodies should devotedly do any work which is in the interests of the people through fire and water.

In order to eliminate bureaucracy and establish the revolutionary mass viewpoint, all our functionaries should acquire the revolutionary work method of going deep among the masses, consulting with them and enlisting them in the fulfillment of the tasks in hand. The functionaries of our state and economic bodies should strictly follow the Chongsan-ri method, our Party's traditional revolutionary method of work, in their activities.

First of all, political work should be given priority in all matters so as to constantly increase the political and ideological preparedness of the masses and encourage the broad masses of the people to volunteer for revolutionary tasks. When undertaking a revolutionary task, leading functionaries should, above all, correctly explain the Party's aim with regard to the task, bring it home to the masses and see that they collectively discuss ways and means for the implementation of the Party policy and persist in their struggle to carry it out with a high degree of revolutionary enthusiasm.

Along with this, guidance should be given more directly to the lower levels, and the method of guidance be radically improved. The principal aim of guiding the lower levels is to help the workers there correct their shortcomings quickly and get great results in their work. Our functionaries of state and economic bodies should not just issue commands and directives when they go to the lower levels, but should give practical assistance to their subordinates, teaching them in a kindly way, cooperating with them in solving knotty problems and helping them do their work well.

The functionaries of our state and economic bodies should not only equip themselves with our Party's revolutionary method of work, but should have the popular trait of being always the first to implement the laws, decisions and directives of the state, setting an example with their own conduct in all work and being modest, unassuming and courteous, thereby becoming models for the masses in actual deeds. Only then will the people really trust and follow our functionaries, and the bonds of kinship between the people's power and the masses of people will be further strengthened.

Work style is not a question of the professional ability of the functionaries or of their personal character; rather it is an ideological manifestation, expressed in their work. We should intensify ideological education for our functionaries of state and economic bodies so that they may rid themselves of bureaucratic work style—the expression of surviving obsolete ideologies—and acquire a truly popular work style and the noble characteristics of boundless loyalty to the Party and the revolution and of resolutely fighting for the interests of our country and people.

While imbuing the functionaries of state and economic organs with class and mass outlooks, their technical and professional levels should be continually raised. This is absolutely necessary if they are to do away with bureaucratic work style and meet their great responsibilities to the Party, the state and the people. All these functionaries must establish the revolutionary habit of studying to completely master economic theory and technical know-how and the practical aspects of their work.

Thus, all our functionaries in state and economic bodies should be revolutionaries who thoroughly defend and implement our Party's lines and policies, and devote themselves to the struggle for the interests of the people, becoming their genuine, faithful servants, deeply loved and respected by the masses of people.

Fifth. The Government of the Republic will consolidate the foundations of the independent national economy of the

*country, further improve the people's standard of living and
fulfill the solemn duty of freeing the working people from
exhausting labor by holding on to the policy of the Workers'
Party of Korea for socialist industrialization and struggling to
carry out the technical revolution in all fields of our national
economy.*

Following the basic orientation for the economic development
of our country in the present stage, set by the Conference of the
Workers' Party of Korea, we should place the main emphasis
on making effective use of the already established economic
foundations through their proper improvement and reinforcement and on normalizing production in all spheres, and at the
same time, undertake new capital construction in a big way in
order to further expand the economic foundations of our
country. In this way, the productive forces of our country as a
whole should be further developed, and industrial production
more than doubled, in a few years.

1.Industry

Giving priority to the electric power and mining industries is
the basic prerequisite for normalizing production in all
branches of industry and for further advancing our national
economy. We will speedily develop our power and mining
industries to fully satisfy the demands of our national economy
for raw materials, fuel and power.

In developing the power industry, we will hold fast to the
policy of combining the construction of hydroelectric power
stations correctly with that of thermal power stations and of
simultaneous construction of large, medium and small-scale
power stations. Making use of the rich water and coal resources
of our country, we should accelerate the construction of
large-scale hydroelectric and thermal power plants and build
many medium and small-scale hydroelectric power stations and
factory thermal power stations everywhere, thus further
solidifying the country's power base. In this way, seasonal
fluctuations in power production caused by natural conditions

should be done away with entirely, and it should be made possible to increase production steadily in all branches of the national economy, unhampered by a limited power supply.

In developing the mining industry, it is important to adhere to three principles: give preference to geological prospecting work, carry out the technical revolution and actively push ahead with scientific research work.

The ranks of our prospectors should be expanded and their technical equipment reinforced in order to develop preliminary prospecting and, particularly, detailed and service prospecting radically; and the tempo and efficiency of prospecting work should be stepped up through the comprehensive introduction of advanced prospecting methods.

It is absolutely necessary that we promote the technical revolution energetically in the mining industry, where much of the work is more difficult and exhausting than in any other branch of the national economy. In coal and ore mines, we should work hard for mechanization and automation of drilling, hauling and all other arduous, labor-consuming operations. We should also introduce advanced mining methods extensively and, particularly, undertake open-cast mining on a large scale.

Meanwhile, scientific research work should be pushed forward actively in all aspects of the mining industry—surveys of underground resources and studies on their rational exploitation, research on the strengthening of the technical equipment in the mining industry and the improvement of extraction methods, studies on the comprehensive processing of ores, etc.

We should keep the mining industry well ahead of the development of the processing industries and further consolidate our country's raw material and fuel bases by carrying through our Party's line.

The development of the metal industry—and particularly the steel industry—is a major index showing the level of industrialization of a country and its economic power. In our country, with its inexhaustible resources of iron ores, the steel industry is one of our most promising industrial branches. We must scale the steel height set in the Seven-Year Plan by concentrating our efforts on developing ferrous metallurgy.

Our capacity for processing raw materials and products will

be augmented, auxiliary facilities will be improved and advanced technical processes including oxygen-blasting be extensively introduced in our existing iron and steel works to raise the production capacity of our metallurgical installations as much as possible. At the same time, reconstruction and expansion projects will be carried out in our metallurgical plants, including the building of new steel and rolling shops in the Kim Chaek Iron Works, to further expand and consolidate the bases of our country's ferrous metallurgy.

With the development of technology, the demand is rising steadily for higher quality and greater variety of steel. We should greatly increase our assortment of steels, and further develop the production of alloy steels. Serious attention will be given to increasing the assortment and gauges of rolled steel and, particularly, to developing the production of thin plate and cold-rolled products and raising the output of second-stage processing.

An especially important task for ferrous metallurgy in the present stage is to introduce domestic fuel on a large scale so as to further consolidate the independence of this branch. In order to develop our iron industry, using the anthracite coal abundant in our country, we should build the necessary material foundations, and, at the same time, keep promoting scientific research work for perfecting the reduced pellet process, the process of continuous steel making from granulated iron, and so on.

Nonferrous metallurgy should be developed further in order to put out various nonferrous metals and rare metals in greater quantities. The proportion of finished products should be raised in the production of nonferrous metals, through extensive nonferrous metal rolling, and work should be briskly carried forward to build up the base of our light metal production.

The engineering industry is the core of heavy industry and is the basis for the development of all branches of the national economy and for technical progress. Without advancing the engineering industry, we cannot hope for the development of our heavy and light industries and agriculture, nor can we satisfactorily perform the tasks of easing the strain on transport and increasing our defense capabilities. It can be said that, in carrying out the task of building up our economy and national defenses in parallel set forth at the Conference of the Workers' Party of Korea, or in fulfilling the Seven-Year Plan as a whole, everything depends, after all, on the development of our engineering industry.

Our country abounds in the ferrous and nonferrous metal resources needed for the development of the engineering industry and has solid metallurgical bases, as well. We should turn these favorable conditions to good account and speed up the development of our engineering industry, thus effecting the industrialization of the country and overall technical innovation in our national economy through our own efforts.

The efficient and economical machinery and equipment that are needed in the mining, metal, chemical, light and fishing industries, in agriculture, transport and all other branches of the national economy should be turned out in larger quantities by reinforcing and fully equipping our existing machine plants as soon as possible, building up many medium and small-sized machine factories and actively promoting specialization and cooperation in production.

In view of prospective requirements of the development of our national economy, the major equipment production bases for turning out large excavators, heavy-duty trucks, large tractors, large vessels, large machine tools, etc., should be further expanded and strenghtened and solid production bases should be built up for turning out high-speed precision machines, thereby raising our engineering industry to a higher level.

Extensive application of chemistry in all fields of the national economy is a major trend in the development of science and technology in modern times and a powerful factor in accelerating the development of the productive forces. By continuously directing great efforts to the development of the chemical industry, we should further expand and consolidate our raw material bases for light industry, and promote chemicalization of agriculture to increase its production and lighten the toil of the farmers.

A solid foundation has been laid in our country for developing the chemical industry with domestic raw materials. Drawing on this, we should further develop the inorganic and organic chemical industries and create such new branches of the chemical industry as oil processing and synthetic rubber industries to further develop and diversify the chemical industry in our country.

In the chemical industry, the output and quality of chemical fibers should be raised; new kinds of chemical fibers should be put out and the production of vinyl chloride and various other synthetic resins be increased. Along with nitrogen fertilizer, phosphorous and kali fertilizers should be produced with domestic raw materials, and weed killers and various other agricultural chemicals should be put out and supplied in great quantities. At the same time, we should step up the fight to produce the raw and other materials necessary for the building-materials industry, synthetic chemicals and various other new chemical products which are needed for the economic development of the country and the improvement of our people's livelihood.

The huge task of capital construction facing us in the parallel building up of our economy and national defenses and in the fulfillment of the Seven-Year Plan, cannot be carried out successfully without correspondingly increasing the production of building materials.

In the field of building-materials industry, the production of cement, metal and chemical building materials should be developed on a large scale. In developing this industry, we will implement the Party's line of improving and expanding the existing building-materials factories and properly combining this with the construction of new building-materials factories, and of simultaneously developing our large-scale central building-materials industry and our medium and small-scale local building-materials industry.

In the field of forestry, we should introduce the rotation cutting method to increase timber production and, at the same time, raise the rate of sawmill lumber output and the production of wood shavings and fiber boards to make a comprehensive and effective use of timber, thus easing our country's shortage of timber.

We should pay great attention to the development of light industry and bring about marked progress in the production of consumer goods in a few years.

The central tasks of light industry are those of raising the quality of consumer goods, increasing their variety and lowering their production costs. We should raise the quality of consumer goods to meet world standards as quickly as we can by increasing our workers' sense of responsibility in the field of light industry, perfecting the production processes, strictly observing the technical processes and standard operation regulations and elevating the technical knowledge and skills of the producers. We must improve the quality of fabrics and increase their variety, and further develop the production of daily necessities and foodstuffs. At the same time, we should produce greater quantities of different kinds of inexpensive consumer goods by striving actively to reduce production costs in light industry.

For our country, seabound on three sides, an active development and exploitation of marine resources is of great significance in promoting the well-being of the people.

We should increase our catch of fish by further cementing the material-technical foundations of the fishing industry, making wide use of advanced fishing methods and developing inshore and pelagic fishing in a big way. Besides increasing our catch, we should also decisively improve our fish-processing work. We should work hard to process all the fish we catch without any waste and raise the quality of processed fish by eliminating backward methods and widely introducing refrigeration, canning and other up-to-date methods of fish processing.

The strain on transport must first be eased in order to achieve a normalization of production and a rapid advance of the national economy.

We should continue to direct great efforts towards developing transport—railway transport in particular. The electrification of railways should be energetically pushed through to completion in the main within a few years, and diesel engines should be introduced in some sections, to increase rail haulage decisively. The production of electric locomotives, freight cars and passenger coaches should be further expanded. Use of the existing railway lines should be raised to the maximum and, at the same time, new lines should be built, with a view to satisfying our fast-growing demands for transport.

Parallel with this, river and ocean transport should be

advanced and automotive transport should further be expanded and developed.

2. Agriculture

In agriculture, all efforts should be concentrated on carrying into effect the *Theses on the Socialist Rural Question in Our Country.*

First of all, technical revolution should be effected in the countryside to ease the labor of the farmers and further increase agricultural production.

To expand and consolidate the successes already scored in irrigation, we should improve and make more effective use of the existing irrigation facilities and, at the same time, continue to carry out new irrigation works, afforestation and water conservation projects on a wide scale. Afforestation and water conservation projects should be well carried out after adequate surveys are made and designs are worked out in detail.

For the speedy mechanization of agriculture, various trailer farm implements and spare parts should be turned out so that sufficient supplies are made available and repair and maintenance work on farm machines should be improved.

We should introduce all-round chemicalization, while continuously pushing ahead with irrigation and mechanization in the countryside. A scientific fertilizing system should be established according to soil conditions and the special characteristics of crops to raise the effectiveness of chemical fertilizers, and crops should be thoroughly protected from all damage by blights and harmful insects through effective applications of various agricultural chemicals. Particularly, the tendency to emphasize nitrogen fertilizer alone should be discarded, and we should produce phosphorous, kali and microelement fertilizers on our own and supply them in large quantities to raise the per-unit-area yields decisively. At the same time, weed killers and other highly effective agricultural chemicals should be produced and applied in quantity.

Without electrification in the countryside, it is impossible to successfully carry out irrigation and mechanization and build the farm villages in a modern way. In accordance with the line of our Party and the Government of the Republic for electrification, electricity has already been installed in 98.2% of all the rural *ri* and 86.1% of all the farmhouses in our country. Only far isolated houses in the mountain areas have yet to be supplied with electricity. While bringing together the scattered farmhouses as much as possible, we should keep promoting electrification to supply electricity to all our villages and farmhouses in a few years.

In order to successfully carry out the huge tasks of the technical revolution in the countryside, productive construction should be undertaken on a large scale.

For this purpose, the size and direction of capital investments should be correctly fixed according to the specific conditions of each farm village. In construction, designing should be kept ahead of other work, and its quality should be raised. The work of building should be done meticulously.

Simultaneously with productive construction, many new, modern houses should be build and older ones rebuilt on modern lines in the countryside. In this way the straw-thatched houses, our rural inheritance of backwardness and poverty through the ages, should be completely eliminated in the next few years.

We should take all these economic and technical measures for the speedy development of all sectors of agricultural production—grain growing, cultivation of industrial crops and vegetables, etc.

While decisively boosting grain output above all, great attention should also be paid to the development of stockbreeding. An energetic struggle should be waged to further consolidate its existing foundations and put stock-breeding on a modern basis so that our backwardness in this field—a hangover from the past—may be eliminated and the output of animal products be decisively increased. The most important task in developing stockbreeding is to create stable fodder bases. To achieve this, double cropping should be introduced extensively in rice paddies and dry fields, and, in addition, high-yield fodder crops should be cultivated in extensive areas and assorted feed factories built in many places. Measures should be taken to establish a system of breeding superior pedigreed stock, and the care of the animals should be improved so that the productivity of our livestock may be raised and the production costs of animal products systematically lowered.

In our country, nearly 80% of which is mountainous, large-scale fruit growing by making use of the mountains is of great significance for the development of the national economy and for raising our people's living standards.

We should set great value on the 133,000-odd *chongbo* of orchards and 100,000 *chongbo* of chestnut tree groves we already have, and take good care of them so that all of them are in production, thus markedly increasing output of fruit and chestnuts. Also, in keeping with the decision of the Pukchong Enlarged Meeting of the Presidium of the Central Committee of the Workers' Party of Korea, the work of planting orchards should be continued, and the total area in fruit trees be increased to 200,000 *chongbo* in the next few years in order to supply the people with delicious fruit in greater quantity. Measures should also be taken actively for storing and processing the fruit as output increases from year to year.

3. The People's Living

Interest in promoting the people's well-being is the supreme principle governing the activities of the Government of the Republic. Our struggle to build socialism and communism is aimed, in the final analysis, at fully satisfying the material and cultural demands of all our people and providing them with a rich and cultured life.

The source of the constant increase in the well-being of the working people lies in the systematic growth of the national income.

The Government of the Republic will do everything possible to increase the national income substantially, by quickly developing industry, agriculture and all other branches of the national economy. At the same time, close attention will be given to the proper distribution of the national income on the principle of rationally adjusting the balance between accumulation and consumption and raising the people's standard of living markedly while ensuring a high rate of expanded reproduction and a successful defense upbuilding.

In the future, we will take all measures to raise the money wages and real incomes of the working people on the basis of increased socialist production and labor productivity.

The Government of the Republic will make greater state investments in various social and cultural services in order to more fully satisfy the demands of the entire working people.

In particular, close attention will be paid to improving trade and the public health services in order to raise the general living standards of the people.

Commerce is the supply service of the working people in our country and an important means of meeting the material and cultural needs of the people.

In the field of trade, greater quantities of foodstuffs, clothes and various articles that go to meet cultural needs should be supplied to the working people and, in particular, the sales of winter goods should be greatly increased.

To improve commodity supply, commercial networks should be properly distributed and further expanded, trading facilities should be modernized and commodities be well distributed to meet the demands of the different regions and social groups according to the season of the year. Trade should be more cultured and give better service by proper organization of the work of packaging and delivery, night sales and sales made on the road.

The number of restaurants of various kinds should be increased and the quality of public catering improved, offering more conveniences to the working people in their everyday life.

Service establishments should be increased in number and so furnished as to give better service to the working people. In this way, conditions should be provided to make it possible for large numbers of housewives to participate in social labor and thus working-classize and revolutionize themselves.

In our system, nothing is more precious than the people. We should develop our public health services to protect the lives of the people and further promote the health of the working people.

In public health, more hospitals and clinics should be built and many medical workers assigned to them, and our doctors' qualifications should be raised decidedly so as to continue improving medical services for the working people. The policy on preventive medicine should be firmly maintained and work in hygiene and of an antiepidemiological nature be carried out regularly in both urban and rural areas. Attention should also be given to the development of our country's traditional *Tonguihak* medicine along with modern medicine, and to the theoretical systematization of folk medicine. The production of medicines should be developed so as to increase the variety of synthetic pharmaceutical products and boost the production of antibiotics.

4. Labor Administration

The laboring masses are the makers of history. Socialism and communism can be built only by the creative labor of the working millions. The labor force is the most active and decisive factor in production. Technology is developed by man, and machines are made and operated by man. All the material and cultural wealth of the world, precious and fine, is created by the labor of the working people.

We can say that whether or not we can build socialism and communism faster and better depends, after all, on how we bring the creative ability and talents of the working people into play, how we organize and use social labor and how speedily we raise labor productivity.

The improvement of labor administration is a very important task throughout the course of socialist construction.

The improvement of labor administration involves a problem of particular importance in our country.

Under the conditions prevailing in our country, where arable land is scarce, intensive farming methods should be employed in order to keep agriculture in step with our developing industry, and owing to the special characteristics of our agricultural production, it will take a long time to complete the mechanization of agriculture. We, therefore, do not have a large rural population that can be enlisted in industry, as other countries do, even after mechanization of agriculture has been carried out.

Further, as we have to push ahead vigorously with economic

construction while continually increasing our defense capabilities, in direct confrontation with the U.S. imperialists, the chieftain of world reaction, we must economize to the maximum on the labor resources of our country and make rational use of them if we are to successfully carry out the political and military tasks facing us and continue accelerating our socialist construction.

At present, improvement of labor administration is one of the most important ways to implement our Party's line of building up our economy and national defenses in parallel and vigorously step up defense construction, while at the same time successfully carrying out the gigantic tasks of the Seven-Year Plan.

It is of primary importance in improving labor adminstration to constantly increase the polico-ideological consciousness of the working masses and bring them to display their labor enthusiasm and creative activity to the fullest in socialist construction.

Work is not only the solemn duty of every citizen but also the most honorable contribution to the good of the state and society. Love of work is one of the most important traits of the new man in socialist and communist society. We must cultivate the respect for and love of work among the working people, so that they will feel repugnance to the idea of loafing or shying away from work as an exploiter-class idea, and participate in collective labor with the responsibility of masters, for the sake of the collective and society, and for their own happiness.

The most important task in labor administration at present is to ensure the full use of the 480-minute workday, doing away with all wastage of labor.

In socialist production in which cooperative production and the division of labor are highly developed and which grows steadily on the basis of advanced techniques, the 480-minute workday can be fully utilized only when each production unit and each worker observes established discipline to the letter. We should fully realize that the eight-hour workday is established by a state regulation under the Labor Law, which no one is allowed to violate, and we should wage an uncompromising struggle against any practices that lead to the slightest waste of manpower and violation of work discipline, making the best possible use of every minute and every second and doing our utmost to attain maximum productivity within working hours.

Moreover, to eliminate wastage of labor and ensure the full use of the 480-minute workday, fluctuations in production should be eliminated and work stoppages be kept to a minimum by providing our working people with adequate working conditions in factories and enterprises. In all fields of our national economy, in all enterprises, the production of raw and other materials and semi-finished goods should be given priority over other work, and cooperative production should be correctly organized so as to ensure that all the participating units observe strict discipline in the fulfillment of contracts. To ensure a regular supply of raw and other materials, detailed planning should be effected and a materials supply system should be established according to which the higher level takes responsibility for delivering materials to the lower units, in keeping with the Taean work system. In addition, top priority should be given to technical preparations in all factories and enterprises.

Primary attention in labor administration must be given to vigorously advancing the technical innovation movement. Technical innovations are the most important factor in easing our present manpower shortage and raising per-capita output value swiftly. In all branches and all units, mystification of and passivism towards technology should be done away with completely and the technical innovation movement be advanced extensively, so as to save every single man-day of work possible and produce more with less labor expenditure.

To improve labor administration, it is also important to maintain a proper manpower balance between the productive and nonproductive branches and between the basic and auxiliary sectors of production within the productive branches and distribute our working people rationally.

Under socialism, balanced distribution of all the working people among the productive and nonproductive branches is of great importance in expediting socialist construction and the development of the national economy as a whole. The more working people there are in the productive branches, the more goods will be put out by heavy and light industry and agriculture—goods that are needed for economic and defense construction and for the people's consumption—thus making it possible to raise output value per head of the population, steadily increase state accumulation and promote the people's well-being. In the distribution of manpower, therefore, it is important to give priority to expanding the number of employees in the productive branches while, at the same time, fixing the number of workers in the nonproductive branches according to the level of economic development. In the future, as well, we should continue to adhere firmly to this principle in distributing the labor resources of the country rationally.

For the rational use of manpower, the proportion of manpower in the indirectly productive branches should also be lowered and that in the basic productive sectors, especially the directly productive branches, should be raised decisively.

Simultaneously with this, the functionaries of our labor administration bodies should pay close attention to allocating manpower correctly, taking into account the sexes, ages, physical conditions, and the technical skills of the working people, so that all may give full play to their abilities.

Implementing the socialist principle of distribution correctly, while constantly raising the politico-ideological consciousness of the masses, is an important factor in guaranteeing the further development of socialist production. In socialism, the development of the productive forces has not yet attained a level where distribution can be carried out according to need; fundamental differences remain between different kinds of labor, and the working people have not yet completely eradicated the survivals of outmoded ideologies. Under these circumstances, only through the correct implementation of the principle of distribution according to work done can we eliminate the outdated idea of trying to idly live off the work of others, stimulate the working people's zeal to raise production and elevate their technical knowledge and skills, and thus promote the development of the productive forces. The necessary measures should be taken in all branches and units of the national economy to distribute shares accurately, according to the quantity and quality of work performed.

We must take decisive action to improve manpower planning. Manpower planning is the basis for the rational organization and effective use of the labor force; a good manpower planning, therefore, is fundamental in the improvement of labor administration. The leading functionaries of state and economic bodies should improve their manpower planning so as to make the best possible use of the manpower resources of the country, distribute the labor force rationally and raise labor productivity.

The Government of the Republic will further strengthen the economic power of the country and its economic independence and raise the people's standard of living radically by carrying out all these tasks of socialist economic construction in full.

Sixth. The Government of the Republic, adhering firmly to the Juche idea of the Workers' Party of Korea, will continue to forcefully strive to step up the development of the country's science and technology and build a socialist culture.

The fulfillment of the all-around technical revolution, which is the most important central task for socialist economic construction in our country at the present stage, urgently calls for the radical advancement of science and technology.

We should wage a vigorous struggle to take the fortress of science and make great strides in this field, thereby adequately ensuring immediate technical reconstruction of all sectors of the national economy.

The fundamental question in scientific research work is to keep developing science and technology in the direction required by our Party and our revolution, holding fast to the Juche stand. Only when Juche is firmly established in scientific research work is it possible to bring the creativity and talents of scientists into full play so as to accelerate the progress of science and technology and develop our economy more rapidly by relying on the resources of our country and our own technology. Scientists and technicians should concentrate their efforts on research work designed to promote industrial production with domestic raw materials, search out those raw materials which are scarce in our country and produce substitutes for the ones we lack, and expedite the technical revolution in keeping with our actual conditions so as to free the working people from arduous toil as soon as possible.

While working out for ourselves those scientific and technical problems whose solutions are vital for us, we should pay attention also to taking in the scientific and technological achievements and experiences of other countries with a view to applying them in the actual conditions of economic development of our country.

The immediate task confronting our scientists and technicians is to find solutions for the scientific and technical problems that arise in connection with utilizing our existing economic foundations to the fullest while, at the same time, constantly exploring new realms of science and technology in view of the prospective tasks for the development of our national economy.

The rapid development of technology, particularly mechanical engineering and electronics, is quite important at present.

Unless we develop mechanical engineering, we cannot fully carry out the task of building up-to-date factories and turning out machinery and equipment of the latest types, the task of increasing the capacities of our existing factories and equipment, or the task of rapidly introducing the achievements of scientific research in our national economy. We must concentrate our scientific forces on developing mechanical engineering to set this branch of science on its feet as soon as possible.

In view of the technical revolution and of the prospects for the development of the national economy, it is a matter of pressing urgency that we develop electronics. The importance of electronics and its role is ever growing, and its sphere of application is constantly expanding as science and technology develop and automation is applied widely in all fields of the national economy. We should actively step up research in all aspects of electronics.

Scientists and technicians should also give close attention to the development of chemistry, biology, agricultural science, forestry and oceanography in order to tap and use the natural resources of our country effectively and gain dominion over nature successfully.

For great success in scientific research work contact and cooperation should be strengthened among scientists and scientific research organizations, and creative collaboration promoted between scientists and producers. Also, instead of taking up new problems at random, efforts should be focused on the solution of those problems which are urgent and important for the national economy and those on which research work has already been begun or has not yet been completed, thereby settling problems one by one, by the method of successive annihilation.

To step up the development of our country's science and technology the qualifications of those who are engaged in this field should be raised decisively. All our scientists and technicians should study hard to become workers who have great command of scientific theory and a wealth of practical experience and are familiar with the trends in the development of modern science and technology, to become able workers who can skillfully solve scientific and technical problems as they come up in actual practice.

We will see to it that scientific research centers are built up more firmly and that better conditions are provided for successful scientific research work.

In the building of socialist culture, it is important to make education available to all the working people and raise their general cultural and technical standards to a higher level.

The most important task confronting us in this field is to substantially provide compulsory nine-year technical education. By carrying it out efficiently, we should bring the training of our technical personnel into step with the rapid pace of development of our country's productive forces and the technical revolution.

Along with our regular full-time educational system, our system of studying while working should be further developed so that all the working people will be provided with better conditions for learning.

Success in the education of the younger generations and the training of cadres depends largely on the role of the teachers who are directly engaged in this work. Our teachers should acquire the habit of studying and decisively increase their knowledge of political theory, and of their own subjects, so that the quality of teaching and training may be further raised. Simultaneously with this, the entire state, all of society, should take an interest in adequately consolidating the material foundations of our educational establishment so as to improve the work of education.

We should continue to strive for the development of socialist literature and art, upholding the literary and art policy of the Party. Workers in the field of literature and art should make a

better contribution to working-classization and revolutionization of the whole of society by creating many revolutionary
works representing the glorious anti-Japanese armed struggle
of our people, and the great present-day struggle of our people,
who are heirs to that tradition, and the pulsating reality.

*Seventh. The Government of the Republic will do all it can to
further increase the defense capabilities of our country and
build up the nationwide, all-people defense system, so as to
meet the prevailing situation.*

One of the basic functions of a socialist state is to keep
increasing its defense capabilities while pushing ahead with
economic construction. The imperialists carry on uninterrupted
acts of aggression and plunder and, as long as imperialism
exists, the threat of war will not vanish. Under these
circumstances, we can safeguard the gains of the revolution
against imperialist aggression and preserve the security of our
people only by reinforcing our defense power and being ready
for action at all times.

Increasing our defense capabilities is an urgent task for us,
particularly in view of our present national situation—our
territory is divided and we are building socialism in direct
confrontation with the aggressive forces of U.S. imperialism.

Since the first days of their occupation of south Korea, the
U.S. imperialists have pursued the sinister aim of committing
aggression against the whole of Korea and Asia and have
completely converted south Korea into the military base for
aggression. They have stationed tens of thousands of their
aggressor troops in south Korea and maintain a huge puppet
army of more than 600,000 men at all times.

In recent years, the U.S. imperialists have taken the course of
further intensifying their war preparations in south Korea. To
carry out their war policy in south Korea, the U.S. imperialists
are reinforcing the puppet armed forces and keep bringing
tactical nuclear weapons, guided missiles and other weapons of
mass destruction into south Korea, as well as military vessels,
aircraft and other combat equipment. They have set up a
system of wartime mobilization aimed at driving the innocent
south Korean people into an aggressive war and perpetrate

frequent provocations against the northern half of the Republic along the Military Demarcation Line, in flagrant violation of the Armistice Agreement.

In an attempt to utilize south Korea more effectively in their Asian aggression, the U.S. imperialists are maneuvering to align the south Korean puppets militarily with Japanese and other reactionaries in Asia and are scurrying around like mad to rig up a new military alliance in Asia, dangling the "ROK-Japan treaty" as bait. They are trying to unleash another war in Korea, using south Korea as an advanced base and the forces of Japanese militarism as "shock troops," and to mobilized the south Korean armed forces easily for their war of aggression in Asia. The U.S. imperialists have already dragged south Korean puppet troops into the aggressive war against Vietnam, and the traitorious Pak Jung Hi clique shipped more troops, and sooner, than any other vassal country to the battlefields of South Vietnam.

The situation is becoming tenser and the danger of war ever greater in our country and throughout Asia.

The prevailing situation requires that we make our country's defenses strong as steel and that we make full war preparations for any surprise attack by the enemy.

To defend our country is to defend the socialist gains of our people and our revolutionary base; it is the most sacred duty and honorable task of all our people. The People's Army should serve the country and the people, and the entire people should love and aid the People's Army; our soldiers and the people should further develop the traditional spirit of unity between the army and people, and, in case of emergency, should closely unite in a body as true revolutionary comrades and fight with single-hearted devotion, to safeguard our country and our socialist gains, sharing life and death, joys and sorrows.

All our people and the men and officers of the People's Army should never be lulled into a pacifistic mood but should keep ever watchful and alert, maintaining the sharpest revolutionary vigilance and should be ready to meet and fight the enemy valiantly without the slightest panic, no matter when he may launch a sneak attack.

To make our defenses invincible, the People's Army should carry on the policy of turning the whole army into a cadre army and making the whole army a modern army, and the people should thoroughly implement the policy of arming all our people and fortifying the whole country, in keeping with the military line of the Party.

We should temper the ranks of the People's Army politically and ideologically, and train them in military technique and prepare all the men and officers for the duties of higher-ranking commanders, thereby further increasing the fighting efficiency of the People's Army and enabling all our people to take part in battle with the standing forces of the People's Army as the core in case of emergency.

The People's Army should be firmly armed with up-to-date weapons and other combat and technical equipment, and our military science and technology should be rapidly advanced, to meet the demands of modern warfare. Combat training should be intensified for all our soldiers so that they will be completely at home with their weapons and will master modern military science and technology.

In this way, our People's Army should be built up into a revolutionary force with the indefatigable spirit of fighting through fire and water for the Party, the working class, our country and people, into an iron force each member of which is a match for a hundred, fully capable of frustrating any reckless adventure the enemy may make.

The arming of all our people and the fortification of the entire country constitute the most powerful defense system, based on the unshakable political and ideological unity of all the people and on the solid foundations of our country's independent economy. We should firmly arm the workers, peasants and all other people so that they may make intensive labor efforts in socialist construction while defending our country, with a hammer and a sickle in one hand and a rifle in the other, and that, in case of emergency, they may not only continue with production but also fight well. At the same time, we should build impregnable defense installations in all parts of the country and turn the whole country into a military fortress so that we can repel the enemy with one blow, no matter when or where he may attack us.

All this is aimed at fully materializing our Party line of self-defense in national defense. Only by so doing can we crush the enemy's incessant subversive activities at every step, and smash armed invasion in any form.

Eighth. The Government of the Democratic People's Republic of Korea, while continuing to hold fast to the line of building an independent national economy by enlisting its own potentials and domestic resources to the fullest under the banner of self-reliance, will also establish economic relations and develop trade with other countries, based on the principles of proletarian internationalism, complete equality and mutual benefit.

The development of an independent, comprehensive economy in our country through our own efforts does not imply that we reject international economic ties or that we produce everything we need for ourselves. Every country differs from every other one in its natural and economic conditions, in the levels of development of its productive forces and science and technology at a given stage, and, accordingly, in the variety and quantity of raw materials and products turned out. Under these circumstances, each country should produce on its own the essentials and those products which are in great demand, and obtain through trade with foreign countries those things which are in slight demand or in short supply, or which cannot be produced at home, on the principle of meeting each other's needs.

In developing our foreign trade we attach primary importance to the world socialist market.

As is generally known, the world socialist market came into being as an economic consequence of the emergence of socialism beyond the bounds of a single country and its transformation into a world system after World War II, when our country and a number of others broke away from the capitalist system.

The formation of the world socialist market promoted economic and technical exchange between the socialist countries, thereby making a great contribution to the development of the national economy, the building of the material and technical foundations of socialism and the improvement of the people's living conditions in each of those countries. This made it possible to frustrate the sinister designs of the imperialist powers of the world headed by U.S. imperialism to throw an economic blockade around the socialist countries, impede their economic development and, further, strangle the world socialist economic system.

The socialist market provides favorable conditions not only for the socialist countries but also for the newly independent states to meet each other's needs for the development of their own national economies. Unlike the capitalist market, in which the economic law of taking monopolistic high profits through unequal exchange and the plunder of backward countries holds sway, the socialist market enables the newly independent states to realize their surplus industrial goods and farm produce and purchase foreign industrial equipment, raw materials and other supplies essential to the development of their economies, on the principle of complete equality and mutual benefit.

In this way, economically backward countries are no longer held in bondage to the capitalist market, where they were limitlessly robbed of their natural resources and the priceless fruits of their people's labor; now they can follow the path to economic independence, casting off the economic yoke of imperialism.

The formation of the socialist market dealt a mortal blow to the imperialist monopolies and the multimillionaires that had held a stranglehold on the world economy through their vast market; in particular, it completely shattered the expansionist policy of U.S. imperialism, the ringleader of modern imperialism, that had sought to monopolize overseas markets, plunder the world of its raw material resources at will and dominate the world; and it aggravated the general economic crisis of the imperialist powers.

If all socialist countries, meeting each other's economic needs, consolidate and develop the socialist market, the development of the national economy of each socialist country will be further promoted; more favorable conditions will be created for the economic independence of the newly independent states; and, in addition, the capitalist market can be driven into an unstable position and the general crisis of the world capitalist economic system be aggravated further still.

Needless to say, consolidating and developing the socialist market and strengthening and developing economic ties among the socialist countries do not mean at all that the socialist countries should not establish economic relations with capitalist countries.

We will develop the relations of trade and commercial

exchange with all countries that have different social systems if they respect our sovereignty and want to have economic ties with our country. The economic business relations of socialist countries with capitalist countries, however, should always be of secondary importance in foreign trade and should not be made the basis of their economic relations with foreign countries. Our first concern should be that of promoting economic and technical exchanges with the fraternal countries and consolidating and developing the socialist market.

The most important thing in consolidating and developing the socialist market is that each fraternal country, on the basis of its political interest in the victory of the common cause of building socialism and communism against imperialism and colonialism, display the lofty spirit of proletarian international-ism and totally renounce hidebound national selfishness in mutual economic relations. In particular, the developed socialist countries should give more material assitance—with no political strings attached and with no selfish motives behind it—to the economically backward countries which aspire to socialism, against imperialism. In this way, conditions should be created for these countries to be able not only to frustrate the economic blockade of the imperialist powers successfully but also to have fewer transactions with the capitalist market, relying on the socialist market. In our foreign trade relations, as in all else, we should never depart from our class stand or neglect communist ethics and comradely obligation.

We will do everything possible to promote close economic ties with the brother countries and consolidate and develop the world socialist market for the victory of the common cause of building socialism and communism, against imperialism, for the unity of national and international interests in revolution and construction.

While preferentially developing economic ties with other socialist countries, the Government of the Republic will endeavour to establish economic relations and develop commercial exchange with the newly independent states of Asia and Africa which have broken the chains of imperialism and achieved political independence, on the principle of complete equality and mutual benefit.

The peoples of many newborn independent states who have gained political freedom are now faced with urgent tasks of eradicating the aftereffects of the colonial rule of imperialism, of building an independent national economy, and of radically improving their life.

However, the imperialists are maneuvering to bring the newborn independent states under the yoke of neocolonialism, the same colonialism in a new guise, in order to dominate the peoples of the liberated countries again. The imperialists pursue a policy of enslaving other countries economically by offering "aid" as bait and, further, of riding roughshod over the sovereignty of those countries. The "European Common Market," the "integration of the world economy" and the like, loudly advertised by the imperialist powers today, all pursue the heinous, aggressive aims of strangling the economic independence of the newly independent states and subordinating these countries to their rule.

By developing economic relations with the newly independent states on the principle of meeting each other's needs without any political and economic strings attached, we should sincerely help them secure complete political and economic independence from the imperialists and assist their peoples in achieving national prosperity.

Ninth. The Government of the Democratic People's Republic of Korea will actively fight to defend the interests and national rights of all the Korean compatriots abroad.

In the past, as a result of the occupation of Korea by the Japanese imperialists, large numbers of our fellow countrymen left their homeland and wandered abroad. As a people without a country, they were subjected to chauvinistic discrimination and all sorts of humiliations, were deprived of all their rights and suffered from extreme hardships in strange lands for a long time.

Today, however, as proud overseas citizens of their beloved fatherland, the Democratic People's Republic of Korea, they have boundless confidence and pride in their nation, and foresee their happy future in the prosperity and development of the Republic. The overseas citizens of Korea support all the policies of the Republic and are making positive efforts to perform their duties as citizens of the Republic.

Our 600,000 Korean compatriots in Japan, solidly united

around the Workers' Party of Korea and the Government of the Republic, and guided by the General Association of Korean Residents in Japan, are now fighting bravely for their democratic, national rights against the unwarranted, chauvinistic persecution and contempt to which they are subjected by the Japanese authorities; and they are keeping up a staunch struggle for the reunification of their country and the prosperity of the nation.

At present, there is a widespread movement among our fellow countrymen in Japan to continue their repatriation. To return to their homeland is a legitimate national right of the Korean citizens in Japan, which no one is allowed to violate; there are still large numbers of them who want to come back to the Democratic People's Republic of Korea, which is their homeland.

Nevertheless, the Japanese authorities have deliberately placed obstacles in the way of the repatriation of the Korean citizens in Japan and are maneuvering to interrupt it, in gross violation of international law, international practice and humanitarian principles. This is proof that the Japanese government is trampling on the democratic, national rights of the Korean citizens in Japan and is openly defying impartial public opinion in Japan and the world over.

The Government of the Democratic People's Republic of Korea and the entire Korean people resolutely denounce the unjustified maneuvers of the Japanese authorities to frustrate the repatriation of the Korean citizens in Japan.

The Government of the Republic maintains that Korean citizens in Japan should be fully guaranteed freedom of travel to their homeland and of democratic, national education and all other democratic, national rights. We strongly demand that the Japanese government duly treat and protect the Korean citizens in Japan as foreign residents and cease all its acts of persecution and repression against them immediately.

No repression and persecution by the Japanese authorities can ever halt the just struggle of the Korean citizens in Japan for their democratic, national rights and for the reunification of their country. The constantly intensified persecution and repression of the Korean citizens in Japan by the Japanese authorities will only arouse still greater national indignation on the part of all the Korean people, and, sooner or later, an end will be put to this unjust act.

The Government of the Democratic People's Republic of Korea considers it a sacred duty to protect our 600,000 Korean compatriots in Japan and all other Korean citizens overseas, and defend their national rights. We will continue to fight persistently against any unjustified acts of infringing on the national rights of the Korean citizens overseas, humiliating and persecuting them, and will always resolutely support and encourage our overseas compatriots in their just struggle.

Tenth. Ever since the first days of the founding of the Democratic People's Republic of Korea, we have consistently affirmed that we will promote friendly relations with all countries that oppose imperialist aggression, respect the freedom and independence of our people and desire to establish state relations with our country on an equal footing, and in the future, we will continue to hold fast to this principle in the field of foreign policy.

The foreign policy of the Government of the Republic is derived from the nature of our state and social system free from all exploitation and oppression, and reflects the noble aspiration of our people to ensure peace, democracy, national independence and the victory of the common cause of socialism. Our independent, principled foreign policy is supported by an increasing number of countries in the world and has consolidated the international position of our country as never before.

Today our country maintains friendly relations with the fraternal socialist nations and scores of other countries in the world. Just since 1962, when the third Cabinet of the Democratic People's Republic of Korea was formed, our country has newly established diplomatic relations with many countries in Asia and Africa, and our friendly relations with these countries are developing steadily. Economic and cultural exchanges between our country and other countries have also been further expanded and developed. Our country now maintains trade and cultural relations with many countries. Mutual exchange is becoming more active every day between a large number of peace-loving peoples of the world and our people, and our friendly ties with them are expanding further still. We have thus many revolutionary comrades and friends in all parts of the world, and international solidarity with our revolution is being ever strengthened.

The Government of the Democratic People's Republic of Korea and the Korean people will continue to strengthen and develop these relations of friendship with foreign countries and strive to make more friends throughout the world.

The international situation confronting our revolution is very complex and tense today.

The imperialists, headed by U.S. imperialism, are incessantly perpetrating armed invasions and subversive activities against the socialist and the newly independent countries. They are brutally suppressing the liberation struggle of the peoples of Asian, African and Latin American countries, and disturbing peace and threatening the security of the peoples throughout the world.

U.S. imperialism is the master enemy of peace, democracy, national independence and socialism. U.S. imperialism is going downhill, but, far from giving up its aggressive ambitions, it is revealing its piratical nature more brazenly than ever.

The basic strategy of the U.S. imperialists for aggressions against the socialist countries and the progressive countries of the world at the present stage is to swallow up, one by one, mainly the divided and small countries, while refraining from worsening their relations with the large countries and shunning confrontation with them as far as possible. In this, the U.S. imperialists are directing their spearhead of aggression especially against Vietnam and other Asian countries. This aggressive maneuvering on the part of the U.S. imperialists aggravates tensions in our country and all other parts of Asia to the extreme and seriously endangers peace throughout the world.

The most urgent task confronting the peoples of the socialist countries and the peace-loving peoples throughout the world today is to check and frustrate the U.S. imperialists' policy of aggression and war. There is no use talking about any kind of victory for the revolutionary cause or about world peace and the progress of mankind without waging an anti-U.S. struggle.

The attitude the socialist countries take toward U.S. imperialism is the proof of whether they are really fighting for the development of the international revolutionary movement at the present time. Their attitude toward U.S. imperialism is a touchstone that distinguishes the revolutionary position from the opportunist position. The socialist countries should do away with all deviations in the anti-U.S. struggle and maintain an unswerving revolutionary position against U.S. imperialism.

To wage a vigorous struggle against U.S. imperialism, joint anti-U.S. action must be achieved and an anti-U.S. united front formed on an international scale. Split in the anti-imperialist forces only benefits the imperialists headed by U.S. imperialism and harms the revolutionary peoples. All the socialist countries and anti-imperialist forces the world over should form the broadest possible anti-U.S. united front, thorougly isolate U.S. imperialism and administer collective blows to it in all areas and on all fronts where U.S. imperialism has stretched its tentacles of aggresion. Only by so doing is it possible to disperse and weaken the forces of U.S. imperialism to the maximum, cut its windpipe everywhere and successfully smash the U.S. imperialists' global strategy of defeating the socialist countries and other international revolutionary forces piecemeal.

The Government of the Democratic People's Republic of Korea and the Korean people will fight resolutely against the imperialist forces of aggression headed by U.S. imperialism, and will continue to wage a stubborn struggle to drive the U.S. imperialist aggressors out of south Korea and accomplish the revolutionary cause of reunification of the country.

The Government of the Republic and the Korean people, regarding the strengthening of their solidarity with the international revolutionary forces opposing U.S. imperialism as an important factor in the victory of the Korean revolution, will unite with all the anti-imperialist, anti-U.S. forces the world over and actively support and encourage the struggles of all peoples against U.S. imperialism.

The primary task of the anti-imperialist, anti-U.S. struggle at present is to check and foil U.S. imperialist aggression in Vietnam and support the Vietnamese people in every way in their just war of resistance against U.S. imperialism and for national salvation.

Vietnam has now become the front where the anti-U.S. struggle is fiercest. A bitter struggle is being waged on the very soil of indomitable Vietnam between socialism and

imperialism, between the anti-imperialist, peace-loving forces
of the world and the aggressive forces of U.S. imperialism. The
Vietnamese people, bearing the brunt of this struggle, are
valiantly fighting not only to safeguard the independence and
freedom of their country, but also to defend socialist countries
and peace in Asia and the world. The heroic Vietnamese people
are inflicting repeated serious military and political setbacks on
the U.S. imperialist aggressors and are driving them into a
dead end.

On behalf of the Government of the Democratic People's
Republic of Korea and all the Korean people, I would like to
extend, from this rostrum of the Supreme People's Assembly,
warmest militant greetings to the Government and the
Democratic Republic of Vietnam, the Central Committee of the
South Vietnam National Front for Liberation and all the heroic
people of North and South Vietnam who have risen as one in the
just war of resistance against U.S. imperialism and for national
salvation.

The Government of the Democratic People's Republic of
Korea and the Korean people consider the U.S. imperialist
aggression against Vietnam to be an aggression against
themselves and are doing everything in their power to support
the brotherly Vietnamese people. The Government of the
Republic and our people solemnly declare once again that we are
fully prepared to fight side by side with the Vietnamese people
whenever requested to do so by the Government of the
Democratic Republic of Vietnam. We fully support the position
of the Government of the Democratic Republic of Vietnam and
the political program of the South Vietnam National Front for
Liberation with regard to the solution of the Vietnamese
question.

The socialist countries and the revolutionary peoples
throughout the world have a solemn internationalist duty to
defend the Cuban revolution and actively support and
encourage the revolutionary struggle of the Cuban people. The
triumph of the Cuban revolution and the existence of the
Republic of Cuba mean a heavy blow to the U.S. imperialists
and have a great revolutionary influence on the liberation
struggles of the peoples of Latin America and the oppressed
peoples of the world. Today the Republic of Cuba represents
the hope and revolutionary future of the Latin American

peoples.

This is why the U.S. imperialists stop at nothing in their evil attempts to stifle the Republic of Cuba and engage in incessant plots of aggression against it, whipping up the reactionaries in Latin America.

No maneuver on the part of U.S. imperialism, however, will be able to stop the heroic Cuban people, who are advancing steadily in the front ranks of the anti-imperialist struggle, bearing aloft the banner of revolution.

The Korean people resolutely support the heroic Cuban people in their struggle to safeguard their revolutionary gains and build socialism under the difficult conditions of direct confrontation with U.S. imperialism in the Western Hemisphere, and firmly denounce the U.S. imperialists for their aggressions and all other subversive activities against the Republic of Cuba. Our people will, in the future, continue to exert all efforts to strengthen their militant solidarity with the fraternal Cuban people.

The Government of the Democratic People's Republic of Korea and the Korean people will endeavor to cement their solidarity with the peoples of all the countries in Asia, Africa and Latin America that are fighting for freedom and national independence, and will give active support to their liberation struggles. In particular, our people will fight in close unity with all the Asian peoples to drive the aggressive forces of U.S. imperialism out of all parts of Asia. We will unite firmly with all the anti-imperialist forces in Asia, including the democratic forces in Japan, and battle staunchly against the revival of Japanese militarism, "shock troops" of the U.S. imperialists for Asian aggression, and its aggressive maneuvers.

The Korean people express firm solidarity with the working classes and laboring peoples of capitalist countries who are fighting against capitalist exploitation and oppression, and for their vital rights, for democracy and socialism, and offer warm support and encouragement to their revolutionary struggles. We will always stand firm by the peoples of all countries fighting for peace, national independence, democracy and social progress and work unceasingly to strengthen our solidarity with them.

Despite the frantic endeavors of the imperialists, the general international situation today continues to develop favorably for the forces of peace and socialism. The ranks of the peoples fighting against imperialism are swelling ever more in Asia, Africa and Latin America and throughout the world.

Imperialism and reactionaries of all shades will eventually be destroyed, and the peoples who have risen in the anti-imperialist struggle for the just cause of revolution will surely emerge victorious.

Holding high the banner of Marxism-Leninism and proletarian internationalism and the revolutionary banner of anti-imperialist, anti-U.S. struggle, the Government of the Democratic People's Republic of Korea and the Korean people will, in the future, as in the past, unite with the peoples of the socialist countries, with the revolutionary peoples of Asia, Africa and Latin America, and with all the progressive peoples of the world and fight on determinedly for peace, democracy, national independence and for the triumph of the common cause of socialism.

Comrade Deputies,

The Political Program of the Government of the Republic embodies our Party's idea of Juche and its revolutionary line of independence, self-sustenance and self-defense—a creative application of Marxism-Leninism to the realities of Korea.

The realization of this Political Program will turn our country into a richer, stronger and more advanced socialist nation, independent in politics and self-sustaining in the economy and self-defensive in national defense, and will ensure a still happier life for our people. It will powerfully inspire and encourage the south Korean people in their struggle against U.S. imperialism and its stooges and afford a firm guarantee for the reunification of our country.

The Government of the Republic will carry out this Political Program faithfully and thereby advance revolution and construction in our country further and live up to the expectations which all our people and you deputies have placed in it.

The entire people, upholding the policies of the Party and the Government, should advance faster, overcoming all difficulties with great uninterrupted revolutionary enthusiasm and patriotic devotion. It is the revolutionary mettle of our heroic people that they do not buckle under when faced with difficulties nor rest on their laurels, but make continuous advances and continuous innovations for fresh victories. There will be a new great upsurge in our revolutionary struggle and work of construction as all our working people keep advancing dynamically with the speed of Chollima in order to carry out the policies of the Party and the Government.

No force on earth can stop the forward movement of our people, who, with the seasoned Marxist-Leninist leadership of the Workers' Party of Korea, hold power firmly in their hands. Our revolutionary cause is a just one, and victory is on the side of the Korean people who are fighting for justice.

Let us all march forward bravely towards the final victory of our revolution and a bright future of socialism and communism, united closely around the Workers' Party of Korea and the Government of the Republic.

LET US DEVELOP THE CHOLLIMA WORKTEAM MOVEMENT IN DEPTH , A GREAT IMPETUS TO SOCIALIST CONSTRUCTION

Speech Delivered at the Second National Meeting of the Vanguards in the Chollima Workteam Movement, *May 11, 1968*

Comrades,

At this meeting of the vanguards in the Chollima Workteam Movement, we have listened with deep interest to the report of Comrade Chairman of the Central Committee of the General Federation of Trade Unions and to the speeches of many vanguards in the Chollima Workteam Movement about the need to continually strengthen and develop the Chollima Movement and thus bring about a new revolutionary upsurge in socialist construction.

On behalf of the Central Committee of the Party, I would like to extend warm thanks to you vanguards of the Chollima Workteam Movement present at this meeting who, deeply conscious of the urgent requirements of our revolution's development and of the historic mission entrusted to you, are waging an unyielding struggle to accelerate economic construction and defense building as rapidly as possible.

Through you, I also send my deep thanks to all the Chollima riders and our heroic working class.

I would like to take advantage of this opportunity to speak about the Chollima Workteam Movement and what we must do to strengthen and develop it. At the First National Meeting of the Vanguards in the Chollima Workteam Movement and at the Fourth Party Congress, I made detailed mention of the significance and tasks of the Chollima Workteam Movement. Therefore, today I would like to stress only a few points.

The Chollima Workteam Movement, which is unique to our country, is a great communist, mass progressive movement to educate the people in communist ideology and rouse them to collective innovation and heroism.

The history of the Chollima Workteam Movement is not very long, a little over ten years. In this period, however, truly enormous progress has been made, and what amount to miracles winning the admiration of people all over the world have been realized in our country.

Without launching the Chollima Workteam Movement as vigorously as we did, we could not have built Pyongyang, our magnificent democratic capital, or many other cities, large and small, we have today; we would not have been able to construct thousands of factories and enterprises equipped with modern technology or develop an advanced socialist agriculture, thus laying the solid foundations of an independent national economy. In other words, we could never have built a paradise of socialism where all the people lead a full, happy life.

In our country today everyone receives an education and anyone who is sick gets free medical care.

Furthermore, we have no unemployment and there are conditions for everyone to work. You may take this for granted, but in fact it is by no means easy to provide all the people with jobs. I was told that a foreign delegation visiting the Hwanghae Iron Works yesterday asked the management if there was any unemployment in our country. The manager of the works answered that on the contrary, far from having unemployment, we are faced with a labor shortage today; accordingly, a very pressing task set by our Party is to carry out the technical revolution and save every worker we can. Without considerably developing the national economy and maintaining the rapid pace of economic growth, it will be impossible to provide jobs for all the employable people whose number is steadily growing as a result of the increase of the population. Therefore, the fact that all these people in our country work means that our economic foundations have attained large proportions and are rapidly expanding.

Our country inherited a very underdeveloped economy from the backward colonial, semi-feudal society which had not gone through the capitalist stage of development in the regular way. Worse still, everything in our country was reduced to ashes in the fierce three long years of war unleashed by the U.S. imperialist gangsters. How, then, has it been possible to build such magnificent modern cities and attractive villages, lay strong economic foundations and make great strides forward in all spheres of social life in such a short time, slightly over ten years?

It was possible only because our people firmly followed our Party's unique and correct line of economic construction which gave priority to the growth of heavy industry simultaneous with the development of light industry and agriculture, and consistently rushed forward with the vigor of Chollima riders to carry through this line, valiantly overcoming all obstacles and difficulties.

It is the requirement of the laws of socialist and communist construction to create more material and cultural riches by steadily raising the people's level of ideological consciousness and boosting their zeal for production, thus encouraging them to make continuous advance and uninterrupted innovation. The Chollima Movement correctly reflects this requirement. The original meaning of the word Chollima is a steed that can cover a thousand *ri* a day, and the term has been used from the time of our remote ancestors to symbolize rapid progress. Conforming to the national sentiments and predilections of our people, the Chollima Movement expresses their desire to charge ahead at the speed of this steed as is required by the law of socialist economic development.

Let us look back on how the Chollima Workteam Movement started in our country, though you know all about it.

The situation of our revolution and construction nationally and internationally was very difficult and complex when the

Chollima Workteam Movement was launched.

Our Party and people had successfully carried out the Three-Year Plan for Postwar Rehabilitation and Development of the National Economy, by and large restoring the ruined economy and stabilizing the people's life to a considerable extent. But the overall situation in our country was very difficult. Many people were ill-clad, rice had to be imported and a large part of the population was still living in shacks in the ground because of the lack of houses.

To add to this, great-power chauvinists pressured us on the pretext that our Party did not follow their guidance. Certain people, opposing our Party's line of giving priority to the building of heavy industry with the machine-building industry as its core and, on this basis, laying the foundations of an independent economy of the country as a whole, argued by saying, "Why do you only buy machines instead of buying consumer goods? Do you plan to live on machines?"

Within the Party, factionalists infected with flunkeyism toward great powers raised their voices against the Party's line with the backing of their masters. They challenged the Party with such nonsense as: "It is wrong to build heavy industry;" "There is no need to develop the machine-building industry;" and, "The people's standard of living is being neglected." At that time a certain scoundrel even vilified us for having built the Nampo Glass Factory. "The Nampo Glass Factory is too big," he said. "There is not such a glass factory elsewhere in the world." What is wrong with building a glass factory and good houses with glazed windows for the working people? Even having built the factory, we are still short of glass and cannot glaze all the new houses in our villages. Therefore, we are going to expand the existing factory and build a few more in the future. Nonetheless, this economic ignoramus came out against the Party's policy with his rubbish.

That was not the only difficulty we faced. The U.S. imperialists occupying south Korea and their stooges, the Syngman Rhee traitorous clique, noisily clamored for a "march north" and made wild attempts to undermine the gains of our revolution and wreck our people's work of construction by encouraging the remnants of the overthrown exploiting classes.

At that moment our Party had no one to trust but the working class, the main force of our revolution and the reliable defender of the Party.

Now, in that trying situation, too, our Party decided to go to the working class, discuss things with them and break through the existing difficulties—just as it had overcome obstacles and difficulties by putting its faith in the working class and drawing on their strength in all the arduous revolutionary struggles in the past.

Authorized by the Political Committee of the Party Central Committee, I went to the Kangson Steel Plant.

At the time our country had one blooming mill with a rated capacity of only 60,000 tons. We had to build towns and villages, erect factories and manufacture more machines. Sixty thousand tons of steel could get us nowhere. So, we asked the leading functionaries of the Kangson Steel Plant if they could not raise the output to around 90,000 tons. Some of them shook their heads dubiously, saying it would be difficult. The workers of Kangson, however, decided to tackle the job in response to the Party's appeal and turned out 120,000 tons that year—120,000 tons at a blooming mill with a rated capacity of 60,000. Thus, we were able to build more houses and factories.

Precisely at the Kangson Steel Plant and in the course of the struggle to produce 120,000 tons of steel, Comrade Chin Ung Won stepped forward with a proposal to initiate the Chollima Workteam Movement. From that moment on, the movement gained ground. This was the beginning of the honored history of our great Chollima Workteam Movement, and the Kangson Steel Plant was its birthplace.

True, the three-year struggle of postwar rehabilitation and construction also represented a grand Chollima advance. But it was in 1957 that the movement got into its stride in industry, and it would therefore be proper to mark down that year as the starting point in the history of the Chollima Workteam Movement.

The Chollima Movement is a movement of communist education, its aim being to convert large numbers of people into activists of socialist construction who make continuous advance and uninterrupted innovation; it is a forward movement of communism to get large numbers of people to display mass heroism and vigorously push ahead with socialist construction.

In other words, the main objective of the Chollima Movement

is to turn the passive elements into activists—ensuring that not even one person lags behind—by educating and remolding all people in the period of transition from capitalism to socialism, and to build socialism and communism rapidly by bringing all people to display mass heroism.

In fact, it is possible for us to press forward at Chollima speed; and far from being criticizable, rapid progress is a positive thing.

Let me give you a few examples.

The steel workers of the Kangson Steel Plant have improved their blooming mill from one that had a rated capacity of no more than 60,000 tons to one that now has a capacity of 450,000 tons. What is this, if not a Chollima advance? What a good thing it is to break away from the old rated capacity instead of leisurely maintaining it and to increase it eight times through unending innovation and advance!

Take an individual.

As Comrade Li Hwa Sun mentioned in her speech, she has become a multi-loom operator in the heat of the great revolutionary upswing and has now established a world record by tending 72 looms by herself. To handle these machines she runs a distance of 180-200 *ri* every eight-hour day. I have heard that she has not missed one day's work until today. Assuming that she works 300 days in a year, it means she has run 60,000 *ri*. They say our country covers 3,000 *ri*. And she has run 60,000 *ri*, which amounts to having made 20 trips a year from one end of our country to the other. The fabrics woven by this comrade in one year alone run to a million meters. She is a genuine Chollima rider, a heroine of our times and a true revolutionary.

If we were to have not one but hundreds and thousands of innovators like Comrade Li Hwa Sun, it will be a good thing and not bad.

Let's look at the brave workers of the Songhung Mine.

Through innovations the mining platoons of the Songhung Mine fulfilled in three and a half months this year's production plan which was two times greater than last year's. The more such platoons increase, the faster our economy will develop and the more prosperous the people will become. And as our country grows in strength, the U.S. imperialists and their lackeys—Pak Jung Hi, the landlords and capitalists of south Korea—will have greater cause to fear us. Therefore, such progress is far from being negative.

Yet villians imbued with revisionist ideas opposed the Chollima Movement. According to information obtained from a recent checkup, a certain fellow crossed out the words "Chollima" and "match for a hundred" from the text of a new song *March of the People's Army* submitted by the General Federation of the Unions of Literature and Arts. It is also said that he gave instructions to strike out the words "match for a hundred" from the report fo be delivered at a mass meeting. The meaning of the words "match for a hundred" is that a man is so strong as to be able to cope with a hundred opponents. From olden times they have been used in our country in referring to a mighty warrior, an illustrious general. So, in 1963 when we visited the 2nd Army, we said that our People's Army should become a match-for-a-hundred army by conducting political work more effectively, intensifying military training in all the units and thus converting the army into an army of cadres and modernizing it. Nevertheless, that fellow, a sheer ignoramus, imprudently opposed the slogan we suggested. Comrades in the People's Army, however, did not comply with his instructions. They said that no one was entitled to erase a slogan put up by the Party leadership.

These rascals imbued with revisionism not only tried to ban the use of the words "Chollima" and "match for a hundred" but actually hindered our working class from driving ahead at Chollima speed.

In his speech yesterday, one comrade told us about a certain individual who visited the Komdok Mine which was ready to rush forward in the spirit of Chollima. He called the workers together and advised them to work with moderation instead of pushing themselves to raise production; and then he arbitrarily reduced their production quota of ore set by the Party to half. Though the scoundrels tried their best to obliterate the "match for a hundred" slogan, the People's Army obstinately refused to accept it. The management of the Komdok Mine, however, listened to their jargon rather than to our words, and fell back in production. This was most regrettable. If the Komdok Mine had followed the Party's instructions to increase production, our annual earnings in foreign currency could have gone up by several million pounds, and we could already have imported many more plants.

You must clearly understand the great harm those scoundrels have done. As we said before at the time of the anti-factionalist struggle, factionalists are never seen in bright places because they are afraid; they sneak around only in the dark and work mischievously like mice. Slinking about in shady places, these rogues also did a lot of evil, opposing the Party slogan.

Such is the behavior of servers of the bourgeoisie who have wormed their way into our revolutionary ranks, a hostile act which benefits our national and class enemies, such as the Yankees and Pak Jung Hi.

No one has the right to oppose the Chollima Movement. Although it started at the Kangson Steel Plant, the Chollima Movement received the unanimous support and approval of all our people, including the working class, and was adopted as the Party's general line in socialist construction at the Fourth Congress of our Party.

The validity and great vitality of the Chollima Movement have more than adequately been displayed in the people's day-to-day struggle to speed up socialist construction.

We must not give up but carry forward with even greater persistence the Chollima Movement and the Chollima Workteam Movement—the general line of our Party in socialist construction and a strong impetus to the development of the national economy.

Furthermore, the present situation in our country makes it imperative for us to push ahead more energetically with the revolutionary struggle and work of construction and further increase our rate of advance, not in the least being carried away by past successes. Our country is not yet reunified and the revolution is not complete. Under such conditions, we have to keep moving ahead with vigor, spurring on the galloping Chollima.

What, then, is to be done to develop the Chollima Workteam Movement in depth in keeping with the reality of today?

The central tasks in the Chollima Workteam Movement are as follows: first, to work with people correctly; second, to work with equipment and materials efficiently; and third, to work with books properly. By working with people we mean to make the ideological revolution; by working with equipment and materials, the technical revolution; and by working with books, the cultural revolution. To do these three kinds of work well, that is, to carry on the ideological, technical and cultural revolutions properly is precisely the basic task of the Chollima Workteam Movement.

The ideological, technical and cultural revolutions are an objective requirement of socialist and communist construction. For Chollima riders and all working people, it is the most honorable duty to fight selflessly for the successful accomplishment of these three revolutions. The Chollima riders who lead the Chollima Workteam Movement should not only set examples for the masses in carrying out the ideological, technical and cultural revolutions but also endeavor to convert all working people without exception into revolutionaries boundlessly loyal to the Party by doing work with people correctly, bring about collective innovations in the economic construction of socialism through an efficient management of equipment and materials, and strive, through the proper use of books, to convert all people into educated and technically qualified men of a new, communist type.

I would like to speak first of the need to work well with people.

The most important element in working with people is to thoroughly establish the monolithic ideological system of the Party.

Chollima riders, more than anyone else, should arm themselves closely with the monolithic ideology of our Party, and make every effort possible to establish that system firmly in all the working people.

If a person fails to arm himself firmly with the Party's monolithic ideology, he cannot correctly tell right from wrong nor bravely fight his way through difficult and complex circumstances.

Due precisely to this failure in the past, the management of the Komdok Mine became passive in ore production by complying with the bad elements' instructions, and the personnel of the General Federation of the Unions of Literature and Arts meekly agreed with the rogues who advised them to eliminate the word "Chollima" from the text of the song *March of the People's Army*.

If the management of the Komdok Mine had fully integrated the Party's monolithic ideological system, they would never have accepted the bad elements' instructions; rather they would have already increased their production of ore to the 100,000-ton mark as the Party Central Committee advised.

The same is true of the personnel of the General Federation of the Unions of Literature and Arts. Had they been firmly armed with the Party's monolithic ideology, they would certainly have defied the scoundrel when he crossed out "Chollima": "How dare you strike out the word 'Chollima' when it is a slogan put forth by the Party Central Committee and when the Chollima Movement is the general line of our Party adopted at the Party Congress?" However, unarmed with the Party's monolithic ideology, they accepted it in silence although clearly aware that it ran counter to the Party's line.

These examples are positive proof that people who are not firmly armed with the Party's monolithic ideology can neither introduce innovations in economic construction nor lay bare the conspiratorial maneuvers of the anti-Party factionalists in good time.

Without thoroughly establishing the monolithic ideological system of the Party, it is likewise impossible to effectively combat any kind of negative idea, including revisionism, "Left" adventurism, great-power chauvinism, flunkeyism toward great powers, dogmatism, capitalist ideology and feudal-Confucian ideas.

Survivals of the old, exploiter society linger in the minds of our people in no small measure. In addition, as long as imperialism exists, capitalist ideology, revisionism and all other kinds of opportunism can infiltrate from without. Pernicious ideas of this kind that come from the outside spread and soon exercise a negative effect first of all on those who still retain many obsolete notions.

We have a good example of this in some leaders in the economic fields. Still captivated by flunkeyism toward the great powers, they used to crane their necks in an attempt to see if there was anything worthwhile imitating in the enterprise management systems of other countries. Some people opposed the Chollima Movement and other lines and policies of our Party mainly because they were affected by flunkeyism and strongly influenced by revisionism.

When a person retains old ideas in his mind, not arming himself with the Juche idea of the Party, it is inevitable that he should be susceptible to evil ideas infiltrating from the outside.

Only when we are well armed with our Party's Juche idea—the idea permeated with the revolutionary spirit of independence, self-support and self-defense—can we uproot the remnants of outmoded ideas from our minds and prevent the influence of all kinds of unhealthy foreign ideas. This is an immutable truth confirmed through our experience in the revolutionary struggle.

In our future work with people, we should concentrate on fixing the Party's monolithic ideological system and, thereby, firmly equipping all the working people with the revolutionary ideas of our Party. This is the most important task facing the Chollima riders today to develop the Chollima Workteam Movement in depth.

Next in importance in our work with people is to educate all the working people to energetically fight individualism and selfishness and love collective life and political, organizational life.

Socialism and communism is a society whose ideological basis is collectivism. Therefore, in order to build socialist and communist society successfully it is imperative that we combat individualism and selfishness and educate people in collectivism. Individualism and selfishness are capitalist ideas. They cannot coexist with communist ideas, collectivist ideas. In order to cultivate collectivist ideas in the people, we must, before anything else, root out individualism and selfishness from their minds.

In order to stamp out individualism and selfishness and educate the working people in collectivism, it is necessary to strengthen collective life and, particularly, political, organizational life among them. Party members should be faithful to their Party organizational life; trade union members, to trade union organizational life; members of the Agricultural Working People's Union, to their union's organizational life; Socialist Working Youth Leaguers, to their league's organizational life; and Women's Union members to the organizational life of the Women's Union.

Party and working people's organizations should properly assign work to every member and sum up the results of its implementation in time; and as soon as one task is fulfilled, another should be given. In this way, everybody should get used to living under the rigid discipline and revolutionary order of his organization and under the strict control of the masses. As for a person who hates collective life and likes to get away from it, it is necessary to admonish him in a comradely manner and persuade him to correct his shortcomings. If a man with defects is left alone without being admonished in time, he will become worse and worse until eventually he slides into evil ways. Therefore, his deficiencies must be corrected without fail by admonishing him ten times if once is ineffective, and a hundred times if ten warnings are not enough.

We should thus train all working people to be honorable Chollima riders, ardent revolutionary fighters who hold the interests of the collective dearer than personal interests and take an active part in socialist and communist construction for the prosperity and development of society as a whole.

While thoroughly establishing the monolithic ideological system of the Party among the working people and strengthening their collective and political, organizational life, we should energetically push ahead with the working-classizing and revolutionizing of the whole society by intensifying communist education as well as education in our revolutionary traditions.

Unless the working people are working-classized and revolutionized, it is impossible to build socialism and communism successfully. That was why our Party presented the problem of working-classization and revolutionization of the working people as an important revolutionary task at the Party Conference.

All the Chollima riders here belong to the working class; they are its most exemplary members. We can say, therefore, that all of you have been working-classized. In our society, however, in addition to the revolutionary working class like you, there are also the peasantry and the intelligentsia. We must working-classize and revolutionize all the farmers and intellectuals.

The working class also has to revolutionize itself. As we often say, no one automatically becomes a revolutionary simply because he belongs to the working class. To a certain degree workers, too, harbor obsolete ideas because they lived under the capitalist system in the past. Moreover, among the working class of our country there are many former peasants and quite a few former small and medium traders and entrepreneurs. They have more remnants of old ideas in their minds than other people. Although these traders and manufacturers have now become workers, they have not yet completely rid themselves of the idea of living in idleness and exploiting others as they did in the past. We must educate all such people to become true members of the working class and ardent revolutionaries.

According to a platoon leader of a certain mine who spoke yesterday, in his platoon there was the son of a man who had been fairly well-off in the old days. Although personally he was on good terms with his mates, he often had ideological differences with them and occasionally made mistakes in his work. The platoon set out to educate him patiently and in the end made a good man of him, so that the whole platoon became honorable Chollima riders. This is an excellent example to follow.

In contrast, however, on the pretext of strengthening the ranks of workers in their factories, some functionaries try to dismiss those who had problems in their social and political life instead of educating them. They are quite wrong. Needless to say, we should tighten the ranks of the working class; this is our Party's policy. But when the Party calls upon us to strengthen the ranks of the working class, it by no means asks us to expel people by administrative means. Rather, it means educating all of the workers to become fine members of the working class.

Former small and medium traders and manufacturers have now become workers according to our Party's policy of socialist transformation. They ceased to be exploiters long ago. They have neither private means of production nor people to hire for work. In other words, they have neither the means nor the objects of exploitation. They are workers today like everyone else. We have converted them into workers, and if we expel them from the factories now, where will they go? We should not oust them from factories but should properly educate and revolutionize all of them.

As I clearly reported to the Party Conference, the class struggle in socialist society should be conducted by methods of educating and remolding, not by dismissing or expelling people indiscriminately. Of course, we must be merciless with those who turn against us. However, we should arm all of those who want to follow us with our Party's ideology, revolutionize them and rally them closely around the Party, thereby taking them along with us.

To proceed. It is necessary to work well with equipment and materials.

Equipment is the most important means of production—our weapon for mastering nature. Just as an army cannot take on its enemy without weapons, so factories cannot carry on production, nor can we successfully dominate nature without equipment.

Our factories and enterprises now have a variety of equipment, including machine tools and boilers, all of which are our precious assets. The tools and goods produced with them are being used for the happy life of our people and the eternal prosperity of the country. Therefore, the Chollima workteams should operate this equipment well so that the machinery and equipment we have may be used more effectively.

When we talk about working well with equipment, we mean, above all, to value and love equipment by taking excellent care of it. Good maintenance is essential in order to prevent problems, work to full capacity and lengthen its years of service.

Careful work with equipment also means being at home with it and knowing how to handle it proficiently. However good it may be, a piece of equipment cannot be worked to full capacity if its operator is inexperienced.

When we visited the Anju Coal Mine in the past one of the pit managers there could not even handle properly a basic piece of mining equipment, although he had worked in the mine for over ten years. Under these conditions, how can we expect him to direct production let alone boost it?

In the same way that soldiers must understand their arms and handle them skillfully, Chollima riders and all the working people should be at home with their equipment and operate it competently. Chollima riders should be well acquainted with the structure, action and efficiency of their tools, be able to repair them rapidly and work them to full capacity.

In addition to taking scrupulous care of equipment and being experienced in its operation, Chollima riders should also constantly try to improve it. In other words, they should continually strive to make technological innovations.

The Chollima riders and all the working people must always be studying ways to increase the efficiency of their machinery and equipment and to mechanize and automate the production processes. They should look to the workers of the Kangson Steel Plant who constantly improved the blooming mill, increasing production capacity from 60,000 tons to 450,000 tons, to the Anju Coal Mine workers who devised a cylindrical hewing machine, thereby increasing production several times and making their work easier, to the comrades of the Songhung Mine who, by making a new, automatic air screw and introducing it into production, boosted their productivity several times and simplified their work. Following these examples all the Chollima riders should be fired in their unceasing efforts for technical renovation and improved efficiency of equipment.

We are living in the age of the technical revolution. Therefore, we should constantly strive for technical renovation and create new techniques in all branches of the national economy; the remodelling of all machinery and equipment to facilitate handling and increase efficiency should be a constant preoccupation.

The industrial foundations of our country today are enormous. If all our Chollima riders and working people make that extra effort to push forward the technical revolution, our factories with their present machinery and equipment will display a force several times greater than they do now.

The conditions are favorable for this dynamic advance in the technical revolution. Our situation today is fundamentally different from what it was ten years ago when the Chollima Workteam Movement began.

The economic foundations of the country have been consolidated beyond compare and almost all the working people have received at least a secondary education. At present the majority of the workers in the factories and enterprises are graduates of middle school and higher. Those old people who did not go to secondary school as children have, for the most part, finished the working people's middle schools or evening middle schools connected with their work centers. Under such conditions, we can expect an even bigger leap in the technical renovation—assuming that the entire working people fully demonstrate their revolutionary spirit of self-reliance, smash the mystification of technology with collective efforts and think and act boldly.

In the People's Army, a struggle should be launched to make the weapons lighter and more efficient.

Of course, the rifles our soldiers are carrying now are far lighter, handier, more powerful and better suited to the physiques of Koreans than those used during the Fatherland Liberation War. The Yankees and the south Korean puppet soldiers dread our rifles today.

However, the army should not be content with this improvement already made. It should keep trying to lighten its weapons even more. It should make continued efforts to improve not only small arms, but also larger weapons and combat and technical equipment of every description—making them efficient, light and handy.

Along with equipment, we should work with materials well and save them to the maximum.

I have visited factories and enterprises that do not even have an adequate place to store goods and, therefore, waste a great deal of materials. Any factory worthy of the name should first build storehouses to protect production materials from exposure or any other potential danger. However, many factories and enterprises have still not built storehouses and are wasting precious materials through careless management. Coal and cement, for example, keep indefinitely if they are stored. But piled carelessly in the open air, they are spoiled by the rain or blown away and uselessly lost. As I also stressed at the recent plenary meeting of the Party Central Committee, there is still too much wastage. If we could eliminate this problem alone, we would be enjoying a far better life today.

With the attitude of a master toward the nation's economic life, Chollima riders should preserve and economize the precious materials of the country, resolutely fight against wastage and strive to raise production and construction using fewer materials.

Third, we should work with books well.

An important task of the Chollima riders and all the working people is to study constantly in an effort to steadily improve their political, cultural and technical qualifications.

In point of fact, successful implementation of the tasks of the ideological and technical revolutions depends largely on how well we conduct the cultural revolution.

We have already achieved enormous success in the cultural

revolution and have prepared conditions to drive it forward more energetically in the future. Compulsory secondary education in our country—and of course, primary—was introduced a long time ago, and a nine-year technical education became obligatory last year. This is a genuine people's system of education radically different from the so-called "compulsory education" in capitalist society which only serves the sons and daughters of the handful of landlords and capitalists.

As a result of this compulsory education, everyone in our country is acquiring the basic knowledge which will enable him to study for himself. Under such conditions, if all the working people strive to study more, we can raise the cultural revolution to a higher plane. The cultural revolution can be successful only if all the working people love books and are anxious to learn.

Books are an indispensable food for revolutionaries. If a person does not read but rather idles his time away, merely filling himself with bread, life becomes meaningless. Books are a rich and diversified source of knowledge on politics, economy, culture, military matters and all other subjects. Without reading books, a revolutionary can neither act nor live. Reading is essential if we are to conduct political or cultural work and develop our economy and technology.

Our working people, however, have not acquired the habit of studying properly. Everyone should always carry a book with him, try to read even a page in spare moments and hold books dear. But many people fail to do this.

The reason our functionaries do not read now as they should is not that books are scarce or expensive. We have plenty of books and have provided people with every condition for study. The point is that our functionaries do not make the effort.

In the past when we were engaged in the guerrilla struggle, it was very difficult to obtain a book. When we were able to get one, we passed it around among us until its pages were worn out and the words were difficult to read. When a word became totally illegible, we would write it in again; and when the pages were falling apart, we repaired them and read the book over and over.

The same applied to newspapers. At that time just getting one page of a newspaper was a major effort. When we could get our hands on it, we circulated it until it was illegible.

It is true that in general books and newspapers are still

somewhat short of the demand. But there are enough of both for working people on the job to study. As for newspapers alone, there are dozens of them including *Rodong Sinmun, Minju Choson*, the paper of the Socialist Working Youth League, and the People's Army paper, all issued in hundreds of thousands or millions of copies. If reading sessions are properly organized and publications are well used, everybody will be reading books and newspapers. The question does not lie in the shortage of reading materials, but rather in the fact that they are not effectively used or properly read.

Therefore, while it is important to produce more paper and print more books and newspapers, our first job is to increase the use we make of reading material we already have.

At present our cadres go to the lower units to give guidance, but they do not ask whether functionaries go over newspapers regularly or inquire about the number of books they read—even though they check on everything else. In the future they must not fail to find out about the study program of the leading personnel and working people. A campaign to build study habits and read more books should be waged in every work center, whether they be Party organs, people's government bodies, schools, factories, enterprises, villages or units of the People's Army. In this way we should encourage a positive attitude toward study throughout society and initiate a movement which has everyone read for two or three hours a day.

What books then should you read?

You should begin by studying Party literature, then material on our revolutionary traditions, books on Marxism-Leninism and on the technology in your field. You should also read literature. A person's cultural life is inseparable from the rest of his life. But the necessity to read should not lead you to decadent, bourgeois novels. We should read books useful for the revolution, useful for socialist construction. We need not and should not read any other kinds of books.

These are the tasks for developing the Chollima Workteam Movement in depth.

We should develop it this way, thus maintaining the great revolutionary upsurge in our construction of socialism.

By "great upsurge" we mean to rise high like the surging tide. Yet, this term can be misinterpreted because the tide falls after a rise; in the same way, socialist construction may also be thought to recede a certain degree after an advance. Therefore, I feel it is necessary to replace the term with a more appropriate one. But since we cannot think of another expression right now, we will use the phrase in this way: "Let us sustain the great upsurge." Our intention is to have the rise without the fall.

The prevailing situation in our country is very tense now, just as it was around 1956-57 when the anti-Party factionalists made their challenge and the great-power chauvinists began to pressure our Party. Today U.S. imperialism is using the incident of the armed spy ship *Pueblo* as an occasion to intensify open military provocations against the northern half of the Republic and is obsessed with preparations for war.

In the light of this situation, we must combine economic construction better still with defense building and thus make national defense impregnable at the same time as we further cement the country's economic foundations and better the people's standard of living through our own efforts. To do this we must launch an intensive struggle to bring about a new revolutionary upsurge in all fields of socialist construction.

Another great revolutionary upsurge has swept across the whole country since the workers of the Songhung Mine and the Ryongsong Machine Plant valorously responded last year to the Party Conference resolution. The upsurge is of great dimensions, and remarkable innovations are being made almost daily in our socialist construction. This impressive revolutionary upsurge taking place today must be sustained.

To do so, it is most important that we intensify the struggle against passivism and conservatism.

Passivism and conservatism are inevitable in the course of social development. It is the rule that in both the revolutionary struggle and our daily lives there are passive elements as well as active ones, cowards and brave men, the old and stagnant alongside the new and progressive. Therefore, the revolution-ary struggle is accompanied by a ceaseless fight between activists and passivists, between the new and the old. The struggle against passivism and conservatism is an important one in the revolutionary process.

Some of our functionaries today are afraid to march forward boldly in socialist construction precisely because they are affected by passivism and conservatism. We must launch a vigorous ideological struggle against passivism, conservatism, mystification of technology and all other "evil spirits."

We will be able to keep up the great revolutionary upsurge as well as push forward socialist construction more dynamically if we wage a powerful battle against all practices that are obsolete and unsound—if we sweep away all "evil spirits." Of course, we may run up against difficulties and sometimes make mistakes in the course of furthering the revolutionary cause and the work of construction. But great victory is certain if we continue to march forward courageously, not yielding to difficulties or losing spirit in the face of failure.

Society develops and revolution advances only when the new and the progressive triumph in the struggle between the new and the old, between the progressive and the stagnant. As a matter of course, the new and the progressive, however small, will win victory sooner or later. This is an objective law. The point, though, is how to speed up this inevitable victory. For an early victory of the new and the progressive, we must expand our ranks of activists; and the new should grow rapidly to become a powerful, irresistible force. When there are many activists and their force is great, they can persuade the passive and conservative elements and move them forward dynamically.

Therefore, in order to shatter passivism and conservatism and sustain the great revolutionary upsurge in socialist construction, we must swell the ranks of the Chollima forerunners, representatives of the new force and the most active elements.

For an army to win a war, it is not enough that one platoon or a company or a unit be good fighters. All platoons, all companies and all units have to fight well. Likewise, in order to build socialism successfully, the example of one or two people, one workteam, one workshop or one factory will not do because all the people, all workteams, workshops, factories and work places have to work well. Therefore, as I already mentioned at the First Meeting of Vanguard Workers in the Chollima Workteam Movement, we should energetically strive to ensure that not one or two workteams, but all workteams, all workshops and all factories alike ride Chollima. Thus, the whole country will be galloping forward at the speed of Chollima.

The more heroes born of the working people while everyone rides Chollima, the better. This, in turn, will stimulate collectivism and mass heroism. As a manifestation of egoism, individualistic heroism is wrong. But heroism of the masses is an excellent thing and more important than anything else.

Through promoting the Chollima Workteam Movement, you should be able to help shatter passivism and conservatism, display a high degree of collective heroism and thereby speed up economic construction and defense building.

The tasks of economic and defense construction were examined in the report and resolutions of the recent plenary meeting of the Party Central Committee, so I would like to emphasize only a few points here.

Every minute and every second is precious to us now. We have to make the most of our time in order to boost production significantly and speed up construction.

The first and foremost task in all branches of the national economy today is to give every possible assistance to the building up of our defense capability.

Under no circumstances should we turn to other countries for arms. It is true that our fraternal allies could probably help us if war should break out. But, more often than not, war supplies are needed urgently. Even if brotherly countries gave us internationalist arms aid, this would not be nearly as good as if we made them for ourselves. In addition, we should never forget the bitter lesson of the Fatherland Liberation War when we were forced to retreat, though temporarily, because we did not have enough guns. We must fully demonstrate the revolutionary spirit of self-reliance and produce for ourselves the munitions we need.

The first task of factories and enterprises in all sectors, including metallurgical and engineering plants, is to produce materials and equipment necessary to build up our national defense.

Afterwards, we should direct our efforts toward developing the mining industry to extract more nonferrous minerals, such as gold, silver, lead, zinc and copper.

The Songhung Mine has resolved to produce 2.3 times more ore this year than last, and the Komdok Mine is also out to more than double their last year's output of nonferrous ore. This is a very good thing. The Songhung Mine and Komdok Mine as well as all others should push themselves to turn out more nonferrous minerals.

Nonferrous metals constitute one of the important sources of foreign currency and are also essential for strengthening our defenses. Among others, copper is needed in great quantities in munitions production. Without this metal it is impossible to make either shell cartridges, telephone wire or various other items for military use. Therefore, we should mine our copper quickly and use it now when it is needed instead of merely boasting about our rich deposits. If we extract a lot of copper ore and make copper wire, we can lay electric wire and speed up the electrification of our railways.

Aside from these reasons, the mining of sizable quantities of nonferrous metals is essential to obtain the foreign currency we need to set up new factories, install new equipment and buy necessary materials, all of which contribute to the consolidation of our economic foundations. We built the Pyongyang Thermal Power Plant with foreign currency earned in the past. Had we not built it, many of our factories would be at a standstill now for lack of electricity. Owing to the long drought since last autumn, the hydroelectric power stations are low on water and cannot turn out much electricity. But we have built the Pyongyang Thermal Power Plant, and it is playing a very important role in the dry season. Before long we can boost the capacity of this power plant. At its new capacity, efficient operation of the plant during a single year will be enough to repay all costs.

The workers in the mining industry should make still greater efforts to hit the target they have set for next year to increase their profits from foreign trade without fail. You have resolved to raise income from foreign trade and must carry out your determination with honor by working harder in the future.

The metallurgical industry should produce steel and structural steel in greater quantities and supply them to the machine-building industry so that more machines and equipment can be produced.

In the electric power industry, the power plants now under construction should be completed at an early date; in the coal industry mechanization should be actively introduced in production to boost coal output. The building-materials industry should turn out more and better products for capital construction.

The central task in light industry is to augment the

production of textiles and daily necessities and improve their quality.

First of all, high-quality textiles should be turned out in large quantities and innovations made in the clothing industry to provide the people with fashionable clothes. Footwear should also be more attractive and durable, and we should produce a variety of well-designed daily necessities.

In agriculture a vigorous campaign should be launched to increase grain output by 500 kilograms per *chongbo*.

It appears that the damage caused by drought this spring is very serious throughout the world. In our country, too, the drought may inflict extensive damage on the grain harvest if we do not cope with it properly. Of course, there will be no big problem for us because we have irrigated hundreds of thousands of *chongbo* of land. However, our early dry field crops may be damaged. Therefore, South Pyongan Province and North and South Hwanghae Provinces should prepare enough fertilizer and seeds so that if the early crops fail, we can make up for them with late crops. Thus, they should be able to harvest a bumper crop this year just as they did last.

It is necessary to produce supplementary food properly along with regular grain production. All the cooperative farms, civil service organizations and enterprises should direct close attention to increasing the output of vegetables and animal products in accordance with the decisions of the recent plenary meeting of the Party Central Committee.

In the fishing industry, we should increase our catch, and fish should be processed carefully to avoid the slightest possible spoilage.

Another important job is to intensify the struggle for economization and create sufficient material reserves in every branch and every unit of the national economy.

To begin with, we should economize on fabrics as much as possible in the summer so that everyone—children and grown-ups alike—will be provided with enough winter clothes.

We must also lay up great reserves of rice. Without food we cannot produce or fight the enemy. Grain should never be wasted just because there was an abundant crop last year. We must vigorously fight grain wastage and store up larger reserves.

In the meantime, we should try hard to economize on the

materials we have to import, such as rubber and gasoline.

Thus, the central task facing us in the present situation is to increase production and practice economy to the maxiumum, improving our work by the minute to produce and build more.

Even if war should break out tomorrow morning, we should struggle until midnight tonight to increase production and economize to the fullest, following the line set forth by the Party and energetically continue the simultaneous work of socialist economic construction and defense building. If we increase the country's economic power and complete positive defense arrangements by struggling to achieve higher production and thrift in all branches and units of the national economy, the Yankees will not dare attack us, and even if they embark on a reckless adventure, we can smash them in one stroke.

Thus, we can be fully prepared for our great revolutionary event only by successfully building up the economy and defenses.

Like all other revolutionary events, the great revolutionary event of our country will not come automatically. It can be brought about only through a purposeful, positive struggle on our part.

As we have mentioned time and again, it is necessary to build up three revolutionary forces if our revolution is to triumph.

First, the revolutionary force in the northern half of the Republic should be increased. We must strengthen the northern half in the political, economic and military spheres alike by keeping up the great upsurge, and thereby speeding up socialist construction, through the continued grand march of Chollima.

Next, in order to achieve the final victory of our revolution, we must constantly assist the people of south Korea to strengthen their revolutionary forces and accomplish the south Korean revolution, while building up our revolutionary base in the northern half of the Republic in all spheres. When the revolutionary forces in south Korea have grown enough so that the south Korean youth and people rise in the struggle to crush the Yankees and their stooges and call for our help, we should give them all possible assistance. When the south Korean revolutionaries ask us for materials, we should give them materials; when they ask for guns, we should give them guns; and when they ask for men, we must send them men.

Meanwhile, we should strengthen our solidarity with the international revolutionary forces and assist the struggle of the revolutionary peoples all over the world.

Today the peoples of many countries in Asia, Africa and Latin America actively support us because we have strengthened our solidarity with the revolutionary peoples and adhere to a principled stand in the revolution. They carry our documents, including the Ten-Point Political Program of the Government of the Republic, in their newspapers and denounce the aggressive acts of U.S. imperialism in our country. When we captured the U.S. imperialists' armed spy ship *Pueblo*, many countries including Vietnam and Cuba and other fraternal parties issued statements of support. All this says that the international solidarity of our revolution has been strengthened a great deal.

We are now helping the revolutionary peoples of Vietnam and many other countries in Asia, Africa and Latin America. True, if we hold back material aid to other countries in their revolution, we will have more to promote our own socialist construction and standard of living. But we should not do this. It is national egoism and revisionism to care only for one's own easy life without assisting other revolutionary peoples.

We must actively support the revolutionary peoples for the sake of the world revolution, for the purpose of crushing U.S. imperialism, our sworn enemy. By doing so, we can help them knock down as many Yankees as possible.

Whether it is in our country or in others, the more Yankees that are killed, the better. Wherever Yankees are smashed and a hundred of them finished off, it will mean a hundred less of the enemy and if a thousand or ten thousand are wiped out, our revolution will benefit that much more.

We must, therefore, do all we can to continue strengthening our solidarity with the revolutionary people of the world and defeat Yankees wherever we find them. By fighting the Yankees all over the world—by tearing off their limbs one by one everywhere—U.S. imperialism will ultimately be destroyed.

Small countries, too, are fully capable of beating U.S. imperialism if they fight in unity. This is a law of dialectics.

Let me cite an example from the course of our socialist economic construction in the past. In 1959 when the First Five-Year Plan was going ahead full steam, our economic foundations were not solid and there was a scarcity of equipment. Therefore, we had to tackle countless difficulties whenever we tried to make anything. At that time the workers of the Ryongsong Machine Plant were assigned to make a sheet-steel rolling machine for the Hwanghae Iron Works, but they did not have the necessary large machine tools to build it. The workers, however, proceeded to cut the big piece of material on all sides with many small machine tools in the same way ants gnaw away at a big bone and, at last, they succeeded in making the rolling machine.

Although the Yankees now brag of their invincibility, they cannot escape their doom when they are attacked in many parts of the world and their limbs dismembered one by one, just as the big piece of material was processed by the workers of the Ryongsong Machine Plant with small machine tools.

One must not think that unless a country is big it cannot smash U.S. imperialism. Of course, it would be more gratifying if large countries were to join us in fighting the Yankees. That is why we try to unite with big countries as well.

But no one can ever say that a country has to be big to fight and defeat U.S. imperialism. In the final analysis, it is flunkeyism to think that only large countries can vanquish the Yankees. If all peoples fighting in the cause of revolution strengthen their solidarity and put up a powerful, united resistance, they are bound to win.

Our tasks, then are to firmly build up the northern half of the Republic through a successful building of socialism, steadily increase the revolutionary forces in south Korea, unite with the revolutionary people of the world and get an increasing number of countries to struggle against U.S. imperialism. This will lead us to an easy victory over the Yankees and achieve the nationwide triumph of the Korean revolution.

Such is our work to prepare to meet the great event of the Korean revolution, and our Party is directing all its activities now in this direction.

The Chollima riders are entrusted with a weighty and honorable task in preparing to greet our great revolutionary event. They should make new leaps forward, bringing about fresh wonders through uninterrupted innovation and continuous advance in all domains of the national economy. And they should sustain the great revolutionary upsurge in socialist construction by putting spurs to the grand Chollima march. At the same time, they should thoroughly arm all the working people with the monolithic ideology of our Party and intensify the struggle for revolutionization and working-classization. Through such efforts they can help rally all the people closely around the Central Committee of our Party and turn them into a unified, powerful political force.

I am firmly convinced that you will make a great contribution to accelerate the final victory of our revolution by continuing to deepen and develop the Chollima Workteam Movement.

ON CORRECTLY IMPLEMENTING OUR PARTY'S POLICY TOWARD INTELLECTUALS (Excerpt)

Speech to Intellectuals in North Hamgyong Province, *June 14, 1968*

2. On Some Revolutionary Tasks Facing Our Intellectuals

Our Party has trusted the intellectuals and assigned them as engineers and chief engineers; it has placed factories in their charge and entrusted them with various important revolutionary tasks. Being a factory chief engineer, for instance, is by no means an ordinary job. It is as important a job as that of a chief of staff in the army. Just as the army chief of staff makes and executes all operational plans, so the chief engineer manages the factory in the technical sphere and guides all the production processes. Our Party assigns such important jobs to intellectuals because it completely trusts them. Some comrades seem to think that it is some sort of diplomacy to keep them in important posts. That is quite mistaken. There can be no diplomacy among revolutionaries. The point is whether or not you make revolution. If we did not trust intellectuals, we would not give them such honorable revolutionary tasks.

Our Party has entrusted intellectuals with important revolutionary tasks. Why then should they become timid, vacillate and fall into the self-preservation frame of mind? There is no reason why our intellectuals should take such an attitude. It is not right to be timid because of their bad class background.

Our intellectuals should be determined to become worthy of the Party's confidence by revolutionizing themselves and faithfully serving the Party and the working class and be active in all spheres and try to avoid making mistakes. Yet, instead of trying to be worthy of the deep trust of the Party, some comrades are not working wholeheartedly.

Let me take the instance of the chief engineer in a certain enterprise. As he did a fine job before, we promoted him to the post of chief engineer in 1962. His family background was somewhat complex. But we did not make a big question of it.

We trusted the man himself and boldly assigned him as chief engineer, though his family background was complex. Therefore, he should have been faithful to his job. But, contrary to the Party's expectations, he did not introduce new technology nor did he work hard. He even had licentious relations with an ideologically bad woman.

The Party organization was also to blame. It did not even criticize him, I was told, lest he should get frightened. That was a wrong method of work. The Party organization should have criticized his mistakes in time. If someone has shortcomings, he should be told frankly that such and such is wrong. That should be enough to make him correct his mistakes painlessly. Absence of timely criticism of mistakes makes the person concerned doubt things more. In fact, the chief engineer at issue grew all the more skeptical and timid and failed to do his work properly because the Party organization did not criticize his mistakes. As we see, a man of bad family background will become worse if, because of that handicap, he is left free of supervision and criticism even when he has made mistakes in carrying out the revolutionary tasks given him by the Party.

Party organizations should promptly criticize and educate intellectuals when they commit errors. Some comrades say it is hard to criticize those who are to some extent of bad origin. You should not think in that way. It is better to criticize those with shortcomings than leave them alone. Of course, criticism should be given after due consideration of whether it is better to criticize a person openly before the masses, or individually or else at a closed meeting of a few people, according to his political level and character when he has made a mistake. It is not a bad thing to bring a person before the masses when he repeats his errors many times. And intellectuals on their part should realize that they well deserve criticism for their mistakes, and accept the Party's criticism as an effective educational remedy to save them.

In the days of our guerrilla struggle we used to expose mistakes to sharp criticism and deal out severe punishment.

I would like to give you a case in point that happened when we were waging our guerrilla struggle. Many comrades were then engaged in underground activities down in the Tanchon and Songjin areas. To establish contact with them we sent a small unit under a comrade named Kim Ju Hyon into the homeland. His job was something like that of deputy commander for logistics as we say nowadays in the People's Army. Comrade Kim Ju Hyon led his small unit into the homeland. But on the way to the destination, he took an action which he had not been instructed to do and came back without fulfilling his mission. He came back believing that he had done a good thing, but we punished him for his failure to carry out his revolutionary assignment. We sharply criticized him: "We told you to give some revolutionary tasks to the comrades who are working in the Tanchon and Songjin areas, and it is a serious thing that you did not carry out your important revolutionary task." We then decided to dismiss him from the post of deputy commander for logistics and assigned him the job of carrying a cauldron for six months. This was certainly no light punishment. How shameful it must have been for a man in a leading post as deputy commander for logistics to find himself carrying a cauldron on his back in the rear of a marching column following those who had formerly been under him! But he knew that was really the way to revolutionize himself. He was an intellectual like you comrades and was good at writing and making speeches. He made up his mind: "I will fight to the last on the road of revolution. I deserve punishment since I have made a mistake. I must correct my mistake by faithfully serving the revolutionary struggle." And then he worked tirelessly, carrying a cauldron on his back. He kept on working hard without the least complaint despite his punishment. So we wrote off his penalty before the six-month period was up and restored him to his former position.

Anyone may be punished if he makes mistakes in his work, and in a serious case he may be demoted. This is what order and discipline mean in the revolutionary struggle. Without such strict revolutionary order and discipline we cannot carry out difficult revolutionary work. Even if you are punished and demoted, you should regard your new job as a revolutionary post assigned by the Party. In the revolutionary struggle you should not have likes or dislikes, be your post high or low. No matter what kind of post you hold, you should faithfully perform your revolutionary task and constantly strive to correct your mistakes.

Today our Party trusts all intellectuals—old and new intellectuals, intellectuals of working-class origin, of petty-bourgeois origin or of bourgeois origin. You comrades have worked for the revolution for more than ten years and some comrades have served the working class and the people for over 20 years. Therefore, you deserve to work in the important position with which the Party entrusts you. That is why intellectuals should stick to the revolutionary post entrusted to them by the Party, work harder and strive to revolutionize and working-classize themselves.

Our intellectuals must first discard all old ideas—timidity, attitudes of self-preservation, egoism, etc. They should defend socialism in every way and be loyal to the revolutionary cause of the working class to the last.

Generally speaking, intellectuals together with the petty bourgeoisie stand on the side of the Party and the working class and go ahead without vacillation as far as the stage in the socialist revolution in which the landlords' land is confiscated and the capitalists' factories are expropriated. But in the course of building socialism and on the road to communism instances are found from time to time of some intellectuals who give up revolution, and flinch and waver halfway. As you all know, many very interesting struggles take place in the periods of the national-liberation struggle, the democratic revolution and the socialist revolution. In these periods, the struggles are waged mainly to solve irreconcilable contradictions and ideological struggle does not yet develop full scale, for it is of a non-antagonistic nature aimed at eliminating the survivals of obsolete capitalist ideas in the minds of people. In these periods, therefore, intellectuals zealously participate in the revolution on impulse.

But in the period of building socialism following the socialist revolution, ideological struggle is carried out on a full scale to completely root out the remnants of capitalist ideas. The struggle against egoism and other survivals of old capitalist ideas is one of the most important revolutionary tasks in the period of the transition from capitalism to socialism. As they enter the period of ideological revolution when egoism and other capitalist ideas are totally opposed some intellectuals begin to vacillate. Old ideas such as egoism survive in everyone to some degree or other. Consequently, all who are not revolutionized should remold their ideology. It is a big problem for the peasants, who are backward in ideology, and particularly intellectuals. This is one of the reasons why intellectuals and petty bourgeoisie waver in the period of ideological revolution.

Another major reason why intellectuals and some sectors of the middle class vacillate during the struggle for the complete victory of socialism, i.e., in the period of the transition from capitalism to socialism, lies in the fact that they do not realize the real advantages of the socialist system, because of their social, class or economic positions in the past and that, faced with the difficulties which may temporarily stand in the way of the building of socialism, they lose confidence in its complete victory.

All this indicates that they have not been thoroughly armed with revolutionary ideas.

It is a matter of much regret that there are cases in which our intellectuals have not discarded egoism and fail to devote themselves to the building of socialism.

In former days our revolutionaries dedicated themselves to the revolution at the cost of their lives—to the cause of creating a socialist society, even though they had never been to a socialist country. Among the people who made the revolution with us were intellectuals. They came from well-to-do families. They never wavered in their revolutionary constancy or forsook their revolutionary conscience even when in the revolutionary struggle they were captured by the enemy and faced death. But nowadays our intellectuals lack such a strong revolutionary spirit.

At present the south Korean intellectuals, too, are taking an active part in the revolutionary struggle. This is by no means because they live in poverty. Although most intellectuals engaged in the revolution in south Korea are the sons and daughters of the well-to-do, they are bravely fighting the enemy to drive out the Yankees and overthrow the corrupt south Korean regime. It is said that they declare: "We are not making revolution because we are hungry. We have land and money. We are from well-to-do families, but we'll carry out revolution. How can we be indifferent to the *chige*-carriers wandering about the streets to earn their bread, the many homeless people sleeping under bridges and the miserable children begging around with tins in their hands or polishing shoes by the roadside, denied the chance of schooling?" The south Korean intellectuals are fighing today without yielding even when they are arrested by the enemy, and they do not give up the revolutionary struggle even when they see their comrades taken to the scaffold.

Thus, the south Korean intellectuals are fighting solely for the revolution at the risk of their lives, their families and their property. Why, then, do some of our intellectuals yield to egoism and fail to devote themselves to socialist construction?

The question depends on whether one has a revolutionary world outlook or not. The fact that many south Korean intellectuals are fighting for the revolution under cruel enemy supression shows that they possess the revolutionary world outlook. This is why they make nothing of their comfortable homes, their large land-holdings and their wealth. They are fighting, defying the scaffold and prison, not for their own prosperity but in order to build a socialist society where everyone has an equal chance in life. Our intellectuals, however, have not yet been thoroughly educated in this revolutionary spirit, nor have they formed a solid revolutionary world outlook. That is why they are not wholehearted in their devotion to the revolutionary cause of the working class. When I say this, however, I do not mean that all our intellectuals are backward people lacking in revolutionary ideas. Needless to say, the absolute majority possess the revolutionary world outlook and are working faithfully for the Party and the people on all fronts of socialist construction. But some, though very few, have not yet discarded selfishness and lack a strong revolutionary spirit.

Our intellectuals should undergo ceaseless ideological tempering. They should eradicate the survivals of old ideas and arm themselves firmly with the communist idea to devote themselves to the Party and the revolution, to the country and the people, and to society and the collective.

When they are revolutionized and see things from the point of view not of egoism but of collectivism and communism, intellectuals will clearly realize the advantages of socialism and work devotedly for its complete victory.

In fact, our socialist system is a social system incomparably superior to the capitalist system. A south Korean intellectual said that in Seoul there were many *chige*-carriers, and a lot of people slept on straw-bags under bridges, whereas in north Korea there were none of such people, and in Pyongyang one could see everyone on the streets in the morning equally well-dressed, regardless of rank, and this really gave an impression of a different world. He also said that some women in Seoul painted their lips thickly, though their underwear was worn-out, but no woman over here did that. When we asked him why those south Korean women went around like that, he replied that it was because they were so badly off that they had no choice but to become prostitutes. He said young south Koreans were even forced to choose to become paid cannon fodder for the U.S. imperialists on the battlefields of South Vietnam, in an attempt to prolong their existence even by a day, for they were in fear of starving to death at home. This shows how wretched the situation is in south Korea. It is, indeed, a great misery inconceivable in our happy northern half of the country.

Capitalist society is the land of promise for a handful of landlords and capitalists but a living hell for the absolute majority of the laboring masses. In contrast, socialist society is a society in which every one of the working people is equally well-fed, well-dressed and well-off, and in which everyone can study and receive free medical care.

Whenever we have visitors from the newly independent countries we tell them about the superiority of the socialist system over the capitalist system. We vividly explain to them, by illustrating with our experience that if an underdeveloped country takes the road of capitalism after its liberation from imperialist colonial rule, it will become a colony again and will become ruined, and that only when it takes the road of socialism, will it become a rich and strong country enjoying a worthwhile life.

The successful building of socialism naturally requires much time and effort because an independent national economy and national culture must be developed and national defense must be strengthened. Difficulties and obstacles will crop up, though only temporarily, in the course of building socialism. How can it be an easy job to ensure that everyone leads a happy life—able to work and study and be equally well-fed and well-dressed? Yet once we achieve the complete victory of socialism and gradually build communism through hard work and great effort, we will find no better society. Communism is the highest ideal of mankind. In that society man will attain his highest development, both mental and physical, and everyone will live a cultured and prosperous life. The fall of capitalism and the victory of socialism and communism is an inexorable law of human history.

By further revolutionizing and working-classizing themselves, therefore, our intellectuals should devote all their wisdom and talents exlusively to the struggle for the defense and complete victory of socialism without vacillating in the slightest under any adversity. Thus, they will help to step up socialist construction in our country and consolidate and develop the socialist system, thereby contributing greatly to making all the people understand better, through their actual life, the real advantages of socialism.

As we always say, for the complete victory of socialism we must conquer two fortresses, that is, the ideological and the material. Therefore the ideological revolution and economic construction should be carried out properly, and in this intellectuals have many things to do.

Intellectuals have indeed tremendous tasks in economic construction alone.

We should endeavor to speed up the industrialization of our country and consolidate the basis of our independent national economy. It would be easy for us to provide temporary abundance for the people. If we imported oil, meat and other subsidiary foods or clothing materials with the money we earn every year, instead of building factories, our people would be able to live well for the time being. However, we must not live in such a way as to eat today when we have money and go hungry tomorrow when we have none. That is not the way to make our country prosperous and powerful. We must build our economy under a long-range program, even if we have to tighten our belts at present, and we must lay a solid economic base for the well-being of the future generations. We must develop the chemical, iron and steel and machine-building industries and also the defense industry. In other words, we must give priority to the growth of heavy industry which constitutes a leading sector of the national economy and provides the material basis guaranteeing a high tempo of extended reproduction. This alone will guarantee a better life for our people in the future and deter the enemy from attacking.

We should not only strengthen the nation's economic base for the sake of the future but also carry on economic construction efficiently in order to improve the people's present living conditions. Our aim in building socialism and communism lies, in the final analysis, in providing all the people with abundance and all the benefits of modern life. The superiority of socialism must find expression not in factory chimneys but in a happy life for the people. For that reason, while concentrating our main efforts on economic construction to ensure plenty in the distant future, we should never neglect today's living conditions of the people.

Of course, with the gradual strengthening of our economic base our people's standard of living has already risen as never before. But we cannot yet say that our people live a life of plenty. We must solve a few questions to raise living standards.

One to be solved at present is that of non-staple foodstuffs. We have not yet satisfactorily solved the question of oil and meat. In order to turn out large quantities of good subsidiary foodstuffs we must develop light industry and agriculture, which in turn requires a rapid growth of those branches of heavy industry that are directly related to the improvement of the people's living standards. In other words, for a plentiful supply of subsidiary food we should develop the machine-building, metallurgical and chemical industries, and thus lay a solid foundation for the efficient production of these foodstuffs. Only when the chemical industry produces fertilizers and agricultural chemicals in large quantities to ensure good farming, can we produce a large amount of feed-grain and, consequently, abundant meat. And only when we develop the engineering industry and thus build many large vessels, will we be able to catch lots of fish on the high seas.

Furthermore, the improvement of our people's standard of living calls for raising the quality of consumer goods. Quality, however, is not high, as you can see for instance in the footwear now made in the shoe factories in North Hamgyong Province. This is true not only of footwear but also of other consumer goods. And the variety of daily necessities is not large at present, to say nothing of their poor quality.

Both the work of laying a solid economic base under the long-range national plan and economic work to raise the people's present living standards can only be successfully carried out when they are pushed ahead vigorously by scientists and technicians with scientific know-how and technique. Indeed, the Party expects much from you intellectuals in economic construction.

But how are you doing things now? You are neither working heart and soul to promote our science and technology, nor tackling the elementary technical problems that need to be solved to improve the people's living conditions nor doing even simple organizational work. That is why our industrialization is not being accelerated nor are the people's living standards raised rapidly.

Take stockbreeding for example. It cannot go ahead because our functionaries are not organizing the work properly and not solving even simple technical questions to do with animal husbandry and veterinary work. I discovered on this visit that many sheep have perished in North Hamgyong Province in the last eight years. If these sheep had been saved, carefully raised and bred, they would no doubt have tremendously increased in number by now. The same situation exists in the fishing industry. At present, small-scale fishing, for instance, is not organized properly, though this is fully possible. And while vegetable growing will be successful if the sprinkling irrigation system is introduced in accordance with the Party's policy, our functionaries do not properly organize that work either. The low quality of the products of light industry is also due to your failure to give effective technical direction and to your neglect of adequate ideological education for the people. You are highly-educated technicians. Our Party has entrusted you with the task of the technical revolution and with scientific research. Yet, you are not working hard to improve quality. Since you are engineers or chief engineers, you ought to try hard to raise the quality of manufactured goods and expand their variety.

We are all materialists and believers in science. Nothing falls from heaven or springs up from the earth by itself. We must make everything we need through our own efforts. Intellectuals in particular should put in a lot of effort to help achieve this, but they fail to do so. As a result, we are not properly making what is well within our capabilities.

Is this clumsy way of doing things, then, due to a lack of adequate working conditions for our scientists and technicians? No, that is not the case. Our intellectuals are not in such difficult circumstances as those in south Korea where their colleagues are doing scientific research under the enemy's cruel suppression. Our intellectuals are provided with all the conditions necessary for doing profound scientific research and for doing their work to the best of their ability. Our Party has entrusted intellecuals with important posts and created favorable conditions for them to do their work without worry. So they ought to work hard to live up to the Party's trust and expectations. You must understand Party policy correctly and endeavor to defend the Party positively, uphold its ideology and translate it into action.

Intellectuals should also become active propagandists for socialism and communism. They should be, so to speak, defenders of socialism not only in the field of economic construction but also in the sphere of ideological revolution. You have studied under the Party's care since liberation, growing up in its bosom, and are better educated than anyone else. Therefore, you should fully rouse other people and explain and propagate socialist and communist ideology among the masses. All our intellectuals will thus make a greater contribution to the revolutionization and working-classization of the whole of society.

Next, our intellectuals should arm themselves firmly with the Juche idea, the revolutionary ideology of our Party, in order to become Red soldiers of the Party.

Our adherence to the Juche idea does not in the least mean that we have adopted nationalism. The Juche idea we advocate does not conflict with internationalism. Instead, it is designed to promote internationalism, for it leads to the development of the sciences and the building of the economy to suit our specific conditions, and thus contributes to increasing the strength of our country and furthering the might of the socialist camp as a whole.

Let us take the food question for example. Suppose we often asked other socialist countries to lend us food because we failed to become self-sufficient. What then would the result of that be? It would hold back the standard of living of the peoples of those countries by that much. However, if we get good crop yields and do not ask others for food, they will be free from such worries and obstacles to their own livelihood. Furthermore, it will help improve food conditions in the socialist camp to that extent. So the building of an independent agriculture does not mean nationalism. On the contrary, it is conducive to promoting internationalism.

Our intellectuals must arm themselves with our Party's ideology and thoroughly establish Juche, and never practice flunkeyism. The path of flunkeyism leads to the ruin of the country and the nation. If individuals practice flunkeyism, they are bound to become fools.

Yet flunkeyism has found and is finding much expression among intellectuals—not only in the past but also at present. Flunkeyism is seldom found among the workers and peasants, but conditions are ripe that give rise to flunkeyism among intellectuals working in the fields of science, technology, literature and art. For the purpose of scientific and cultural research, they read books written by foreigners as well as those published in their own country, and many go abroad for study or training to acquire advanced experience. In such cases those who are not firmly equipped with the Juche idea will be infected with national nihilism and flunkeyism which regard things of their own country as unworthy of attention and indiscriminately consider that everything foreign is good.

Let me take a few examples.

In former days some of the government-patronized scholars infected with flunkeyism prattled that the Koreans were the descendants of "Kija." History books by those ancient scholars made a fiction that a foreigner named "Kija," who hated serving the king of his country, rebelled against him and took several hundred technicians to Korea to build a country. These books say that among these technicians were blacksmiths, weavers and others with all sorts of skills, and that they developed our science and culture. Those scholars even had what they called the "Kija mausoleum" built in Pyongyang. In the days of Japanese imperialist rule this was extolled in a popular song as a spot of scenic beauty and historic interest in Pyongyang.

Under Japanese imperialist rule flunkeyism with respect to Japan was also serious. In those days a man called Li Gwang Su went to the length of babbling that the Koreans were of the "same blood" as the Japanese; in other words, the Koreans had the same ancestor and the same origin as the Japanese.

Flunkeyism of this kind has not been eradicated from the minds of our intellectuals even now.

A certain archaeologist was so full of flunkeyism that he tried to establish the origin of our nation in an absurd place. Without doing any scientific research he said that our ancestors had probably come from a foreign country because of the similarity in the shape of the skulls of Koreans in primitive society and those found in an old tomb somewhere in that country. Thus he tried to regard our people as the descendants of another nation and as a very backward nation. This allegation is really nonsense.

Our present-day musicians also have tendencies to flunkeyism. A certain singer, I was told, insists on singing Italian songs, considering them the best in the world. This attitude is prompted by a fundamentally wrong ideology. Our country is beautiful by nature, our mother tongue sounds fluent and the pronunciation is articulate, and our songs, too, are melodious. Why do they only worship foreign music rather than developing our own fine national music?

The tendencies to flunkeyism are now revealed even in the way some people speak. When they have a fine language of their own, they introduce words of Chinese origin into their speech to show how learned they are. When they mention one's age, for example, they say "sibose" (15 years old—Tr.) instead of "yoldasossal" which itself sounds good. This means, in effect, that they make little effort to develop things of our nation.

In south Korea the idea of U.S.-worship is widespread among intellectuals. It was reported that a south Korean dance troupe visited Indonesia not long ago. As they were in the habit of copying American "jazz," they danced naked on the stage even in that country—only to be expelled. What a lousy show they must have put on to be kicked out even by a country not ruled by Communists! As you see, American "jazz" dance is all the rage in south Korea, not among the workers and peasants, but among actors and actresses who are intellectuals. U.S.-worship is also dominant in other spheres in south Korea, to say nothing of the realm of art.

We should resolutely combat this practice of hindering the development of our national culture, as well as that of distorting the history of our nation.

You would be wrong if you thought that flunkeyism existed elsewhere but not a bit here in North Hamgyong Province. Quite a lot of it exists in this province, too. When we were here in 1959, we found many manifestations of flunkeyism. On that visit I went to the theater where I noticed a display of many quotations from foreign writers, but there were none of our own. So I asked the manager of the theater if he knew anything about the foreign writers, and he answered he knew nothing about them. How deplorable it is to be so ignorant and to practice flunkeyism!

We should root out this flunkeyism and establish Juche more thoroughly in all spheres of social sciences.

Juche should be thoroughly established not only in social sciences but also in natural sciences. By establishing Juche in natural sciences we should see to it that domestic raw materials meet at least 70% of the demand set by industry. Otherwise our industry will not develop on a stable basis.

This has been fully proved by our experience. This year our iron production was retarded by the shortage of coking coal. Though they talk much about establishing Juche, our functionaries have not yet discarded flunkeyism in practice and, therefore, they are not trying hard to make wide use of domestic fuel in our iron industry.

We should endeavor to develop the iron industry with domestic fuel. As we mentioned on our recent visit to the Kim

Chaek Iron Works, you in North Hamgyong Province should use iron ore produced in this province rather than bringing ore from the western region, and do research on making granulated iron by using coal available in your province instead of anthracite.

The correctness of the Juche idea advocated by our Party is now widely known to the world, and it is finding an echo among large numbers of people. The revolutionary intellectuals in south Korea also actively support our Juche idea, the idea of independence, self-support and self-defense, and are fighting for it. The *Theses on the Socialist Rural Question in Our Country*, the Ten-Point Political Program of the Government of the Republic and other documents of our Party are now widely studied in many countries.

Thus, even foreigners support and study the Juche idea, the line of independence, set forth by our Party. Why, then, should we, who directly initiated the Juche idea and are building socialism, practice flunkeyism? We should never practice flunkeyism.

North Hamgyong Province in particular is vulnerable to flunkeyism because it borders on big countries. You comrades should, therefore, intensify the struggle to oppose flunkeyism and establish Juche.

But that does not mean we intend to follow a policy of national isolationism or closed-doorism. Even things foreign, if acceptable, should be turned to good account. Foreign experience should be studied—if it does not suit us it should be rejected, and vice versa. Flunkeyism means blind worship of everything foreign and contempt for everything of one's own. It never implies the exchange of good experience with foreign countries or the introduction of scientific and technological achievements that are suited to one's own country. Certainly we should introduce foreign things, if necessary. Nevertheless, we should value our own things highly and guard against flunkeyism at all times.

You should not misinterpret our urging to oppose flunkeyism and establish Juche as an encouragement to the restoration of the old. Restorationism has nothing in common with Juche. Nowadays certain persons claim that a husky voice should be the vocal basis of our music as in old times, and that this alone is genuine national music. They maintain that even the musical instruments used by our forefathers in ancient times should be popularized without improvement. According to them, there can be no progress in national music. We must not tend to restorationism because of our emphasis on national music. The old feudal songs tuned to *sijo*, which the feudal rulers liked to sing, were decadent and moribund. If you were to revive and sing those songs as national music, who would want to hear them? Such outmoded, corrupt songs would have no educational value at a time when you ought to sing songs that suit the proud reality of socialism rushing forward in the spirit of Chollima. Rather than following restorationism in music, you should develop our national musical instruments and sing the songs expressing the emotions and feelings arising from the present-day life of our people, songs that throb with the thrilling reality of socialist construction.

In conclusion, in order to establish Juche thoroughly, we must completely eliminate dogmatist attitudes to the universal principles of Marxism-Leninism, blind worship of big powers and reliance on them and national nihilism. At the same time, we must oppose national chauvinism and national isolationism and strictly guard against restorationism which attempts to revive the ancient uncritically on the pleas of valuing our own things. This is precisely the revolutionary essence of the Juche we advocate.

For the thoroughgoing establishment of Juche an ideological struggle against outmoded ideas should be intensified among the people. No doubt, it would be impossible to measure offhand how much each man is infected with flunkeyism. But this is not so difficult a job. If ideological struggle is conducted and each man's acts examined, everything will become clear. You should root out flunkeyism from your minds through effective ideological struggle. Our intellectuals will thus be able to take the lead in holding high the banner of anti-flunkeyism and championing the Juche idea of our Party.

Lastly, you should be honest in your Party life and other organizational life. Anyone will lag behind in ideology if he is not under organizational supervision and has no organizational life. Those who dislike organizational life will be badly affected by the old ideas and will be the first to be infected with the venom of capitalist ideology from outside. Therefore, you should not regard organizational life as a nuisance but actively participate in it and constantly temper yourselves ideologically.

All intellectuals will be bold and brave in their work, will find it interesting and be more faithful to the Party, overcoming all obstacles and difficulties, if they clearly understand our Party's policy toward intellectuals, actively safeguard the socialist system, form the revolutionary world outlook and thoroughly arm themselves with the Juche idea of our Party.

North Hamgyong Province today has many tasks to perform, which require an intense struggle. In this province there are enormous construction projects for you to undertake: the steel and rolling mills at the Kim Chaek Iron Works, the Sodusu Hydroelectric Power Station, the building of an oil refinery, and so on. It is you who have to design and undertake all these vast projects. Therefore, the tasks for scientists and technicians in this province are really important.

All your learning and energy should be devoted to the successful fulfillment of your glorious revolutionary tasks. Indolence and slackness are taboo in revolutionary work. How can you afford to be idle and easy-going when we have yet to reunify the country and perfect its economic base and especially when you have huge construction tasks in North Hamgyong Province? I was told that it took a certain enterprise six years to build a mine shaft. You should not work in such an easygoing way. You should strive to carry out your revolutionary tasks faster and better, devoting all your learning and talents to them, without slackening in the least degree.

For the successful completion of the huge construction projects in North Hamgyong Province all reserves should be mobilized in every field. The technicians in every field of the national economy—the engineering, metallurgical and local industries, construction and transportation, etc.—should all endeavor to tap reserves.

North Hamgyong Province has abundant available reserves. It has a large population, a great many factories and enterprises as well as rich natural resources. All these should be actively enlisted in tapping reserves.

The engineering industry, above all, should be run at full capacity so as to increase production still more. The metallurgical industry also should put its existing facilities into full operation.

You should briskly mobilize all potentialities for construction in your province. All sectors of industry, the engineering and iron industries in particular, must actively support it.

All the intellectuals in North Hamgyong Province should work more energetically. Technicians in factories and enterprises as well as teachers in schools and colleges should do their utmost to carry out the province's construction projects faster and better. You should thus turn North Hamgyong Province into a still greater industrial base by doing an excellent job of completing your projects.

I firmly believe that all intellectuals in North Hamgyong Province will thoroughly arm themselves with our Party's revolutionary thinking and live up to the expectations of the Party by devoting their all to the successful fulfillment of their glorious revolutionary tasks.

THE DEMOCRATIC PEOPLE'S REPUBLIC OF KOREA IS THE BANNER OF FREEDOM AND INDEPENDENCE FOR OUR PEOPLE AND A POWERFUL WEAPON FOR BUILDING SOCIALISM AND COMMUNISM (Excerpt)

Report at the 20th Anniversary Celebration of the Founding of the DPRK, *September 7, 1968*

2. On Further Consolidating and Developing the Socialist System in the Democratic People's Republic of Korea

Comrades,

The great triumph of the Korean people in the struggle waged under the banner of the Republic over the past 20 years for the flourishing development of the country and the prosperity of the nation is entirely due to the fact that they have vigorously advanced along the socialist path, firmly relying on the indestructible vitality of socialism. Our triumph is striking proof of the superiority of the socialist system over the capitalist system.

The socialist system is a most advanced social system: power is in the hands of the people, and on the basis of the public ownership of the means of production, there is a steady development of a planned production on a highly scientific and technical basis for the purpose of systematically improving the welfare of the people. Every kind of exploitation and oppression has been abolished once and for all, and each works according to his ability and takes his share according to the quality and quantity of his work.

Unlike capitalist society where the people have neither political rights nor freedom, the socialist system actually provides genuine democratic rights and freedom to the masses of the people in all spheres of politics, economy and culture. In our society, everyone participates freely in the political life of the country, exercises his sovereign rights for the revolutionary cause, chooses his occupation and profession according to ability and propensity, and works, studies and lives happily. In capitalist society where the means of production are private property and the aim of production is to squeeze out more profits for the capitalists and landlords, the producer masses have to work to keep body and soul together and have no interests in the development of production and technology. In a socialist society, however, the means of production are public property and the working people work for the country, the society and for themselves. This encourages the people to give full play to their inexhaustible creative initiative and talents for developing production steadily and swiftly. In a socialist society all branches of the national economy and all enterprises are organically linked with each other on the basis of common aims and interests. Therefore, there is no anarchy of production or crisis of overproduction as there is in a capitalist society. The national economy develops in a planned and proportionate manner and all the manpower and material resources and potential of our country for production can be tapped and turned to account most efficiently. Moreover, under the socialist system there exist neither exploiters nor exploited and the fruits of labor are entirely devoted to the promotion of the welfare of the working people, and the living standards of the people continually rise in correspondence with the rapid growth of production.

The capitalist path is the path of exploitation and oppression, slavery and ruin, while the socialist path is the path leading to the abolition of class exploitation and national oppression, to the freedom and happiness of the entire people and complete independence and prosperity of the country.

The two diametrically different realities, that in the north and that in south Korea, furnish a striking example of what we are saying. In the northern half of the Republic, the most progressive system—the socialist system—free from exploitation and oppression, has been established, the foundations of a powerful independent national economy have been laid, and the people enjoy genuine freedom and happiness. In contrast, south Korea has been turned to U.S. imperialism's colony and military base for aggression, its economy has been utterly ruined and the people are groaning under a regime of terrorism and tyranny, deprived of all political freedom, even elementary democratic rights, and are suffering hardships without precedent in thousands of years.

Historical experience shows that when a people throw off the colonial yoke of imperialism they must take the socialist path. A people who have won their independence must work hard to crush the subversive maneuvers of foreign imperialism and domestic reactionary forces, and tear down the imperialists' colonial ruling machine and wipe out the economic foothold of imperialism and domestic reaction. They must positively strive to strengthen the revolutionary forces, establish a progressive social system, and build an independent national economy and national culture. Only by doing these things will they be able to advance dynamically along the short cut to freedom and happiness, national independence and prosperity, bypassing the bitter history of misery and distress which capitalism has inevitably gone through.

Capitalism has already lived out its days. It is rushing incessantly toward its doom. Socialism and communism represent the bright future of mankind. It is an inexorable law of historical development that all nations go toward socialism and communism.

We will continue to advance steadily along the socialist path without the slightest vacillation.

Our people are confronted today with the historic task of ensuring the complete triumph of socialism by promoting revolution and construction even more vigorously on the foundations of the brilliant successes already achieved in building a new society.

We have already built a firm base for socialism in the northern half of the country. But we still have much to do to win complete victory for socialism. Even after the achievement of a socialist base, the socialist state should continue to carry out the revolution thoroughly in all spheres of political, economic and cultural life.

Although the exploiting classes have been liquidated and the socialist transformation of the relations of production has been accomplished, the class struggle continues throughout the period of transition from capitalism to socialism. It is true that when the socialist transformation is effecuated in town and country, the exploiting classes are totally liquidated as classes and their socio-economic foothold ceases to exist. But the remnants of those classes survive. They never give up the dream of restoring their old positions and continually carry out subversive activities. Even after the triumph of the socialist system, therefore, hostile elements remain in a socialist society for a prolonged period. Though insignificant in themselves, these hostile elements should never be ignored, for they are tools and agents of the foreign imperialists. While they resort to direct armed intervention to commit aggression against socialist countries, the imperialists also maneuver to wreck them from within by bringing together and abetting the remnants of the overthrown exploiting classes and other reactionaries in these countries.

Particularly in our country, the chieftain of world reaction, U.S. imperialism, entrenched in south Korea, is constantly instigating the reactionary classes in the southern half and the remnants of the exploiting classes in the northern half to carry out subversive and sabotage activities as well as to penetrate ideologically, with the aim of overthrowing the socialist system in the north.

Even after the establishment of the socialist system, the old thinking left over from thousands of years of exploiter societies survives for a long time in the minds of the working people. The triumph of the socialist system puts an end to the economic base that engenders obsolete ideas and it creates the social and material conditions for arming people with new ideas. But since the development of the ideological consciousness of people lags behind the changes in the material conditions of society, even after the socialist system has triumphed, old ideas left over from the exploiter society persist for a long time among the working people. Also, the venom of bourgeois ideology infiltrates ceaselessly into socialist society from the outside owing to the ideological and cultural penetration of the imperialists.

At the same time, there remain distinctions between town and country, and also class distinctions between the working class and the peasantry, for many years after the socialist relations of production have been established in the whole of society. The lag of the countryside behind the towns is expressed above all in the fact that agriculture has weaker material and technical foundations than industry, the cultural level of the rural population is lower than that of the urban population, and the farmers are behind the workers as regards ideological consciousness. This backwardness is a legacy of the old society. It is due to this backwardness that the cooperative economy remains the predominant form in agriculture, whereas all-people property rules supreme in industry. Accordingly, there remain the class distinctions between the working class and peasantry.

We also have much to do in the way of developing the productive forces. By establishing the advanced socialist system over the past years, we have paved a broad path for the development of the productive forces and the improvement of the people's living standards. But we have only laid the basis for industrialization and taken the first step in the technical revolution; we have as yet a long way to go to attain the high level of development of the productive forces commensurate with a socialist and communist society. Also, as for the people's living standards, we have eliminated the social sources of exploitation and poverty and have developed production at a fast tempo, thus solving the most essential problems in the material and cultural life of our people. But we have not yet been able to make their life very bountiful and modern.

A society cannot yet be called a completely triumphant socialist society where the hostile classes persist in insidious maneuverings; where old ideas continue to exert corrosive influence; where there still remain distinctions between town and the countryside and class distinctions between the working class and peasantry; where industrialization has not been realized fully and where the material and technical basis of socialism has not been firmly laid.

In order to achieve the complete victory of socialism and win the historical cause of the working class, the socialist state must further strengthen its role as a weapon of class struggle and of the building of socialism and communism. In other words, the socialist state should strengthen the dictatorship of the proletariat, carrying on the class struggle on the one hand and vigorously pushing ahead with the building of socialist economy on the other.

Only when the socialist state acquits itself well both in exercising dictatorship against hostile elements and in carrying out the ideological revolution and economic work, can it occupy the two fortresses, ideological and material, which must be captured on the way to socialism and communism, to guarantee the complete triumph for socialism. If any one of these tasks is neglected or overlooked, it will cause great difficulties and irretrievably grave losses to the whole course of socialist construction.

If the socialist state neglects the dictatorship of the proletariat and the ideological revolution to the slightest degree and slackens the class struggle, it will become impossible to consolidate and develop the triumphant socialist system or defend it against the encroachment of the internal and external enemies. The intrinsic superiority of socialism and its great vitality lie above all in the fact that the working people, freed from exploitation and oppression, unite firmly and cooperate closely with each other as comrades and display creative initiative and voluntary zeal in their work for the common goal and interest. Experience shows that without increasing the working people's class awareness and raising their level of ideological consciousness by intensifying the class struggle, this superiority of socialism cannot be brought out and the working people are prone to indolence and slackness, thereby making it impossible to carry out the tasks of economic construction and the technical revolution successfully.

On the other hand, it is also wrong to put stress only on the class struggle and ideological revolution and slight the building of the socialist economy. The ideological revolution is an important revolutionary task which the socialist state must carry out without fail. The ideological revolution is important because it roots out the old ideas that remain in the minds of the working people and calls forth their voluntary zeal and creative initiative so as to build socialism and communism successfully. The Communists not only fight for the freedom and liberation of the people but also strive to make their life happy. An important task which confronts the Communists after they have overthrown the old system and liberated the people from exploitation and oppression, is to build the socialist economy efficiently. Concern for the growing welfare of the people is the supreme principle governing the activities of the Party and the state of the working class. Our struggle for the building of socialism and communism is aimed, in the final analysis, at fully satisfying the material and cultural requirements of all the people and ensuring them a bountiful and cultured life. Only when economic construction is carried out well, can we attain the high level of development of the productive forces demanded by a socialist and communist society. Only then can the country be made rich and strong and the living standards of the people raised decisively. And only when the material and technological basis of socialism is firmly laid by vigorously promoting economic construction, can the political independence and sovereignty of the country be secured firmly and, also, its defense capabilities strengthened.

If stress is put only on the ideological revolution and the technical revolution is neglected, the revolutionary task of liberating the working people from backbreaking labor cannot be accomplished, nor can the ideological revolution itself be carried out successfully. The ideological consciousness of people is determined by the material conditions of society. So in socialist society it is also transformed as technology develops and the people's living standards rise.

Guarding against every kind of Right and "Left" deviation which might manifest itself, we should continuously strengthen the dictatorship of the proletariat and the class struggle and carry on economic construction efficiently. We should give definite precedence to the ideological revolution and forcefully push ahead with the technical revolution at the same time. Only by so doing is it possible to remold the ideology of people, and build up the solid material and technological foundations of socialism and thus achieve the complete victory of socialism.

We should first strengthen dictatorship over the class enemy, and thoroughly carry out the ideological revolution, thereby to revolutionize and working-classize the entire society.

The historical mission of the dictatorship of the proletariat lies in educating and transforming all the working people to revolutionize and working-classize them, in gradually eliminating all class distinctions and building communism, while liquidating the exploiting classes and putting down their resistance. We should correctly combine the Party's class line and mass line to isolate and suppress the handful of hostile elements and, at the same time, educate and remold the broad masses to rally them closer around the Party.

As you all know, the dictatorship of the proletariat means suppression for the few hostile elements and democracy for the absolute majority of the population—the working class, peasantry and other sections of the working people. To correctly link these two aspects of the proletarian dictatorship means to properly combine the work of rallying the absolute majority of the people through education and remolding with the class struggle against the intrigues and maneuvers of the paltry handful of hostile elements. One will commit a "Leftist" error if one only emphasizes and exaggerates class struggle, forgetting that the unity and cooperation of the working class, peasantry and working intelligentsia constitute the basis of social relations in socialist society. In that case, one may tend to distrust people, treat innocent people as hostile elements, divorce the Party from the masses and bring about unrest in the society.

In contrast, a grave Rightist error will be committed if what some call "democracy" and "freedom" is granted to everybody in disregard of the fact that in socialist society, too, there exist hostile elements, the survivals of old ideology remain and class struggle continues. Democracy as a political concept intrinsically assumes a class character. The dictatorship of all exploiters is dictatorship over the exploited laboring masses and their democracy is democracy solely for the few exploiters. On the other hand, the dictatorship of the proletariat is dictatorship over the exploiting classes and democracy for the broad masses of the people. As there has been no state detached from classes in the history of mankind, so there has not been, and cannot be, democracy which does not bear a class character. In any state, democracy is democracy for the class that maintains power, and is combined with dictatorship over the hostile classes. Under the conditions in which remnants of the overthrown exploiting classes are maneuvering insidiously and class struggle continues, there can be no "pure democracy" or "complete freedom" for all. Bourgeois democracy provides the billionaires with the freedom to exploit and plunder the working people for profit and oppress them at will, but it allows the toiling masses only the freedom to wear rags and starve to death. If the class character of democracy is denied in socialist society and so-called "pure democracy" and "complete freedom" for all under the dictatorship of the proletariat are advocated, it is, in fact, tantamount to forcing bourgeois democracy and the freedom to be slaves upon the people. We are against an abstract and supra-class conception of democracy.

At present, the Western imperialists and the renegades of revolution are cheering over the so-called "democratic development" and "liberalization" fusses being made in some socialist countries, describing them as a "lawful process" in the development of socialist society, a "new wind in Eastern Europe that brings hope to the Western world," a "deep-going process of transformation for further democracy" and so on. However, in the last analysis, this is an insidious maneuver of the imperialists and the renegades of the revolution to whittle away the achievements of socialism and open up the way to the restoration of capitalism in the socialist countries. We must heighten our vigilance against the intrigues and maneuvers of the imperialists to subvert the socialist countries from within.

If the peoples of the socialist countries are to enjoy genuine freedom and democracy, the dictatorship of the proletariat must be strengthened. Proletarian democracy consists of finally liquidating the exploiting classes, fully guaranteeing true political freedom and rights as well as material and cultural welfare to the working class and other sectors of the working people, and strengthening comradely cooperation and mutual assistance among them in every way. There can be no better democracy than proletarian democracy. Should there be a higher form of democracy than proletarian democracy, it would not be democracy. It is wrong to think that the dictatorship of the proletariat has become unnecessary before the class distinctions between the working class and peasantry are obliterated, before the ideological survivals of the old society are eradicated, and particularly at a time when the enemies at home and abroad continue to intensify their aggressive and subversive activities against socialism. If we avoid a principled class struggle, obscuring the class lines between bourgeois democracy and proletarian democracy and negating the class character of democracy, vigilance against hostile elements may grow dull, the leading role of the Party and the working class may be nullified and the corrupting influence of the bourgeoisie be increased in society.

In short, both the Right and "Left" deviations make it impossible to clearly distinguish friend from foe, and do great harm to the construction of socialism and communism. Our Party's consistent line is to properly combine dictatorship with democracy and class struggle with the work of strengthening the unity and cohesion of the people, while opposing all Right and "Left" deviations in state activities.

We should continue to strengthen the role of proletarian dictatorship of the Government of the Republic, and thereby successfully frustrate all intrigues and maneuvers of the enemies, within and without, against our socialist system. We should apply strict sanctions against the remnants of the overthrown classes of landlords and capitalists who still do not give up the dream of restoring their old positions. We should opportunely make a resolute counterattack and smash to smithereens the imperialists' counterrevolutionary attempts to attack our social system in collusion with the hostile elements within. We should thus strongly defend the gains of our revolution and firmly guarantee the complete victory of socialism in our country.

While suppressing the hostile elements, we should intensify the leadership that the working class gives to all other social strata and carry out the ideological revolution thoroughly, thus revolutionizing and working-classizing all members of society.

True, suppression of the hostile elements is the basic function of the state of the proletarian dictatorship and a form of class struggle which the socialist state must carry out to the end. But this is not the only function of the proletarian dictatorship nor does it represent the only form of class struggle. Besides the class struggle to suppress the hostile elements, there is the basic form of class struggle in socialist society whose major content is the ideological revolution. This aims at rooting up obsolete ideas in the minds of the working people and arming all of them with communist ideas. Even after the triumph of the socialist system the class struggle continues, but it should then differ somewhat in content and form.

Indeed, the struggle against the survivals of old ideas among the working people in a socialist society is a class struggle in that it is a struggle between working-class ideology and bourgeois ideology. But it is entirely different from the previous class struggle. The class struggle during the socialist revolution was primarily a struggle for complete liquidation of the exploiters as a class, whereas after the establishment of the socialist system it is not designed to liquidate people but is primarily an ideological struggle to transform the people ideologically. The ideological revolution in socialist society is an internal affair of the working people who advance hand in hand to attain the common ideal. Its goal is to educate and remold all the working people into Communists. The ideological revolution should not be carried out by force as is the struggle against the hostile elements, but always by means of persuasion and education. It should become a work of cementing the unity and cohesion of the working people.

In socialist society the main targets of the ideological revolution are the remnants of old feudal, bourgeois and petty-bourgeois ideas that survive in the minds of the working people and the virus of reactionary capitalist ideology that infiltrates from outside. Through vigorous ideological revolution the socialist state should root up all survivals of old ideas among the working people and totally prevent the penetration of bourgeois ideological poison from the outside. This is especially true in our situation where the country remains divided and we are directly confronted with the U.S. imperialists, the chieftain of world reaction. For these reasons the struggle against the enemy's schemes for subversion and sabotage and his ideological infiltration acquires greater importance, and we must always pay deep attention to this. While steadily enhancing the leadership role of the working class, we should conduct patient education on the Party's policies and revolutionary traditions, communist education with class education as its basic theme and education in socialist patriotism. In this way we will revolutionize and working-classize all the working people.

The final solution of the rural question and raising of cooperative property to the level of all-people property is one of the most important tasks confronting the state which exercises proletarian dictatorship after the triumph of the socialist system and one of the basic conditions for the complete victory of socialism. Only when the rural question is finally solved and the backwardness of the countryside is completely overcome, will the socialist state have swept away the hangouts and footholds where the reactionary bourgeois virus coming in from the outside, and the remnants of the overthrown exploiting classes within, breed and engage in insidious scheming. And only when cooperative property is raised to the level of all-people property, can the agricultural productive forces be highly developed. Only then will the selfishness remaining among the farmers be rooted out, only then will all working people be guided undeviatingly along the path to collectivism under which they work for the whole of society and the entire people with a high degree of conscious enthusiasm. Our Party, generalizing the achievements and the experiences gained in our rural work, has already set forth the basic principles and the concrete ways to solve the rural question in socialist society. In accordance with the clear-cut policy set by the Party, we should vigorously step up the technical, cultural and ideological revolutions in the countryside to put an end to the technical lag of agriculture behind modern industry, the cultural back-wardness of the countryside in comparison with the advanced towns and the ideological lag of the peasantry behind the working class, the most revolutionary class. Moreover, we should continue to strengthen the leadership and assistance given to the rural areas by the working-class Party and state and develop all-people property and cooperative property as an organic whole while steadily bringing the latter closer to the former.

To win complete victory for socialism, socialist economic construction should be vigorously promoted, while every kind of class distinction is eliminated and cooperative property is elevated to the level of all-people property. Our task in the domain of socialist economic construction is to carry through the industrialization of the country and also the technical and cultural revolutions, thus assuring that the material and technological foundations of socialism are laid out solidly and that all working people have the know-how and skill to handle up-to-date machines efficiently.

We should continue to develop industry at a fast rate and introduce modern technology into all branches of the national economy including agriculture, thus forging a modernized industry and advanced agriculture in our country. We should rear all people into well-rounded, competent builders of communism. In this way our people, who have already rid themselves of exploitation, will be relieved from backbreaking labor. There will gradually be obliterated the distinctions between industrial and agricultural labor, heavy and light work, physical and mental labor, allowing for the production of a greater amount of material wealth with less expenditure of manpower. On the basis of the rapid growth of industrial and agricultural production we should raise the material and cultural level of all the working people to at least that of the old middle classes. Doing so, we will guarantee that all the people see the true superiority of the socialist system more clearly in their daily experience and devotedly fight for its consolidation and development, firmly confident of the complete victory of socialism. Only when this is realized can we say the triumph of socialism is complete.

An important immediate task confronting us for the complete victory of socialism is the thorough implementation of the line of simultaneous economic and defense construction, while vigorously tackling the problem of working-classizing and revolutionizing the entire society by giving definite precedence to the ideological revolution in accordance with the policy set forth in the decision of the Party Conference and in the Ten-Point Political Program of the Government of the Republic.

What acquires prime importance for the implementation of the Party Conference decision is the early overfulfillment of the national economic plan for the current year and the thorough preparation for the coming year's productive effort to scale the main heights of the Seven-Year Plan which are of decisive importance in the socialist construction of our country.

We should direct primary attention to giving definite

precedence to the electric power and extractive industries, which are a prerequisite for the normalization of production in all branches of the national economy.

In the power industry, we must fully improve the installations and equipment of the existing power plants to increase their capacity to the maximum. We should also actively push ahead with the building of large power stations to consolidate the power bases. Specifically, the existing thermal power plants should be managed more efficiently and the building of new ones should be stepped up, so that fluctuations in electric power output will be eliminated. In this way the requirements of industry, transport and other branches of the national economy for electric power will be met more satisfactorily and rural electrification should be completed by 1970.

There should be no complacency in the coal industry even if the height of the Seven-Year Plan is captured this year. Rather, we should continue our vigorous struggle to increase coal production. Geological prospecting and tunnelling should be kept substantially ahead of other processes to provide enough cutting faces. Dynamic technological innovation drives should be launched to spur the introduction of mechanization and automation in the operations, and advanced methods including open cast mining should be widely introduced. Continued innovations should be made in coal production, so that the national economy's fast growing demand for coal can be met satisfactorily.

While existing ore mines are expanded, the development of new nonferrous ore deposits with big prospects should be stepped up. At the same time, the construction of ore dressing plants now under way should be terminated quickly and all necessary types of mining equipment supplied, so that the output of ores can be increased.

It is of very great importance for the development of the national economy as a whole to normalize production of the ferrous metallurgical industry that supplies iron and steel to the engineering industry, to capital construction and other branches of the national economy. Scientific research should be carried on more energetically in this sector to make the iron and steel industry more independent. We must push ahead vigorously with the building of iron and steel centers using domestic supplies of anthracite so as to ensure adequate production of pig iron, steel and structural steel.

The engineering industry, and in particular, the production of heavy machinery, should be further developed, to fully guarantee that many large-scale projects for remaking nature can be carried out in the future. We should expand and bolster the bases to produce heavy equipment such as heavy-duty excavators and trucks, big tractors, vessels and machine tools.

In order to fully ensure the vast amount of construction work scheduled for the coming year, we should direct great efforts to radically advancing the building-materials industry, particularly the production of cement.

There is a great strain on transport in our country, particularly on the railways. Easing this strain is a vital condition for guaranteeing the success of our production efforts next year. To diminish the strain on the railways, we should push ahead dynamically with their electrification, expand the production and repair capacity of rolling stocks, lay more shunting tracks and mechanize the loading and unloading operations so as to make more efficient use of our rolling stocks in every way.

In the field of agriculture, every effort should be directed to finishing the forthcoming harvest quickly, to increasing grain output and developing livestock breeding next year. The rate of mechanization and chemicalization should be increased steadily in order to shore up the material and technological bases of agriculture. Preparations should be stepped up energetically for an extensive land reclamation and development program in the future.

Next year's plan must thus be fulfilled so that we may capture all the major heights of the Seven-Year Plan, our epic program for socialist construction. The completion of the Seven-Year Plan will be an epoch-making event which will signify great progress in the consolidation and development of the socialist system in the Republic and in the struggle for the complete victory of socialism. With the fulfillment of the Seven-Year Plan our industry will have become firmly independent, with a more perfected structure, a dependable raw material base and new technology. It will be capable of turning out larger quantities of diverse types of high-quality means of production and consumer goods needed for the development of the national economy and the improvement of the people's living standards. The material and technological bases of agriculture will have been consolidated and the achievements of advanced agronomical science will have been introduced widely. As a consequence, all sectors of agricultural production including grain growing can develop rapidly and our farmers will be freed, to a large extent, from arduous labor. Our towns and villages will be more beautiful and the life of our people will have become more bountiful and cultured. Our country will have been converted from an industrial-agricultural nation into an advance socialist industrial state.

All the working people should work in a more revolutionary way, never slackening their high revolutionary spirit in the least. They should make the best use of the economic foundations already established and of all our potentialities in order to step up production and construction, thereby further expediting the fulfillment of the Seven-Year Plan.

Comrades,

To achieve the final victory of socialism, it is necessary to strengthen the class alliance of the socialist countries, the unity and cohesion of the socialist camp. It must be made invincible.

Individual countries where the proletariat has seized power under conditions of international capitalist encirclement cannot be free from the danger of imperialist aggression and capitalist restoration until communism is triumphant on a worldwide scale. Therefore, in order to win final revolutionary victory, the proletariat of each country that has assumed power should consolidate its own internal revolutionary forces in every way, while receiving active support from other contingents of the world socialist revolution and cementing true internationalist solidarity with the working class of all countries and the oppressed peoples of the entire world.

Here is where the formation of the socialist camp and its expansion and development are of great significance. The historical mission of the working class is to do away with all systems of exploitation and to build socialism and communism, the highest ideal of mankind, on a worldwide scale. The final victory of the world revolution will be achieved by the complete victory of socialist revolutions in numerous countries, and the gradual expansion, consolidation and development of the socialist camp. The socialist camp is the invincible revolutionary base of the international working class for the ultimate victory of socialism and communism, the reliable bulwark of victory for the oppressed and all progressive peoples of the world and the powerful fortress of world peace.

That is why the imperialists headed by U.S. imperialism together with all other reactionaries, fear the existence of the socialist camp more than anything else. That is why they are making desperate attempts to destroy it. They are scheming to smash by force of arms, one after another, those countries which march forward along the path of revolution, holding aloft the banner of anti-imperialist, anti-U.S. struggle. They are maneuvering to disintegrate from within, through intensified ideological and cultural infiltration, those countries which refuse to follow a positive revolutionary path, spreading illusions among the people about imperialism and only insisting on an unprincipled compromise with imperialism.

These circumstances make it necessary for the socialist countries, through their unified efforts, to frustrate the schemes of the allied forces of world imperialism for aggression and subversion and to jointly defend the socialist camp. This requires the monolithic unity of the socialist camp.

The unity and cohesion of the socialist camp are an important guarantee for firmly defending each socialist state against imperialist aggression and for ensuring the final victory of the socialist revolution for the socialist camp as a whole.

The existence of the socialist camp and its united forces constitute an essential factor that is decisive to the destiny, not only of the peoples of the socialist countries, but of mankind as a whole. The solution to all the problems of the world revolution at the present time depends largely on the united efforts of the socialist countries.

Only by steadily strengthening the unshakable unity and might of the socialist camp, can we successfully expedite the cause of socialism and communism. Only in this way can we provide powerful support and encouragement to the anti-imperialist national-liberation struggle of the peoples in the colonial and dependent countries and newly independent countries and the revolutionary struggle of the working class in the capitalist countries.

Unity is the mightiest weapon of the working class. Since its first days in the arena of history, the working class has always regarded unity as its most precious weapon in the struggle against international capital, and on the strength of unity it has won arduous struggles. Even today, the success of the world revolutionary movement in breaking the chains of capitalism which are linked together internationally, can be won only by the united force of the international communist movement based on the principle of proletarian internationalism. It can be firmly guaranteed only by strengthening, in the first place, the unity of its center, the socialist camp.

Every condition for unity exists in the socialist countries. In the socialist countries power is in the hands of the working class and the exploitation and oppression of man by man has been liquidated on the basis of the establishment of the public ownership of the means of production; Marxism-Leninism is the guiding doctrine for revolution and construction in these countries. The socialist countries are all opposed to imperialism and colonialism and fight for the common goal of building a socialist and communist society which represents freedom and happiness. The socialist camp is not an artificial product, nor is it the outcome of any international treaty, nor is it a temporary alliance. It developed as a result of the fact that the international working class, winning victories in the course of its revolutionary struggle against international capital, became united into a permanent alliance in accord with the inevitable need for class solidarity.

If every socialist country firmly adheres to the class position and proceeds from the fundamental interests of the revolution, the unity and cohesion of the socialist countries will be constantly strengthened.

Differences may arise between fraternal parties and countries. Differences may come either from the different historical and geographical conditions within which the activities of the fraternal parties and countries are carried out and from their different national duties or from their mistaken conception of Marxist-Leninist principles and their lack of a consistent revolutionary stand. Such differences do not represent any contradiction between the differing state and social systems nor do they mean fundamentally incompatible interests between hostile classes. However serious they may be, the differences between the socialist countries are an internal affair of the socialist camp and the international communist movement; they are a problem which should be solved through the method of ideological struggle proceeding from the desire for unity of class brothers. The fraternal parties and states, the class comrades-in-arms who should share life and death, the sweet and the bitter in the struggle for the common cause of socialism and communism, should never feud and quarrel or be antagonistic to each other because of ideological differences. Communists should always be able to distinguish between class brothers and class enemies and should under no circumstances depart from the class point of view. The international communist movement cannot exist and the socialist camp is inconceivable without the principle of class solidarity. If fraternal countries feud and quarrel and are antagonistic to each other, it can only gladden the imperialists and bring losses to the international communist movement.

Communists cannot remain indifferent to this grave situation that affects the very existence of the socialist camp and the destiny of the world revolution. Splits should be healed and unity should be safeguarded and strengthened.

If the fraternal parties and countries desire genuine unity, they must abide strictly by the standards governing their mutual relations, the main content of which is complete equality, independence, mutual respect, noninterference in each other's internal affairs and comradely cooperation. When fraternal parties and socialist countries strictly apply these standards of mutual relations, the unity of the socialist camp and the cohesion of the international communist movement will then have a really conscious and lasting basis. If these standards are violated, complicated problems will arise between fraternal parties and countries and the unity of the socialist camp will be badly affected.

The socialist countries and Communist and Workers' Parties are completely equal and independent. Because of the class solidarity of the working class, each of them, as an equal and independent national detachment of the international revolutionary ranks, is not only responsible to its own people for the revolution in its own country but also to the world's people for the world revolution. No one can lay claim to a privileged position in the ranks of the communist movement and there can be no relationship of superior and inferior between the socialist countries. To cement the class solidarity of the socialist countries, all fraternal countries should respect each other and provide sincere mutual assistance on the basis of equality.

At the same time, they should not renounce their autonomy under pressure from outside and blindly follow other parties and countries. To follow others blindly, forfeiting one's own independence, does not help to strengthen the unity of the socialist camp nor does it mean loyalty to proletarian internationalism. On the contrary, it will do serious harm to revolution and construction in one's own country and, accordingly, result in weakening the international revolutionary forces as well. Only when each of the Communist and Workers' Parties and socialist countries maintains autonomy and independence in its activities, can it work out correct policies suited to the peculiarities of its own country and successfully promote its revolutionary cause and the work of construction. In leading revolution and construction, the Communists should never relinquish the universal truth of Marxism-Leninism nor should they ignore national peculiarities and dogmatically copy the experiences of fraternal countries.

The socialist countries, while strengthening independence in politics, should have confidence in their own strength and endeavor to develop the economy through the labor of their own people and with their own domestic resources. Only by building an independent national economy, can each country accelerate socialist construction and thus increase the might of the entire socialist camp. The economies of all the socialist countries, as independent units of the world socialist economic system, develop steadily in close mutual relationship and cooperation. The might of the socialist economic system as a whole will be reinforced when each of its units grows powerful. If the national economy of each of the socialist countries fails to develop in an all-round way and thus is incapable of standing on its own two feet and fulfilling its own functions, each link in the whole chain of the socialist camp will be weakened and, in the end, the world socialist economic system as a whole will become undermined. The important thing is that mutual economic cooperation be strengthened in line with the principles of proletarian internationalism, equality and mutual benefit, on the basis of the development of a sound economy in all socialist countries which will allow each of them to play its independent role fully, so that the world socialist economic system as a whole can function smoothly and manifest its potential to the full. Only in this way will the unity of the national and international interests be ensured in the construction of socialism in each country. And only by so doing, can the socialist countries successfully foil the imperialist powers' policy of economic aggression and blockade and, moreover, aggravate the general crisis of the world capitalist economic system.

The independence we advocate does not by any means conflict with proletarian internationalism. It is, on the contrary, aimed to strengthen it still further. Independence should serve to strengthen proletarian internationalism and should never weaken it. There can be no internationalism apart from independence, and vice versa. If one turns his back on Marxism-Leninism and proletarian internationalism and takes to national egoism, under the pretext of maintaining independence, he is making a grave mistake. What is more, the renunciation of the principle of class solidarity and the rejection of joint action and joint struggle by class brothers, using "independence" as a rationale, is not an attitude befitting a Communist. Such acts will do enormous harm to the development of the world revolution and, moreover, result in undermining the revolution in one's own country.

The defense of independence and at the same time the cementing of the proletarian internationalist unity of the socialist countries, unity and cooperation on the basis of complete equality and independence—this is the position which our Party and the Government of the Republic have consistently maintained. Proceeding from the national and international duties of our revolution, we will, in the future too, exert all our efforts to strengthen friendship and unity with the socialist countries on the principles of Marxism-Leninism, proletarian internationalism, complete equality and independence.

LET US STRENGTHEN THE TRAINING OF TECHNICAL PERSONNEL TO MEET THE NEW REQUIREMENTS OF SOCIALIST CONSTRUCTION

Speech to the Faculty and Students of the Kim Chaek Polytechnical Institute, *October 2, 1968*

To begin with, I warmly congratulate the faculty and students of the Kim Chaek Polytechnical Institute on the 20th anniversary of its inauguration.

Over the past 20 years the Kim Chaek Polytechnical Institute has trained armies of technical personnel and sent them out to many branches of the national economy. They are now playing an important role at varied posts of socialist construction—in our factories and enterprises and state and economic institutions. This means that the Kim Chaek Polytechnical Institute has rendered great service, and this is a valuable result of the tireless efforts its teaching staff has made in upholding the Party's educational policy. The institute, whose growth coincides with the history of our Republic, has contributed greatly to the country's prosperity, development and socialist construction.

On behalf of the Central Committee of the Party and of the

Government of the Republic, I extend warm thanks to the faculty and students of the Kim Chaek Polytechnic Institute.

Our Party's educational policy is correct and our achievements in education are tremendous. This is clearly proved by life itself, and foreigners, too, have a high opinion of our policy and achievements.

Representatives of many countries attending our Republic's 20th anniversary celebration sometime ago were unanimous in their unstinted praise for our educational system and very much envied our pupils and students. They particularly admired our students who were active in supporting and defending the Party's line and policies and who showed themselves firmly united around the Party.

In our country today, students are a source of great pride and a valuable asset, not a source of trouble and anxiety. This is a great victory won in the implementation of the Party's educational policy.

We have achieved great successes in the development of science and technology as well as in education.

True, we still have much to do to catch up with the advanced industrial countries. But under the leadership of the Party our people have performed a great miracle in a short historical period of time—abolishing technological and economic backwardness, a legacy of the old society, and building a powerful independent national economy with a modern industry and a developed agriculture.

Today our industry has a fairly strong foundation. The foundation of heavy industry is especially firm. This is graphic evidence of the correctness of our Party's line on the building of the economy, the line of giving priority to the growth of heavy industry while simultaneously developing light industry and agriculture.

Over the past years we have won truly great victories in socialist construction and, in particular, have achieved a big success in education. However, we must not become at all complacent over this. We have much more work to do than we have done so far.

Our task now is to raise our industry to a higher level by relying on the industrial base we have already laid. This requires the continued, energetic promotion of the technical revolution.

The Party's Fourth Congress set the technical revolution as one of the central tasks of socialist economic construction. This task is now proceeding successfully, but it cannot be completed within the Seven-Year Plan period. The complete victory of socialism and the laying of the sound material and technical foundations of socialism and communism make it imperative to advance the technical revolution to a higher plane.

The first and foremost task in this is the development of electronics.

This is the age of electronics, and we must develop electronics quickly. The development of electronics is essential for the extensive introduction of automation in all branches of the national economy. This will enable us to produce more material wealth with less manpower while making work lighter. It will also help us eliminate the distinctions between heavy and light and industrial and farm labor and, furthermore, between mental and physical labor.

The rapid development of electronics is also necessary for the defense industry. With our present industrial base, we can produce all the conventional weapons we need. However, if we are to develop the defense industry to manufacture large quantities of modern automatic weapons, we must improve the automation system and electronics. At one time we told you to stop building helicopters and the like. But it is now high time to make helicopters and other types of planes and modern automatic weapons such as rockets in our country. You should now put your minds to producing such modern automatic weapons. When we develop electronics, we will be able to manufacture as many of these modern weapons as we want.

As you see, the development of electronics is very important for the advancement of the country's productive forces, for the final emancipation of the working people from heavy labor and for boosting national defense power.

But electronics is a field which we have only just begun to explore because our country had a very weak industrial base in the past. The industrial base must reach a certain level for the development of electronics. In the complete absence of this base, electronics is out of the question. Today, however, a firm industrial base has been laid and the engineering industry, in particular, has attained a pretty high level. So it is with full confidence that we say it is high time to place the question of developing electronics on the order of the day. We should develop electronics on a large scale.

Another important problem in the field of science and technology, if the technical revolution is to be carried to a higher level, is to increase the production of light and pure metals and alloy steel.

Of course, the establishment of Juche in the production of iron is very important, and metallurgy should continue to concentrate on the work of strengthening the independence of the iron industry. But the production of light and pure metals and alloy steel should never be neglected. Without expanding production of these, it is impossible to make further advance in the engineering, electronics and defense industries or to carry out the tasks of the higher phase of the technical revolution successfully.

First of all, the work of establishing our own aluminum production base must be speeded up. Until recently no deposits of bauxite were found in our country and the technical problem of producing aluminum from nephelite, which we do have, was not solved. This compelled us to defer construction of an aluminum factory. Our prospectors, however, found bauxite deposits recently. Therefore, we must speed up the construction of the factory and turn out aluminum ourselves as soon as possible. In addition to aluminum, we must produce magnesium, and further the production of alloy steel and various pure metals including titanium.

The new and higher phase of the technical revolution urgently demands a corresponding improvement in the training of technical personnel. So a very important and honorable task faces the Kim Chaek Polytechnical Institute, our country's biggest integrated center for training technological cadres. Up to now the institute has undertaken the duty of training technical workers needed in the stage of industrialization. Now it faces the task of training more technical personnel capable of carrying out the higher phase of the technical revolution.

We have quite a few fields of science and technology to be explored and many scientific and technological problems to be solved. That explains why we need larger numbers of competent technical personnel.

Let me take an instance.

To rapidly raise the cultural and technical levels of the

working people as a whole, we are planning to cover the whole country with a TV network. We have already built a TV broadcasting station with a big tower. However, a broad section of the working people cannot watch television because there is a shortage of TV sets. Though we import a small number every year, this is not enough to bring the nation under a TV network soon. To solve this problem we must mass-produce TV sets by the hundreds of thousands every year. But we are still barred from this because our country does not have many electronics technicians and the electronics industry is underdeveloped.

In order to open up new branches of industry and advance industry as a whole to a higher level, technicians are needed in every field. The training of technical personnel must be decisively improved so that our technicians will be able to meet the rapidly growing demands of socialist economic construction.

This is why the Kim Chaek Polytechnical Institute, an important training center for technicians in our country, must strengthen its work. It must increase its enrollment to train more competent technicians.

We should continue to encourage night and correspondence courses. Since this form of education is an excellent one which enables working people to study and work at the same time, it must be consolidated. It is possible that students following these courses fall somewhat behind their counterparts taking regular courses, but this problem can be solved if the school term is extended a little.

Next, the work of revolutionizing the students must be carried forward unremittingly.

As everyone knows, the building of socialism and communism necessitates the capture of two fortresses, the material and ideological. Consequently, in addition to the technical revolution, the ideological revolution must be energetically pushed forward. It is incorrect to emphasize only the technical revolution and neglect the ideological one which is aimed at getting rid of the backward ideas in people's minds. Nor is it correct to emphasize only the ideological revolution and neglect the technical one. Undue emphasis on one or the other will prevent the successful building of socialist and communist society.

We must energetically struggle to conquer the ideological as well as the material fortress throughout the course of socialist and communist construction. In the training of technicians, too, the ideological education of the students must be intensified along with technological education. The colleges must revolutionize all the students, in other words, bring them up to be true Communists before sending them out into society. A dynamic struggle is now under way in our country to root out the bourgeois, feudal-Confucian and revisionist thinking and all other unsound ideas remaining in the minds of the working people and to revolutionize and working-classize the whole of society.

Colleges, too, must thoroughly revolutionize all their students, not to mention the teachers through an energetic struggle against the old ideas. They must not send half-baked graduates out into society only to become objects of remolding. Some of the old intellectuals might need remolding. But why should the new intellectuals who have been trained in our colleges be made objects of remolding after graduation?

Experience shows that as long as the old ideas remain in their minds, people tend to become lazy and degenerate as economic growth gives rise to abundance and makes work easier. Consequently, the ideological education of the working people, and particularly of intellectuals, must not slack off in the least throughout the course of the building of socialism.

It is difficult for a college to revolutionize the students completely in four or five short years. Therefore, the proper combination of ideological education with science training and of social with natural sciences is important not only in higher education but throughout the school system, from the early stages.

Infected with the theories of time-worn bourgeois pedagogy, some people once asserted that children only needed the cultivation of the emotions confined to the appreciation of such things as the property of red, blue and other colors and that revolutionary ideological education should not be given them. They were entirely wrong. People must be systematically given revolutionary education from childhood so that their minds are kept free of all manner of unsound ideas, including bourgeois ideas, and they arm themselves firmly with the revolutionary world outlook as they grow up. It will not do to neglect ideological education and then try to rid people's minds of obsolete ideas only after they have already become seriously infected with them. If proper college education is given to those who have received a systematic ideological education from childhood, cases where graduates become objects of reform will not occur.

The Kim Chaek Polytechnical Institute must not neglect politico-ideological education by giving only technological education to the students just because it is a technical college. All college life must be so organized as to give the students intensive ideological training to help them enhance their revolutionary world outlook while equipping them with a high degree of technological knowledge. The education program at the institute should be perfected along such lines. Of course, many social science subjects are included in the institute's curriculum, along with technological subjects. In the future, too, importance should be attached to teaching social sciences, including Party policy.

In revolutionizing students it is important to adhere strictly to the Party's policy on college enrollment. Our experience proves the excellence of the system under which middle school graduates are tempered in the army or in society for a few years before they are admitted to college. We must continue to encourage this.

True, after a break of a few years in their studies, the students may have some initial difficulties in tackling technological subjects on entering colleges. However, if they are well taught in primary and middle schools, they will not forget what they have learned during their period of military or civilian service. Even if they have forgotten some, six months or a year of good individual tutoring in college will enable them to catch up quickly. Having been tempered in society or in the army, all of them will become fine intellectuals meeting the Party's requirements, provided they are given a good college training.

Some people used to say that to become a genius one needs systematic studies from childhood, and he should be kept away from all other pursuits. They maintained that middle school graduates should go to college immediately. We cannot agree with their concept. Indeed, if a boy enters college straight from middle school as those people insisted, he might show fairly good progress in certain technological subjects. But his revolutionization will be that much slower, because he lacks social training. This will inevitably lead to the turning out of a half-baked intellectual who will have to go through the process of revolutionization again after he goes out into society. No matter how many there may be, we have no need of genteel, half-baked intellectuals who have to be remolded after graduation. We need Red communist intellectuals who have been working-classized and revolutionized. A few years of social training after secondary education will be of far greater benefit than any "loss" resulting from it. Some people used to allege that demobilized soldiers were only capable of taking a social science course at best, and that if they took a natural science course, they would not be able to cope. This does not hold water. Experience shows that demobilized soldiers can become competent technicians if they are given a good individual tutoring when they are admitted to technical colleges.

We must categorically reject the outmoded viewpoint which goes in for education of the best brains and stick to the Party's policy on college enrollment. Institutes of higher learning should thus turn out fully revolutionized intellectuals who befit this era of the Workers' Party.

To proceed. We must continue to establish Juche thoroughly in all fields.

Some of our people are not yet completely free of flunkeyism toward great powers. Intellectuals especially retain much of that tendency.

When, then, will our country be rid of flunkeyism? The complete establishment of Juche is conditional on the elimination of flunkeyism and to abolish flunkeyism altogether we need a higher level of economic development and standard of living and, especially, more advanced science and technology than other countries.

True, intensified ideological struggle alongside ideological education will help overcome flunkeyism to a considerable degree. But ideological struggle alone is not enough to wipe it out. Only when our country is far more advanced than other countries in all fields of science, whether social or natural, or has at least come abreast of them so that our people will no longer cast envious eyes at them over the fence, will flunkeyism finally disappear and Juche be firmly established in our country. Within our time we must put an end to flunkeyism which has been handed down through the ages in our country. This requires accelerated development in all branches of science and technology, concomitantly with the economy. A huge responsibility in this rests on scientists and professors.

Here the question arises: Is it possible for our country to outstrip developed countries in science and technology? It is our belief that we can definitely overtake and outstrip them if all of us put our shoulders to the wheel.

Are Koreans inferior to other peoples in intelligence? Cannot Koreans study and solve problems if others can? Cannot we develop science and technology when they do? If the entire Party and people buckle down to the job and tackle things with determination, we can and must get ahead of developed countries.

In the realm of social sciences, we can say we are now making rapid progress.

We have solved many difficult and complex problems of socialist construction in a unique manner suited to the actual conditions of our country. We have accumulated a wealth of valuable experience in the building of the state, the economy and national defense and in education, culture, the health service and all the other spheres of the revolution and construction. Our Party's lines and policies are correct, and time is proving their great vitality.

But this should never make us complacent. We have yet to tackle many problems in the domain of social sciences. We must continue to develop social sciences. Society advances constantly and so do the revolution and construction. Thus we are confronted with many new problems. Look at our own situation. With regard to systems of management in industry and agriculture, we have formulated correct theories and policies and accumulated a certain amount of experience, but we still have a number of problems in regard to trade, for instance. Although the basic principle that socialist trade should be a supply system for the people has been clarified, we cannot yet say that a series of questions such as how to ensure quicker and more equitable supplies have been completely solved. We should never allow ourselves to become complacent, but should make further progress in social sciences and creatively solve the new, urgent problems arising in the revolution and construction.

Natural sciences in our country, we should note, are lagging behind social sciences. Our level is still low in the field of natural sciences and so are our scientists' and technicians' qualifications.

Let me take an instance from several years back.

Sometime after we gave guidance at the Changsong Joint Conference of Local Party and Economic Functionaries, we visited a stock farm and had a consultative meeting there with scientists and workers in the field of stockbreeding. I said at the meeting that a wide use of microelements was necessary if we were to improve our stockbreeding, and asked if we had any good solution to the problem. None of them could give a definite answer.

After the meeting, our scientists studied the problem in real earnest and succeeded in using microelements in poultry farming. As a result, poultry raising made rapid progress in a few years. As is the case with all other scientific and technological problems, the use of microelements is not such a difficult problem to someone who has gone into it. Naturally, science seems difficult to the uninitiated, but you will find it easy as soon as you become acquainted with it. Science which is accessible only to a few persons serves no purpose; it is not science but magic.

We have hardly begun to explore many fields of science, such as electronics and the metallurgy of pure metals. Our scientists and technicians should make strenuous efforts to open up new areas of science so that they can conquer as soon as possible the new peaks of science which mankind has already reached.

In order to make advance in science we must lay a sound material basis for scientific research.

Despite our great efforts to promote the sciences, the economic conditions and tense situation in our country have prevented us from laying satisfactory foundations for scientific research.

Up to now you have worked hard to make a lot of apparatus for yourselves and to build your own laboratories. This is very good. But your experimental apparatus leaves much to be desired and you have a long way to go to equip your laboratories to the standards required by modern science and technology. In the future, you should equip your laboratories better. To do so, you must make all the apparatus you can yourselves and import only that which is beyond you.

Practical work and field trips should be widely organized. I have heard that you have not yet visited our electron tube factory and semiconductor plant. This is a great mistake. If it is necessary for you to go on inspection tours to foreign countries when it helps to push our science and technology forward, why then not go and see our own factories? If you students of the Kim Chaek Polytechnical Institute visit these factories you might be able to make ingenious suggestions for improving their equipment. From now on, the institute should widely organize practical work and field trips. They are indispensable to scientific research.

It is also advisable for you to use foreign books on science and technology extensively.

You should thus take bold steps forward in your scientific research and soon overtake and outstrip advanced countries in science and technology.

The history of industrial development in capitalist countries such as Britain and Japan dates back a century or even a few centuries, but ours, even when counting from the establishment of the Republic, covers no more than 20 years. If we leave out the time spent on recovering from the ravages of war, our modern industry has a history of only a little more than ten years. This, however, should not lead us to think that it will take our country 100 or 300 years to overtake the developed countries. We must and can outstrip them in the near future.

Only a few years ago our agricultural workers considered the production of 4.8 tons of rice per *chongbo* in a foreign country something extraordinary. But now the average per *chongbo* rice yield amounts to 5.7 tons in Mundok and Sukchon Counties, South Pyongan Province, and in Anak County, South Hwanghae Province. So these counties have already outstripped foreign countries.

Now that sound foundations have been laid for it stockbreeding can make swift progress.

If we apply microelements and vigorously step up the chemicalization of agriculture, we shall be able to overtake and surpass the advanced countries in the next few years.

In metallurgy, too, we can reach world levels before long. Even now, for example, we are by no means behind others in alloy steel production. Steel plants in our country have a comparatively long history and have accumulated a considerable amount of experience in alloy steel production. The level of their workers and technicians is very high. The alloy steel produced in our country, though still limited in quantity, is not in the least inferior to that of other countries in terms of quality.

In the production of light and pure metals, too, we can quickly overtake and outstrip the advanced countries provided we tackle the job boldly and exert ourselves.

We must intensify our struggle to establish Juche in the iron and steel industry.

I think it necessary to introduce the semi-steel process which is being studied in the Kim Chaek Polytechnical Institute to production. Semi-steel is said to contain a considerable amount of sulphur. But that does not matter much. It is better to produce steel from domestic raw materials, though it is slightly inferior in quality, than to have to ask other countries to sell coke to us. Moreover, if we promote research on the elimination of sulphur, we will definitely be able to solve the problem. We cannot build up a Juche-motivated iron industry if we are passive, only worrying about the problem instead of daring to have a go at it. When the new iron works in the western region is completed, the semi-steel process must be boldly introduced. You should concentrate your energies on research on semi-steel and complete it at an early date.

In order to develop a Juche-motivated industry, those raw materials which we still have to purchase from other countries should be sought in our own country by stepping up geological prospecting. Intensified geological surveys will enable us to discover new sources of raw materials.

It would indeed be expecting too much to find every raw material we need in our own country. But in accordance with the Party's policy we must locate every single mineral deposit through intensified geological prospecting, and make substitute materials through the development of science and technology or, if this is impossible, strive to use less imported raw materials. We should enhance the independence of our industry in every respect.

South Korea today depends upon the United States and Japan for almost all its industrial raw materials. If they stopped supplying them even for a single day, all its factories and mills would have to suspend operations.

We must not build industries that are entirely dependent on other countries for raw materials, as is the case in south Korea.

Let me emphasize once again that if we want to eliminate flunkeyism toward great powers completely, we must build a stronger economic base in our country and raise our living standards above those enjoyed in other countries. We should far surpass others in everything—policy and theory, science and technology. To do this, we must make faster progress in social and natural sciences. In orther words, the ideological struggle alone is not enough to get rid of flunkeyism. It must be matched by the material base, the building of which requires the rapid advancement of science and technology.

Some people may ask: We are internationalists, so why should we constantly stress the need to get ahead of others? I would like to ask them in return: Why should we always tag along at the heels of others? We must catch up with the advanced countries in all spheres as soon as possible. There is nothing wrong in our being in the lead.

It is my firm belief that all the faculty and students of the Kim Chaek Polytechnical Institute, one of the biggest palaces of science and technology in our country, will make new and greater progress in their scientific research and in the training of technical personnel, fully living up to the expectations of the Party.

ANSWERS TO THE QUESTIONS RAISED BY ABDEL HAMID AHMED HAMROUCHE, GENERAL MANAGER OF DAR-EL-TAHRIR FOR PRINTING AND PUBLISHING OF THE UNITED ARAB REPUBLIC

July 1, 1969

Question: *Comrade Premier, the revolutionary spirit of self-reliance is the most important thing I have learned about on my visit to Korea. During my stay here I have seen that this spirit is embodied splendidly in all aspects of your domestic and foreign policies. I have seen clearly how the principle of self-reliance is actually carried through at home, in particular. But I cannot say I have fully understood everything in such a short time. So could you please tell me something more about it, Comrade Premier?*

Answer: As for the situation in our country, you have heard about it from the Chairman of the Central Committee of the Journalists' Union, Editor-in-Chief of *Rodang Sinmun*, I suppose.

As you have probably noticed, we had no mean success in creating a new society and a new life in the past. We owe our past success entirely to the correct policies and sagacious leadership of our Party and Government and to the courageous struggle of our people who strove to implement the Party's policies.

In leading the revolutionary struggles and the work of construction our Party has taken the idea of Juche as its invariable guiding compass, and our people, armed with the Party's idea of Juche, have waged an indomitable struggle in the revolutionary spirit of self-reliance.

We are making the Korean revolution. As far as the Korean revolution is concerned, Koreans know about it better than anyone else. The masters of the Korean revolution are the Korean people and our own strength is the decisive factor in its victory. No foreigners can tell us how to bring about the Korean revolution or carry it out in our stead. In order to ensure that the Korean revolution is a success, its masters, the Korean people themselves, must use their own brains, solve all problems that arise through their own efforts and settle them in conformity with the interests of the Korean revolution.

That is why we have held that the most important task is to establish Juche in all fields of the revolution and construction, and have fought to this end ever since the first days of liberation.

To establish Juche means, in short, to live by your own sense and your own strength without following others blindly or trying to live with help from others. It means to hold a consistent position in tackling everything in conformity to your own actual circumstances, in the interests of the revolution of your own country.

We have firmly established Juche in ideology, and embodied it thoroughly throughout the political, economic and military fields. Juche in ideology, independence in politics, self-support in the economy and self-defense in national defense—this is our Party's consistent stand.

Our Party has so far adhered firmly to the stand of Juche, solving all the problems of the revolution and construction independently in conformity with the specific conditions of our country and, in the main, through our own efforts. Our people have all carried on the struggle in the revolutionary spirit of self-reliance which calls on us to accomplish the revolution and build socialism and communism in our country through our own efforts and using our national resources, ridding ourselves of the idea of dependence upon others.

As a result of the establishment of Juche and self-reliant efforts, we have been able to advance the country's revolution as speedily as possible and win victories and successes surmounting manifold hardships and trials. Juche and self-reliance—these are the basic guarantees for all our achievements.

You might have seen our film shot right after the armistice; the war destroyed so many things in our country. Everything was burnt down and destroyed and only ashes were to be found in our towns and villages. In Pyongyang, for example, nothing was left after the war but a few houses and even they were badly damaged. Our country was truly in a very difficult situation, confronted with a mountain of hardships.

But we were not at all discouraged. We set out on the postwar rehabilitation and construction, fully convinced that we could rise to our feet again in any adversity, so long as the Party, the power, the people and the territory were there. Our Party convinced the people that they could rise again from the debris, though everything was almost destroyed by the war, if they relied on their own efforts, and it energetically aroused the people to a gigantic struggle for postwar rehabilitation and construction. The Party called upon people from all walks of life to contribute what they had to the sacred cause of building the socialist homeland: those who had physical strength gave their physical strength, those who had wisdom their wisdom, and those who had technical skill contributed their technical skill.

The entire people of our country, in active response to the Party's call, rose as one and waged a courageous struggle, devoting all their energies, wisdom and technical skill. Our working people manufactured machines for themselves and rebuilt factories, producing what they previously lacked and searching out more of what was not enough. Furthermore, they made new scientific inventions, technical innovations and creative suggestions, thus solving tough and knotty problems facing our country through their own efforts. Our patriotic intellectuals especially made a great contribution.

Let me cite a few examples.

Under Japanese imperialist rule there was hardly any textile industry in the northern half of our country. There were no more than a few thousand spindles and the per capita output of fabrics was barely 14 centimeters. Even after liberation it was not so easy to ensure adequate clothing for the people. Our country has a poor harvest of cotton because we have much rain in summer, so the question of fibers still remained a headache.

Our scientists, displaying the spirit of self-reliance, satisfactorily solved this difficult question. Some scientists devised the method of making vinalon from limestone which abounds in our country, and others invented a method of producing fiber from the reeds which grow in plenty in Korea. Thus we came to solve completely the problem of clothing for the people using the efforts of our own scientists and domestic raw materials.

Our iron industry, too, faced many unresolved problems. Coking coal is not produced in our country, and we had to import it to produce iron. But our scientists succeeded in producing iron with anthracite of which we have inexhaustible supplies. The result was that we opened up an avenue to the production of iron with our domestic raw materials. This was another great contribution to consolidating the foundations of the country's independent economy.

Now some countries produce fertilizers by means of electrolyzing water. But this method requires too much electricity, so it does not suit us. Our scientists, therefore, devised a method of producing fertilizers by gasifying the coal of our country.

In addition, various kinds of minerals have been found, which were formerly regarded as nonexistent in our country and they have aided the rapid development of industry. A great deal has also been done in the rural irrigation as we have devised ways and means unkown outside Korea. Again, the work of construction could be pushed ahead rapidly because it was done using our domestic raw materials and building materials.

The idea of Juche and the spirit of self-reliance have likewise been embodied creditably in the fields of education and culture.

The cadres and people of our country are inured to self-reliance and have developed great courage. Whatever task the Party may set forth, they readily accept it, without the slightest hesitation, and always carry it through to the end by their own efforts and talents, however difficult and hard it may be.

When we were rebuilding and constructing blast furnaces soon after the armistice, we had no technicians and were short of equipment and materials. To make things easy, we could have invited foreign technicians and procured equipment from abroad. But we did not have enough money to do so at the time. So we took bold measures. We provisionally graduated the third-year students of the technical college in advance and asked them to design and build furnaces. There were about 200 of them, and they worked hard day and night and succeeded in building excellent furnaces in a little over a year.

Had we built furnaces with foreign help, it would have cost us much time as well as much money. It would have taken a year to design them, another year to manufacture the equipment plus a very long period of time to bring them in; it would have taken four or five years at least to complete the construction of furnaces.

If we rely on foreign countries to build a furnace, large amounts of funds and time must be spent, but if we rely on our own efforts, we can build a good furnace in the short period of a year. How nice it is to rely on our own efforts!

Large funds are also necessary to import such things as electric locomotives. We could not afford to buy from foreign countries large numbers of electric locomotives needed in our country. Therefore, we assigned our college students and technicians to the task of designing and building locomotives by themselves. Our technicians are now in a position to turn out fine electric locomotives using their own techniques and efforts, and we are electrifying nearly all the railway lines in the country with homemade locomotives.

Whenever we got a good machine, we copied it and opened up let-one-machine-tool-make-machine-tools movements everywhere and thus developed the nation's machine-building industry. Today we manufacture automobiles, tractors and different kinds of weapons on our own; we make almost everything we need through our own efforts.

By relying on our own efforts in this way, we have laid down solid foundations for an independent national economy and built up an impregnable defense power for the country and have been able to fully solve the problems of food, clothing and housing for the people.

In our country today homemade up-to-date machines are

working at the construction sites, our own tractors ploughing the fields, and strings of *Charyokgaengsaeng* (Self-Reliance) motor vehicles running along the roads. Our brave People's Army is impregnably safeguarding the nation's defense line with the weapons made by our working class. It is true that our people's livelihood is not so generous as that in advanced countries. However, we all eat our fill with the rice we produce in our country, and do not have to purchase it from foreign countries. We all lead decent lives in the houses built by ourselves; we are dressed in clothing made of our own fabrics, and use the daily necessities of our own make.

As a result of the establishment of Juche and our self-reliant efforts we have turned our country, once a backward colonial agrarian nation, into this advanced socialist industrial-agricultural country in a very short span of time. Today our people have become a dignified nation whom no one would dare to flout.

Some say that a small country need not have a comprehensively developed industry and others say that it would be better if we produced only some of the things which are needed in the country, and bought the rest from foreign countries. Certainly, at a given stage of development of the productive forces we may buy from abroad things which are not produced or are in slight demand in our country. But the main thing is to set it as a principle to build an independent national industry through our own efforts and using our own resources. In particular, we ourselves must produce things which are in great demand at home, along with important raw materials and other materials. Only by so doing can we ensure the independence of the national economy.

The idea of Juche and the spirit of self-reliance do not involve nationalism. We establish Juche and rely on our own efforts in order to build socialism and communism faster and better. Koreans are bound to build socialism and communism in Korea and live in Korea. They could not abandon their country to live in some other country, could they? If we build socialism and communism well in Korea through self-reliance, it means we carry out our national duty and, at the same time we are faithful to our international duty. All this will be conducive to the advancement of world revolution.

In establishing Juche and relying on our own efforts we do

not intend to reject international solidarity, mutual cooperation and assistance among fraternal countries and solve everything by ourselves. We consistently insist that international solidarity among the fraternal countries should be further strengthened, and we think it is vital that we cooperate with and assist one another.

We were given active support and encouragement by other socialist countries and the peace-loving people of the world during the difficult days of postwar rehabilitation and construction. We also received no small assistance from the fraternal socialist countries. The successes achieved in the postwar rehabilitation and construction of our country are also associated with these friends' helping hands. We are grateful for this and remember this.

We benefit from the advanced learning of foreign countries and draw on their good experience. We also get foreign help when we undertake something we have no previous experience of or tackle something new to us. And we purchase from abroad things unobtainable in our country. We have built a thermal power station with the help of Soviet technicians. We are also building an oil refinery with their help because oil is not yet produced in our country. It is certain that next we will build thermal power stations and oil refineries using our own technicians.

We consider it necessary that fraternal countries should cooperate and assist each other. We get help from other countries, but we do not depend entirely upon it. Even in the days of postwar rehabilitation and construcion we always made it a rule that we should rely on our own efforts and we did not attach all importance to foreign assistance. It is all the more so today. Foreign assistance has limitations, however sincerely intended it may be, and can only play an auxiliary role in building the national economy. It is impossible to satisfactorily meet our own demands in time with the assistance of foreign countries.

If too much stress is laid on foreign assistance or an attempt is made to rely entirely on others, it will make people lose faith in their own strength and neglect their endeavors to tap the inner resources of their own country, blindly pinning their hopes on others and simply imitating them. Then, in the end, it will be impossible to succeed in building a sovereign, independent state. You are a writer, so you cannot write a good article nor improve your writing if you merely imitate or copy others' articles. You can write a good article and raise your writing standards only if you use your own brains.

Our experience shows that it is possible to successfully build an independent national economy, bringing prosperity and progress to the country, only when Juche is thoroughly established and the main stress is put on self-reliance.

You speak very highly of our country's success made in socialist construction. But it is, as yet, no more than an initial success. We are not at all self-complacent with our successes to date.

We have a lot of things to do. We have not yet reunified our country. The southern half of our land is still under the occupation of U.S. imperialism, the ringleader of world imperialism. Our nation's supreme revolutionary task is to chase the U.S. imperialists away, so as to accomplish the reunification of the country.

In order to reunify the divided land and hasten the nationwide victory of the revolution we should effect the socialist construction better in the northern half of the Republic and further strengthen our revolutionary forces in all the political, economic and military fields. Especially, we are faced with the vital task of consolidating more firmly the foundations of the independent national economy by rapidly developing the nation's industry.

It is true that we have many difficulties and hardships ahead. However, they are not the difficulties of marking time or the hardships of retreating; they are the difficulties and hardships on the way of our advance.

By our people's revolutionary mettle we mean that we do not sink in despair before difficulties or yield to hardships; on the contrary we make continuous innovations and continuous advances to fresh victories. We will, in the future, as in the past, continue to firmly establish Juche in all spheres of social life and display to the full the revolutionary spirit of self-reliance, thereby surmounting all difficulties and hardships with courage and discharging the national and international duties that fall to us with credit.

Question: *Comrade Premier, in your report at the 20th*

anniversary celebration of the foundation of your Republic you said it is a sad thing that there are differences within the socialist camp, differences which should be overcome. Do you think that the differences within the socialist camp have deepened any further since September 1968?

Answer: As we said before and say still now, there are differences between the socialist countries and we are not by any means going to conceal them.

But the differences between the socialist countries must in no way be identified with the contradictions between the imperialist powers or with the contradictions of the different state and social systems which exist between the socialist and imperialist countries. In all the socialist countries power is in the hands of the working class and communal ownership of the means of production is established, with the result that exploitation and oppression of man by man is eliminated. Between the socialist countries, therefore, there can be no contradictions such as those which reflect the fundamentally different interests between the hostile classes.

The differences between the socialist countries are, in all respects, the differences between fraternal countries fighting together for the common goal. If there are differences between the socialist countries, they are mainly differences over the estimation of imperialism and over strategic and tactical questions in the anti-imperialist struggle.

Some overestimate the strength of imperialism, U.S. imperialism in particular, and do not wage an active anti-imperialist, anti-U.S. struggle, thinking that once the imperialists explode an atom bomb the whole world would perish. We cannot agree with this.

Imperialism should not be underestimated, of course, but it should not be overestimated either. Imperialism, U.S. imperialism above all, is already on the decline.

If the U.S. imperialists are not on the decline, why did they suffer defeat in the Korean war? If the U.S. imperialists are not doomed like the sun setting behind the western hills, why are they suffering such setbacks in South Vietnam? These examples show that the days of U.S. imperialism are already numbered.

The imperialists did not dare to ignite war when the people of the UAR, who had been freed from the yoke of imperialism and were embarking upon the creation of a new life, nationalized the Suez Canal under the leadership of President Nasser.

The Algerian people fought valiantly against the French imperialists and won independence and many other African countries have set out to build a new life, emancipated from the imperialist yoke. The colonial ruling system of imperialism is collapsing irresistibly on the African continent.

Then, is it quiet in Latin America? No, certainly not. Anti-U.S., anti-dictatorship struggles are being forcefully unfolded by the peoples; the U.S. imperialists are helpless and hard hit here in a continent which used to be called the "quiet backyard" of the United States. The revolutionary Cuban people are gallantly building socialism right under the nose of the U.S. imperialists. Not long ago, Nixon's "special envoy" met the surging anti-U.S. resistance of the peoples in Latin American countries and was in the end turned away at their doors.

Imperialism is attacked not only from without but also from within and is confronted with an acute crisis. The black people's struggle against racial discrimination and for freedom and democratic rights and an anti-war movement of the masses of the people are going on extensively in the United States, and in France as well the working class and the broad masses launched a struggle and forced De Gaulle's dictatorial regime to resign from power.

All these are manifestations of the decline of imperialism.

As you see, there are differences between the socialist countries over the questions of how to estimate imperialism, how to struggle against it and how to support the liberation movement of the peoples.

The differences between the socialist countries are, as it were, something like a casual family conflict. Even brothers quarrel with each other occasionally, and how is it most unlikely that there would never be differences between the fraternal countries?

This is our view on the question of differences between the socialist countries.

Well, the question you are interested in is whether such differences have recently been aggravated, but we do not view the matter in that light.

Quarrels may increase or diminish sometimes, since the differences between the socialist countries still remain unsettled. Yet, this does not mean that the differences have deepened, much less can it be considered that the socialist countries are completely split from each other.

If any of the socialist countries had completely gone over to the side of imperialism, that would be a different matter. But as no single socialist country has done this since the differences arose, and as such a thing is impossible, it cannot be considered that the socialist countries are completely severed from each other. The peoples of all the socialist countries struggle to attain the common goal of building free and happy socialist, communist society and the socialist countries are united in the alliance demanded by the class solidarity of the international working class which has triumphed in the struggle against world imperialism and colonialism. Accordingly, the peoples of the socialist countries will never separate from each other.

The socialist countries will eventually get over the differences and have the same view, and fight on together against imperialism for the victory of socialism and communism.

Any maneuver on the part of the imperialists to estrange and split the socialist countries is bound to end in a shameful fiasco.

Question: *Do I understand that the reason why your Party did not attend the recent international conference of Communist and Workers' Parties convened in Moscow was based precisely upon this analysis of the differences within the socialist camp?*

Answer: In principle, our Party has no objection to an international conference of the Communist and Workers' Parties. It is a necessary and good thing for the fraternal parties to sit at the same table and discuss together, as comrades, important questions for the advancement of the international communist and working-class movements and lay down common tasks in the struggle to achieve unity of action. This sort of conference will lead to the development of world revolution and contribute to the cause of unity.

However, to achieve the aim of the international conference of the fraternal parties, the conference should be convened after ample preparations, when all conditions have matured. If an international conference is convened under the present conditions, it may further expose the differences between the fraternal parties to the enemies. And such a meeting will not benefit the cause of solidarity either.

Our Party, proceeding from the desire for solidarity among all the fraternal parties and in the interests of the Korean revolution and the international revolutionary movement, refrains from participating in any international conference of the fraternal parties under the present circumstances, believing that the conditions are not yet ripe. This is our Party's consistent stand.

Question: *Comrade Premier, haven't you anything to say to the people of the UAR through newspapers of Dar-El Tahrir?*

Answer: The people of the UAR under the leadership of President Nasser are valiantly battling against imperialism led by the U.S. imperialists and their henchmen, the Israeli aggressors, and for defending national independence; they are registering great successes in their struggle to build a new society.

The Korean people sincerely rejoice over the successes of the people of the UAR and extend full support and encouragement to them in their righteous struggle. Our people regard your anti-imperialist, anti-colonial struggle as support for our own cause of national reunification.

The Korean people are happy to have the people of the UAR as their comrades-in-arms and will always march ahead shoulder to shoulder with them in the common struggle against the U.S. and other imperialists.

Availing myself of this opportunity, I sincerely wish the people of the UAR fresh successes in their struggle to force the Israeli aggressors out of the occupied territory and defend the dignity of the Arab people and build a prosperous country.

ON SOME THEORETICAL PROBLEMS OF THE SOCIALIST ECONOMY

Answers to the Questions Raised by Scientific and Educational Workers, *March 1, 1969*

In April 1968 I received some questions from scholars, through the Science and Education Department of the Party Central Committee, concerning problems of socialist economic theory. But, as the situation in the country was tense and we had the celebrations of the 20th anniversary of the foundation of the Republic last year, I had little time to spare for a prompt answer. Recently, I was told that some leading economic functionaries and scholars still have no clear understanding of these problems and are disputing about them. Therefore, I am now going to give my opinion on these questions.

1. The Problem of the Relation Between the Scale of the Economy and the Rate of Production Growth in Socialist Society

A "theory" is now in vogue among certain economists to the effect that although the economy grows without interruption in socialist society, its rate of growth cannot exceed 4-5 or 6-7 % a year after a certain stage of development is reached. I am told that some of the leading workers in our state economic bodies, too, argue that, even if our industrial output should increase by only 6 or 7% a year, that would be high enough, inasmuch as in capitalist countries production barely increases by 2 or 3% a year.

They base such an argument on the assumption that the reserves for production growth diminish in the period of reconstruction as compared with the previous period of rehabilitation and that, accordingly, as the economy develops and its scale expands, the possibilities for increasing production are reduced. In other words, they contend that the further industry advances, the more the reserves for growth diminish and the slower the rate of increase of production becomes. In our country, too, they say, there were plenty of growth reserves in the postwar rehabilitation period, but such reserves are no longer abundant today, when the basis of socialist industrialization has already been laid and we are in a period of all-out technological reconstruction of the national economy, and therefore production cannot be multiplied at an ever high rate.

People who think in this way are either unaware of the true advantages of the socialist economic system or are unwilling to see them.

Socialist society has unlimited potentialities for developing the economy continuously at a high rate inconceivable in capitalist society, and the further socialist construction advances and the stronger the economic basis grows, the greater these potentials become.

In capitalist society production cannot grow steadily, because the process of reproduction is periodically interrupted and much social labor wasted owing to overproduction crisis. In socialist society, however, all the labor resources and natural wealth of the country can be utilized in the most rational way, and production can be raised continually according to plan. This potential for production growth will always increase so long as the balance among the branches of the national economy is rationally maintained and the country's economy is coordinated well by strengthening the economic organizing functions of the state of proletarian dictatorship and improving the economic management capacity of the functionaries. Since the socialist state controls coordinately and carries out production and distribution, accumulation and consumption according to plan, it can allocate large amounts to accumulation and make the most rational use of funds, and in this way carry on socialist expanded reproduction steadily on a big scale.

The production relations of socialism open a broad highway for unrestricted development of the productive forces; the socialist state, by making use of this potential, can develop technology rapidly, according to plan. The replacement of outmoded technology with a new one and then with a still newer one, the mechanization of manual labor and the further development into semi-automation, and then from semi-automation on to automation: This is a law that governs the construction of socialism and communism. It is a self-evident truth that in socialist society, with the rapid development of technology, labor productivity increases constantly and production grows at a high rate.

In socialist society, the people's high revolutionary zeal is the decisive factor forcefully pushing the development of the productive forces. The essential superiority of the socialist system lies in the fact that the working people, freed from exploitation and oppression, work with conscious enthusiasm and creative initiative for the country and the people, for society and the collective, as well as for their own welfare. In capitalist society the working people are not interested in the development of production and technology at all, for they work against their will, forced by the threat of unemployment and hunger. But in socialist society the working people work with enthusiasm for the development of production, because they are deeply aware that the fruits of their labor are their own, their people's and their country's. The more the proletarian party and state fulfill their proper functions of strengthening the ideological revolution among the working people and gradually eliminating the survivals of old ideologies from their minds, the more the working people will devote their talents and stamina to the development of socialist production. In this way, continuous improvement and innovation will be brought about in all aspects of economic management, the organization of production and manpower, and the advancement of technology.

All this testifies to the sheer fallacy of the "theory" that in socialist society the reserves for increasing production gradually diminish and that production cannot be kept growing at a high rate as the economy develops and its scale expands.

Practical experience in the building of socialism in our country also irrefutably proves the incorrectness of such a "theory."

To begin with, let me tell you what happened when we were working on the Five-Year Plan. The economic life of our country at that time was very hard in general, although our Party members and working people had, on the whole, rehabilitated the ravaged economy and stabilized the people's living conditions by successfully carrying out the Three-Year National Economic Plan. Moreover, the enemies at home and abroad were hysterically trying to encroach on the gains of our revolution and demolish our people's work of construction. Under such circumstances we were confronted with an urgent task, that of quickly laying the foundations of industrialization, in order to drive the country's economy ahead and improve the people's living conditions; and this required large quantities of rolled steel.

At that time our country had only one blooming mill and its rated capacity was only 60,000 tons. However, 60,000 tons of rolled steel were far from enough, for we had to build up the towns and countryside, erect factories and turn out more machines.

In all the previous arduous revolutionary struggles our Party had trusted the working class and relying on their strength, broken through bottlenecks and difficulties. This time, too, our Party decided to go to the working class, consult them and overcome the existing difficulties.

Entrusted by the Political Committee of the Party Central Committee, we went to the Kangson Steel Plant. When we asked the leading personnel there if they could not increase the output of rolled steel to 90,000 tons, some of them shook their heads and said that it would be difficult. So we called the workers together and told them: We have barely managed to rehabilitate the ravaged economy, and now the factionalists have reared their heads against the Party and the great-power chauvinists are putting pressure on us, and the U.S. imperialists and the Syngman Rhee puppet clique are going wild with their "march north'' shriekings. But can all this be an excuse for us to get disheartened and yield to the grave difficulties before the cause of revolution and construction? Unthinkable. We trust only you, the working class, the main force of our revolution, and we have no one but you to rely on. Therefore, to tide over these grave difficulties facing our Party, you must be in high spirits and work hard to produce plenty and construct well and thus push economic construction more vigorously.

We did our political work in this way, and the workers of Kangson responded with a resolution to produce 90,000 tons of rolled steel. Roused to activity, they worked hard, improving the existing machines and equipment and solving difficult problems, with the result that 120,000 tons of rolled steel were turned out that year instead of 90,000. This steel plant was able to raise the capacity of its blooming shop to the present level of 450,000 tons, that is, nearly eight times the rated capacity.

Not only in the Kangson Steel Plant but in all branches of the national economy and all factories and enterprises, the old rated capacities were scrapped and great innovations were made. Miracles were wrought day by day that astounded the world, and our country's economy developed at a very high rate. Thus, the Five-Year Plan envisaging a 2.6-fold increase in total industrial output value was carried out in two years and a half, and the plan for major manufactured goods was also fulfilled or overfulfilled on all production indices in four years.

During the seven or eight years that have passed since the fulfillment of the Five-Year Plan, the tasks of the overall technical revolution have been vigorously carried forward in our country, with the result that a number of new branches of industry have been opened, our installed industrial technology has been radically improved, and the volume of production expanded several times. If the "theory" held by some people, that with the expansion of production scale the rate of growth decreases, were correct, it would have been impossible for our country to keep up the high rate of production growth in the period that followed the fulfillment of the Five-Year Plan. But in the Seven-Year Plan period, too, the economy has developed continually at a high speed, though our country allocated more of its accumulation than planned for defense construction in view of the U.S. imperialists' more pronounced aggressive maneuvers. Above all, the national economic plan for 1967, the plan for the first year the Party Conference decision was in effect on simultaneous construction of the economy and defenses, was a tight plan envisaging a 12.8% increase in total industrial output value over the previous year. But we actually overfulfilled the plan by far and raised industrial output by 17% that year. If it had not been for the extraordinary flood damage that year, industrial output would have risen more than 20%. This is attributable to the fact that our Party intensified the ideological revolution among the working people, arousing their conscious enthusiasm and waging a resolute struggle against passivism, conservatism and all other kinds of old ideas that were hampering our forward movement.

Take the Songhung Mine for example.

In 1967 when the mine's management came up with a very low target plan, the Cabinet persuaded them to raise it a little. Yet, even this was too low to meet the Party's requirements. So the Party Central Committee, in order to conduct political work among the workers of the Songhung Mine, summoned its cadres, from platoon leaders on up, to a meeting. There we told them: In order to successfully carry out the line of simultaneous economic and defense construction set forth by the Party Conference, the Songhung Mine will have to extract more nonferrous metal. They immediately pledged themselves to mine more than the target set by the Cabinet. In the end, they produced nearly twice as much as they had promised at first.

Let us take another example.

Officials in the machine-building industry said that they had no potential for expansion, so we went to the Ryongsong Machine Plant in 1967 and kindled the flames of innovation. The workers there all rose to the task and fulfilled the tightened-up plan for that year, including the extra production plan, by October 10, two months and 20 days ahead of schedule.

Great reserves for growth were also found in the course of the struggle to carry out last year's national economic plan.

Responding to the U.S. imperialist war hysteria following the *Pueblo* incident, the Party Central Committee addressed an appeal last year to the factories and enterprises in all fields of the national economy to fulfill all their production and construction assignments ahead of schedule and produce more with the manpower, materials and equipment thus economized.

This revolutionary call by the Party met response in all the factories and enterprises, and many of them, inspired with a burning desire to drive the U.S. imperialists from our soil and reunify the country at the earliest possible date, asked for greater assignments and did a fine job of fulfilling their commitments.

All this shows that we can develop the economy as fast as we want, no matter how big its scale is, if we do our political work well, in accordance with the line set by our Party, and thereby raise the political consciousness of the masses, arouse their revolutionary zeal and constantly improve technology.

The "theory" that as industry reaches a certain stage of development the reserves diminish and a high rate of growth cannot be ensured in industrial production has nothing to do with Marxist-Leninist economic theory. The "theory" that large-scale economies cannot develop rapidly is just a sophistry brought forward by some people to justify the fact that their technological progress is slow and their economy stagnant because they have been talking about "liberalization" and "democratic development" instead of educating their working people, who as a result have slackened ideologically, fiddle about and loaf on the job.

Referring to the immediate tasks of Soviet power after the victory of the October Socialist Revolution, Lenin put forward the famous proposition: Communism is Soviet power plus the electrification of the whole country. This proposition, though simple, has a profound meaning. I think it is of great importance for building socialism and communism that we have a correct understanding of this proposition and translate it into practice. What is meant by the Soviet power Lenin mentioned? It means proletarian dictatorship itself. Therefore, the working-class state must continue the class struggle and carry out the ideological and cultural revolutions, and thus remold the consciousness of the people and raise their technical and cultural levels, and carry out the program of working-classizing and revolutionizing the whole of society. Electrification means that we should develop technology to such a high level as to be able to make all the production processes automatic and greatly consolidate the material-production basis of society. To sum up, this proposition of Lenin's teaches us that communism will be achieved only when, on the one hand, the ideological and cultural revolutions are accomplished and the whole of society is revolutionized and working-classized through the strengthened dictatorship of the proletariat and when, on the other, a solid material and technical basis for a very high level of the productive forces is laid, relying on the fulfillment of the technical revolution.

If we neglect either the dictatorship of the proletariat or the technical revolution alluded to by Lenin, we can neither develop the socialist economy steadily at a rapid pace nor build a communist society. We should therefore strengthen the dictatorship of the proletariat and step up the technical revolution dynamically in order to build a communist society. As Lenin passed away before he himself could build communism, we must correctly interpret his proposition and carry it into effect. Some people, however, refuse to correctly understand and put into effect this proposition of Lenin's. We must categorically oppose Right opportunism in the field of economic theory in order to boost socialist construction at a higher rate. If we do not oppose the Right deviation in the economic field, and instead weaken the proletarian dictatorship and fail to do political work, thus foster individual selfishness among the people, and try to move the people merely with money, we cannot arouse their collective heroism and creative initiative, and accordingly, we cannot successfully carry out the tasks either of technical revolution or of economic construction. If we followed the Right opportunist theory and failed to develop the economy rapidly, we could even find it difficult to provide everyone with jobs and food. In that case, with the very backward productive forces we inherited from the old society, how can we catch up with the advanced countries and build a communist society where everybody works according to his abilities and gets his share according to his needs? We must reject the Right opportunist theory, thoroughly defend our Party's revolutionary ideas, our Party's theory of economic construction, and carry them through to the end, thus keeping up the grand march of Chollima in building socialism.

2. Problems of the Means of Production in the Form of Commodity and the Use of the Law of Value in Socialist Society

I have heard that some economists are arguing about the questions of whether the means of production are commodities in socialist society and whether the law of value operates in the domain of their production and circulation.

I do not think these questions should be handled indiscriminately. In socialist society the means of production are sometimes commodities and sometimes not, as the case may be. The law of value will operate when they are commodities and not when they are not, because the law of value is a law of commodity production.

Then, when are the means of production commodities and when are they not? To find the right solution to this question, I think it necessary, first of all, to have a clear idea of the properties of commodities and the origin of commodity production.

Commodities are produced not for one's own consumption but for sale. In other words, not all products are commodities; only things produced for the purpose of exchange are commodities. As is clear from this, in order for a product to be a commodity there are required: first, the social division of labor through which different kinds of goods are produced; second, the seller and the buyer — the man who gives up the right to possess a thing by selling it and the man who buys and acquires the right to possess it. That is to say, commodity production presupposes the social division of labor and the differentiation of appropriation of the products. Therefore, where there is no social division of labor and ownership is not differentiated but remains in a unified form, there can be no commodity production.

The continuance of commodity-money relations in socialist society is also due to the existence of the social division of labor and different forms of ownership of the products. As everybody knows, in socialist society the division of labor not only exists but develops day by day. As for ownership, there exist both state and cooperative property of the means of production and private ownership of consumer goods as well, though in the course of the socialist revolution private property is abolished and different forms of economy that existed early in the transition period are gradually fused into a single, socialist form. Besides, the socialist states must carry on foreign trade while communism has not yet triumphed on a world scale and national frontiers still exist.

All these are conditions that give rise to commodity production in socialist society. It goes without saying that in socialist society commodity production is a production of goods without capitalists and, therefore, the law of value does not operate blindly as in capitalist society but within a limited scope, and the state uses it in a planned way as an economic lever for effective management of the economy. Later, when the transition period is over and cooperative property is transformed into property of the entire people so that a single form of ownership is established, the product of society, leaving aside for a moment the consideration of foreign trade, will not be given the name "commodity" but simply called "means of production" or "consumer goods," or some other names. Then the law of value will also cease to operate. Needless to say, even then the social division of labor will continue to develop, but there will be no more commodity production.

Scholars, leading economic functionaries and many other people are now committing Right or "Left" errors both in the domain of theory and in economic management, because they have not fully understood the question of whether or not the means of production are commodities in socialist society. As a result, some fall into the Right tendency to manage the economy in a capitalist way, overrating the importance of commodity production and the law of value in the wake of revisionist theory, while others commit the ultra-"Left" error of failing to streamline management of enterprises and causing great wastage of means of production and labor power by totally ignoring commodity production and the role of the law of value, taking no account of the transitional character of our society. A correct understanding and treatment of this question is of great importance in socialist economic construction. After all, the question of utilizing commodity-money relations is an important one which the working-class state must settle properly in the period of transition from capitalism to socialism. Right or "Left" mistakes on this question can do serious harm.

The factor determining when the means of production are commodities and when they are not in socialist society should also be found in the differentiation of ownership. In socialist society the means of production, even when shifted from one place to another, are not commodities as long as they do not change hands, and they are commodities when they do change hands. An obvious conclusion follows from this:

First, when means of production made in the state sector are transferred to cooperative ownership or vice versa, they are commodities in both cases and the law of value is therefore operating; second, when means of production are exchanged within the bounds of cooperative ownership—between cooperative farms or between producers' cooperatives, or between the former and the latter—they are just as much commodities and here, too, the law of value is operating; third, when they are exported the means of production are commodities and are traded at the world market price or at the socialist market price. For instance, when countries such as Indonesia or Cambodia ask our country for machine tools, the machine tools sold to these countries are commodities for which we should receive due prices. And when a Confederation of the north and the south, though not yet realized at this time, is established in our country in accordance with our Party's proposal for national reunification, and businessmen in south Korea ask us for machines and equipment, we will have to sell them. In that case the machines and equipment we sell them will be commodities, and the law of value will be bound to come into consideration.

What, then, are the equipment, raw materials and other supplies that are transferred between the state enterprises? They are not commodities, because means of production such as these are turned out on the basis of socialist cooperation between production enterprises, and even when they are turned over from one enterprise to another they remain under the ownership of the socialist state, and such means of production are supplied not through free trade but under state planning of equipment and material supply. When the state believes it necessary, it provides the enterprises with the means of production, even if the enterprises do not ask for them, just as it provides the army with weapons. Therefore, the machines, equipment, raw materials and other supplies, which are transferred between the state enterprises, cannot be called commodities realized through the operation of the law of value.

Then, what shall we call these means of production transferred between the state enterprises, if not commodities, and what shall we say is being made use of, if not the operation of the law of value, in fixing the prices of the means of production when they are turned over, or in calculating their costs when produced? It would be correct to say that the means of production transferred between state enterprises according to the plans for equipment and material supply and for cooperative production are not commodities, but assume the commodity form and accordingly, that in this case the law of value does not operate in substance as in the case of commodity production, but only in form.

In other words, such means of production are not commodities in the proper sense of the word, but merely assume the commodity form, and accordingly, what is made use of here is not the operation of the law of value in the proper sense of the word, but the law of value in its outward form; and in the case of the production and exchange of means of production, it is not value itself but the form of value which is made use of simply as an instrument of economic accounting.

Then, how do you explain that the means of production transferred between state enterprises are not really commodities but only assume the form of commodities? This occurs because the state enterprises are relatively independent in using and managing the means of production and in running the economy, just as if they were under different ownership, when in fact they are all under one and the same state ownership. Though all the cost-accounting enterprises in the state sector are owned by the state, they independently use the means of production received from other enterprises according to unified state plan, and must net a certain profit for the state over and above their production costs.

Although such cost-accounting state enterprises are under the same ownership, their independence in management gives the impression that the means of production transferred between them are commodities like those handed over to different owners. Thus, when one enterprise delivers means of production to another, it does not give them free or dirt-cheap, but hands them over at prices fixed uniformly by the state according to the expenditure of socially necessary labor on the principle of equivalent compensation, though they are all cost-accounting enterprises in the state sector. Even between state-owned enterprises control is kept of things that are mine and thine, and transactions in means of production have to be conducted on a strict cost-accounting basis.

Why, then, should the enterprises within the state sector be granted independence in management, and, if the means of production are not commodities, why should they be delivered and received under strict accounting, on the principle of equivalence? That has something to do with the specific feature of socialist society, which is a transitional one. In socialist society the productive forces have not developed to such an extent that each person works according to his abilities and each receives according to his needs. And not all people possess so great a collectivist spirit as to value and take responsible care of state properties like their own. In quite a few cases, even those who are educated enough do not care so much about the affairs of other state bodies or enterprises as about their own affairs, nor do they devote themselves to them, to say nothing of those who still harbor such old ideological debris as stodgy departmentalism and parochialism, gnawing away at the interests of the state or other institutions and enterprises, putting the narrow interests of their own institutions and localities above everything else. Further, under socialism labor has become, of course, an honorable and worthwhile thing but not yet life's prime requirement as in communist society. All these things require that under socialism equivalent values be strictly calculated in transactions between the enterprises, though they are all state-owned. If our society had a great abundance of goods and if the managing staffs and working people of all enterprises were free from selfishness, were concerned about all the state properties as about their own, and conducted all the state affairs as devotedly as their own, then there would be no need of keeping accounts on the basis of equivalent exchange.

A proper use of the commodity form and the commercial form in the production and circulation of the means of production is of definite significance in methodically increasing the profits of the enterprises and state accumulation, by eliminating the wastage of social labor and strengthening the regime of economy. It is therefore necessary to make proper use of them in all branches of the national economy and in all enterprises.

Above all, efforts should be made to properly use the value form in the manufacture of the means of production, so as to strengthen the strict accounting system and control by the *won* over the use of raw and other industrial materials as well as labor power and systematically lower the norm of materials consumption per unit of output.

In the domain of circulation, too, the commercial form should be fully utilized, while good plans of equipment and materials supply are mapped out, so as to do away with the wastage of machines, equipment, raw materials and other industrial supplies and use them in a rational way. When we set up the materials supply agencies and saw to it that raw and other industrial materials were bought and sold through the medium of these agencies, we aimed at ensuring their smooth supply.

Our economic functionaries, however, fail to do this properly. The textbook of political economy, too, simply says that the means of production are excluded from the sphere of commodity circulation and are supplied to enterprises according to plan, but it makes no mention whatever of how and in what form they are supplied. The question of supply of means of production is all but left out of the textbook of political economy and, particularly, the question of purchase and sale of raw and other materials between the state enterprises is not even touched upon.

Such being the case, many shortcomings have appeared in the supply of materials. When securing raw materials and other supplies, the enterprises take them without caring much about their prices, high or low. Moreover, it is not infrequent that valuable materials lie idle in heaps at some enterprises, while at others production is interrupted for lack of these same materials.

True, this is partly owing to the defective plans of materials supply mapped out by the State Planning Commission, but the real problem is the lack of understanding of the fact that the supply of raw and other industrial materials is carried out in the form of trade. That is to say, their supply is carried out in the form of commodity circulation, inasmuch as the form of selling and buying is adopted between the state enterprises, too. But this has been ignored. As a result, if the planning organs make erroneous plans for the supply of materials, nobody is responsible for them being kept idle or wasted, and no one notices the defect.

To straighten out this question, it is necessary, first of all, to enhance the role of the materials supply agencies. When these agencies do their work well, they will not be besieged by crowds of people coming to get materials; even when scarce, the materials will be put to effective use, being supplied in adequate quantity to the enterprises which most need them; and the enterprises, on their part, will stop receiving whatever materials they can get, without considering the need for them, only to keep them idle or waste them.

We must realize that when means of production such as machines, equipment, raw materials and other supplies produced in factories and enterprises, while remaining under state ownership, are transferred between the enterprises, they assume the form of commodity circulation. Then, as prices are the issue in this case, if defects occur in the plans, it will be possible to straighten them out during the actual supply process.

Of course, in our society everything is produced, supplied, and consumed according to plan. Moreover, under the ownership of the entire people, production, supply and consumption are completely planned. It is by no means an easy thing, however, to have everything correctly planned. We have had a planned economy for over 20 years and we have continually stressed the need for the plans to be objective. But planning is still not being done as well as it should be.

The same is true of the supply plans for raw materials and other supplies. Some kinds of materials are left out of the plan and some unnecessary things are included in the supply plan. Then, where should the defects be detected? They should be detected at the supply agencies. That is, they must be complemented and corrected in the course of selling and buying raw and other industrial materials through the agencies.

Besides, even if a materials supply plan has been all correctly drawn up, it cannot be executed when the supply work is not actually carried out properly. If the commercial form, that is, the selling-and-buying form, is ignored in the supply of raw materials and other supplies and if they are simply supplied according to plan, materials may be used at random and squandered at the enterprises. Such practices may be quite frequent so long as our functionaries and working people are not all Communists.

It is therefore necessary to raise the role of the supply agencies and make the most of the form of commodity circulation in the supply of raw and other industrial materials. Thus, things must be so arranged that if an enterprise should purchase too much of some kinds of materials, it would not be able to buy other kinds, and if materials should be wasted, the activities of the enterprise would be greatly affected. Only when such conditions are established in the supply of raw materials and other supplies, will the personnel of enterprises check up closely on their prices and transport costs, value and take better care of these materials, and make efforts to lower the norm of their consumption per unit of output.

Now I should like to present my views on the question of making proper use of the law of value in the production and circulation of commodities.

Most important of all in the use of the law of value is to fix the prices of commodities properly. Prices should be calculated by taking full account of the requirements of the basic economic law of socialism and the law of value.

First of all, the assessment of prices should be based correctly on the socially necessary labor contained in goods. If prices were not fixed on the basis of the outlay of socially necessary labor, the price equilibrium could not be maintained, nor could socialist distribution be handled properly and the development of social production would be unfavorably affected.

Let us take an example. Once I walked into a shop in Changsong County of North Pyongan Province, and I found there a meter of twisted-yarn fabric woven with 200 grams of yarn priced at three *won,* and a thread-ball weighing 50 grams at 5.4 *won.* This meant that a thread-ball was priced twice as high as a piece of cloth made of twisted yarn equivalent to four thread-balls, which had been woven into fabrics and dyed. Indeed, it would seem that a lot of manpower and fairly large production costs were needed to spin thread at the local industry factory, because it was poorly mechanized. But, since the thread was not spun on hand spinning-wheels, its cost cannot be greater than the cost of fabrics. And even if the production costs were so high, the price cannot be fixed without taking into account the expenditure of socially necessary labor, and it is irrational to fix the price so preposterously.

Further, when fixing prices, low prices should be assigned to the basic consumer goods. It is a matter of course, as I have mentioned above, that the values of commodities should be taken into account in assessing their prices. But this by no means signifies that the price of a commodity cannot be deviated from its value. The working-class party and state should set low prices for the mass consumption goods by deliberately deviating the prices of commodities from their values. That is to say, rice, cloth, footwear, mosquito nets, thread, matches, school articles and other goods indispensable for the people's material and cultural life should be cheap. This means precisely a proper use of the law of value, and accords with the essential requirement of the socialist system to feed and dress all the working people equally and to make them equally well-off.

Otherwise, if we price the basic consumer goods high, we cannot fully display the superiority of the socialist system and may possibly inconvenience the people in their everyday life. If, for example, the prices of fabrics such as the vinalon mixtures much demanded by our people were set high, it would not be possible to have all the people dress decently. And if the prices of such school supplies as textbooks, pencils, notebooks and school-bags were set high, children would not be duly educated despite compulsory education.

Nevertheless, there is a tendency among our functionaries to increase the state budgetary revenues by unwarrantedly raising the prices of fabrics and other basic consumer goods. As a result, though we turn out a large volume of fabrics, 20 meters per capita, the working people cannot afford to buy enough to dress their children well, because the prices are high. No doubt, the major reason why many fabrics do not reach the people is that our country does not yet turn out different kinds of low-cost fabrics. But it should be clearly borne in mind that the erroneous position of the functionaries who seek to secure revenues for the state by raising the price of cloth is also largely accountable for the small cloth supply to the people. Owing to this erroneous act on the part of the functionaries, the prices of fabrics have kept rising unreasonably over the past few years.

Unless our functionaries rectify such wrong ideas and work attitudes the people's living standards cannot be improved rapidly. In fact, it often happens that fabrics do not sell because of their excessive prices and lie on the counter for a long time and at last have to be sold off at reduced prices. This, in the end, will not only be harmful to the people's living conditions but make it impossible to secure the state budgetary revenues.

Our Party and Government, therefore, fix definite rates on sales taxes and assign lower prices as far as the basic consumer goods are concerned and, particularly, see to it that the goods for children are priced so low that their production costs can barely be recovered, even if the state budgetary revenues are not raised. This principle should continue to be observed.

On the contrary, however, articles of luxury, sumptuous goods, high-quality suit material and other things which are in limited supply as yet, should be priced higher than the basic consumer goods in order to control the demand for them. The charges for houses and welfare facilities should also be fixed on the same principle as the prices of commodities. The rents on ordinarily-furnished one- or two-room apartments, for example, should be cheap, but those on well-appointed homes with three or more rooms should be high because we do not have many of them. Of course, when our productive forces are developed highly enough to fully ensure all the goods and facilities needed by the people, it will become unnecessary to go to the trouble of taking such measures.

To fix the prices of commodities correctly, we must make them uniform. The unfair prices found so far in some cases were caused by the failure on the part of the leading functionaries of the State Planning Commission, the Ministry of Finance and some other economic organs to exercise control over the fixing of prices on the goods produced by locally-run enterprises, leaving it up to the chairmen of the provincial people's committees, on the pretext that these goods were supposed to be of only local significance. Therefore, just as the regional planning commissions have been set up to unify planning, regional price commissions should be established to unify the assessment of prices on all goods, including those turned out by the local industry enterprises, and the economic organs such as the State Planning Commission, the Ministry of Finance and the Price Assessment Commission should strengthen their control over the fixing of prices.

3. Problems of the Peasant Market in Socialist Society and of the Way to Abolish It

The peasant market represents a form of trade whereby, at definite places, the peasants sell directly to people part of the agricultural produce, both of the collective economy of the cooperative farms and of the sideline work of individual cooperative members. Though a form of trade in socialist society, the peasant market retains a number of features that have survived from capitalism. What, then, are the capitalist survivals in the peasant market? They are to be found in the fact that in the peasant market prices are determined spontaneously according to supply and demand, and therefore, the law of value operates somewhat blindly. The state does not plan supply and demand or prices for the peasant market. Of course, the spontaneous character of the peasant market undergoes certain restrictions as state trade develops and the coordinating function of the state over the market grows. Yet at the socialist stage the peasant market cannot be done away with completely.

The word *chang* (market—Tr) was engendered neither under the socialist system nor under the capitalist; it is a term that comes to us from feudal society. *Chang* came into being as handicrafts developed in the feudal period. From of old the Koreans call a merchant *changsagun* which means a person who does business at *chang*. Thus, *chang* is a backward form of trade that has its origin in feudal society. It is therefore preferable in principle that there be no peasant market—a backward form of trade —under the advanced, socialist system.

But, since the cooperative economy and individual sideline production are in existence under socialism, it is inevitable that the peasant market exist, and this is not such a bad thing. Some comrades seem to consider that the state should even purchase all the sideline products and supply them in a planned way, but they are wrong, and it is not practicable either. As for individual sideline products, the producers should be allowed to consume them and take the surplus to the market to sell or barter for other goods according to their wish. As for the animal products and industrial crops turned out by the collective economy of cooperative farms, the greater part should be purchased by the state, but part of them should be divided among the peasants. They may consume them or sell them to the purchasing agents or take them to the peasant market for sale. The peasants should not be forced to sell them exclusively to the purchasing agents, but should be allowed to sell them to anybody they like. That is the way to facilitate the people's life.

The textbook of political economy does not give a good account of the peasant market. It only says that the peasant market produces an unfavorable effect on the development of the collective economy and fosters the peasants' petty-bourgeois ideas and selfishness. But no clear account is provided as to why the peasant market is necessary in socialist society, what role it plays and when it can disappear.

There is more good than bad in the continued existence of sideline production and the peasant market in socialist society. We are not yet in a position to supply everything necessary for the people's life in sufficient quantities through state channels, especially miscellaneous goods for daily use like brooms and calabash-ladles, and subsidiary provisions like meat, eggs, sesame, both wild and cultivated. Under the circumstances, what is wrong with individuals producing these things on the side and selling them in the market? Even though it is a backward way, it should still be made use of when the advanced ways are not sufficient to cover everything.

Some functionaries are afraid that sideline production, or the peasant market, could revive capitalism right away. But there is no basis for this fear. If too large kitchen gardens were allotted to cooperative farmers, they might become engrossed in their individual farming, neglecting collective labor, and this could foster capitalist elements. But the kitchen gardens of our farmers are no bigger than a few dozen *pyong* each, and their individual sideline animal raising amounts to no more than a couple of pigs or a dozen chickens or so per household. Just because a peasant grows a few tobacco plants on his garden plot, that will not make it a capitalist economic unit and even if he takes a few chickens to the peasant market and sells them at a somewhat high price, he will not become a capitalist.

But what would happen if the peasant market were abolished by law on the supposed ground that sideline production as well as the peasant market had a harmful effect on the collective economy and fostered selfishness? The market place would disappear, of course, but the black market would remain. Peasants would knock at kitchen-doors or hang around the back streets to sell chickens or eggs they raised on the side. Then they might be caught and fined or otherwise punished by law. So forcible abolition of the peasant market would lead to no solution, but might rather inconvenience the people's life and senselessly turn many people into delinquents.

Therefore, as long as the state cannot produce and supply enough of all the goods necessary for the people's life, we must strictly guard against the "Left" tendency to abolish the peasant market so hastily.

When, then, will individual sideline production and the peasant market disappear?

Firstly, they will disappear only when the country is industrialized, technology highly developed, and there are plenty of all the consumer goods required by the people. No one will bother to go to the peasant market when he can buy anything he wants from state-owned shops, and it will not be offered on the peasant market either. Suppose cheap and good-quality chemical fibers gush forth in plenty from the factories. Then people will not take the trouble to go to the market place to buy expensive cotton; and even if some peasants want to sell it high, it will not sell. Even under the present circumstances, those goods which meet the demands of the people are not traded in the peasant market, they are sold at uniform prices in all parts of our country, alike in big cities such as Hamhung and in remote mountain villages such as Potae-ri at the foot of Mt. Paekdu-san. When goods are plentiful and sold at uniform prices in this way, it amounts to a supply system.

It must be borne in mind, however, that goods which do not meet the demands of the people are traded on the sly or resold at the peasant market, even when uniform prices are fixed on them by the state. It happens that some people buy goods from the shops and hoard them and sell them at higher prices when they are badly needed by others. Let me take the sale of eggs for example. At present we produce eggs at the chicken plants built in Pyongyang and many other places. But we do not yet produce enough of them to meet the people's requirements. So there exists a discrepancy between the state and the peasant-market prices of eggs. Taking advantage of this, the practice of reselling eggs has appeared.

We cannot, of course, be taking the people who have resold some eggs and sending them to prison as criminals. As for other methods of control, we can only take some technical measures such as regulating the volume of sale per buyer. Of course, such measures should also be taken, but all we can do with them is just to limit somewhat the tendency toward concentration of goods in the hands of a few people. Such measures can by no means do away completely with the reselling in the peasant market or black-marketeering.

In order to solve this problem large quantities of goods must be produced. If more egg factories are built and enough eggs are produced to fully meet the needs of the people, black-marketeering in eggs will disappear and buying and selling in the peasant market, too, will naturally come to an end. If the state satisfies the demands of the people in this way and eliminates from the peasant market the goods traded there, one by one, then the peasant market will no longer be needed in the end.

Secondly, individual sideline production and the peasant market will cease to exist only when cooperative ownership is turned into ownership of the entire people.

As was pointed out in the *Theses on the Socialist Rural Question*, too, there will be no more buying and selling in the peasant market when we have converted cooperative property into the property of the entire people by integrating the two forms of ownership while steadily enhancing the leading role of property of the entire people over cooperative property.

One of the major reasons why the peasant market exists at present is that the cooperative and individual sideline economies exist, side by side with the state economy.

Therefore, when the two sorts of ownership are integrated into the single ownership of the entire people, the individual sideline economy will vanish, due to the developed productive forces, and consequently, the peasant market will disappear and the circulation of commodities as a whole will become unnecessary. Then products will be distributed under a supply system. At present, we distribute rice and some other indispensable goods to the workers and office employees under a supply system. Needless to say, this supply system was not introduced because of an abundance of these goods, nor was it introduced under the single ownership of the entire people. We have this system with a view to exercising control so that people eat and live on an equal basis under conditions where goods are not plentiful. The system of produce supply that we intend to introduce, when the productive forces are very highly developed and the two forms of property are welded into the single property of the entire people, will be different from the one we have now for purposes of control; it will be a supply system aimed at providing the people more effectively with the consumer goods turned out in large quantities according to their diverse needs.

To conclude, both the peasant market and black-marketeering will disappear and trade will go over finally to the supply system only when the productive forces have developed to such an extent that the state can turn out and supply enough of all the kinds of goods required by the people, and when cooperative ownership has grown into ownership of the entire people.

ANSWERS TO THE QUESTIONS RAISED BY ALI BALOUT, CORRESPONDENT OF THE LEBANESE NEWSPAPER AL ANWAR

November 22, 1969

Question: *Your Excellency Mr. Premier, you have achieved prodigious successes for the heroic Korean people.*

These successes will be immortal and will serve as a beacon for the people who are working out their destinies through their own efforts. They will also serve as a guide for the people who want to build the best society possible.

Your Excellency Mr. Premier, could you tell the Arab people, through the Lebanese newspaper Al Anwar, *about achievements to be made in the near future under your wise leadership in each of the political, economic, social and cultural domains?*

Answer: To begin with, let me express my thanks to you for your deep appreciation of the successes achieved so far by our people.

The Korean people set great store by all the successes they have made in their struggle to build a new society under the leadership of the Workers' Party of Korea. They have a warranted confidence and great pride in them. But no matter how great our victories may be, we are by no means self-complacent about them. The successes we have already scored in the revolutionary struggle and work of construction are no more than the foundations for further advancing the revolution and winning fresh victories. We are still on the path to revolution. We have more work ahead, more work than we have already done.

Our people should fight not only for the complete victory of socialism in the northern half of the Republic. They must also drive the U.S. imperialists out of south Korea, accomplish the national-liberation revolution and reunify the country. For this purpose, socialist construction in the northern half of the Republic must be pushed forward vigorously, and the revolutionary force in the north, which is the base of the Korean revolution, must also be firmly built up into an invincible force in all fields, political, economic, military and cultural. This is a very weighty and complex revolutionary task. However, our people's revolutionary zeal and fighting spirit is very high and well able to carry it out. Their confidence in victory, too, is firm. Our people have firm confidence not only in their ideals for the distant future but also in the shining prospects of the years immediately ahead.

In the future, as in the past, all the victories of our people will be achieved by observing closely the line of independence, self-support and self-defense—the embodiment of the Juche idea of the Workers' Party of Korea in all fields of state activity.

We will continue to hold fast to the principle of solving all problems arising in our revolution and construction independently. We will solve them in conformity with the Juche idea of the Workers' Party of Korea. In particular, we will pay special attention to firmly arming the entire working people with our Party's Juche idea, and to further revolutionizing and working-classizing them so as to rally them closely around the Party and the Government. By so doing we will transform the political force of our revolution into an invincible power which no force can ever destroy.

The goal we are to achieve in the coming few years in socialist economic construction is huge and inspiring. Our country's economy will develop at a very fast rate, relying on the solid basis of the independent national economy laid by our people during their hard struggle of the past years.

We will continue to push ahead energetically with the technical revolution in all branches of the national economy. In the field of industry, we will strive for complete mechanization and semi-automation and full automation in the next few years. We will thus make the labor of the workers easier and more efficient and expand production on a much larger scale.

There will be a great leap forward especially in the development of branches of heavy industry such as engineering, metal, chemical and mining industries. A radical change will also take place in light industry, including textile, food and daily necessities industries.

At present our people are making the final efforts to reach the climax of the Seven-Year National Economic Plan, a magnificent program of socialist construction. When this plan is fulfilled, our country will be transformed from an industrial-agricultural state into a powerful socialist industrial state and will be able to hold its own among the advanced countries of the world.

Our socialist rural economy will also develop very rapidly. We are planning to complete irrigation and electrification in the next few years and carry out extensive mechanization and chemicalization and widely introduce advanced methods of farming. We will do this by vigorously pushing forward the rural technical revolution in line with the *Theses on the Socialist Rural Question in Our Country*. With the realization of this plan our farmers will be freed to a greater degree from the conditions of arduous and difficult labor under which they have suffered for thousands of years. They will be able to farm in an easy, enjoyable and efficient way with up-to-date farm machines and diverse chemical fertilizers, weed killers, vegetable growth stimulants and other agricultural chemicals. Not only that, with rapid growth in the output of various agricultural products including grain and animal products, our country will become more affluent in food and will be in a position to supply the working people with sufficient nonstaple foodstuffs including meat, eggs and vegetables.

Our science and culture will also advance more rapidly as the nation's political and economic might increases. Scientists and technicians will continue to involve themselves in active research, in order to solve any scientific and technical problems that arise in the building of a more Juche-oriented industry and a more developed socialist agriculture. The state will take measures to enable a far greater number of youths and working people than at present to receive higher education, while, at the same time, consolidating the successes of the already introduced compulsory nine-year technical education. In addition, the entire masses will wage a vigorous struggle to eliminate once and for all the influence of a decayed reactionary imperialist culture and to make our socialist national culture shine more brilliantly.

When these goals have been achieved in all domains of politics, economy and culture, our country's political and economic power will be augmented incomparably and our science and technology, literature and art will be developed onto a new, higher plane, while our people will enjoy a more abundant and cultured life.

It is true that our goals to be achieved are very high and we have many difficulties ahead. We are building socialism under difficult circumstances—our territory is divided into north and south and the maneuverings of U.S. imperialism and its stooges to unleash a new war are becoming more pronounced every day. Therefore, the building of the economy and culture in our country cannot but be hindered to a certain degree. It will meet with various difficulties.

But our people, who have matured in the trials of the revolutionary struggle and have the wise leadership of the Workers' Party of Korea, will courageously surmount all these difficulties and will certainly carry out with credit all their revolutionary assignments, firmly grasping a rifle in one hand and a hammer or sickle in the other.

Question: *The friendly Korean people who enjoy your inspiring leadership have clearly proven that the U.S. gangsters cannot deprive them of their national sovereignty or dampen their desire to drive out the colonialists and reunify their country in the near future.*

Your Excellency Mr. Premier, do you think that the U.S. imperialists are planning new aggression against the heroic Korean people?

Answer: The aggressive maneuverings of the U.S. imperialists in Korea are already widely known to the world. Out of their brigandish ambition to seize the whole of Korea and use it as a springboard for invading Asia and the socialist countries, the U.S. imperialists have turned south Korea into their complete colony and military base for aggression. They have daily continued their maneuverings of aggression and war provocation against the Democratic People's Republic of Korea for more than 20 years, from the first days of their crawling into south Korea till now.

The U.S. imperialists' maneuvers to launch a new war in Korea have become more intensified particularly in the last few years.

The U.S. imperialists' already had enormous aggressive military potentialities in south Korea and, of late, are further stepping up their augmentation. They illegally shipped into south Korea large quantities of tactical nuclear weapons, guided missiles and various other types of weapons of mass destruction in gross violation of the Armistice Agreement. Some time ago, they again brought large numbers of fighter-bombers to the military bases in south Korea and even newly organized what they call the 71st task fleet with scores of war vessels including a nuclear aircraft carrier and large-size battleships, deploying it in the waters off the DPRK.

U.S. imperialism is greatly increasing the numerical strength of the south Korean puppet army and further strengthening its military technical equipment. In particular, the U.S. imperialists have created the so-called "Homeland Reserve Force" with the aim of increasing the number of local mercenaries in south Korea. They have pressganged a huge number of south Korean youths and middle-aged people into it and are hurrying to arm it fully.

Various military bases and military installations have also multiplied rapidly in south Korea.

Meanwhile, the U.S. imperialists perpetrate more frantic armed provocations against the northern half of the Republic. Owing to this there is not a single day when gunfiring does not take place along the Military Demarcation Line.

As was fully exposed through the incident of the U.S. imperialists' armed spy ship *Pueblo* in January last year and the shooting down of their large-size spy plane EC-121 in April this year, the U.S. imperialists have perpetrated their espionage activities more and more openly against our country.

Today the U.S. imperialists have established a "wartime structure" throughout south Korea, issued emergency mobilization orders to the U.S. troops occupying south Korea and to the south Korean puppet army and entered a "special alert" while reinforcing the armed forces along the front line.

All these facts show clearly how frantically the U.S. imperialists are again working to unleash a war of aggression in Korea.

Owing to the naked aggressive maneuvers of the U.S. imperialists, the situation in Korea is so tense and dangerous that war may break out at any moment.

No military threat of the U.S. imperialists, however, can frighten the Korean people. If, in the end, the U.S. imperialists and their stooges unleash a new war against the DPRK, in defiance of our people's patient efforts to prevent war and maintain peace and the unanimous condemnation of the peace-loving people of the world, the Korean people will rise as one in a sacred war to safeguard their beloved country and revolutionary gains. They will completely annihilate the aggressors.

Question: *The imperialist and colonialist press and news agencies try to impair the good relations existing between the DPRK and the Soviet Union, and China, claiming that your young country is leaning to one side in the dispute between the two great socialist powers.*

What effect do you think the continuance of this dispute can have on the unity of the socialist countries in the struggle against world imperialism?

Answer: As you have correctly pointed out, the imperialists and their reptile press are prattling that our country is on the side of this or that country in the differences between the socialist countries. It is nothing but a foolish trick to create antagonism and drive a wedge between our country and other socialist countries. There is nothing strange about the fact that this mean trick is employed by the imperialists and reactionaries of all types throughout the world. They hope the differences between the socialist countries will widen, and are perpetrating all sorts of crafty machinations to weaken and undermine the unity and cohesion of the socialist countries.

The Marxist-Leninist parties are independent and autonomous by nature. Because the Communists are fighters who out of their faith in Marxism-Leninism, struggle for the emancipation of the working class and working people in their own countries and for the freedom and liberation of the world's people, they hold fast to their independent conviction and fight on for it unyieldingly, through any adversity. If the Communists lose independence and autonomy and follow in others' steps, they cannot uphold principle and consistency in their lines and policies, and this will, in the long run, not only spoil the revolution and work of construction in their own countries, but also inflict a great setback to the progress of the international communist movement and world revolution.

Our Party, guided by the Juche idea in its activities, is a revolutionary party that adheres solely to the principles of Marxism-Leninism and determines all its lines and policies independently, to suit the actual conditions of our country. Our Party develops its struggle against imperialism and opportunism of all hues not blindly on orders or instructions from anyone else, but always on the basis of its own faith. Firmly maintaining independence in our activities in this way, we endeavor to unite with friends fighting for the common goal on the principles of Marxism-Leninism and proletarian internationalism. We also strive to learn from their experiences if they are worthy of learning, when they conform to Marxist-Leninist principles and when they suit our actual conditions. The fraternal parties, too, fully understand this position of our Party and consider it correct.

No crafty maneuver of the imperialists and reactionaries can impair the independent, principled position of our Party and Government or weaken the unity between our country and other socialist countries.

As for the differences between the socialist countries, they are, in all cases, ideological and theoretical differences existing between class brothers who have the same political and economic basis and fight against imperialism and colonialism for the common goal of building socialism and communism. These differences do not express antagonistic contradictions such as those between the imperialist powers or between nations with differing social systems; they are merely temporary differences which arise from different views on such questions as how to appraise the present times, how to fight imperialism and support the liberation struggle of the peoples. They are rooted in the different historical and geographical conditions of each socialist country, different national duties and different understandings of Marxism-Leninism.

In the course of the joint struggle against imperialism, the peoples of the socialist countries will eventually overcome their differences and march forward shoulder to shoulder in their battle for victory in the common cause of building socialism and communism.

Question: *Your Excellency Mr. Premier, you are probably well aware that the Arab people are suffering from the continued aggression of Israel, an aggressive country, and its patron, the United States, and that more than two million Arabs have been driven away from their native land.*

Could you please give us your opinion of the Middle East crisis?

Answer: The Middle East crisis has resulted from the aggressive maneuvers of the imperialists headed by U.S. imperialism, who, putting up the Zionists as a "shock force," are trying to suffocate the growing anti-imperialist national-liberation struggle of the Arab people and bring this area under their control. It is entirely because of the brazen aggressive machinations of the Israeli aggressors and their manipulators, the U.S. imperialists, that the crisis has not yet been solved and the situation in the Middle East remains tense.

The anti-U.S., anti-Israeli struggle waged by the Arab people today is a righteous struggle to safeguard national independence and dignity, to restore the usurped Arab territory and accomplish the Palestinian people's cause of liberation.

The Korean people resolutely condemn the U.S. imperialists and the Zionists for their aggressive maneuvers in the Middle East, fully support the Arab people in their just struggle and express firm solidarity with them.

Question: *Your Excellency Mr. Premier, you triumphantly*

organized and led the guerrilla warfare against the Japanese invaders and fought for 15 long years, thereby bringing a great victory to the Korean people in the end.

Today the Arab people of Palestine have begun their liberation war in the occupied areas following the path you opened up.

Then, what advice could you give the Arab guerrillas from the experience of your glorious struggle?

Answer: The Palestinian people have started the armed guerrilla struggle against the U.S. imperialists and their faithful stooges, the Zionists. This is the correct way of achieving freedom and liberation.

You have asked me to give some advice to the Arab guerrillas, but I would like to tell you briefly about our experience of struggle rather than giving advice.

As you know, the fine sons and daughters of the Korean people had waged an arduous anti-Japanese armed struggle for 15 long years under the leadership of the Communists and defeated the Japanese imperialist aggressors, thereby accomplishing the historic task of the country's liberation. The Korean people's anti-Japanese armed struggle was the highest form of national-liberation struggle to resist the counterrevolutionary forces with their own revolutionary forces. During this struggle we underwent many trials and gained valuable experience.

Our experience shows that the oppressed people must resolutely fight against their oppressors in order to achieve the country's liberation and national independence, and that armed combat is the most active and the most decisive form of that struggle.

History has not yet seen any instance of the imperialists making a gift of independence to colonial peoples, nor any case of a people deprived of their country that received independence from others without waging a struggle themselves. That is why, in order to restore the lost country and achieve genuine national freedom and independence, the oppressed people need to discard all illusions about imperialism. Only by an active struggle against imperialism, can they advance the revolution and accomplish the cause of liberation.

The imperialists leave no stone unturned in maintaining their colonial rule and, with the approach of their doom, they become all the more desperate. The imperialists cruelly and ruthlessly suppress the liberation struggle of the colonial peoples by using all the machinery of power and violence at their disposal. That is exactly what the Japanese imperialists did in Korea before. Therefore, the Korean Communists had to rise in arms and fight for the restoration of the fatherland and we finally won victory after waging a long, arduous armed struggle. Violence must be countered with violence and counterrevolutionary forces must be smashed by revolutionary violence. The experience of the people's liberation struggle shows that a struggle which begins on a small scale develops gradually into a massive struggle and can emerge victorious in the end. We are firmly convinced that the Palestinian people who have embarked on the road to liberation with arms in their hands will certainly triumph if they have firm confidence in victory and stubbornly carry on the armed struggle to the last in all areas, whether the scale of the struggle is big or small.

To ensure steady growth of the revolutionary forces is one of the basic conditions for winning victory in the revolutionary struggle. Throughout our anti-Japanese armed struggle, therefore, we set as the most important task the building up of the revolutionary forces of our own and we persevered energetically to that end.

Our primary concern was directed, first of all, at strengthening the Anti-Japanese Guerrilla Army politically, ideologically and militarily, in order to consolidate the revolutionary forces. We endeavored to ensure the organizational and ideological purity and unity of purpose of the anti-Japanese guerrilla ranks and equip all the guerrillas with the firm consciousness of Juche, ardent patriotism and warm revolutionary comradeship and voluntary discipline. Also, we improved the military equipment of the guerrilla army with weapons captured from the enemies in the course of incessant battles with them. We further expanded and developed the guerrilla ranks.

While strengthening the Anti-Japanese Guerrilla Army, we strove to lay the firm mass basis of revolution and unite all the masses who loved the country and nation, to organize and mobilize them to the revolutionary struggle.

In view of the fact that the armed struggle was being waged

in the form of guerrilla warfare, it was very important that we
strengthened the ties between the anti-Japanese guerrillas and
the masses of the people, induced the people to render support
and encouragement in every way to the guerrillas and actively
organized and mobilized them in the anti-Japanese struggle.

Under the slogan of "As the fish cannot live without water,
so the guerrillas cannot live without the people," the
Anti-Japanese Guerrilla Army strove for closer kinship with the
people anywhere anytime. They also worked to rally all the
anti-imperialist forces around the armed struggle and combine
this struggle with diverse forms of mass struggle under the
correct strategical and tactical leadership. The founding on
May 5, 1936 of the Association for the Restoration of the
Fatherland, the first organization of the anti-Japanese national
united front in our country, was an event of epochal significance
in consolidating the mass basis of revolution. With the founding
of the association, the anti-Japanese national united front
movement developed more organizationally, systematically and
rapidly on a nationwide scale in close combination with the
anti-Japanese armed struggle. It became possible firmly to
organize and mobilize all the anti-imperialist forces in the
struggle to liberate the country.

The strengthening of the Anti-Japanese Guerrilla Army,
consolidation of the mass basis of revolution, close combination
of the anti-Japanese armed struggle with diverse forms of mass
struggles—all these constituted an important factor in our
victory in the anti-Japanese national-liberation struggle.

Victory will be hastened if the Palestinian people strengthen
their armed guerrilla force organizationally, ideologically and
militarily, lay the solid mass basis of the struggle, closely rally
all the revolutionary and all the mass organizations so as to
cement the unity of the revolutionary forces and, further,
vigorously wage the anti-U.S., anti-Israeli struggle on a
nationwide and all-Arab scale in firm unity with the entire Arab
people.

Availing myself of this opportunity, I sincerely wish the
Palestinian people greater victories in their guerrilla struggle
for the liberation of their country.

REPORT TO THE FIFTH CONGRESS OF THE WORKERS' PARTY OF KOREA ON THE WORK OF THE CENTRAL COMMITTEE (Excerpt)

November 2, 1970

Comrades,

Nine years have elapsed since the Fourth Congress of our Party, at which a magnificent program of socialist construction was drawn up. This has been a period of harsh trial, in which very complex and difficult circumstances were created in our revolution and construction, but it has also been a proud period, in which revolutionary events of great historic significance have occurred in our people's advance toward socialism and communism.

During the period under review, audaciously breaking through manifold hardships and obstacles, our Party opportunely convened a conference and plenary meetings in order to take stock of the changes in the situation and presented unique strategic and tactical policies for successfully promoting the Korean revolution as a whole and skillfully organized and mobilized the masses of the people for their implementation.

Thanks to the wise leadership of the Party, great victories and achievements have been obtained on all fronts of socialist construction, and the revolutionary base of the northern half of the Republic has been consolidated as firmly as a rock.

The impact of our brilliant successes in socialist construction in the northern half of the Republic has given added momentum to the revolutionary advance of the broad masses of the people—the workers, peasants, student youth and intellectuals —in south Korea, and the colonial rule there of the U.S. imperialists has been shaken to the core.

During the years we are reviewing our Party has waged a dynamic struggle, holding aloft the banner of Marxism-Leninism and proletarian internationalism, the revolutionary banner of anti-imperialist, anti-U.S. struggle, and thereby enhanced our country's international prestige still further and contributed greatly to the general advance of the revolutionary movement all over the world.

In the course of its arduous struggle for the revolution and construction, our Party has developed into a militant party capable of weathering any storm, into an invincible revolutionary party all of whose members are closely united with one idea and purpose around the Party's Central Committee and maintain ties of kinship with the masses.

Today we are to greet the Fifth Congress of the Workers' Party of Korea, the organizer and inspirer of all the victories of our people, with deep conviction in the justness of our cause and with great pride and self-respect in the tremendous achievements attained by our people under the leadership of the Party. All our Party members and working people, our overseas compatriots and our close friends in other lands, warmly congratulate us on this congress and wish us success in our work.

This congress will mark another milestone in our Party's struggle to consolidate and develop the socialist system in our country, give powerful support to the revolutionary struggle of the south Korean people, achieve the independent reunification of our homeland and cement solidarity for our revolution all over the world. It will powerfully encourage and inspire our Party members and the entire Korean people to new and greater victories.

I. Great Results

Comrades,

The Fourth Congress of our Party reviewed our historic victory in building the foundations of socialism and adopted a magnificent Seven-Year Plan, the main tasks of which were to carry out all-round technological reconstruction and a cultural revolution and to radically improve the people's standard of living, relying on our firmly established socialist system; and it forcefully roused our entire people to the struggle for its realization.

All our Party members and working people, hopefully confident of their bright future, rose in the struggle to implement the new, militant program set forth at the Party congress and successfully carried the great Seven-Year Plan into effect, coming up with fresh innovations and miraculous achievements every day.

However, our revolution and construction have been faced with great difficulties and hardships during the past few years, as the aggressive maneuverings of the U.S. imperialists have become more and more blatant and as a complex situation has developed in the international communist movement. This state of affairs urgently required our Party to arm all our people firmly with the revolutionary ideas of Marxism-Leninism and, in particular, to lead them to make thoroughgoing politico-ideological preparations for coping with war. At the same time it also demanded that the Party direct tremendous additional efforts to strengthening our nation's defenses, even if this should mean a readjustment of the rate of development of the national economy, so that we would possess a strong national defense that would guarantee the security of our country and people.

The Party held a historic Conference in October 1966 at which it took steps to build up our revolutionary ranks politically and ideologically and to reorganize all the work of socialist construction in line with the requirements of the prevailing situation; it also advanced a new revolutionary line of simultaneously carrying on economic and defense construction in order to strengthen our defense capabilities in the light of the intensified aggressive machinations of the enemy. In view of this, it was decided to extend the Seven-Year Plan for three years.

Ensuing developments have clearly shown that the measures taken by the Party suited the fundamental interests of our revolution extremely well and that they were daring, active and intelligent measures for dealing with the changing situation. All our Party members and working people, true to the new revolutionary line put forward by the Party, have waged a heroic fight on the two fronts of economic and defense construction, fulfilling the Seven-Year Plan creditably, achieving firm politico-ideological unity throughout our society and turning our entire country into a mighty fortress that can stand up against any surprise attack by the enemy.

1. Conversion of Our Country into a Socialist Industrial State

Comrades,

Our greatest achievement in socialist construction during the period under review is that the country has been converted into a socialist industrial state as a result of our splendid fulfillment of the historic task of socialist industrialization.

Socialist industrialization was vital to reinforcing our socialist system and furthering socialist construction in the northern half of the Republic. And it was the cardinal task of the Seven-Year Plan.

Relying on the foundations of an independent national industry and the material base laid for introducing modern technology in all branches of the national economy during the period of the Five-Year Plan, our Party saw to it that a powerful struggle was waged under the Seven-Year Plan to create a comprehensively developed, independent modern industry with a solid raw material base of its own and the latest techniques, and to effect the overall technological reconstruction of our national economy.

In accord with the correct policy of the Party, our industry developed very rapidly, and its outlook changed radically under the Seven-Year Plan.

Thanks to the successful implementation of the Seven-Year Plan in the field of industry, the value of our gross industrial output this year will be 11.6 times that of 1956—13.3 times as much in the manufacture of the means of production and 9.3 times as much in consumer goods. This means that industrial production has made a great annual increase of 19.1%, averaged over the entire period of industrialization from 1957 to 1970. Today our industry makes as many industrial products in just 12 days as were turned out in the preliberation year of 1944.

Industry as a whole has developed rapidly, and this is especially true of heavy industry.

In the period of the Seven-Year Plan our Party made sure that emphasis was laid primarily on the improvement and reinforcement of the key branches of heavy industry, while, at the same time, extensive work was carried out to expand and consolidate our heavy industry bases. As a result of this policy, our heavy industry became fully equipped, with its own powerful machine-building industry at the core, and its strength was increased beyond compare during the period we are reviewing.

The greatest success achieved in the growth of heavy industry was precisely the establishment of our own machine-building industry, the basis for the development of our national economy and technological progress.

Owing to the great efforts directed by the Party to the development of the machine-building industry under the Seven-Year Plan, our country—which could not even make simple farm implements properly before liberation—is now in a position to manufacture such large machines as 6,000-ton power presses, heavy-duty trucks, large tractors, excavators, bulldozers, electric and diesel locomotives, vessels of the 5,000-ton class, and precision machines; it can also produce not only individual machine units and pieces of equipment but also complete sets of equipment for outfitting modern factories. Under the Seven-Year Plan alone, our machine-building industry produced and supplied aggregate plants for more than 100 modern factories, including power stations and metallurgical and chemical plants.

The power bases of the country, too, have been further consolidated to meet the demands of our rapid industrial development and overall technical revolution. Giant hydro- and thermo-power plants were built during the Seven-Year Plan, with the result that the total generating capacity of our country has grown considerably, the one-sidedness of the electric power industry—which had relied exclusively upon hydraulic power—has been eliminated and the nation's power bases have been consolidated qualitatively.

Rapid development of the ferrous metallurgical industry was one of the key tasks in achieving overall industrialization. Under the Seven-Year Plan our iron-producing bases were expanded and a new iron works was built in the western region. This resulted in an increase in our pig and granulated iron production capacity, the strengthening of an independent iron industry, rapid progress in the production of steel—particularly rolled steel—and the setting up of a number of new second-stage metal-processing branches. Our country's ferrous metallurgical industry, equipped with perfect production processes for everything from pig iron to steel, rolled steel and goods of second-stage metal processing, has become a powerful branch, and it can now satisfy all our demands for different metals needed to develop our national economy.

The look of the chemical industry, as well, has undergone a fundamental change. During the period of industrialization, the bases of our chemical-fertilizer production were reinforced and a new branch producing agricultural chemicals and other branches producing vinalon and other synthetic fibers and synthetic resins were created. Thus, powerful bases for both an organic and an inorganic chemical industry have been laid in our country, enabling us to further step up the use of chemicals in our national economy.

Rapid progress has also been made in the coal industry, mining industry, building-materials industry and in other branches of heavy industry.

This year our heavy industry will turn out 16,500 million kwh of electricity, 27.5 million tons of coal, 2.2 million tons of steel, 1.5 million tons of chemical fertilizers and 4 million tons of cement.

Our heavy industry, with a powerful machine-building industry at its core, is a guarantee of the country's political and economic independence. In addition, as the solid material foundation for the accelerated development of our national economy, it plays a great role in developing light industry and agriculture and in bettering our nation's defenses.

Great headway has also been made in the development of

light industry. The Party, firmly maintaining its policy of concurrently developing large-scale nationally-controlled industries and medium and small-scale local industries for the production of consumption goods, saw to it that modern factories of centrally run light industry were established under the Seven-Year Plan while, at the same time, many local industry factories were set up with local reserves and the technological reconstruction of this industry was actively pushed ahead along with the development of heavy industry. As a result our country now has all sectors of light industry production, including a textile industry with an annual capacity of more than 400 million meters of high-quality fabric, a food industry and industry for daily necessities. Moreover, up-to-date light industry bases have been set up which can fully meet our working people's demand for consumer goods ranging from draperies to products for cultural use.

With its rapid advance and great expansion, industry came to play a more decisive role in the production of gross national product and national income. Industry's share in the value of our total industrial and agricultural output rose from 34% in 1956 to 74% in 1969, and its share in our national income from industrial and agricultural production increased from 25 to 65% during the same period.

Furthermore, there has been a marked rise in the per capita output of basic manufactured goods, an important index to a nation's economic strength and level of industrial development. This year the per capita output of our country will be 1,184 kwh of electricity, 1,975 kilograms of coal, 158 kilograms of steel, 108 kilograms of chemical fertilizers and 287 kilograms of cement. This proves that our country has caught up with the advanced industrial countries in the per capita output of major industrial products and surpassed them in some items.

The task of effecting an overall technical revolution has also been successful in every field of the national economy, thanks to our powerful heavy industry bases. With the development of our machine-building and other heavy industries, the technical equipment available for use in all fields of our national economy has been radically improved. Moreover, electrification and automation have been introduced on a large scale throughout our national economy.

Powerfully supported by heavy industry, we have also

realized the technological reconstruction of our rural economy successfully.

The Party has directed great efforts to this technological reorganization, following the policy set forth at its Fourth Congress, particularly, along the path indicated by the *Theses on the Socialist Rural Question in Our Country* adopted at the Eighth Plenary Meeting of the Fourth Central Committee of the Party in 1964, and it has achieved brilliant successes in this field.

The most noteworthy success attained in the rural technical revolution during the period under review is the completion of all our irrigation projects.

We pushed work ahead on large-scale irrigation projects while, at the same time, making maximum use of the existing facilities, thereby completing the irrigation of our paddyfields and irrigating many non-paddyfields as well. Great efforts had also been made by the state on drainage projects over the past few years; consequently the major rice-producing areas of our country are now completely freed of the harmful effects of stagnant water. Large numbers of river improvement projects, dyke projects for controlling tidewater and reforestation works were undertaken all over the country, and paddy and dry fields and crops have been better protected against natural disasters. In short, during the period we are reviewing a perfect irrigation system has been established in our country, ensuring rich, stable harvests every year, regardless of the weather, be it flood or drought.

The Party singled out mechanization as the principal task in the rural technical revolution under the Seven-Year Plan and worked hard to carry it out. During the period under review, the number of farm-machine stations, the bases of rural mechanization, increased considerably, and they were set up in every city and county throughout our country. Also, countless new farm machines were introduced in the rural areas. The number of tractors serving the rural economy was multiplied by 3.3—and trucks, by 6.4—between 1961 and 1969, and several kinds of new farm machines were devised and manufactured so that more of our farm work could be done with the help of machines.

The task of electrification in the countryside was also

admirably carried out under the Seven-Year Plan. An all-out campaign was waged to guarantee that not one *ri* or farmhouse was left without electricity, and as a result, every *ri* in our country now has electricity and every farmhouse has electric lights. In the countryside electricity is used extensively not only in the home life of the farmers but also as a source of power for machines and of heat in agricultural production. Annual consumption of electricity in the countryside today amounts to 1000 million kwh, most of which is used in production. The proportion of our total electric power output that is consumed in rural areas is considerable, and our country already compares favorably with the advanced countries in the field of rural electrification.

We have also made great progress in the use of chemicals in agriculture. There was 3.2 times as much chemical fertilizer applied per *chongbo* of paddy and dry fields last year as in 1960, and the qualitative composition of these fertilizers was markedly improved. In addition, an increase in the use of chemical sprays meant that crops were better protected against blights and harmful insects and the countryside had large supplies of highly effective herbicides.

All branches of agricultural production made rapid progress as the rural technical revolution gathered headway.

Despite some fluctuations in agricultural production caused by unusually severe natural disasters which hit our country repeatedly during the past few years, we reaped a good harvest every year, and this year we have also brought in a bumper crop. Our food problem has now been completely solved, and a firm basis of grain production has been laid which will allow us to develop all other fronts of our rural economy more rapidly. Having laid the solid material and technical foundations for stockbreeding, our country's animal husbandry has entered a new phase of development based on modern techniques. The poultry industry has experienced an especially noteworthy advance in the past few years, and now, by using industrial methods we can produce over 700 million eggs and large numbers of chickens every year.

The electrification of our railways is one of many major achievements wrought in the technological reconstruction of our national economy. Under the Seven-Year Plan 850 kilometers of railway have been switched over to electric traction so that the electrification of the major trunk lines has been substantially completed.

All this shows that the historic task of socialist industrialization has been carried out successfully in our country and that a once colonial agrarian land far removed from modern, technical civilization has now been turned into a socialist industrial state with modern industry and highly developed agriculture.

Comrades,

The implementation of the Party's line of industrialization was far from an easy task; there were many obstacles and hardships that had to be overcome by our people who turned out to create a modern industry and effect the technological reconstruction of our national economy.

What industry we inherited from the former, colonial society was negligible, and even that was almost entirely destroyed in the war unleashed by the U.S. imperialist aggressors. During the postwar Three-Year Plan we successfully rebuilt our war-ravaged national economy, but the colonial lopsidedness of industry was not fully eradicated and the foundations of our heavy industry were extremely weak. We had limited funds, insufficient raw and other materials and only a small technical force. Moreover, we had to wage our struggle to achieve the industrialization and the technological reconstruction of our national economy in the midst of the highly complicated internal and external conditions faced by our revolution, outstanding of which is the strained situation caused by the ever intensified maneuverings of the U.S. imperialist occupying forces and their lackeys in south Korea, who are trying to provoke another war.

In spite of these difficulties, our Party carried through the line of socialist industrialization without the slightest vacillation, correctly leading our people to a tremendous display of revolutionary self-reliance, as a result of which they solved all the difficult and intricate problems that arose in the course of creating a modern industry and achieving the technological reconstruction of our national economy without recourse to outside aid.

All of our working people, upholding the Party's line, joined in the struggle for the socialist industrialization of our country and the technological reconstruction of the national economy.

Responding to the Party's call, "Let us rush forward at the speed of Chollima!" our heroic working class and the rest of the working people waged an untiring battle to implement the Party's line of industrialization, smashing any passivism and conservatism that stood in the way and overcoming all hardships and difficulties.

Thanks to both the accuracy of the Party's line of industrialization and its wise leadership in carrying this line out, and to the heroic and devoted struggle of our people in their work, the difficult and complex task of industrialization—which took the capitalist countries a full century or even a few centuries—has been creditably accomplished in our country, in a short time, in only 14 years.

The conversion of our country into a socialist industrial state is an event of great historic significance in the struggle to accelerate the building of socialism and communism in our country and attain a nationwide victory for the Korean revolution.

With the accomplishment of socialist industrialization our country has been provided with the firm material and technical foundations for socialism and is now capable of meeting all the demands of its economic and defense construction as well as the people's needs for industrial products and agricultural produce. The conversion of our country into an industrial state as a result of industrialization turned our revolutionary base into an impregnable fortress and provided us with a solid asset for powerfully supporting the revolutionary struggle of our compatriots in south Korea and securing the reunification of our homeland and its future prosperity.

With the founding of an independent, modern industry and the introduction of modern technology in all the branches of the national economy, including agriculture, our country has finally done away with the economic and technical backwardness it inherited from the old society and has joined the ranks of the advanced countries of the world as full-fledged member. Our people, never again to suffer all those insults and contempts because of their backward economy, can now proudly enter the international arena as a mighty and advanced nation on an equal basis with all the other nations of the world, large and small.

2. Achievements in the Cultural Revolution

Comrades,

The cultural revolution was a matter of tremendous importance in our country, formerly a backward colonial, semi-feudal state. The Party has always given the most careful attention to combatting the cultural backwardness that was our legacy from the old society and to developing, as rapidly as possible, a new, socialist national culture, and it has worked especially hard in this regard during the period covered by the Seven-Year Plan.

In its work to bring about the cultural revolution, the Party attached primary importance to public education and the training of our own cadres, giving top priority to these tasks. It took a series of radical measures aimed at training the younger generation to be able builders of socialism and communism and at creating large numbers of technicians and specialists, in keeping with the swift pace of the technical revolution.

The most important success achieved in the work of public education during the period under review was the introduction of universal compulsory nine-year technical education. Based on the further consolidation of successes achieved under the compulsory secondary education system which had been introduced earlier, this system of universal compulsory nine-year technical education was put into practice by our Party from 1967. As a result, all children and young people in our country from the ages of 7 to 16 receive free, compulsory technical education at regular schools. This compulsory nine-year technical education, a full embodiment of the Marxist-Leninist theory on education, is the most advanced educational system that blends general studies with basic technical training, education with productive labor.

While putting compulsory nine-year technical education into effect, we have paid close attention to improving the content and methods of our teaching. In line with the correct educational policy of the Party, our socialist science of teaching has been further perfected, Juche and the working-class line have been fully integrated in our school education and the quality of our scientific and theoretical training has been raised even higher.

Benefiting from the compulsory nine-year technical education, the members of our younger generation today are all reliably growing into a new communist type of men with all-round capabilities, able builders of a new society who are firmly armed with the Juche idea of our Party and have a wide general knowledge and a mastery of the fundamentals of modern science and technology. With members of the younger generation who have completed their compulsory technical education now starting to join all fronts of socialist construction in large numbers, the ranks of our educated working people are steadily increasing and the general technical and cultural levels of our society are being raised.

The introduction of compulsory nine-year technical education is a great victory for the educational policy of our Party, marking another milestone in our country's cultural revolution.

The realities of rapid socialist construction called for more technicians and specialists. In view of the practical requirements of socialist construction, our Party continued to exert great efforts to train technicians and specialists and achieved many successes in this field as well. During the period we are reviewing the number of institutions of higher education increased from 78 to 129, and 376 higher technical schools were newly established to train technicians and specialists in large numbers. Paralleling our regular system of higher education, various plans offering higher education for those who are on the job have also made progress.

Today more than 497,000 engineers, assistant engineers and specialists—4.3 times as many as in 1960—are working in the various fields of our national economy, excellently managing and operating state and economic organizations, scientific and cultural institutions, modern factories and enterprises and cooperative farms with their own talents and efforts.

In line with our Party's correct educational policy, comprehensive bases for training cadres have been firmly established all over the country. At present, we have at least one higher technical school or higher school in every county, higher technical schools and colleges in the factories in our major industrial districts, and agricultural colleges, schools of medicine, normal colleges, teachers' training institutes, colleges for kindergarten teachers, communist colleges and various other colleges in all the provinces. Thus, all local areas are excellently training the technical personnel, Party officials and state administrative personnel they need, in line with their specific conditions.

As they have come to basically meet their demands for cadres, our localities have eliminated their previous dependence on the central authorities for cadres and are now in a position to tackle their tasks in socialist construction more satisfactorily through their own efforts. The establishment of the comprehensive bases for training cadres in the local areas is of great significance, as well, in raising the cultural levels of all parts of the country to a uniform high. These colleges and higher technical schools, distributed throughout the provincial and county seats and other localities, are the bases of the cultural revolution. They have contributed greatly to introducing modern technical civilization in the local areas and raising the cultural and technical levels of the working people. This shows that our work in education and in training cadres for the nation has attained a very high level, and that a solid foundation has been laid for training greater numbers of technical personnel and specialists in the future.

Socialism and communism cannot be built with the knowledge of a few people alone; they can be successfully built only by arming the broad masses of the working people with a vast knowledge of nature and society. Over the past period our Party has gone all out to raise the general cultural and technical levels of the working people while simultaneously pushing ahead with the training of technical personnel. Thanks to the strengthening of adult education and the improvement of our radio propaganda and press coverage and circulation, the general cultural and technical levels of the working people have been raised appreciably, and the Party's policy of having every working man and woman master at least one technical skill is bearing good fruit. As a result, all our working people are now taking part, purposefully and with a definite degree of knowledge and techniques, in the dedicated struggle to remake nature and society.

During the period under review, great advances have also been made in the field of science. Upholding the Party's policy of firmly establishing Juche in scientific research, our scientists succeeded in solving a number of pressing scientific and technical problems by directing their efforts to research aimed at further increasing the independence of our national economy, thus making a great contribution to socialist construction in our country.

Our socialist literature and art are in their heyday. Thanks to the successful implementation of the Party's policy in this area, all revisionist elements and restorationist tendencies have been removed. Our writers and artists are all busy creating revolutionary literature and art works thoroughly based on the working-class line; and workers, farmers and broad sections of other working people are actively participating in literary and artistic activities. Our literature and art have become the literature and art of the Party, of the revolution and of the people in the truest sense of the term and are becoming a powerful means in educating our working people along communist lines.

Having successfully fulfilled the tasks of the cultural revolution, our country has now become a land where all the people, young and old, are studying, a land where science and socialist literature and art are developing and flowering on every hand. The cultural backwardness which we inherited from the old society has been overcome, and the centuries-old desire of our people to lead a cultured, happy life is being fully realized in the era of the Workers' Party.

3. Consolidation of the Political and Ideological Unity of All the People

Comrades,

During the period under review, our Party has made strenuous effort to educate and transform the masses of our people, rallying them closely around the Party and further strengthening our revolutionary ranks.

The policy invariably followed by our Party in building up the revolutionary ranks and cementing the politico-ideological unity of society was that of pushing ahead energetically with the work of revolutionizing and working-classizing the working people, while strengthening the dictatorship over the hostile elements through a proper combination of the class and mass lines. This correct combination of dictatorship with democracy, of class struggle with the work of strengthening the unity and cohesion of the people, along with the winning over of broad masses while isolating a tiny handful of hostile elements, is a fundamental requirement of the revolution and a basic work method of the Communists. The Party has put a lot of energy into strengthening its revolutionary ranks politically and ideologically, guarding against both the "Leftist" tendency to ignore the unity and solidarity of the working class, cooperative farmers and laboring intellectuals—which constitutes the basis of our social relations—and to lay undue emphasis on the class struggle, distrusting and shunning people for no reason at all, and the Rightist tendency to neglect the class struggle against hostile elements and the survivals of outmoded ideologies and focus all attention on the unity and cohesion of the masses of the people.

It is essential that we isolate and put down all hostile elements in order to be able to reinforce our revolutionary ranks and ensure the success of our revolutionary struggle and work of construction. Our Party has opportunely smashed all attempts to weaken the class struggle and has wielded proletarian dictatorship as an effective weapon in that struggle.

In the recent past some of our people, following this ideological trend toward Rightist capitulationism which appeared in the international communist movement, asserted that the class struggle came to an end with the establishment of a socialist system and there was no need to exercise a dictatorship over the remnants of the overthrown exploiting classes. We made a powerful attack on these dangerous revisionist ideas promptly and utterly routed them.

Our Party stood firm by the principle of educating the broad masses, actively drawing them in the struggle against counterrevolution and bringing them to a class awakening through struggle against the enemy. Under the Party's correct guidance we fought energetically against the counterrevolutionary elements as an all-Party, all-people movement smashing the conspiratorial maneuverings of our class enemy before it was too late and completely isolating the handful of hostile elements, firmly safeguarding the gains of our revolution and further solidifying its class position.

During the period we are reviewing, our Party vigorously pushed ahead with the work of revolutionizing and working-classizing the whole of society, while increasing the dictatorship over the hostile elements.

This work is a requirement of the law that guides the construction of socialism and communism, and is one of the most important responsibilities of the dictatorship of the proletariat after the establishment of the socialist system. In the period of the socialist transformation of production relations the task of liquidating the exploiting classes and turning all the working people into socialist working people is of paramount importance. However, the principal task after the establishment of the socialist system is that of reeducating all the working people as members of the working class from the point of view of both their socio-economic status and their ideological and moral qualities, thus gradually doing away with class distinctions and turning them into true builders of socialism and communism.

In carrying through the policy of revolutionization and working-classization of the whole of society, our Party has firmly maintained the principle of steadily enhancing the leadership role of the working class and of educating and remolding the farmers and intellectuals on the pattern of the working class.

In this strengthening of the leading role of the working class in the building of socialism and communism so that it may carry out its historic mission, it is imperative that its ideological and cultural levels be raised and its organization increased and that it temper itself in all aspects in a more revolutionary manner. Ours is a young working class with a number of characteristic features in its development. The ranks of our working class which had not been very large, registered a sharp rise in a short period of time as industry developed by leaps and bounds following liberation, and our workers were joined by a large number of erstwhile peasants, small traders, handicraftsmen and members of the younger generation who had had no revolutionary training.

Our Party therefore waged a powerful struggle to revolutionize the working class. The Party stepped up its politico-ideological work among the workers in order to increase their class consciousness and lead them to steel themselves perseveringly in productive activities, and went all out to strengthen the ranks of the working class organizationally and ideologicaly. As a result, the vanguard role of the working class in revolution and construction and its revolutionary influence on the working people have grown. Our working class is now fulfilling its honorable mission creditably as the leading class in the Korean revolution.

Working-classizing and revolutionizing the farmers, a main detachment of our revolution, is one of the basic prerequisites for creating a classless society and assuring the victory of the cause of socialism and communism.

As there have never been many hired farm hands in our country, our rural population consists mainly of former poor and middle peasants. A small proprietor's mentality, egoism and other obsolete ideas are thus deeply rooted in their minds. Our farmers not only lag behind the working class technically and culturally; they are far behind ideologically, as well. The socialist revolution has wrought a radical change in the socio-economic position of the farmers and also effected a great change in their ideological awareness, but the lag of the farmers behind the advanced working class in ideology remains a major contributing factor to the class distinctions that still exist between our working class and farmers even after the establishment of the socialist system.

During the period under review, our Party has paid special attention to intensifying the ideological revolution as well as the technical and cultural revolutions in the countryside. The strengthening of our farmers' ideological education and organized life as well as their training through socialist collective labor all led to a marked rise in their level of ideological awareness and a further promotion of their collectivist spirit and organization. As the technical and cultural revolutions progressed successfully in the countryside, the technological and cultural levels of our farmers rose ever higher, and their socio-economic position approximated that of the working class. Today our farmers, reliable allies of the working class and genuine masters of socialist construction, are staunchly defending the rural outposts of socialism.

Our Party has all along devoted much effort to including our intellectuals, as well as our workers and farmers, in the revolutionizing, working-classizing process.

One major task facing a Marxist-Leninist party which has

assumed power is how to correctly solve the problem of the old intellectuals who served the old society, while at the same time training new intellectuals. Fundamentally speaking, the intelligentsia, as a social stratum, has a dual nature: it can serve not only the exploiting classes, but the working class as well. Most of the old intellectuals in our country came from wealthy families and served the exploiter society in the past. But, as intellectuals of a colonial and semi-feudal society, they were subjected to racial oppression and discrimination by the Japanese imperialists and, therefore, the majority of them had anti-imperialist leanings and a democratic, revolutionary spirit. In view of these characteristic features of the old intellectuals, our Party adopted a policy of active transformation and patiently educated them, while, at the same time, training large numbers of new intellectuals from among the working people. Now, in the stage of socialist construction, the question of the dual nature of the old intellectuals, that is, who they serve, has been solved, and there remains only the question of how best they may serve the working class and other working people.

During the period of socialist construction, when an all-out battle against bourgeois and petty-bourgeois ideas is the order of the day, our Party has devoted special attention to the revolutionization and working-classization of the intellectuals, who harbor the most hangovers of obsolete ideologies and have the least opportunity to temper themselves. The Party has energetically tried to turn them into true intellectuals of the working class who will serve our homeland and the people more faithfully. Thanks to the Party's steady work of ideological education and to revolutionary organizational life, a campaign against individualism and egoism was promoted among the intellectuals, tendencies to flunkeyism and dogmatism that remained in their minds were successfully overcome, and all our intellectuals have been more tempered politically and ideologically. Our experience shows that it is possible not only to enlist the services of the old intellectuals but also educate and remold them into true builders of socialism and communism. Today our intellectuals as socialist working intellectuals, are confidently advancing along the road indicated by the Party and serving our revolution and construction well. This is a shining victory for our Party's policy with respect to the intelligentsia and one of our greatest achievements in the revolutionary transformation of the whole of society.

Revolutionizing and working-classizing all of society is a class struggle to root out all manner of retrogressive ideas and nonworking-class elements from every sphere of social life. And, precisely as a question of reeducating the working people themselves, who are striving to build socialism and communism ever faster and better, it is a duty that should be tackled in leading all the working people to communist society. Our Party, therefore, has conducted its work of revolutionizing and working-classizing the working people by means of explanation and persuasion, putting the main stress on ideological education. We have worked unceasingly to revolutionize and working-classize the masses of all strata on the principle of boldly trusting any person who wants to follow our Party and winning him over to the revolutionary cause even though his origin, environment and social and political backgrounds are problematic.

Revolutionary struggle and the work of construction can be fully carried out only with the conscious efforts of the masses. Our Party found the key to a successful revolutionization and working-classization of the society as a whole in the voluntary activity of the masses, and stepped up its organizational and political work among the working people, infusing them with enthusiasm for revolutionary training. We combined practical activities closely with education and reformation, using the proper mixture of general and individual education, with emphasis on eliminating negative phenomena through positive examples, and the masses themselves took on the task of revolutionization and working-classization.

One thing of vital importance in expanding the struggle for the revolutionization and working-classization of the working people is the Chollima Workteam Movement. More than a collective innovation movement in production, it is also an excellent vehicle for educating and remolding the working people in a communist way and a mass movement to speed up the revolutionization and working-classization of all society. We increased the depth and scope of the Chollima Workteam Movement, thereby also stepping up our efforts in educating and transforming the working people in line with the building of a socialist economy and culture. Thus, the reeducation of the people was pushed forward vigorously in all fields and in all units as a movement of all the masses along with a constant struggle for the successful fulfillment of our Seven-Year National Economic Plan.

Through the struggle for the revolutionization and working-classization of all the working people, we have overcome all manner of opportunism, flunkeyism, dogmatism and factionalism; we have armed them firmly with the revolutionary ideas of our Party and actively aroused their revolutionary enthusiasm, thereby achieving a great victory in socialist construction.

Today, as a result of the successful implementation of the Party's policy of revolutionizing and working-classizing all of society, the ideological and moral qualities of our people have undergone a radical change, and our society has been consolidated as never before. Our working people are now imbued with the fine spirit of fighting devotedly for society and the collective, for socialism and communism, and all society lives and works as a revolutionary whole. The unity of our working class, cooperative farmers and working intellectuals has been further cemented, with all of society now constituting a Red family whose members advance in solid politico-ideological unity, helping each other and leading each other forward; our revolutionary ranks have been turned into an invincible force.

4. Establishment of an All-People, Nationwide Defense System

Comrades,

Increasing the nation's defense capacity is both one of the most important tasks facing a Marxist-Leninist party that has taken power and a vital issue for the building of socialism and communism in a world in which imperialism is still extant. Strengthening the defenses of our country has been a matter of particular importance for us, who are building socialism with our territory partitioned and in frontal confrontation with the aggressors of U.S. imperialism, the ringleader of world reaction.

This is why our Party has always devoted special attention to the work of national defense, correctly combining the building of defenses with the work of economic construction. During the period under review, in particular, we took a number of radical steps to boost our nation's defense capabilities, in view of the U.S. imperialists' stepping up their aggressive maneuvers and war provocations and the resultant increase in tension. Carrying out our Party's policy, we did a tremendous work to strengthen the People's Army, arm all the people and fortify the entire country, thus creating our own defense power strong enough to guarantee the security of our homeland against enemy invasion.

Our Party began by waging an untiring campaign of politico-ideological education among the officers and men of the People's Army, in order to maximize its politcal and moral superiority as a revolutionary armed force. Carefully guarding against the tendency to neglect political work and cling only to military-technical affairs in the army, we have held fast to the principle of increasing the political and ideological awareness of our soldiers, combining it correctly with military-technical work. Today the morale of the officers and men of our People's Army is high, and they are well prepared ideologically. The ranks of our People's Army are filled with great political enthusiasm and staunch revolutionary will to serve our Party and the revolution and fight for our socialist homeland and people, come what may; they exhibit the fraternal unity between officers and men and bonds of kinship with the people that have been a tradition with us. Due to the splendid implementation of the Party's policy of turning the entire army into an army of cadres and modernizing it from top to bottom, our People's Army has become an army of cadres—each of our men being the equal of a hundred enemies—further steeled politically, ideologically, and in military techniques; it has grown into an invincible revolutionary armed force, fully equipped with powerful means of attack and defense.

One of the most significant achievements made in strengthening our defense capacity during the period under review was the arming of all our people and the fortifying of our entire country. All of our people know how to fire guns and carry arms with them. Furthermore, we have built impregnable defenses throughout the country and have even fortified all of our major production installations. This is the most powerful system of defense, one that can be established only in our socialist society in which monolithic politico-ideological unity of all the people has been attained and a solid independent economic system established.

Great success has also been registered in the development of our national defense industry. Formerly, our country had but an insignificant munitions industry which was confined to the production of a limited number of rifles. Now, however, thanks to the establishment of firm bases for an independent national defense industry, we are in a position to manufacture various types of up-to-date weapons and all the combat and technological equipment needed for the defense of our homeland.

This increase in our national defense capacity has been obtained at a very great price, however. Frankly speaking, our spendings on national defense have been too heavy a burden for us, in the light of the small size of our country and its population. Had we been able to divert even a part of our nation's defense spendings to economic construction, our national economy would have developed more rapidly and the standard of living of our people been raised markedly. But the situation never allowed us to do so. We could not throw the fundamental interests of the revolution to the winds in seeking temporary comfort, nor did we want to once more become a people without a country. Therefore, we devoted our great efforts to increasing our defense capacity to perfect the defenses of our homeland even though this meant delaying our economic development and the raising of our people's standard of living.

That is why we were able firmly to safeguard the security of our homeland even in the face of frenzied activity by the imperialists; the enemy did not even dare to provoke us. Things were extremely tense in our country at the time of the U.S. imperialist armed spy ship *Pueblo* incident in 1968 and again when the huge *EC-121* spy plane incident occurred last year. The U.S. imperialist gangsters massed armed forces at the very doorstep of our country and brazenly attempted an armed invasion of the northern half of the Republic. The situation was really serious. The whole world waited on developments and expressed its deep concern. However, thanks to our powerful all-people, nationwide defense system, with the People's Army at the core, we were not scared in the slightest, and we took a strong stand, stating that we would retaliate for the "retaliation" of the enemy and wage all-out war against all-out war, and finally we forced the aggressors to their knees. Our enemies are still running amuck, trying daily to set off a new war of aggression in our country. But we are sure that we are able to knock down any and all aggressors, thanks to the wise leadership of our Marxist-Leninist Party, the boundless strength of our people, united closely around the Party, our powerful, independent economy, our invincible revolutionary army, our armed citizenry, and our fortified territory.

5. Thorough Establishment of the Socialist System of Economic Management

Comrades,

In order to take the fullest advantages of the socialist economic system and build socialism and communism successfully after the socialist reorganization of production relations has been effected, we must work constantly to improve the guidance and management of our national economy.

The circumstances under which we brought about the socialist transformation of production relations and pushed overall technological reconstruction in our country urgently demanded a new solution for the question of guidance and management of our national economy. Although we had established a unitary rule for the advanced, large-scale socialist sector of our economy with the creditable fulfillment of our historical task of laying the foundations of socialism, the system and methods of guidance for our national economy as a whole had not yet been adapted to it, and the qualifications and ability of our officials also failed to measure up. These deficiencies, brought out by the new historical circumstances, would have to be overcome before we could make any more rapid advances in socialist economic construction.

These requirements brought out by the new circumstances could only be met by establishing a thoroughgoing socialist system of management in industry, agriculture and all other fields of our national economy.

Setting up and perfecting a new socialist system of economic management is an extremely hard and complex revolutionary task, as it implies making drastic changes in the old system and methods of work, which are rooted deep in tradition and order built up through a long-historical process.

However, our Party, basing itself on all the experiences gained in the socialist construction of our country and creatively developing Marxist-Leninist principles, scientifically worked out an original orientation and specific methods for socialist economic management, thus laying the groundwork for solving this urgent question in practice.

Our guidance at Chongsan-*ri* in February 1960 marked a qualitative change in improving our system and methods of work and in establishing a socialist system of economic management, in line with changing conditions. In the course of generalizing the Chongsan-*ri* spirit and Chongsan-*ri* method, which were an embodiment of the traditional, revolutionary mass line of our Party in the actual socialist construction, new changes were effected in the work of the state and economic organizations.

Following this guidance our Party took radical steps to establish the Taean work system of industrial management, so as to facilitate putting the Chongsan-*ri* spirit and Chongsan-*ri* method into practice in the guidance and management of the national economy.

The Taean work system is a system of economic management admirably suited to the nature of a socialist system, for it stipulates that the factories and enterprises conduct all their management activities under the collective leadership of Party committees and carry out their economic tasks by giving precedence to political work, infusing the producing masses with an enthusiasm for work; that superiors do everything they can to help their subordinates and that the economy be managed and operated in a scientific and rational way.

Our Party put an end to one-man management by directors, the outmoded method of enterprise management; defined the Party committee as the highest leadership authority at every economic unit; and set up a system of collective leadership by the Party committee in enterprise management. Thus, the Party committee steers economic activities by discussing orientations collectively, deciding on the ways and means for settling important questions that arise in the economic work in each period and directing and supervising their implementation. In addition it scrupulously attends to Party organizational work and ideological education, thus actively organizing and mobilizing all the working people for carrying out revolutionary tasks. The use of this system has made it possible for us to eliminate the subjectivity and arbitrariness of individuals in enterprise management and to enlist collective wisdom in managing and operating our large-scale modern, socialist economy efficiently. Moreover, it has also made the broad masses creative and active in production with the attitude of masters.

In addition to this, our Party established a well-organized system under which the officials of ministries, bureaus and other higher organizations and the management personnel of enterprises actually go to the production sites to solve their knotty problems in good time, and under which the higher, more centralized units responsibly provide their branches with all the equipment, materials and other goods needed for production. Thus, the old autocratic, bureaucratic methods used in the guidance of our economy are on the way out at last.

Moreover, in order to rationally manage and operate the economy the Party has introduced a system of unified, concentrated guidance in production. This did away with the irrationality—caused by independent, unrelated systems of planning, technical guidance and production guidance—that had made it impossible for us to direct production efficiently in the past, and it enabled us to coordinate productive and technical guidance and carry it out effectively and, especially, strengthen technical guidance.

The Taean work system is, indeed, a new socialist form of economic management which fully embodies the mass line and scientific principles in enterprise management and has completely done away with all hangovers from the outmoded, capitalist method of economic management. The Taean work system is also a form of industrial management materializing communist principles in a large measure. Here superior and subordinate personnel as well as producers learn from one another, help one another as comrades and work together as one, and the economy is managed on the basis of the great revolutionary enthusiasm of the producer masses.

Our Party has also striven to improve the guidance and management of the rural economy.

The Party transferred the direction of the rural economy from the county people's committees to the newly established county cooperative farm management committees, placing all the agro-technicians and state enterprises directly engaged in agriculture under their authority. The county cooperative farm management committees were thus charged with the task of giving direct guidance to the cooperative farms and providing material and technical assistance from the state to the rural economy. While organizing the county cooperative farm management committees, our Party also established provincial rural economy committees and reorganized the Ministry of Agriculture—now the Agricultural Commission—so as to strengthen the scientific and technical guidance of agriculture.

The introduction of this new system of agricultural guidance with the county cooperative farm management committee as the basic unit has enabled us to direct agriculture by industrial rather than old administrative methods. As a result, it has become possible to approximate the methods of agricultural management and operation more closely to the advanced methods of industrial enterprise management, to plan and organize all management activities better and to increase technical guidance in agricultural production. The establishment of the new system of agricultural guidance has also made it possible to organically link cooperative ownership with ownership by all the people and to create closer productive ties between industry and agriculture. This increases the leading role of all-people ownership in the development of agricultural production and greatly accelerates the process of turning cooperative ownership into ownership by all the people.

After establishing these systems of industrial and agricultural management, our Party saw to it that unified and detailed systems of planning were effected in order to strengthen the democratic-centralist discipline in overall economic management and develop our economy in a more planned and balanced way.

For unified planning, the Party has set up regional planning commissions and state planning departments in the cities (or districts), counties, factories and enterprises, both under the direct control of the State Planning Commission. Moreover, the

planning departments for all sectors of our national economy—
including those of the ministries and organizations of the
national level—were subordinated, with regard to planning,
both to the State Planning Commission and to their respective
enterprise or organization. Thus, a unified system of planning
was established which coordinates all the planning of our
national economy, from the work of the central management
bodies to that of the individual localities, factories, and
enterprises.

Thanks to this new, unified system of planning, Party and
state policies reach all the planning units promptly and are
accurately carried out as all the work of planning done at the
various localities and enterprises has been placed in the hands
of personnel from planning bodies who have a thorough
understanding of the intentions of the Party and the needs of
the state. This has enabled us to do away with localism and
departmentalism, thoroughly subordinate the plans of ministries, administrative bureaus, provincial organizations and all
factories and enterprises to the national strategic plan, and
work out mobilizing and active plans. The new system has also
enabled us to eliminate subjectivism and bureaucracy from the
state planning bodies and fully ensure the objectivity and
feasibility of plans by having the planners personally work with
the producer masses, actively enlisting their creative initiative
and familiarizing themselves with the specific conditions at
each production site.

The new system of detailed planning, along with that of
unified planning, is an important guarantee for the most
scientific planning possible of our national economy.

Detailed planning makes it possible for the state planning
agencies to closely coordinate general economic development
with the management activities of every factory and enterprise
and to draw up plans to suit the actual conditions in all the
branches of our national economy, localities and enterprises, so
that everything—even down to the smallest detail—will
dovetail. The introduction of detailed planning has enabled us
to develop our nation's economy rapidly without a hitch by
totally eliminating the factors of imbalance and spontaneity in
economic development and by ably reflecting the laws of a
well-planned, proportionately developed economy.

From our own experience we can say with great pride that the socialist system of economic management established in all spheres of our country fully accords with the revolutionary principles of Marxism-Leninism and with the specific conditions of our country and that it consitutes the best economic management method for further consolidating and developing our socialist economic system and for giving great impetus to the development of our productive forces.

The overall introduction of the new economic management system has enabled us to more than meet the requirements of the economic laws of socialism, properly combining political and moral incentives with material incentives, and centralism with democracy in economic management. In particular, it has enabled us to completely overcome both the "Leftist" deviation of ignoring the transitional character of socialist society in economic management and the Rightist inclination toward decentralization in economic guidance and liberalization of enterprise management, that is, putting all the emphasis on material rather than political or moral incentives.

Comrades, thanks to our successful implementation of the lines set forth at the Fourth Congress of the Party and the Party Conference, we have achieved great victories and successes in socialist construction.

The historic task of turning our country into a socialist industrial state has been splendidly carried out, and the independent national economy built by our people in a spirit of self-reliance during the course of a hard-fought struggle has grown mightier. The newly established socialist system of economic management is forcefully promoting the development of our nation's productive forces. Culture and art are flourishing, and beautiful new towns and villages are going up all over every day. Our revolutionary forces have become invincible and now we have a stronger national defense. Our people have made giant strides in their battle to scale the high peak of socialism and are leading happy, worthwhile lives in our prospering socialist homeland.

We may state with confidence that we have amassed strength enough to ensure the complete victory of socialism and to attain the reunification of our homeland and the nationwide victory of the revolution.

On behalf of this Party congress, I would like to warmly thank all our Party members, workers, farmers and the rest of the working people who have performed brilliant exploits on every front of socialist construction, upholding the lines and policies of our Party.

II. On the Consolidation and Development of Our Country's Socialist System

Comrades,

Today our Party and people are faced with the urgent task of further consolidating and developing our country's socialist system and hastening the complete victory of socialism on the basis of the achievements already gained in revolution and construction.

In order to strengthen the socialist system and attain the complete victory of socialism, we must carry on a powerful struggle to capture the material and ideological fortresses, which must be seized without fail on our way to communism.

We must develop our productive forces continuously by carrying the technical revolution to a higher stage. We must bring about a further development and efflorescence of socialist national culture by speeding up cultural construction. We must vigorously push ahead with the revolutionization and working-classization of all of society by giving priority to the ideological revolution.

1. Central Tasks of Socialist Economic Construction

Comrades,

During the Seven-Year Plan we have founded a modern industry, self-supporting in structure, and put all branches of the national economy mostly on a modern technical footing by vigorously accelerating the socialist industrialization of the country and the all-round technological reconstruction of the national economy.

However, we still have much work to do in the field of economic construction if we are to lay the solid material and technical foundations for socialism. We must bring the might of our modern industry into full play by equipping it better and strengthening its independence. We must develop the nation's productive forces still faster by steadily introducing technical progress in all fields of the national economy.

The basic task of the Six-Year Plan in the field of socialist economic construction is to cement the material and technical foundations of socialism and free the working people from heavy labor in all fields of the national economy, by consolidating and developing the successes gained in industrialization and advancing the technical revolution onto a new, higher plane.

During the period of the new prospective plan we should, above all, perfect the inner-structures of the industrial branches and further strengthen the Juche character of our industry.

With socialist industrialization now a fact, our industry is a well-balanced structure, equipped with new techniques, and one with enormous potentialities, relying mainly on domestic raw material resources. Our industry, however, does not take full advantage of its strength, since some of its branches have not yet been perfected and some minor, secondary sections and production processes are not in good shape. In particular, we still depend on foreign countries for some raw materials, and this inevitably affects the secure and normal development of our industry to a certain degree.

We should continue with the work of improving all branches of industry, reinforcing weak sections and creating new branches so as to perfect our industry quickly. At the same time, we should wage a dynamic struggle to base its expansion entirely on the raw materials available in our own country. In this way we can bring the power of our industry into full play and base all our industrial branches on Juche so firmly that they will be, at least, 60 to 70% self-reliant in regard to raw materials.

Great efforts should also be directed to strengthening the independence of our iron and steel industry.

Our country has rich iron-ore resources and very bright prospects for the development of this industry. However, we are now meeting the iron industry's demand for coking coal through trade with fraternal countries, because it has not yet been found in our country. Such cooperation, of course, is very valuable to us, and in the future, we shall continue to promote economic cooperation with other countries on the principle of satisfying each other's needs. But we cannot afford to import all the vast amount of coking coal we need for our iron production, which is expanding rapidly in keeping with the demands of our developing national economy.

While intensifying the struggle to increase pig-iron output with the least possible expense of coke, we must actively develop the iron industry by using home-produced fuel. During the period of the new prospective plan we must increase the production of granulated iron and semi-steel and industrialize the production of sponge iron and reduced pellets as soon as possible. We must also continue our research in electric iron-manufacturing.

The variety and quality of steel should be increased; the variety and standards of rolled steel should be expanded sharply and the production of second-stage metal-processing goods should be developed rapidly, so that we may have an adequate supply of the different ferrous materials required for the development of the national economy and the technical revolution.

The nonferrous metallurgical industry should be rapidly developed so as to effectively exploit and utilize nonferrous metal resources abundant in our country. We should produce the light metals essential to technical progress and to the improvement of our people's living standards, especially aluminum.

The development of the chemical industry is of very great significance in expanding the raw-material bases for industry and increasing our economic independence. Relying on the existing foundations of the chemical industry, we must continue to develop the inorganic and organic chemical industries and to establish new branches in order to diversify our chemical industry.

In order to realize full-scale chemicalization of agriculture, the production of chemical fertilizers, herbicides and insecticides should be increased.

The expansion and consolidation of the raw-material bases for light industry is an important task of the chemical industry. We must enlarge existing production bases for chemical fibers and synthetic resins and, at the same time, make great efforts in the Six-Year Plan period to build new and large bases for a petroleum chemical industry so that we ourselves can produce more than 70% of the fibers needed for light industry. The production of synthetic resins should also be increased quickly.

In addition, we should rapidly build up bases for synthetic rubber production to meet the domestic demand for rubber, and should intensify our attempts to produce and supply our own chemical materials for light industry.

The question of advancing the technical revolution to a new height and increasing the nation's productive forces as a whole depends largely on the growth of the engineering industry. In the Six-Year Plan period, big efforts should be continuously made to develop this industry so that it can turn out larger quantities of more efficient and economic machinery and equipment, needed for our gigantic nature-transforming projects and for the various sectors of the national economy.

Bases for the production of heavy machinery should be expanded and reinforced to manufacture heavy equipment on a large scale: large equipment needed by the metallurgical, cement and chemical industries; turbines and generators, boilers and other big-capacity generating equipment; the same goes for 25-ton heavy-duty trucks, 300-hp bulldozers, big excavators and other kinds of large-size equipment needed for the extractive industries and our huge nature-remaking projects.

The development of the fishing industry and water transport system demands a speedy growth of the ship-building industry. Under the Six-Year Plan, we should build more big vessels, including 5,000-ton refrigerator-transports and freighters. We should even build our own factory mother-ships and freighters of 10,000 tons and over.

The extensive introduction of semi-automation and automation in all spheres of the national economy has placed before the engineering industry the important task of developing the electronics and automation industries. Electronics and automation industry bases should be reinforced to produce different automation elements, instruments and gauges in large quantities. All the varieties of rare and pure metal materials needed in the electronics and automation industries should also be manufactured and supplied in sufficient quantity.

One of the important problems to be solved in the engineering industry is to mass-produce different kinds of single-purpose equipment needed for the production of consumer goods. During the period of the new prospective plan, we should set up many single-purpose equipment factories to rapidly increase the production of these machines in demand by the foodstuffs and daily-necessities industries.

The tremendous tasks confronting the engineering industry call for stepped-up production of machine tools. The output of machine tools should be boosted rapidly and, especially, special machine tools, automatic and semi-automatic machine tools, large-size and efficient single-purpose machine tools should be produced in quantity.

Active exploitation of the rich natural resources in our country's subsoil is very important not only in accelerating the nation's economic construction but also in promoting trade with foreign countries. We should expand the bases of magnesia clinker production and the capacities of our cement factories; at the same time, we should build many new medium and small-size local cement factories, so as to achieve a sharp rise in the output of magnesia clinker and cement.

The major task to be tackled in light industry is to quickly shore up the daily-necessities industry. The articles of daily use put out in our country still lack variety and quality. We should exert great efforts to develop this industry and, especially, strive to tap local reserves in order to bring about a new increase in the production of daily necessities in the next few years.

The central task facing the rural economy is to make agriculture highly intensive.

Above all, two-crop acreage should be expanded through the extensive introduction of irrigation in dry fields. When non-paddy irrigation is effected, dry-field farming will be freed forever from crop failure as is the case with rice farming, and the per *chongbo* yield of dry-field crops can be increased considerably. During the period of the new prospective plan a vigorous struggle should be waged to introduce irrigation, including water sprinkling, in 300,000 *chongbo* of dry fields with main emphasis on the area suitable for two-crop cultivation. This can be done by properly readjusting and effectively utilizing the already-existing irrigation facilities.

At the same time, the chemicalization of agriculture should be pushed ahead. In the period of the Six-Year Plan, we should increase to one ton or more the amount of chemical fertilizers applied per *chongbo* of cultivated land; their qualitative composition should be improved and microelement fertilizers suitable to the soil and the peculiarities of the crops of our country should be produced and supplied in larger quantities. Along with the increased application of chemical fertilizers, their effect should be heightened to the utmost through the establishment of a scientific manuring system. Insecticides and other agricultural chemicals should be used on an extensive scale so that crops may be completely protected from all kinds of blights and harmful insects.

A great possibility for raising the per *chongbo* yield of crops lies in strengthening biological research and extensively applying its results to agricultural production. All varieties of crops should be replaced by new superior strains by improving seed selection and increasing the production of high-yielding choice seeds fitted to the climatic and soil conditions of our country.

Tideland reclamation should also be undertaken on a large scale to obtain new land. In the Six-Year Plan period we should obtain plenty of new fertile land by concentrating our efforts, first of all, on those areas with favorable natural and geographical conditions, that can be reclaimed comparatively quickly.

One of the very urgent tasks confronting us today is to eliminate the waste and loss of agricultural and industrial products while rapidly increasing their output.

Although our country produces an enormous amount of fruit and vegetables and catches hundreds of thousands of tons of fish evey year, a lot of these products spoil. This is because measures have not been taken to facilitate their keeping and to industrialize and streamline their processing. Frequently, careless packing spoils precious agricultural and industrial products.

Decisive steps should be taken to improve the storage, processing and packing of agricultural and industrial products to stop this waste completely. We should launch a mass movement to build fruit storages in areas of production and consumption, so that more fresh fruit can be kept. We should also build many factories to process fruit, vegetables and fish everywhere and process them in time, using industrial methods, without a bit of waste. Kraft paper, cardboard and other high-quality packing materials should be turned out in great quantities for the radical improvement of the packing of manufactured and agricultural products.

Easing the strain on transport is a very urgent question at present in accelerating the overall economic construction of the country. We should make big efforts to develop transport service to fully meet the fast-growing demands of our country.

At present our country has only one railway line linking the east with the west, and this constitutes the main factor in the strain on railway transport. We should speed up the Ichon-Sepo railway construction now underway so as to hasten the opening of another railway line connecting the east and west coasts, and push forward actively the construction of a new railway between Kanggye, Hyesan and Musan to connect the east and west portions of the northern inland region.

We should, at the same time, continue to electrify some overworked branch lines in the eastern and inland areas which have steep gradients and heavy freight traffic. Diesel traction should be introduced on the non-electrified lines and the traction-load and the operation speed of the locomotives should be increased in order to raise railway transport capacity.

Water transport should be further developed with a view to ensuring the efficiency of the rapidly increasing cargo shipment for foreign trade and to easing the strain on railway transport. We should energetically open up new routes to expand the network of coastal and river shipping, develop joint railway-water transport and increase the use of our vessels in foreign trade. We should also develop motor transport to a greater extent on a par with the advancement of the automobile industry.

Comrades,

To continue to push ahead vigorously with the technical revolution is an important task for us to liberate the working people from backbreaking labor. The technical revolution is also essential to ease the present labor shortage.

Our working people have been notably relieved from heavy, backbreaking labor by the full-scale technological reconstruction carried out in all fields of the national economy during the

Seven-Year Plan. But there is still the contrast between heavy and light labor and we have not yet eliminated work in excessive heat or under other harmful conditions. There remains a big disparity between industrial and agricultural labor and the women, who account for one half of the population, have not yet been completely freed from household drudgery.

We have to launch a widespread technical renovation movement in industry and agriculture and all other branches of the national economy so that we will narrow down to a considerable extent the distinction between heavy and light labor, between agricultural and industrial work and free women from the heavy burden of household chores. These are precisely the three major tasks of the technical revolution which we should aim to fulfill in the next few years.

In the first place, a great effort should be exerted to narrow the differences between heavy and light labor, to eliminate heat-affected and other harmful labor and to introduce on a broad scale both semi- and full-scale automation in all fields of the national economy.

The foremost task should be the launching of a widespread movement to introduce advanced technology into the mining industry where, more than in any other branch, arduous, labor-consuming jobs remain. The aim should be to make work in this field easier, safer and highly productive.

Ore and bituminous coal mines should introduce comprehensive mechanization and gradually go over to semi- and full-scale automation. A radical upswing should be brought about in mechanization at the anthracite mines which are responsible for the overwhelming proportion of coal produced in our country and where the degree of mechanization is still low.

The degree of mechanization should be raised in every phase of the lumber industry. The fishing industry should provide itself with large, modern all-purpose boats that would allow for the comprehensive mechnization of fishing.

Capital construction, like the mining industry, is also characterized by the prevalence of excessively heavy labor. Efficient construction machinery should be supplied in a greater quantity and the proportion of prefabricated construction should be increased still more to radically raise the degree of mechanization in the construction field.

The mechanization of loading and discharging operations is a vital necessity if we are to eliminate excessively heavy labor. These operations have not yet been fully mechanized on the railways, at wharves, on construction sites and in other branches of our economy. Not only does this mean that many people are engaged in tough work but also that the rapidity of operations is not ensured. This is one of the reasons why we have failed to utilize our means of transportation more efficiently. During the period of the new long-term plan we should manufacture and introduce different types of efficient loading and discharging machines in larger quantities and thus speed up the mechanization of these operations.

A technical renovation movement should be vigorously unfolded in industry to eliminate work in excessive heat or under other harmful conditions.

Production processes should be completely automated to eliminate heat-affected labor once and for all in the iron and steel, chemical and cement industries as well as in all other industries where work is done in excessive heat. We should begin with the branches of industry where there is exposure to high temperatures and switch over to remote control step by step.

The health of workers and production itself are still affected to a certain extent by gas, dust and other noxious matter emitted in the course of production in the chemical, nonferrous metallurgical, mining and building-materials industries and in a number of other fields. We should facilitate technological reconstruction in these branches to do away with these harmful conditions as soon as possible.

By taking these measures, we can convert harmful working conditions into harmless ones and thoroughly prevent the health of workers and production itself from being negatively affected by heat, gas, dust or humidity in every branch of industry and every work place.

The promotion of the rual technical revolution represents an urgent task for us at the present time. Overall mechanization and chemicalization of agriculture in the Six-Year Plan period should be introduced to drastically narrow down the distinction between agricultural and industrial labor and considerably cut down on the labor force in the countryside.

We should make more effective use of the existing farm

machinery, design and manufacture diverse types of modern farm machinery in greater quantities, particularly those efficient kinds suited to the topographical conditions of our country, thereby introducing mechanization into agriculture on a comprehensive scale. During the period of the new prospective plan we should first introduce it in the two-crop dry fields under irrigation and the paddyfields where rice is sown directly and then gradually generalize its success so that a nationwide movement will be undertaken to materialize the comprehensive mechanization completely in the near future.

Extensive levelling of fields and readjustment of their boundaries is an urgent task if all-round mechanization of agriculture is to be realized at the present stage.

It is mainly because the fields have not been readjusted and levelled adequately that we have failed to impel mechanization of agriculture at a more rapid pace, although we now have a considerable number of tractors, trucks and up-to-date farm machines of diverse types. Such land improvement should be launched as a mass movement with the aim of enlarging and evening the borders of the fields and terracing the sloping ground so that machines can work effectively in both rice paddy and other fields.

Machines alone cannot replace all the manual labor used in the rural economy. Therefore, farm work which cannot be performed by machines should be done with the help of chemistry. Weeding, one of the most painstaking and labor-consuming chores in the countryside, should be accomplished by chemicals through the wide application of different highly-effective herbicides.

By bringing about substantial advances in the rural technical revolution we should, in the near future, be able to reduce the labor power expended on a *chongbo* of rice paddy to a level of 60 to 80 man-days on an average and on a *chongbo* of dry-farming land to a level of 20 to 30 man-days. Therefore, a single farmer will be cultivating at least five to six *chongbo* of rice paddy or eight to ten *chongbo* of dry-farming land. The eight-hour workday could thus be gradually introduced in the cooperative farms as in the factories and other enterprises, and the difference between town and country as regards working conditions would be markedly reduced.

One of the vital tasks in the technical revolution is that of freeing women from the burden of kitchen and household work.

Our Party has not only brought about the social emancipation of the women but it has also made untiring efforts to provide better conditions for them so that they can participate widely in public life. Due to the profound interest of our Party, our women, as proud masters of the country along with the men, are now making an active contribution to the revolutionary struggle and constructive work.

But our women still have to devote a great deal of time to household work even though they are engaged in public activities side by side with men. Therefore, they bear a double burden, that of public activities and that of housework. We should interest ourselves very seriously with the technical revolution as a means for freeing the women from household chores and for increasing still more their role in revolution and construction.

The most important thing we can do to lighten the women's kitchen chores is to introduce innovations into the food industry. The processing of different kinds of complementary food products should be developed on a large scale, as well as that of the basic food items. Thus all the foodstuffs will be processed by industrial methods so that women can prepare meals quickly and easily at home.

At the same time as we develop the food industry, we should manufacture large quantities of refrigerators, washing machines, electric cooking pots and other kitchen utensils so that women need not spend so much time in the kitchen and in doing general household chores.

When all these tasks, vital to the technical revolution, are carried out successfully, all our working people will be free from backbreaking, labor-consuming and inefficient work. Their labor will not only be safe and easy but will have attained a high level of productivity, and they will be much better off materially.

2. The Construction of Socialist Culture

Comrades,

Socialism and communism not only require highly developed productive forces, they also demand working people with a high cultural level. Only when the cultural revolution, along with the technical revolution, is continuously and vigorously pushed forward can we hasten the complete victory of socialism and satisfy the essential requirements of a socialist and communist society.

One of the most important tasks in building a national, socialist culture today is the struggle against cultural penetration by imperialism.

The fight against the outmoded culture of the exploiter society and reactionary capitalist culture responds to the laws that guide the building of a national, socialist culture. Especially, under the present conditions when the imperialists are maliciously machinating to spread reactionary bourgeois culture among us, the struggle against every expression of reactionary culture is imperative.

Cultural penetration, one of the principal methods used by the imperialists to carry out their neocolonialist policy, paves the way for their foreign aggression. Through cultural penetration the imperialists, led by U.S. imperialism, maneuver to destroy the national culture of other countries, dull the people's revolutionary spirit and their consciousness about national independence, demoralize and corrupt them. An outstanding example of this is the ideological and cultural penetration by the U.S. imperialists and the Japanese militarists in south Korea. As a result of the policy to obliterate our national culture, pursued by the U.S. and Japanese reactionaries and their stooges, it is wantonly trampled on today, and degenerate "Yankee culture" and Japanese fashions and way of life predominate in south Korea, corroding the spiritual life of the people. The U.S. imperialists try unscrupulously to implant their reactionary culture not only in south Korea but also in the northern half of the Republic, employing every means at their disposal including radio, printed matter, literature and art.

Unless such cultural penetration by imperialism is thoroughly checked, we will be unable either to develop a healthy national, socialist culture or firmly defend our socialist gains. From historical experience, we know that if imperialist cultural penetration is not energetically blocked and if reactionary bourgeois elements are tolerated to the slightest degree in the development of a new culture, national culture is gradually eaten away; the people develop illusions about imperialism, and suffer ideological confusion; and the revolution and construction face grave difficulty and crisis.

Therefore, the principal target of the cultural revolution is cultural penetration by the imperialists. We must vigilantly prevent the infiltration into our ranks of any manifestation of corrupt bourgeois culture or life style promoted by the imperialists. However trivial, bourgeois elements in the construction of culture should never be tolerated.

If a national, socialist culture is to develop on a sound basis, we must also resolutely oppose the tendency toward restorationism.

Restorationism is an anti-Marxist current in ideology which advocates the uncritical restoration and glorification of anything old while ignoring the needs of the times and class outlook. If restorationism is permitted in the field of cultural construction, every variety of the old, pernicious culture will rise again and reactionary bourgeois concepts, feudal-Confucian ideas, and other outmoded ways of thinking will breed in the minds of the people.

A relentless struggle must be waged against this tendency to blindly copy antiquated and reactionary examples from the past and embellish them on the pretext of reclaiming our national cultural heritage. We must discard what is backward and reactionary in our cultural inheritance and critically assimilate and develop what is progressive and popular in accordance with the socialist reality of today.

We have to develop all spheres of socialist culture including education, science, literature and art more speedily and on a sound foundation. To do so, we must block imperialist cultural penetration completely and overcome the trend toward restorationism through a vigorous ideological campaign in the area of cultural construction.

The main task facing education is that of forming large contingents of technicians and specialists, the nation's huge army of intellectuals.

The productive forces of our country today have reached a very high stage of development and the economy has grown markedly. Unless we train more technicians and specialists, we can neither properly run the national economy, equipped with up-to-date technology, nor successfully carry out the aims of the technical revolution.

We must train technicians and specialists on a large scale to meet the practical demands of socialist construction. Thus, during the period of the new long-term plan, the number of engineers, assistant engineers and specialists from colleges and higher technical schools should reach more than 10 per cent of the labor force at all factories, enterprises and cooperative farms. Within the next few years, the total number of technicians and specialists should exceed one million.

In order to train a large number of technicians and specialists, the work should be improved and enrollment increased at existing colleges and higher technical schools. We should build more colleges in both the capital and the provinces after making a correct assessment of the demands for technical personnel in every branch of the national economy. There should also be significant increase in the number of factory colleges and higher technical schools as well as a further improvement in the work of night schools and correspondence courses.

Along with the training of a large army of intellectuals, we must energetically continue our struggle to raise the level of the working people's general and technical knowledge.

As a result of the new system of universal compulsory nine-year technical education, all children in our country today receive technical training before going out into the world. Consequently, an important way to raise the general cultural and technical levels of the working people is to improve the quality of this compulsory technical education. The material assets of schools should be enlarged, the ranks of teachers should be strengthened and education should be constantly improved in terms of both content and methodology.

In order to raise the general technical and cultural levels of the working people, we must continue the work of educating the adults who never had an opportunity to learn under the exploiter society of the past. We must guarantee all working people a place in some branch of our educational system so they can study on a regular basis in the future as well.

With the aim of raising the working people's cultural and technical levels, the distribution of publications and propaganda by radio should increase and improve. Particularly necessary in this respect would be the broadening of our television network to cover the whole country as soon as it is feasible.

The work of bringing up children under state and public care should be developed. This is an important task in the cultural revolution and in building a socialist society.

Bringing up children by society is both an important communist policy and a communist pedagogical method. Man's character and thinking are formed from childhood; accordingly, a proper education and the cultivation of good habits from the earliest years exert a powerful influence on a child's future development. Raising children under public care trains them to be organized and disciplined, fosters in them the spirit of collectivism and a communist character and accustoms them to organizational life from childhood. Their schooling and social education, therefore, can be more effective when they are older.

We have to enlarge the capacity of our existing nurseries and kindergartens and build many modern ones to provide the best facilities for the education of our little children all over the country. All our preschool children must be brought up in nursery schools and kindergartens at state and public expense.

The gigantic tasks we face today in socialist construction—especially the new goals of the technical revolution—require a radical improvement in our scientific research. Main efforts in the natural sciences should be directed toward solving scientific and technological problems which relate to the more effective use of our present economic base, the strengthening of the Juche character of our industry and the development of the technical revolution to a higher stage. At the same time, new areas in science and technology should be actively explored. In the social sciences, it is necessary to make theoretical generalizations about the achievements and rich experiences of our people in their revolutionary struggle and work of construction and demonstrate in a more profound way the correctness of our Party's lines and policies.

Literature and art play an important role in the communist education of the working people and in the revolutionization and working-classization of the entire society.

Our central task here is to create more revolutionary works of literature and art which will arm the working people with a communist world outlook. Writers and artists should produce more works that are based on our glorious revolutionary traditions—the deep roots of our Party and revolution, and that depict the heroic feats of the soldiers of the People's Army and the people who carried forward the brilliant revolutionary traditions of the anti-Japanese armed struggle and fought bravely during the Fatherland Liberation War. They should also vividly portray the epic reality and the full life of our people today in which, like a hurricane, mounted on Chollima, our people drive ahead filled with revolutionary zeal. The struggle of the south Korean revolutionaries and the patriotic people who are valiantly fighting for the revolution in south Korea and for the reunification of the country needs to be skillfully represented. In order to produce numerous revolutionary works that will have an emotional impact on our people and inspire them in their march forward, writers and artists should delve more deeply into reality, seriously study life and make an admirable use of socialist realism in their creative activity.

It is the popular masses who make socialist culture. Literature and art in our society can advance rapidly only with the broad participation of the working people. We have to strictly guard against professionalism in literary and artistic activities, destroy the mystification of creative work and develop literature and art on a broad popular basis.

Language is one of the characteristics common to a nation. It is a powerful weapon for scientific and technological progress and a major ingredient in determining specifically national forms of culture. Therefore, a national, socialist culture cannot be successfully built without developing the national language.

Our language, a priceless treasure and the pride of our people, is undergoing a grave crisis in south Korea today. Under the U.S. imperialists' policy of destroying our national language, it is gradually losing its purity and degenerating into a hodgepodge of many languages. This gives rise to serious concern among all Koreans. For the development and flowering of a brilliant national, socialist culture, for the everlasting prosperity of our nation, we must organize a vigorous nationwide campaign to defend our mother tongue from the attempts of U.S. imperialism and its stooges to adulterate it. Meanwhile, we should energetically strive to bring into common usage pure Korean words, developing them to conform to present-day needs.

The strength and health of the working people are vital to the revolutionary struggle and the building of a rich and powerful society. We must popularize physical training and sports and extensively improve our physical preparation for national defense. This will further increase the physical strength of all the working people and firmly prepare the entire people for work and defense. Juche must be thoroughly applied in physical training and sports, and the science and techniques of physical culture must be rapidly developed.

We must turn our culture into a true people's culture at the service of our socialist working people—a militant and revolutionary culture actively contributing to the revolutionary struggle and construction work. The way we can do this is by successfully carrying out all these tasks of the cultural revolution.

3. Ideological Revolution, Revolutionization and Working-Classization of the Entire Society

Comrades,

The ideological revolution represents a sharp class struggle for the final liquidation of capitalism including the domain of man's consciousness. It is a vital revolutionary task that must be fulfilled in order to completely free the entire working people from the fetters of all obsolete ideologies and to arm them with progressive working-class ideas, with the ideas of communism. Whether or not to carry out the ideological revolution thoroughly is tantamount to whether or not the revolution will be carried to its final conclusion. Accordingly, this is one of the fundamental determinants for the success of the construction of socialism and communism. A Marxist-Leninist party which has seized power can only triumph in the revolutionary cause of the working class when it repudiates all deviations and solves this crucial question correctly. Historical experience has proved that if a Marxist-Leninist party does not continually raise the class awareness of the masses and strengthen the ideological revolution among them, the influence of bourgeois ideas increases and the revolutionary consciousness of the working people becomes paralysed. As a consequence, not only is there difficulty in consolidating and developing the socialist system but, even more, the achievements of the revolution are put in jeopardy. On the basis of the consistent line of the Party, we must continue to energetically drive forward the ideological revolution and give it definite precedence in all our work.

To realize the working-classization of all of society while steadily revolutionizing the working people by giving priority to the ideological revolution is a vital task that must be fulfilled in the period of transition from capitalism to socialism. Only by working-classizing all the members of society, is it possible to obliterate class distinctions, build a classless society and win complete victory for socialism. However, even after the whole of society has been working-classized and the tasks of the period of transition from capitalism to socialism have been carried out successfully, there still remain some survivals of outworn ideologies in the minds of people and, it cannot be claimed as yet that all working people have become real Communists. Even after the complete victory of socialism the Marxist-Leninist party should coninue the struggle to revolutionize all the working people, consolidating the success made in working-classizing them. Only in this way, can the ideological fortress of communism be conquered completely.

During the period under review we have vigorously carried through the Party's line of revolutionizing and working-class-izing the entire society. We have registered no little success in this endeavor. This is only the beginning, however. We have just started to work. On the basis of our successes and experiences we must develop the revolutionization and working-classization of the working people in a more profound way.

The working-classization and revolutionization of the entire society requires, first of all, the intensification of ideological education among the working people.

We must continue to vigorously conduct communist education among the working people.

What is fundamental to communist education is class education. There can be no communist doctrine apart from the revolutionary doctrine of the working class, nor can there be communist education apart from class education. The class consciousness of the working class forms the kernel of communist ideology. Therefore, only when the working people are firmly armed with proletarian class consciousness can they be transformed into real Communists. We should imbue all the working people with a working-class outlook so that they will learn to hate the class enemies and fight relentlessly against imperialism and the system of exploitation. In particular, the hatred of the working people for U.S. imperialism and Japanese militarism, the main objects of our struggle, should be further deepened. We must give solid ideological preparation to the entire people so that they are ready at any time to staunchly fight to force the U.S. imperialists out of south Korea and carry the revolutionary cause of national reunification to its final conclusion.

Collectivism is one of the intrinsic characteristics of the working class. It is the basis of social life in socialist and communist societies where the working people are closely united and strive to attain common goals. We should continue to pay profound attention to strengthening the education of the working people in collectivism. In order to equip our people with this idea it is most important to step up the struggle against individualism and egoism. Educational work should be intensified among the working people with the aim of cultivating in them the revolutionary idea of cherishing the collective and organization and devotedly working, any time and anywhere, for the benefit of the society and the people, and the Party and the revolution, as opposed to a preoccupation with an easy and gay life for oneself. In this way all the working people will learn to work, study and live in consonance with the communist spirit of "One for all and all for one."

The fostering of a communist attitude toward work holds an important place in communist education. We should educate the working people to esteem labor, regarding it as the most honorable activity, display voluntary enthusiasm and creativity in their work and sincerely participate in communal labor for the good of the collective and society.

Education in socialist patriotism should also be emphasized among the working people. Socialist patriotism means love for the socialist homeland whose revolutionary achievments are the power of the proletarian dictatorship, the socialist system and an independent national economy. It is only when the working people are firmly armed with the idea of socialist patriotism, that they can resolutely fight for the prosperity and progress of our homeland and for the victory of the revolution. We should fully convince the working people of the revolutionary essence of the power of proletarian dictatorship, the true superiority of the socialist system and the might of our independent national economy. They will then have great pride and sense of honor living in their socialist country, they will supremely treasure the socialist gains won and guaranteed by our people at the cost of their blood and sweat and they will work harder for the consolidation and development of these achievements. We should patiently educate all the working men and women to value and protect the property of the country and the people, conscious of the fact that they are the masters of the nation's economic life, and to strive with all their wisdom, talent and energy to make greater contributions to the building of a rich and strong socialist homeland.

The communist education of the working people must necessarily be conducted in close combination with education in revolutionary traditions.

Our revolutionary traditions were formed in the course of creatively developing Marxist-Leninist theory to suit the specific conditions of the Korean revolution and thoroughly combining revolutionary theory and practice. They are a priceless revolutionary heritage grown out of the flames of unprecedentedly arduous and sanguinary anti-Japanese armed struggle. Experience shows that communist education, when linked up with education in our revolutionary traditions, has a decisive influence and an unlimited power to move people. Education in revolutionary traditions is necessary for everyone, but it is most essential for the younger generation who have not undergone the ordeals of revolutionary struggle. The revolution continues and one generation inexorably replaces another. Only if the new generation is educated in the revolutionary traditions will it be possible to form them into genuine continuators of our revolution, who carry it on.

The education of the working people in revolutionary traditions must be made more profound. We should fully acquaint everyone with the historical roots of our Party and our revolution and imbue them with their forerunners' infinite fidelity to the cause of revolution, with their indefatigable fighting will and revolutionary optimism; the working people should also assimilate the experience of the revolutionary struggle and the communist method and style of work acquired during the period of the anti-Japanese armed struggle.

Our Party's lines and policies are a creative application and development of the universal principles of Marxism-Leninism in accord with the specific realities of our country. They guide all our action, being the most accurate strategy and tactics for the successful accomplishment of our revolution. Only when Party members and the working people in general are firmly armed with the revolutionary ideas, the lines and policies of our Party, will they become true revolutionaries, loyal to the Party and the revolution. Only then will they correctly carry out the revolutionary tasks assigned to them. We have to intensify the education of Party members and the working people in the policies of the Party so as to clearly understand their quintessence, fully grasp their correctness and make them a sturdy faith. Therefore, everyone must firmly arm himself with the monolithic ideology of our Party and make its lines and policies an integral part of himself, working in strict conformity to these policies at all times and everywhere, resolutely striving to defend them and carry them through under any difficult conditions.

Revolutionary practice is a powerful instrument for remolding ideological consciousness. It is in the course of the arduous and complex practical struggle for transforming nature and society that people are tempered at all times and formed into revolutionaries. We should link the ideological work of educating and remolding the working people closely with the revolutionary struggle and practical activities for the building of socialism and communism. They will thus steel themselves ideologically and cultivate in themselves a strong revolutionary will in the course of performing their revolutionary tasks. The intellectuals in particular who are not directly connected to practical productive activities should constantly be made to enter into the midst of the actual socialist construction, not only to consolidate their book knowledge and meet with new scientific and technical problems but also to learn from the sense of organization and militancy of the working class and its loyalty to the Party and the revolution.

An essential means of revolutionizing and working-classizing people is to strengthen their revolutionary organizational life.

A major criterion of a Communist is his strong sense of revolutionary organization. To be called a true Communist one must possess this attribute as well as sublime ideology, pervaded with a communist revolutionary spirit. The sense of revolutionary organization of the Communist is formed and strengthened through a revolutionary organizational life.

Organizational life is a furnace for ideological training and a school for revolutionary education. Only through a disciplined organizational life, can one be steeled revolutionarily and formed into a real revolutionary, loyal to the revolutionary cause of the working class. We should wage a vigorous struggle to strengthen the organizational life of the working people. Every person should be encouraged to take an active part in organizational life, observe organizational discipline of their own accord, faithfully carry out what is entrusted to them by their organizations, live under the guidance and supervision of their organizations and attend constantly to their revolutionary education.

What is most important in the development of organizational life is the intensification of criticism. Ideological struggle by means of criticism and education and remolding through ideological struggle—this is the policy consistently followed by our Party in revolutionizing people. All organizations must strengthen criticism and conduct a strong ideological battle against unsound ideological elements of every description.

In this regard it is necessary to fight resolutely, first and foremost, against an incorrect approach to criticism. People must be taught to take a principled attitude toward it. Under all circumstances criticism should be aimed at saving comrades and cementing unity; it should on no account be criticism for criticism's sake. In making criticisms, one must not try to shift the responsibility for one's own faults onto others, take vengeance after being criticized, frivolously mark others with political stigmas or reprimand those criticized in a peremptory manner. Furthermore, criticism should be conducted patiently and on a regular basis, not in a shock campaign. We must educate all our people in this spirit of principled criticism, thus creating a favorable atmosphere for revolutionary criticism and tempering everyone through it. In this way we will ensure the people's timely and uncompromising struggle against errors, in the course of which they will be constantly educated, transformed and revolutionized.

A vital question posed in carrying out the task of revolutionizing and working-classizing society is that of sweeping away what is left of the old way of life in all spheres and establishing a new socialist way of life throughout society.

The socialist way of life means the way people act in a socialist society. Therefore, to establish this way of life means seeing to it that everyone conducts his activities in all spheres—political, economic, cultural and moral—in accordance with socialist standards of social life and behavior.

Many successes have already been scored in the work of instituting a new socialist way of life. However, the way of life inherited from the old society still lingers on to a considerable degree in every sphere ranging from state activity to private life. This represents an obstacle to the building of socialism and to the work of educating and remolding the working people.

We must eliminate the old way of life and thoroughly introduce the socialist way of life in all fields so that everyone lives and behaves in keeping with the intrinsic nature of our society which is based on collectivism. Capitalistic administrative rules and regulations must be done away with in all spheres of state activity; new socialist administrative rules and regulations must be perfected, and particular emphasis should be placed on fully introducing socialist order into our economic work. Socialist order should be fully established in a way that leaves no room for outworn ideas in any of the functions of economic management and administration, from registering, itemizing, maintaining and managing the property of the country and the people to utilizing and handling common property. It is also necessary to establish appropriate order in socialist community life as regards the daily social life of the people and constantly develop norms of culture and morality commensurate with socialist and communist society. Educational work should be intensified in order to obliterate outdated moral standards existent among the working people. At the same time, models of a new morality must be developed and popularized systematically through a social movement and the norms of communist morality must be gradually perfected.

All our Party members and the working people in

general—the working class, cooperative farmers and working intellectuals—should uphold the Party's line of revolutionization and working-classization and continue the dynamic struggle to carry it through. Our Party members and working people must strive to remake themselves along communist lines and revolutionize their families. Especially the leading functionaries, before anybody else, must revolutionize themselves and their families. We should begin revolutionizing our families, and then the sub-workteams, workteams and people's neighborhood units passing to the work centers and the *ri* and gradually revolutionizing and working-classizing the entire society by creating models and generalizing the experiences. All our working people will thus become ardent revolutionaries, true builders of socialism and communism. All of society will have become firmly united with a single ideology, the monolithic ideology of our Party, and will vibrate with revolutionary enthusiasm and creative zeal. All this will bring closer the day of ultimate victory for our revolution.

4. The Strengthening of the Nation's Defense Capabilities

Comrades,

The situation in our country is still critical and tense. The aggressive maneuverings of the U.S. imperialists are being intensified and their plots to provoke another war are becoming more undisguised. Under the wing of U.S. imperialism, the Japanese militarists are again stepping up their aggressive maneuvers against Korea. The puppet clique of south Korea, the stooges of both U.S. and Japanese reactionaries, are running about recklessly in an endeavor to execute the war policies of their masters. In our country the danger of war is augmented with every passing day.

To cope with the prevailing situation we must speed up our socialist construction to the maxiumum and simultaneously build up our national defense capabilities. We should continue to hold fast to the line already put forth by the Party, that of arming all the people, turning the entire country into a fortress, converting the entire army into an army of cadres and modernizing it from top to bottom. Furthermore, we should implement more thoroughly the principle of self-defense in guarding the nation.

The most important thing in increasing the defense capabilities of the country is to arm the entire people more perfectly. Everyone should learn military science in earnest and take a more active part in military training. The workers, farmers and all other working people should continually keep themselves in readiness to annihilate the aggressors anywhere they may attack, at the same time that they should accelerate socialist construction, with a hammer or sickle in one hand and a rifle in the other. When all the people are under arms, when all the people learn to hate the enemy, when all the people join in fighting against the aggressors, it will be possible to defeat any enemy.

Our People's Army is entrusted with the honorable mission of protecting our magnificent socialist achievements and the freedom and happiness of the people from the encroachment of the enemy. The People's Army should keep itself fully ready at all times to rapidly deal the aggressors crushing blows and annihilate them even in the case of a surprise attack by the enemy.

The important task to be fulfilled for strengthening the combat power of the People's Army is that of solidly arming the soldiers politically and ideologically and, on this basis, having them continually study and perfect the art of war suitable to the actual conditions of our country, thus modernizing the army.

Ours is a country with many mountains and rivers and long coast lines. If we make good use of such topographical conditions, skillfully employing mountain warfare and night actions and properly combining large-unit and small-unit operations and regular-army warfare with guerrilla warfare, we will be fully able to destroy an enemy, even if he is armed to the teeth with the latest military hardware. This was proved by the experiences of our Fatherland Liberation War, as it is today by those of the war in Vietnam.

Therefore, we have to base ourselves strictly upon our own specific conditions in modernizing the People's Army and developing military science and technology. If instead, we try to mechanically copy or dogmatically bring in foreign art of war, foreign weapons and other military hardware on the pretext of modernizing the People's Army, it may mean a serious setback to our nation's defense construction.

We must perfect our art of war in such a way as to make up for defects in the People's Army, reinforce its weak links and develop its strong points in line with the requirements of the Party's military strategic thought based on a full consideration of the concrete conditions of our country and the experience of the Fatherland Liberation War. On this basis, we must advance our military science and technique and constantly improve the weapons and other military hardware of the People's Army. We must adhere always to the principle of producing many weapons suitable to the specific conditions of our country and modernizing our military equipment in line with the level of our industrial capacity. The combat training of the People's Army soldiers should also be conducted in such a way that they master the art of war best suited to the actual conditions of our country and fully develop our own military science and technique.

Ours is a small and newly developed country. Frankly speaking, we are not in a position to compete with developed countries in military technical equipment, nor are we required to do so. The destiny of war is by no means decided by modern weapons or military technology. Although the imperialists have a military technical preponderance, our People's Army has politico-ideological superiority. The lofty mission and revolutionary spirit of fighting for the freedom and liberation of our homeland and people, and noble traits such as comradeship between officers and men, conscious military discipline and bonds of kinship with the people, are characteristic features of our People's Army which no imperialist armed forces of aggression can ever possess. Precisely because of this politico-ideological superiority our People's Army can readily defeat an enemy who is technically preponderant.

In order to reinforce our nation's defense capabilities the whole Party and the entire people should also buckle down to the job of further accelerating war preparations. The Party members and the working people in general must combat indolence and laxity and constantly maintain keen revolutionary vigilance. They should be on the ready, alert to fight and repel the enemy without the slightest perturbation no matter when the surprise attack may come. We must never become victims of a pacifistic mood and, in particular, we must strictly guard ourselves against the revisionist ideological current of war phobia and prevent it from penetrating into our ranks.

The outcome of a war depends largely on whether or not the manpower and material requirements of the front and the rear are fully met over the long run. We should guarantee ample reserves of the necessary materials by intensifying the struggle for increased production and economization in all fields of the national economy, develop the munitions industry, reorganize the economy as the situation demands and prepare ourselves in advance so as to be able to continue producing even during a war. In this way, we will build up a firm material base for the more thorough implementation of the principle of self-defense in safeguarding the nation.

Comrades, our national defense capability is literally of defensive nature and is designed to defend the security of our country and our people against imperialist aggression. We have no intention to threaten or carry out aggression against anybody. Threats and aggression against others have nothing to do with the policies of our Party. Our country is a peace-loving socialist country, and our people is one that ardently loves peace. Our consistent advocacy of peace stems from the inherent nature of our state and social system. We are doing all we can to preserve and consolidate peace. No one should, however, take our desires and persevering efforts for peace as a sign of weakness. Our people have no interest in provoking others but they will never allow anyone to toy with them. We are striving to prevent war, but we are not afraid of it. If the imperialist aggressors lunge at us with their armies, we will destroy them to a man and not one will return home alive. We will strengthen the nation's defense capabilities and decisively smash any surprise attack by the enemy, firmly safeguard our socialist achievements and indomitably defend the eastern outpost of socialism.

5. Balanced Improvement of the People's Living Standards

Comrades,
Our Party's activities are governed by the supreme principle

of systematic promotion of the welfare of the people. After all, our struggle to build socialism and communism is aimed at bringing a more abundant life to all people and making them equally well-off. As in the past, so also in the future, our Party will continue to direct endless concern to systematically improving the people's living conditions.

We have already made great strides in socialist construction and our economic gains are enormous. If we could devote them all to raising living standards, our people would be much better off than they are now and able to live as well as others. But we are still carrying on the revolution. Under present conditions, with the U.S. imperialists occupying one half of our territory and incessantly perpetrating provocations against the northern half of the Republic and with the reunification of our homeland not,yet achieved, it is unthinkable that we live in luxury and extravagance. Our way of life must be frugal, befitting a people in this age of revolution. We must save and economize wherever possible, giving priority to war preparations against every type of enemy invasion and to material accumulation for meeting the great revolutionary event of national reunification with full readiness. At the same time, we must strive to make the working people's lives free of inconvenience and improve their living standards on the basis of equality for all.

At present the most important task we must confront in order to better the lives of the people is to rapidly eliminate distinctions between workers and farmers in living standards and between urban and rural inhabitants in living conditions. Indeed, during the period under review, our Party changed the appearance of the countryside, rapidly improved the living conditions of the farmers and did a great deal of work to build the socialist countryside by strengthening working-class leadership among them and by boosting industry's assistance to agriculture and urban support for the countryside. But the rural villages of our country were so backward in the past that they are still behind the towns economically and culturally; and our peasants were so badly off before that their living standards are still not as high as those of the workers. We must pay close attention to solving this matter, finally rid the countryside of its backwardness as soon as possible and raise the living standards of the farmers up to those of the workers.

The most important thing for the improvement of peasant life is to build up the counties and enhance their role.

The county is the lowest unit of administrative leadership, which gives direct guidance to the rural areas and is in direct contact with the life of the farming population, and it is the base for linking the towns with the countryside in all political, economic and cultural spheres. Therefore, the development of the countryside and the betterment of the farmers' lives depend largely on the role of the counties. We should develop the counties correctly and enhance their role, and thus further accelerate construction of the socialist countryside and rapidly improve the living conditions of the rural population. Development of the role of the county as a supply base for the rural villages should be given top priority. It is necessary to build refrigeration plants, fruit- and vegetable-processing factories, meat-processing factories, and to provide many mobile processing facilities for evey county so that meat, fruits, vegetables and other agricultural produce from the farmers may be purchased and processed in good time. Meanwhile, the work of supplying the countryside with processed foodstuffs and a variety of manufactured goods should be further improved by building a strong county supply base and rationally distributing the rural network of stores. If the county's purchase of farm produce and its supply of commodities to the countryside work smoothly, the farmers' incomes will increase more rapidly and they can buy what they need in the countryside as readily as in the towns.

One of the urgent problems in eliminating the difference in living conditions between urban and rural inhabitants is to introduce bus service in every rural *ri*. The opening of bus service to the rural *ri* will not only free the rural working people from inconveniences in travel, but strengthen the ties between town and country in all political, economic and cultural spheres. This will be a great help to speedily ridding the countryside of its backwardness. In the next few years we should improve the roads interlinking counties and *ri* and open bus service to all rural *ri* where it is not yet available.

Water service is of great importance in bettering the living conditions of the rural population. We should lay water lines in all rural villages as well as in those county seats which have no water service yet, so that rural women need not carry water jars on their heads and so that all rural dwellers may live a more hygienic and modern life.

While placing primary emphasis on enhancing the living standards of the farmers and improving the conditions of modern life for the rural population, we should take a series of measures to ensure a better life for all working people.

We should continue building many houses to solve people's living problems adequately. We will launch a general mass movement to build 100,000 family units in towns and 150,000-200,000 in the countryside every year in order to cover the present housing shortage and fill future housing demands for our growing population. As a matter of course, great concern should be given to building comfortable, convenient, modern and sanitary dwellings. At the same time, central heating systems should be installed in Pyongyang and other major cities so that working people enjoy a more convenient and pleasant life.

In the next few years, we should raise the wages of factory and office workers as a whole and, in particular, sharply increase the wages of the factory and office workers in the low-wage category. Prices of all consumer goods should be cut drastically in keeping with an increased production of daily necessities and various other consumer goods, and prices of mass consumer goods which are in great demand should be reduced by more than 50%.

We should further develop the public health service so as to better protect and promote the health of the working people. We should build more hospitals, increase the number of medical workers and produce and supply more medicines and medical instruments of various kinds to further improve both preventive and curative medical care for the working people. In particular, we should build up the county hospitals, improve maternity facilities for the rural women, develop the clinics in rural *ri* into hospitals, and set up children's wards in all *ri*, so that medical services for the rural inhabitants are improved radically.

We should thus improve and equalize living standards for all workers and farmers and ensure all the working people of our country a better life.

ANSWERS TO THE QUESTIONS RAISED BY THE IRAQI JOURNALISTS' DELEGATION (Excerpt)

October 11, 1971

Question: *We would like to tell you of our admiration and wonder at the experience acquired by the Workers' Party of Korea under your wise leadership.*

Would you please tell us what you consider to be the most important experience of the fighting people of Korea and what they have contributed to the treasure house of mankind in their struggle for socialism?

Answer: First of all, I would like to say how grateful I am for your high estimation of our experience.

As you know, our country was formerly a colonial, semi-feudal society. Our people inherited a backward economy and culture from the old society, and even these were totally destroyed during the three-year war started by the U.S. imperialists. In addition, we faced the task of building a new society in a country divided into north and south, opposed face to face with the U.S. imperialist aggressors.

Though they were faced with many difficulties and ordeals as they advanced, the Korean people, always deeply convinced of the justness of their cause, fought an unyielding struggle. They thus put an end to age-old backwardness and poverty and rapidly built a new, decent socialist society. Today, an advanced socialist system under which all people work and live happily, helping each other, has been established in our country where exploitation and oppression once prevailed. Our country has become a socialist industrial state with modern industries and a developed agriculture.

Our people owe all their victories and achievements in socialist revolution and construction to the wise leadership of the Workers' Party of Korea.

The most important characteristic of the guidance by the Workers' Party of Korea of our people's revolutionary struggle and work of construction is that it has thoroughly established Juche.

We have consistently followed the principle of settling all problems of revolution and construction independently, in the context of the actual conditions of our country, by relying mainly on our own efforts. We have creatively applied the universal principles of Marxism-Leninism and experiences gained by other countries in a way which suits our own country's historical conditions and national peculiarities. Thus we have made ourselves responsible for solving our own problems, whatever the circumstances, rejecting the spirit of dependence on others and displaying the spirit of self-reliance. The word Juche, widely known to the world, is a term which expresses this creative and independent principle and position adhered to by our Party in revolutionary struggle and work of construction.

Experience has proved to the full the correctness of the Juche idea.

By struggling to establish Juche in our ideology we have brought about the complete spiritual emancipation of our people from the shackles of flunkeyism, dogmatism and other archaic notions which had long been corroding our spirit of national independence. Our people's tendency to thoughtlessly discard things Korean in favor of swallowing foreign ways whole, has disappeared. Our national pride and spirit of independence has been more awakened and our people have been increasingly encouraged to rely on their own efforts.

While establishing Juche in ideology, our Party has thoroughly embodied the Juche idea in all fields of revolution and construction.

Our Party's line of independence is the embodiment of the Juche idea in the political context.

In shaping its guidelines and policies for revolution and construction our Party has opposed any tendency to cling only to the existing formulae of Marxism-Leninism or swallow whole the experiences of other countries. It has used its own brains to map out original lines and policies suited to Korea's specific conditions, and has implemented them by organizing and mobilizing the masses. On the question of the country's reunification, too, we maintain an independent position: the issue must be settled by our own people, without the interference of any outside forces, under the condition that the aggressive army of U.S. imperialism be withdrawn from south Korea.

In external spheres, too, our Party has steadfastly maintained independence. We have developed friendly and cooperative relationships with other countries, both big and small, on the principles of complete equality and mutual respect. We have also continued to wage the anti-imperialist, anti-U.S. struggle and the fight against opportunism of all hues, in conformity with our actual conditions, basing our actions strictly on our own judgment and beliefs.

Our Party's line of building an independent national economy is the embodiment of the Juche idea in economic construction.

By relying largely upon our own technical skills and resources, and using our own cadres and people, we have maintained the revolutionary spirit of self-reliance. This has been our principle in developing the country's economy. Our Party's line of building an independent national economy illustrates our people's real hope for complete national independence and prosperity, and it has been behind the startling achievements in the socialist construction of our country.

Our country's economy is now independent, equipped with

modern techniques and developed all round. As a result of this we have been able to develop the national economy at a steady, high rate and to improve the people's living conditions through our own efforts. Our independent national economy serves as a solid material guarantee for the political independence of the country and for the increase of our defense capacity.

In implementing Juche and relying on our own efforts we do not intend to build socialism in isolation. We fully recognize that it is necessary for states to supply each other's needs and cooperate with each other, and we are striving to expand and develop such relations. We believe that mutual cooperation between states should be conducted with a view to building an independent national economy in each country. This factor alone makes it possible to expand and develop economic cooperation between states on the principles of complete equality and mutual benefit.

We have held fast to a policy of self-defense in the development of our nation's defenses. As a result of the implementation of the Party's self-reliant military line, our country has today come to possess its own defense forces, which are strong enough to crush all aggressors and enemies.

As I have explained, all the lines and policies of our Party proceed from, and are imbued with, the Juche idea. Juche in ideology, independence in politics, self-support in economy and self-defense in guarding the nation represent the revolutionary stand consistently adhered to by our Party.

Under the revolutionary banner of the Juche idea, our country has become a developed socialist country which has complete political sovereignty, a powerful independent national economy, strong self-defense potential and a shining national culture. As a result of the implementation of Juche, and reliance on our own efforts, we are now able to cooperate with other countries on the principle of complete equality, and make a better contribution to the cause of international revolution.

In guiding the revolution and construction, our Party has striven to carry through the revolutionary mass line, while establishing Juche.

Socialism can be built only with the voluntary and creative labor of millions of people. Our Party, therefore, found the basic guarantee for the promotion of socialist construction in giving the major role to the revolutionary zeal and creative activity of the masses.

In our country, revolutionary struggle and work of construction have been conducted in all fields as a mass, popular movement. We have succeeded in all the huge and difficult tasks of revolution and construction by relying on the high degree of revolutionary zeal and creative energy of the people. An important key to the rapid progress of our socialist construction lies precisely in the fact that we have solved all our problems by the revolutionary method of relying on the masses and rousing them to action.

When we met with major difficulties and trials in socialist construction, we placed faith in the masses of the people, went among them, and had serious consultations with them on means of solving problems and effecting innovations. Through this, the working masses grasped the Party's intention and started a movement for collective innovation, carrying through the Party's lines and policies. This developed into the well-known Chollima Movement of Korea.

The Chollima Movement is our people's mass innovation movement to step up socialist construction to the maximum. It is the most brilliant embodiment of our Party's mass line in socialist construction, and through this very movement all the wisdom, enthusiasm and creative energy of our people have been brought into full play. With the spread of the Chollima Movement, innovations have taken place in all spheres of our economy, culture, ideology, and morality, and splendid achievements have been made in our socialist construction.

All our victories are the great victories of our Party's Juche idea and, at the same time, the brilliant victories of its revolutionary mass line.

Our experience shows that when Juche is firmly established as an ideology and is thoroughly embodied in all domains of revolution and construction and when the creative zeal and talents of the masses are brought into full play, it is possible, in a country, however backward it was in the past, to build rapidly a new, rich and strong society, rout any imperialist aggressors and defend national independence and the dignity of the people and achieve prosperity for the country and the people.

You have expressed your admiration for our experience, and we consider it to be encouragement in our work.

We have already worked a great deal, but we have much to

do in the future. We have not yet reunified the country. The U.S. imperialists continue to occupy the southern half of our country, maintaining a brutal colonial fascist rule.

The greatest national task confronting the Korean people is to drive the U.S. imperialist aggressors out of south Korea, accomplish the national-liberation revolution and realize the reuinification of the country. In order to accomplish the task, we are striving to build up more solidly the revolutionary base of the northern half of the Republic politically, economically and militarily, increase in every way the revolutionary forces in south Korea and, at the same time, strengthen solidarity with the international revolutionary forces.

ON THE CHARACTER
AND TASKS OF THE TRADE UNIONS
IN SOCIALIST SOCIETY

Speech at the Fifth Congress of the General Federation of Trade Unions of Korea, *December 14, 1971*

Comrades,

I consider the report and the debate by many comrades here at this Fifth Congress of the General Federation of Trade Unions of Korea to have been highly instructive and valuable. The report and debate fully convinced us once again that our working class is built up with revolutionary ranks unboundedly faithful to the Party.

I am satisfied that our heroic working class has accomplished much in the revolutionary struggle and the work of construction, displaying a boundless loyalty to the Party and a lofty revolutionary spirit. I highly estimate this.

The Party Central Committee and all the people firmly trust and have great expectations of the working class. Only when the working class, the leading class of the revolution, struggles well, is it possible to rebuild and develop our country quickly and hasten national reunification, the unanimous desire of our people.

I firmly believe that following this congress our working class, deeply conscious of its weighty mission, will work more actively and will definitely meet the expectations of the Party and the people.

Availing myself of this opportunity, I would like to touch briefly on the character and tasks of the trade unions at the present stage.

Internationally speaking, the working-class movement has a long history of development. Ever since its emergence the working class has constantly fought against the oppression and exploitation of capital and for the liberation from its yoke.

The history of the working-class movement in our country is not short. Our working-class movement started in the 1920s. Around this time our working class grew rapidly and began its active struggle; from then on the national-liberation movement in our country developed under the leadership of the working class.

At a time when we were deprived of our country and all our people were groaning under Japanese imperialism's colonial rule, the Korean working class was confronted with the task of achieving national liberation by crushing Japanese imperialism and of freeing itself from capital's exploitation. In its early days, however, our working-class movement could not develop greatly; being weak and having neither a leader capable of guiding the struggle along the right path nor a revolutionary Marxist-Leninist party, it was torn into factions.

Only in the early 1930s as a Marxist-Leninist leadership and a correct line of struggle emerged, did our working-class movement enter a new phase of development. From this time onward the Korean working class fought more dynamically in varied forms against the Japanese imperialist aggressors and capitalists. Particularly, the awakened workers, arms in hand, fought bravely in the sacred anti-Japanese armed struggle to liberate the country. Through a long-drawn heroic struggle, the anti-Japanese armed ranks centering around the working class defeated the Japanese imperialist aggressors and accomplished the historic task of national liberation, opening up before our people a bright prospect of building a new society.

After liberation a people's government was established in the northern half of our country and the workers and other working people became the masters of the country. Under these circumstances the fighting tasks of the working class were fundamentally different from those before liberation. So were the character and tasks of the trade unions, the mass organizations of the working class.

However, the factionalists and local separatists infected with dogmatism failed to see the changed reality and clamored that even in the situation where the working class was in power, the trade unions must fight the government just as in capitalist society; they attempted to oppose the working class to the people's power and maneuvered to lead the working-class movement in the wrong direction. Our Party gave a severe blow to this maneuver of the factionalists in good time and made clear the trade unions' character and tasks under the people's government.

The trade unions' main task at the stage of democratic revolution was that of protecting the people's government, actively supporting all the policies mapped out by the working-class party and people's government and organizing and mobilizing the working class to struggle for their implementation. At the same time, the trade unions, assisting the people's government, performed the function of supervision making sure that the factories and enterprises guaranteed the factory and office workers the vital rights and working conditions as provided for by the state.

Following liberation our people's government allowed the national capitalists to carry on limited business activity, because it was a government that relied on a united front of broad democratic forces based on the worker-peasant alliance led by the working class. Such being the case, it was necessary for the masses to supervise the private enterprises to ensure that the workers and office employees were guaranteed their democratic rights and working conditions and that the private entrepreneurs did not exploit their employees at will. Therefore, our Party saw to it that the trade unions made collective contracts with the entrepreneurs and exercised supervision over their correct implementation of the stipulations of the Labor Law such as on the eight-hour day, labor protection and social insurance.

Another reason for the trade unions supervising the

management of the enterprises was that the workers had no experience in running the factories and enterprises. As a result of the enforcement of the Law on Nationalization of Industries the factories, mines, railways and other major industries formerly owned by Japanese imperialism, pro-Japanese elements and traitors to the nation came under the ownership of the state and the workers became their masters. However, because the workers had neither experience nor knowledge of economic management, the factories and enterprises were run by old technicians and experts as before. Therefore, the trade unions, the organizations of the workers, had to exercise supervision over the factories and enterprises in order to ensure that they were run as demanded by the Party and the Government.

After the socialist system was established and the Taean work system introduced, it was no longer necessary for the trade unions to supervise the management of the factories and enterprises and, accordingly, the character and tasks of the trade unions changed.

The successful socialist revolution brought about a great change in socio-economic relations in our country. All private enterprises were eliminated and the socialist sector of economy held undivided sway; the factories and enterprises were run by the new technicians and experts coming from the working people. Particular mention should be made of the fact that with the establishment of the Taean work system, the one-man management by directors, the capitalist method of enterprise management, was replaced by the system of collective leadership by the Party committee. Now the factory Party committee collectively discusses and adopts decisions on all problems related to enterprise activity and supervises their implementation. The factory Party committee is not only composed mostly of those with a working-class background but also of the active workers directly engaged in production. In this way the factory Party committee is directly linked with the masses of the workers and organizes and guides all work of enterprise management according to the collective will of the workers. In this situation supervision by the trade unions became entirely superfluous.

Since the factory Party committee is the highest leadership body of the factory, the trade union supervision over enterprise management runs counter to the organizational principle of the Marxist-Leninist party. The Marxist-Leninist party is the organized detachment of the progressive elements of the working class and is the highest form of organization of the working masses. The trade unions and all other mass organizations are under the Party's leadership and must actively fight to carry out its lines and policies. If the trade unions supervise enterprise management at the factory, which is directly led and supervised by the factory Party committee, it would, in the last analysis, be tantamount to controlling the Party's activity, to placing the trade unions above the Party.

Therefore, our Party has long abolished the system of the trade unions making collective contracts with the factory management and their right to supervise the enterprise administration. The trade unions have at the same time been converted from a semi-ideological educational, semi-administrative organization into a full-fledged ideological educational organization which revolutionally educates the working class and the trade union membership and rallies them closely around the Party, organizing and mobilizing them to implement the political and economic assignments given by the Party.

Our Party was quite justified in turning the trade unions into ideological educational organizations. This has been clearly proved by the life of our country.

Thanks to the trade unions' increased role as educator and to their intensified ideological education of the workers, our working class' revolutionary zeal is now very high and, owing to their heroic struggle, our nation's economy is developing at a high rate every year. It is true that we have many difficulties in the building of the socialist economy. Because of the Fatherland Liberation War we are suffering from an acute shortage of manpower; and we are feeling a strain on electricity because due to the droughts over the last few years our reservoirs are not filled with enough water. However, these difficulties are just temporary and will be overcome before long. The manpower problem will be solved in a few years to come. If machines are built on a large scale and the technical revolution stepped up as proposed by the Party, this problem may be solved more rapidly. The problem of electricity will also be solved soon because we have already built large thermal power stations and are carrying out the construction of new power stations. Once these two problems are solved, our nation's economy will develop far more rapidly.

There is also the possibility of considerably raising the people's standard of living in the coming few years. So far we have allocated a huge amount of funds for the building of the nation's defenses, and have not been able to exert great efforts to improve the people's living standard. However, the opportunities are now at hand for speeding up this task. If we build a few more synthetic fiber plants including an Orlon factory, the problem of clothing will be solved once and for all. As for the food problem, we do not import rice now; and we are planning to supply everyone with 100 grams of fish daily beginning next year, though the population is not yet supplied with enough fish. In addition, the newly-built chicken plants are beginning to have an effect and large pig factories are being built. The grain needed for meat production will be produced in plenty through two crops with the help of the sprinkling irrigation system on dry fields.

Thus, as far as the socialist economic construction and the people's living conditions are concerned, our general situation is highly favorable now.

In order to build socialism and communism successfully, it is necessary, as the revolution and construction develop in depth and scope, to further strengthen the Party's leadership and the dictatorship of the proletariat, and the trade unions and all other mass organizations must actively support the Party and Government and unconditionally accept the Party lines and policies and carry them through. People still have the remnants of old ideas. So, if the workers were allowed to act as they please, free from the Party's leadership, liberalism and egoism would appear, causing the inroad of capitalistic ideas from outside and thus destroying the revolution and the work of construction.

In socialist society the trade unions, as the Party's transmission belt, must vigorously organize and mobilize the working class for the struggle to occupy the ideological and material fortresses of communism. Therefore, they must, first of all, intensify the ideological education of the working class. The trade unions' main task in socialist society is to strengthen the ideological education and working-classize and revolutionize their entire membership.

At present, some of our officials talk a lot about working-classization and revolutionization but they have no clear idea of these notions. What, then, are working-classization and revolutionization? In a word, working-classization means transforming non-working-class people on the pattern of the progressive working class; and revolutionization means teaching people to be ardent revolutionaries, to be true Communists, equipped with a revolutionary world outlook.

Though the trade unions are organizations of the working class, they must work to working-classize their membership. Their membership includes not only the working class but also office workers, teachers, and many others who are engaged in other occupations. So the trade unions must strive to transform all non-working-class members on the pattern of the working class.

While working-classizing their membership, the trade unions must wage a dynamic struggle to revolutionize and communize them.

At present some people claim that because the word revolution means the struggle to crush the old social system, this word must not be used once the socialist system is set up. This is a wrong interpretation of the term revolution and one which denies the necessity of continuing with revolution in socialist society.

The work of rooting out the traces of outworn ideologies in the minds of people and arming them with communist ideology is a sharp class struggle between what is feudal and capitalistic and what is communistic—a revolution in the sphere of ideology. Therefore, in order to educate and reform people along communist lines, revolution must be carried on in the ideological sphere even after the establishment of the socialist system and a struggle must be conducted to revolutionize and communize people. Only when the working people are not only working-classized but also revolutionized and communized, can they hold fast to revolutionary principle in any adversity and fight for the triumph of the communist cause. The trade union organizations should, therefore, strive to working-classize and revolutionize those who do not belong to the working class and revolutionize and communize those who have become workers.

The revolutionization and communization of our working class is a particularly urgent problem because of its characteristic features. Our working class is young. After liberation, particularly during the postwar period when industry developed at a high rate, the ranks of the working class expanded quickly. As a result, they were joined by many people who had never been exploited or oppressed in the former society, and in particular, by many former peasants, small merchants and handicraftsmen. These latter are now industrial workers, but they still retain selfishness and many other survivals of old ideologies. Hence the necessity of stepping up the ideological revolution to root out the remnants of old ideas in the workers and arm them with a communist world outlook.

In working-classizing and revolutionizing the trade union members the most important aspect is firmly equipping them with our Party's monolithic ideology, the Juche idea.

The Juche idea is Marxism-Leninism creatively applied to the reality of our country, and the most powerful weapon in carrying out our revolution and construction. When all the working people are closely armed with our Party's revolutionary Juche idea, they can fight resolutely against flunkeyism, dogmatism, revisionism and all other evil ideas and push ahead successfully with the revolutionary struggle and the work of construction.

Holding high the revolutionary banner of the Juche idea and fully establishing Juche in all the spheres of politics, economy, culture and military affairs, our Party has been able to defend the purity of Marxism-Leninism and consistently lead our revolution and construction to victory, even under the complicated circumstances where the opportunist trends which emerged in the international communist movement have been obstructing the development of the revolutionary movement and the imperialists have been intensifying more than ever before their ideological offensive against communism.

The imperialists and international reaction took advantage of the crop failures in certain socialist countries to slander the socialist system; they alleged that cooperativization had ruined agriculture and that the agricultural problem could not be solved in a socialist society. Around this time our Party announced the theses on the socialist rural question and developed agriculture rapidly, bringing a bumper crop every year. This fully demonstrated the superiority of the socialist agricultural system to the whole world and utterly smashed the imperialists' reactionary ideological offensive.

And, when in certain countries the economy had come to a standstill instead of developing rapidly, some people attempted to justify this, by spreading the revisionist theory that the socialist economy could not indefinitely develop at a high rate. Our Party answered it with a new socialist economic theory. The Chollima Movement and the great revolutionary upswing in the construction of socialism initiated by the heroic Korean people under our Party's leadership, and the whole course of the development of our national economy proved that the revisionist theory—that as the scale of the economy expands, production cannot develop at a continued high rate—was nothing but an entirely unfounded sophistry.

Through our practical struggle for the revolution and construction we have clearly shown the correctness and vitality of the Juche idea. Today our Party's revolutionary Juche idea is arousing sympathy among many people of the world.

Striving to defend and enrich the Juche idea is the glorious, sacred duty of our working class and of the working people as a whole. The trade union organizations must educate the working class and their membership to continue to arm themselves firmly with our Party's Juche idea and actively struggle to defend and carry it through.

To revolutionize and working-classize the working people, we must strengthen their communist education.

I am only going to refer to this matter briefly because I have dwelt on it on many other occasions.

The most important part of communist education is to rid the working people of individualism and selfishness and equip them with collectivism.

Individualism and selfishness are the legacy of capitalist society. Capitalist society is a society based on individualism that makes people content with their own affluence and comfort, not caring about others. Present-day south Korean reality is a good example of society founded on individualism and selfishness.

In south Korea today a handful of landlords and capitalists eat and live well while the great majority of the working people including the workers and peasants are living stifled in matchbox houses and hovels, and millions of unemployed wander about the streets in quest of jobs and food. South Koreans now criticize their society, saying that "the rich get ever richer and the poor get ever poorer" there. They mean that the rich people amass wealth while the poor people are further impoverished. In south Korea a handful of rich people are getting richer and richer and the overwhelming majority of the people are becoming poorer and poorer because that society is a society for the landlords and capitalists.

Not long ago a capitalist journalist wrote a story which ridiculed the south Korean reality. He said that south Korea had built nice-looking expressways, but they were lined with dilapidated thatch-roofed houses and the streets swarmed with beggars.

A socialist, communist society, unlike a capitalist society, is a society based on collectivism; it is a society where everybody helps and leads each other forward, engaging in productive activity and living happily together. In this society people are not allowed to have an individualist, egoistic desire to live in comfort for themselves.

Individualism and selfishness have nothing to do with communist ideology. In order to build a happy socialist, communist society where everybody is well-fed and well-clothed, lives in a good house, can study to his heart's content and is entitled to free medical treatment, it is necessary completely to eliminate individualism and selfishness from the minds of people and arm them with collectivism. And everybody must devotedly strive anywhere anytime not for his comfort and pleasure, but for the society and people, for the Party and revolution.

To eliminate individualism and selfishness, ideological education must be intensified among the working men and women.

These ideological remnants will not disappear automatically from the minds of the working people just because a socialist system has been established. Experience shows that even though the socio-economic basis for individual selfishness has been eliminated as a result of the establishment of the socialist system, individualism and selfishness will continue to manifest themselves unless the ideological education of the working people is conducted well. When these ideas are allowed to breed, people seek their own comfort and pleasure rather than work for the interests of the state and people; for this purpose, they do not hesitate to do harm to others' lives and property or defame their country and people. Needless to say, we cannot expect these individualists and egoists to love their revolutionary comrades and collectives or fight devotedly for the party and the revolution.

Eliminating individualism and egoism rooted deep in the minds of people is the point of departure in the revolutionization of the working people. The trade union organizations must intensify the ideological education of their membership to root out individualistic, egoistic ideas.

The revolutionary opera *A True Daughter of the Party* recently produced by the People's Army Song and Dance Ensemble is an excellent work for educating the working people in communist ideology. This moving opera truthfully depicts the lofty comradeship and collectivism of a People's Army nurse who sacrifices her life for her revolutionary comrades and collective. Unhesitatingly dedicating one's life to the interests of one's collective is a noble characteristic of the Communist.

From now on, the trade union organizations must strengthen collectivist education so that all their members work and live in accordance with the communist principle: "One for all and all for one."

In order to eliminate individualism and egoism, it is imperative to intensify the education of the women.

As we mentioned at the Fourth Congress of the Women's Union, only by strengthening the education of the women can we not only revolutionize and working-classize them but also facilitate the work of rooting out individualism and selfishness of men. Being mistress of the household, the woman's mentality considerably affects her children and husband. When the women still in the grip of individualism and egoism grumble at home or moan at their husbands for this or that, their husbands inevitably become greedy and fail to revolutionize themselves. Therefore, the women's education must be particularly strengthened so as to revolutionize and working-classize them all.

What is important in eliminating the individualism and selfishness of the women and revolutionizing and working-classizing them is to send them out into the world so that they take part in organizational life. If they are not given a chance to

live in public life but are just kept at home, they will not know
what is going on around them and they will have the egoistic
tendency to enjoy comfortable lives for themselves.

We must send many more of them out into the world and
strengthen their organizational, political life. In such a way all
of them will be revolutionized and working-classized, so that
the revolutionization and working-classization of the whole of
society will be stepped up.

We are striving to build a society where everybody will live
well, not a society where a handful of people will be well-off.
Therefore, when organizing and conducting any work we must
always oppose individualism and selfishness resolutely and
give full scope to collectivism.

Another important aspect of communist education is
fostering in all working people a communist attitude toward
labor.

Communism can be built successfully only when all the
working people love labor and participate in it earnestly. The
word communism itself means that production is run along
communal lines. A handful of persons cannot produce enough
to provide every member of society with an affluent life. So we
must see to it that everybody participates in labor and works
harder.

Should people hate to work and just want to eat the bread of
idleness, it would be impossible to occupy the material fortress
of communism or, moreover, maintain any society. In order to
put into effect the communist principle under which people
work according to their abilities and receive their shares
according to their demands, all the members of the society
must, first of all, love work, consciously take part in it and
dedicate all their efforts and talents to the welfare of the
society.

Loving work and earnestly participating in labor is one of the
most important traits of the Communist. By observing whether
people love work or not, honestly participate in common labor
or not, whether or not they are prepared to work devotedly for
the country and people throughout their lives, we can gauge the
extent to which they are revolutionized and working-classized.

Let me tell you a story about a communist mother who truly
loves labor and works hard for the Party and the revolution.

Sometime ago we visited Comrade Ma Dong Hui's mother.

She sacrificed all her family—husband, son, daughter-in-law and daughter—for the revolution. And she herself had been severly tortured in prison by the Japanese scoundrels, and still has trouble with her leg. But she had never revealed this fact to anybody lest it should worry us. Though she is old and in poor health, this year she voluntarily took part in the movement to raise castor silkworms, which was initiated by the Women's Union. She planted and tended castor-oil plants in her yard and presented them to the local members of the Women's Union as feed for the silkworms.

Comrade Ma Dong Hui's mother has lived all alone, without any help from others. More than once we advised her to keep a person who would take care of the kitchen work for her because she was too old to look after all the household chores. But she refused; she said she lived in comfort under the grateful care of the Party and the state, even though she could not give any help to the country, and she could not take a hand from the nation's precious manpower pool just to take care of her domestic work. Not long ago we arranged for a hospital nurse to live with her and help her in the evening after her work at the hospital.

This mother is a true communist mother who works as hard as she can and is firmly determined to give the country what little help she can.

The trade union organizations must intensify the ideological education of the working class and their membership and equip them with a communist attitude toward labor, so that they will regard the nonparticipation in labor as the greatest shame, always love labor, consciously observe work discipline and devote all their efforts and talents to the construction of socialism.

The trade unions must educate their members to take loving care of and economize the common property which belongs to the state and society.

In our society all property of the state and society is the people's common property. This property has been created by the blood and sweat of the workers, peasants and the rest of the working people and is a valuable asset guaranteeing our people and posterity happy lives. Unless the common property is protected and economized, we cannot make our nation rich and strong nor our people well-off, however much we may produce or build.

What is more, we have not yet reunified our country and are building socialism in confrontation with the enemies. Recently, under the pretext of the "threat of invasion from the north" south Korea's puppet clique has even declared a "state of emergency" and is madly preparing for war. In this situation we must make war preparations, while carrying on economic construction at the same time. Building socialism and simultaneously preparing for war is by no means an easy task for our country which has a small territory and population. Therefore, we must thoroughly prevent wastage in all spheres and maximize production and economy.

However, some of our officials and working people are not economical enough and more often than not, carelessly handle or squander the nation's property.

The neglect of the state property is to be seen in any sphere, at any unit. There are a lot of people who do not take care of the fine homes built by the state, and everywhere machines and equipment, automobiles and tractors break down through the lack of care. Very often materials are wasted and merchandise handled carelessly and damaged. Those who are engaged in agriculture work zealously from the time of rice planting till harvest but after harvesting they do not take good care of the precious grain. In the countryside you can still see plenty of grain stacks in the fields and in some cases the harvested grain stalks are littered there. A considerable amount of grain produced by the hard efforts exerted over the whole year is lost this way because it is not taken in and threshed in good time.

The common property of the state and the society is carelessly handled and wasted because egoism remains in the minds of people. The trade union organizations must conduct a powerful ideological struggle against the wastage and encroachment on the common property and strengthen the education of all their members so that they take responsible attitudes toward the nation's economy.

The trade union organizations must teach their membership to hate the exploitative system and have a deep love for the socialist system.

To educate the working people to have a boundless love for the socialist system and devotedly strive to consolidate and develop it, they must be clearly informed of the essence of the exploitative society and of the former days when our people were oppressed and humiliated.

Among the workers there are many who have never been exploited or oppressed or undergone the harsh trials of the revolutionary struggle. They are not well aware of how the present happy socialist system has come into being, how much blood the revolutionary forerunners shed and how many lives were sacrificed for this system.

The trade union organizations must thoroughly acquaint their members with the essence of the exploitative system and the superiority of the socialist system and with the hard-fought struggle waged by our people to set up and defend this system, so that they may dedicate their all to the struggle to stoutly protect the socialist system from the encroachment of the enemy and further consolidate and develop it.

Another important task facing the trade union organizations is that of raising the workers' technological and cultural levels.

To achieve the complete victory of socialism and build communism, the technical revolution must be carried out along with the ideological revolution. Only by making the technical revolution can we eliminate the difference between heavy and light labor, between agricultural and industrial labor and between mental and physical labor and occupy the material fortress of communism.

We are now confronted with a weighty task of successfully carrying out the three major tasks of the technical revolution proposed at the Fifth Party Congress. These are proud revolutionary tasks aimed at freeing all our working people from arduous labor and guaranteeing them affluent and cultured lives. In order to implement these tasks splendidly, we must quickly complete mechanization in all spheres of the national economy and widely introduce semi-automation and automation.

Ours is an era of automation. If we work hard and extensively introduce semi-automation and automation, we can enable our working people to work with much more ease and efficiency in all spheres of the national economy.

Some time ago I saw a scientific film produced by an advanced country. In this country a large iron works with a capacity of two to three million tons is run by automatic apparatuses. A few people work in a room; when they push buttons, ores enter the furnace automatically and pig iron gushes out, entering the oxygen converter and emerging as steel. When automation reaches such a level we can say that the difference between physical and mental labor has been eliminated completely.

If we also extensively study science and technology and develop them, we can produce steel without making our smelters work in high heat at the open-hearth furnace or electric furnace and go to the trouble of throwing limestone into it with shovels; and we can also automate the production processes of the extractive industries or capital construction. And if we step up the technical revolution in agriculture and raise the level of mechanization and chemicalization, we can liberate the peasants from backbreaking work.

We should raise the level of mechanization in both industry and agriculture and all spheres of the national economy and introduce semi-automation and automation so as to free our working people from difficult and arduous labor. This is a glorious revolutionary task which the working class must undertake. It is mainly they who must carry out the technnical revolution not only in industry but also in agriculture. The technical revolution in agriculture cannot be carried out successfully with the efforts of the peasants alone. Only when many workers equipped with progressive ideas and techniques go to the countryside, can the mechanization and chemicaliza- tion of agriculture be pushed ahead forcefully.

Some time ago we visited the Huichon Machine-tool Plant. On our way back we dropped in at a ri in Hyangsan County and met many people and exchanged views on how to raise the level of mechanization and save manpower in agriculture. I told them that new factories, enterprises and workshops were snowball- ing and this was causing a heavy strain on the nation's manpower, and asked them whether they could farm with machines and save the rural manpower and transfer it to industry. But an official who was said to have had a long experience in farming there was reluctant to accept mechaniza- tion, claiming that farming had better be done with hands rather than machines. However, one of the workteam heads, a demobilized soldier and former worker, actively supported the mechanization of agriculture. He asked for a truck and tractors, saying that if other people were reluctant to mechanize, his workteam would try it out. He said that if his workteam was provided with a truck and three tractors, they would save plenty of manpower and produce much more grain than now. A tractor driver who was present there agreed with the workteam head and stressed the need to mechanize farming. This shows that the rural technical revolution can be stepped up forcefully only when many workers with progressive ideas and techniques go to the countryside.

When large numbers of workers go to the countryside, and farming is done with trucks, tractors and different farm machines, chemical fertilizers and agricultural chemicals in large quantities, we can not only increase grain production but also eliminate the difference between agricultural and industrial labor and enforce the eight-hour day in the countryside, also. The successful acceleration of the technical revolution in agriculture will facilitate the working-classization of the peasants, too.

To carry out splendidly the tasks of the technical revolution devolving on them, the working class must have a high technological and cultural level. So the workers must strive to raise their technological and cultural level, while continuing to revolutionize themselves.

To raise their technological and cultural level, the workers must study hard. Along with the Party's policies, they must diligently study technology to possess a profound and extensive knowledge of the latest developments of science and technology.

We have long set up an excellent system of higher learning such as correspondence courses and factory colleges under which the working people can study while on the job; and we have introduced the Saturday studies and the system of studying two hours every day. Upholding the Party's policy for the whole Party, the whole army and the whole nation to study, the workers must make the best use of their favorable conditions and study hard to constantly raise their technological and cultural level.

The trade union organizations must enhance their role in encouraging the workers to study well. As we pointed out at the Second National Meeting of the Vanguards in the Chollima Workteam Movement, one of the central tasks of this movement is to do work with books to raise the working people's technological and cultural level. The trade union organizations must always take deep care that the workers study well and regularly and must provide them with every condition for continually raising their technological and cultural level.

Then all our workers will be equipped with as much knowledge and technology and cultural attainments as the intellectuals.

The trade union organizations must also vigorously organize and mobilize their members to carry out the immediate economic tasks.

Our major task in the construction of socialism today is that of successfully fulfilling the three major tasks of the technical revolution proposed at the Fifth Party Congress. The trade union organizations must forcefully organize and mobilize the working class for the fulfillment of these tasks designed to free the working people from backbreaking labor.

In order to carry out these tasks successfully, it is necessary, first of all, to quickly develop the machine-building industry and, in particular, step up the production of machine tools.

Increasing the production of machine tools is the key to the fulfillment of the technical revolution. The technical revolution can be called a machine revolution. Without machine tools, it is impossible to develop the machine-building industry itself and succeed in carrying out any of the tasks of the technical revolution. Our success in carrying out the three major tasks entirely depends on the production of machine tools in large quantities. That is why our Party concentrated on the production of machine tools during the battle in the first year of the Six-Year Plan.

Early this year we visited the Huichon Machine-tool Plant and appealed to its workers to bring about a great innovation in the production of machine tools. Upholding the Party's call they boldly buckled down to streamlining the equipment and worked hard to automate the process of production. As a result, this plant which had barely managed to turn out 2,500 machine tools annually, has now surpassed the 10,000 mark.

Following the torch of technological innovation kindled by the heroic workers at Huichon, dynamic struggles were waged by the workers of machine-tool plants in Kusong and Mangyongdae and by other men and women engaged in the machine-building industry across the nation; as a result, we are witnessing a great innovation in the production of machine tools. At present the working class in this field are determined to turn out 30,000 machine tools by April 15 next year and are carrying on a decisive battle to put their resolve into practice.

To occupy this height the machine-tool factories must step up their production, while the related branches of industry must supply them in good time with enough raw materials, supplies and equipment needed for the production of machine tools.

The metal industry must produce plenty of different steel materials for the production of machine tools. As the national economy develops rapidly, the demands of steel are daily increasing. At present the machine-building industry uses a tremendous amount of steel. If the metal industry does not supply an adequate amount of steel, the machine-building industry cannot scale the height of 30,000 machine tools. The working class of the metal industry must fight more actively to meet the increasing demands for steel.

To increase steel production we must develop the mining industry and provide plenty of iron ore to the metallurgical industry. The workers in the mining industry must achieve the comprehensive mechanization of the mining industry and bring about a great innovation in the production of iron ore.

For the production of 30,000 machine tools, the factories taking part in the cooperative production must produce accessories for the machine-tool plants in plenty of time. However many machine tools the machine-tool factories make, if they do not supply electric motors and other accessories in time, the machines will be useless. They say that at the Huichon Machine-tool Plant large quantities of machines are kept in the storehouse half-finished because electric applicance factories do not produce electric motors. They must make many more electric motors and supply them to the machine-building industry and other different branches of the national economy.

To produce more electric motors copper must be supplied. The demands for copper in the electric machinery industry and other fields of the national economy are very high now. A great deal of copper is used particularly by the national defense industry. Since we are building socialism in confrontation with the enemies, we cannot but develop the national defense industry. As long as our enemies remain, we must continue to develop this industry however much copper it needs.

To satisfy the increasing demands for copper, we must develop many new copper mines and wage a dynamic struggle to increase production at the existing mines.

We must strive to economize on copper in all spheres which use it. At present, however, the electrical machinery industry and other spheres of the national economy do not do this. If those at electric motor factories use their brains and work a bit harder, they can save much copper but they do not do so. From now, these factories must conduct an extensive technological innovation movement and endeavor to turn out highly efficient electric motors in large quantities, using less copper. Meanwhile, in all spheres of the national economy, we must do our utmost to economize copper by reducing its consumption to the minimum.

While producing more machine tools, we must, at the same time, strive to increase their variety and raise their quality.

To equip our nation's industry with modern technology, we need more than 130 kinds of machine tools but we only produce 40 or so kinds. Therefore, the Third Plenary Meeting of the Fifth Party Central Committee set forth the task of increasing the variety of machine tools. The working class in the machine-building industry must uphold the decision of this plenary meeting and work hard to increase the variety.

Today our rapidly developing national economy equipped with modern technology needs highly efficient and precise machine tools. Unless we radically improve the quality, we cannot further develop the economy and carry out the three major tasks of the technical revolution properly. Our present situation is different from that in 1959 when our nation started the let-one-machine-tool-make-machine-tools movement. The trade union organizations must strive to improve the quality of machine tools at all the machine-building factories in conformity with the requirements of the developing modern science and technology.

If we work well and increase the number and variety of machine tools and decisively raise their quality, we will considerably hasten the fulfillment of the three major tasks of the technical revolution designed to free our working people from backbreaking work.

In order to properly fulfill the three major tasks of the technical revolution, we must also develop the power industry.

Electricity is the main power that keeps all industries moving. Without it, we can expect neither the successful carrying out of the technical revolution nor our nation's economic advance. We must further develop the power industry and supply enough electricity to the different fields of the national economy and for the implementation of the three major tasks of the technical revolution. The workers engaged in the construction of power stations must step up the projects already undertaken and complete them as soon as possible, and those power stations which are now producing electricity must work vigorously to raise their output to the maximum.

In order to smoothly carry out the three major tasks of the technical revolution, an energetic struggle must be launched for the semi-automation and automation of production processes in all spheres of the national economy.

Therefore, we must develop the electronics and automation industries. Today our country has modern centers of these industries, which produce electronic tubes, semi-conductors and other electronic elements. We must, on this basis, expand and reinforce the large electronics and automation industry centers, at the same time as we set up, through a mass campaign, small and medium branch factories which produce automation gauges and instruments at various places. By producing quantities of electronic elements and automation gauges and instruments needed for automation, we will successfully fulfill the task of semi-automating and automating every sphere of the national economy.

For the fulfillment of the three major tasks of the technical revolution it is imperative to eliminate the difference between agricultural and industrial labor and free the peasants from backbreaking labor.

To do this we must first mechanize agriculture. Therefore, the working class in the machine-building industry must turn out more tractors, trucks and modern farm machines and send them to the countryside. For the present, the working class must provide the farming villages with plenty of equipment and materials needed for the sprinkling irrigation system.

Now, let me touch briefly on the question of national reunification.

We have more than once referred to this question and again, at the Fifth Party Congress, we made clear our policy of reunifying the country.

As we always say, the south Korean revolution must be carried out by its masters—the working class and people of south Korea. As for the people in the northern half of the Republic, who are of the same nation, they are duty bound to give active support to the south Korean people's revolutionary struggle. They must always be fully prepared to come to the aid of the south Korean people in their revolutionary struggle.

Today the south Korean people are unanimously aspiring for the independent, peaceful reunification of the country and are fighting to actualize it.

Particularly, the south Korean people are still demanding that their authorities accept our eight-point peaceful reunification proposal advanced at the Fifth Session of the Fourth Supreme People's Assembly and the proposal on the north-south negotiation made in our August 6 speech. Nowadays the south Korean people are asking Pak Jung Hi why he does not visit north Korea when, in his last-ditch effort, Nixon has visited Peking and Moscow; why he cannot respond to north Korea's proposal for negotiation with the Democratic Republican Party.

As the people began to call more loudly for the north-south negotiation, south Korea's puppet clique was so frightened that they could not but agree to the talks between the north and south Korean Red Cross organizations. In the light of their persistent objection to our proposal for the north-south negotiation, it is apparent that they had agreed to hold the preliminary talks because their masters, the U.S. imperialists, had egged them on to hold a dialogue with our side.

Though the south Korean puppet clique have agreed to hold the north-south Red Cross talks, they are deeply worried about how to handle the talks. Since the north-south Red Cross talks were proposed, they have been only proposing a movement to search for families that have lost touch with each other. Obviously they expected that our side would not agree and that the talks might in the long run be foiled.

Though this movement is unimportant, we agreed to hold talks on this matter. Then we proposed that, instead of confining the subject to searching for the families scattered in north and south, discussions be held also on searching relatives and friends, correspondence between the north and south and free travel. However, the south Korean side is not willing to accept this just proposal of ours. Because the south Korean rulers also know that once free travel starts and the people in the south come up to the northern half of the Republic and witness everybody here secure about food, clothing and housing, studying and working to their hearts' content and living in happiness, the south Korean people's complaint and resistance will increase.

Today the south Korean puppets are at a dead end, and the U.S. imperialists, their masters, are also hard pressed.

The plight the U.S. imperialists are in is clearly seen from the fact that Nixon visited China with which his country has no diplomatic relations and then the Soviet Union. At present they are facing a grave political, economic and military crisis and are being isolated from their allies and colleagues. In this situation the reactionary U.S. rulers apparently thought that they would not get over their present crisis by war alone, and visited China and the Soviet Union in an endeavor to find another way out. But this does not mean that there has been a change in U.S. imperialism's policy of aggression. It still remains unchanged. Through his visits Nixon has tried to improve Sino-U.S. relations and temporarily relax tension, and reach an agreement with the Soviet Union on the cessation of the arms race and the reduction of the production of nuclear weapons. In this way he is attempting to get out of the present crisis and secure time to intensify preparations for aggressive war. In a word Nixon visited China and the Soviet Union to ask them for mercy. So we see nothing strange about his visits.

However, the south Korean puppets are deeply apprehensive of Nixon's China visit. This is seen from an article written by a reporter of *The New York Times* some time ago. He said that it is an Asian tradition that the weak always visits the strong to pay his respects, so the south Koreans consider that through his China visit Nixon recognized the Chinese leaders as his superiors.

Alarmed by the internal and external situations which are turning unfavorable for them, the south Korean puppet clique have declared a "state of emergency" and are harshly repressing the people on the pretext of the fictitious "threat of invasion from the north." The "state of emergency" was declared by them to frustrate contact and negotiation between the north and south and suppress the south Korean people's daily increasing trend to peaceful reuinification, and thus prolong their days.

They declared the "state of emergency" under the pretext of the "threat of invasion from the north" but no one will be hoodwinked by this sort of deceptive artifice. The south Korean puppets' cruel fascist repression is arousing great protest and indignation among the south Korean people and the people the world over. Since the declaration of the "state of emergency" on the pretext of the "threat of invasion from the north" the world's public opinion has been unanimously condemning the south Korean rulers for this action directed at repressing their opposition. Even some of the reactionary rulers and reptile press in the U.S., Japan and West Germany regard the "state of emergency" in south Korea as a political trick carried out on account of their internal circumstances rather than a step to cope with the threat of "invasion from the north." The declaration of the "state of emergency" on the unfounded pretext of the "threat of invasion from the north" has isolated the south Korean puppet clique still more and driven them into a predicament.

It seems that they are looking for a way out of the tight corner now. This is seen from the fact that since we expressed our readiness to hold negotiations with the Democratic Republican Party also, they are endeavoring by every means to confirm whether this is true or not.

Our attitude to the north-south negotiation is clear. If south Korea's present rulers demand the withdrawal of the U.S. imperialist aggressor army, do not bring the Japanese militarist forces into south Korea, if they release patriots and political prisoners, refrain from repressing the people and guarantee political parties and social organizations free activity, we are ready to negotiate with them anytime. Only when the south Korean puppet clique agree to our conditions, will their crimes against the country and the people be condoned.

Today the domestic and international situations are developing very favorably for our struggle for the country's independent, peaceful reunification. Under these circumstances we must continue to step up our peace offensive for national reunification.

At the same time, we must make full preparations for war.

The U.S. imperialists are on the decline but they are still occupying south Korea and do not give up their aggressive ambitions. In addition, there still remains the danger of the revived Japanese militarists igniting a new war against our country in alliance with the south Korean puppets. Therefore, in order to be ready to cope with any maneuvers of the enemy, we must strive to further increase the political, economic and military might of the northern half of the Republic.

In order to achieve national reunification successfully, we must strengthen our solidarity with the international revolutionary forces while, at the same time, increasing our own revolutionary forces.

Since the 15th Plenary Meeting of the Fourth Party Central Committee we have intensified our propaganda abroad and established Juche in our external activities more firmly; as a result, we have many supporters and sympathizers in foreign countries. Today we have so many of them in every part of the world. If we carry on our external activities still better, we will be able to win many more friends.

The trade unions must strive to unite with the working class in many countries of the world, strengthen solidarity with the international working-class movement and win more supporters and sympathizers. We must even win the irresolute forces which support and sympathize with our revolutionary cause in a passive way.

Our active support and encouragagment of other peoples' revolutionary struggles is the fundamental way to increase our solidarity with the international revolutionary forces. We must actively support those peoples who are fighting imperialists led by U.S. imperialism and the newly independent nations. It is true that since our country is small and one half of it has been usurped by the U.S. imperialists, it is no easy task for us to aid other countries. However, we must overcome our hardships and assist other peoples in their revolutionary struggles. Only by doing this, can we accelerate world revolution and win many more supporters and sympathizers for our revolution.

We must work harder in order to give material and moral assistance to the fighting peoples and newly independent nations. We will never allow ourselves to shorten our working hours and do less work as they do in other countries. The more successful we are in socialist construction, the harder we must work to consolidate and develop our country's socialist system and actively support the revolutionary struggles of the peoples of the world.

Our working class must stand in the van of the whole people and keep stepping up the revolution and construcion, and under the Marxian slogan "Workers of all countries, unite!" they must strive to strengthen unity with the working class of all countries and increase solidarity with the international revolutionary forces.

I hope that our heroic working class and the trade union members will firmly unite around the Party Central Committee and struggle more dynamically for the country's independent reunification and for the final triumph of the revolution.

ON THE THOROUGH IMPLEMENTATION OF THE PRINCIPLES OF SOCIALIST PEDAGOGY IN EDUCATION

Speech Delivered at a National Meeting of Teachers, *December 27, 1971*

Comrades,

On behalf of the Central Committee of the Party and the Government of the Republic, I should like to express my warm congratulations and gratitude to your presence here and to all our educators who, upholding the Party's policy of education, are working devotedly on the educational front to bring up the rising generation in the spirit of communism.

Our educational workers, revolutionary fighters loyal to the Party, have successfully carried out the line of education chartered by the Party at each stage of the revolution since the days of the democratic revolution after liberation, and scored great achievements in the education of the younger generations. Our Party highly appreciates the great achievments and outstanding endeavors of the educational workers in the past years in their worthwhile, honorable struggle to train reserves of revolutionaries.

I would like to talk to you now about perfecting socialist pedagogy and carrying out its principles more thoroughly in education.

The most important task in education today is to bring up the new generation as worthy successors to the revolution, as reliable reserves of builders of communism.

Under the wise leadership of the Party and through an arduous struggle, our people established an advanced socailist system in our country, and have achieved brilliant victories in socialist construction. However, our revolutionary cause is yet to be realized. We are confronted with the revolutionary tasks of reunifying our nation, building socialism and communism in our country and wiping imperialism off the face of the earth.

In order to fulfill these honorable and important revolutionary tasks, we must continue with the revolution and train the new generation as staunch communist revolutionaries who will carry forward the revolution.

In order to bring up the new generation as a reliable successor to our revolution, we must educate them in communism from childhood. The establishment of the socialist system by no means signifies that the people will become Communists of their own accord. Only when the new generation are educated along revolutionary and communist lines at kindergartens and schools, can they grow up to be ardent revolutionaries and true Communists.

In any society the primary aim of education is to train people to serve the existing social system faithfully.

In feudal society education served to defend the feudal system by instilling in people respect for the feudal order. In capitalist society it serves to foster selfishness in people and make them yield to capitalist exploitation and oppression.

In socialist society the aim of education is fundamentally different from that in exploiter societies. Education in a socialist society should imbue the new generation with communist ideology and impart to them knowledge essential for the building of socialism and communism. Hence, it must serve the purpose of making them oppose the exploiting system, defend the socialist system and work with devotion to build a communist society free from class distinctions and where everybody enjoys a happy life. In a socialist society education must therefore be based on a new theory and methods of teaching radically different from those in preceding societies and have entirely new content. It must be a revolutionary and communist education which clarifies the distinctions between the working class and the capitalist class, and between communism and capitalism.

If a socialist state fails to educate the children and youth in a revolutionary and communist fashion, and gives them a mixed education which is neither socialist nor capitalist, it will be impossible to train them to be successors to the revolution and builders of communism. A mixed education can only make people mixed-up. People without communist education cannot succeed to the revolution or build a communist society, the ideal of mankind.

In certain socialist countries, there are a variety of negative factors which impair the building of socialism and communism. What is the explanation of this? Of course, there could be many reasons, one of the main being the failure to educate the rising generations in a communist spirit. If the new generation, because of the absence of communist education, are loath to work, loaf on the job, do not cherish the socialist system won by their revolutionary forefathers at the cost of their blood and dislike the revolution, the revolution cannot be furthered and the building of socialism and communism cannot be a success in the country concerned. There can be no doubt about this.

It is wrong to think that socialist education consists only in the teachings of *Capital* and other Marxist-Leninist classics and the general principles of Marxism-Leninism regarding political economy, dialectical materialism and historical materialism at universities, colleges and various other schools. Moreover, if a mixture of socialism, feudalism and capitalism is taught in schools, this will be, so to speak, a hodgepodge education.

It is true that some literary and artistic works of feudal and capitalist societies were progressive. Though these works are regarded as "classics," they should not be wholly included in textbooks or given as reading matter to schoolchildren whose revolutionary world outlook has not yet been shaped.

For example, Pushkin's *Evgeni Onegin* and our *Tale of Chun Hyang* might have been progressive when they were written. However, they contain the limitations of the age and class limitations; they cannot contribute to the communist education of the children and youth in our era.

Evgeni Onegin is a story of some young men from aristocratic families who fall in love with a girl and fight a duel with pistols out of jealousy. The progressive aspect of this work, if any, is in its criticism, though mild, of the aristocracy. As for the *Tale of Chun Hyang*, it criticized social inequality between the nobility and the common people in feudal society and showed that young men and women could love and marry despite their difference in property and social status. For its time it was progressive. However, it is only the son of a nobleman who opposes the social discrimination imposed by the nobility, and the spiritual world of the characters differs too greatly from that of today's youth.

We cannot hope for young people of our age who read such old works as *Evgeni Onegin* and the *Tale of Chun Hyang* to derive from them a revolutionary fighting will and a zeal for production activities. On the contrary, the extravagant and depraved life of the feudal nobility and capitalists described in such old works may exert harmful effect on the children and youth, infecting them with feudal and capitalist ideas and with the bourgeois way of life. In some socialist countries today the children and youth are inclined toward a fast and indolent life and toward the capitalist system and the bourgeois way of life. This is by no means an accident.

We have learned a serious lesson from the realities of other countries and from our own experience: if you give the children and youth a hodgepodge education instead of a communist one, they and even the whole society will not be homogeneous. Therefore, our Party resolutely discarded the old theory and method of education and advanced the policy of creating a new socialist pedagogy to meet the needs of the building of communism. Our Party has already clarified the basic principle of socialist pedagogy and is actively working to carry it through.

The basic principle of socialist pedagogy is to revolutionize and working-classize the children and youth through communist education.

It is a legitimate demand of the building of socialism and communism to revolutionize and working-classize the people. In order to build a socialist and communist society, we must conquer the ideological fortress by revolutionizing and working-classizing all members of society, at the same time capturing the material fortress by developing the productive forces.

Advancing the theory of building communism, Marx and Engels laid great stress on its economic aspect, but wrote little about its ideological aspect. They thought that once the working class in power dispossessed the capitalists · of the factories, railways, land and other means of production and placed them under state ownership and developed the productive forces a little more, a communist society would arrive where all would work according to their ability and receive according to their needs.

There are facts which we must take into account when studying the theory of Marx and Engels on building communism: they evolved their theory without having had personal experience in the building of communism; they lived in the era of premonopoly capitalism; they studied the question of building communism bearing in mind the conditions in the developed capitalist countries where they lived. They believed that the proletarian revolution would break out almost simultaneously or successively in the major capitalist countries and that world revolution would triumph relatively soon. They thought that once the working class in a country had taken power and nationalized the means of production, it would take a rather short time to lay the material and technical foundations of communism. Consequently, they thought that the period of transition from capitalism to communism would be short. They failed to foresee clearly that the remnants of the old ideas in the minds of people and the bourgeois ideology infiltrating from outside would greatly impede the building of communism, and that many difficulties would crop up in the course of communist construction.

Lenin carried out the revolution in Russia, then a backward capitalist country, and personally guided the building of socialism. Therefore, he did not consider the period of transition from capitalism to communism to be as short as Marx and Engels did, but relatively long. However, Lenin did not specify the need for the state of proletarian dictatorship to carry through an ideological revolution in the period of transition from capitalism to communism.

Lenin formulated his idea of communist construction in the

proposition that Soviet power plus electrification of the whole country is communism. In this context the word electrification would have to be construed as meaning that through a technical revolution all production processes should be automated and the country's material foundations built solidly. And by Soviet power he meant the dictatorship of the proletariat. Of course, if we stretch the meaning of this word, it can be interpreted as signifying that the state of the working class should carry on the class struggle and an ideological revolution. However, Lenin failed to expound the idea that in order to build socialism and communism, people have to be revolutionized and working-classized through the ideological revolution, and the ideological fortress as well as the material fortress must be conquered without fail.

The building of communism cannot be said to have been completed simply when the working class has taken power and the country has been electrified. In our country today, every *ri* has electricity, every farmhouse has electric light and electricity is widely used even in farm work. Thus, the country has attained a very high degree of electrification. The Soviet Union has also achieved electrification far beyond Lenin's electrification plan. Yet, it still has a long way to go to realize the communist principle that each works according to his ability and receives according to his needs. Even if production processes have become highly automatic and material wealth is sufficient, the building of communism cannot be declared complete.

In order to realize the communist principle of distribution, we must educate and remold people along communist lines through an ideological revolution, while augmenting the material wealth of society. It is true that if the material wealth is increased by successful economic construction, the people can live in affluence. But if we fail to remold the thinking of people along communist lines, only emphasizing economic construction and neglecting the ideological revolution, it would be impossible for us to build a communist society.

Indeed, people's thoughts are influenced by their material environment, yet they cannot be remolded along communist lines of their own accord even when the economy has developed and the material standards of living have risen. Only when economic construction and the ideological revolution are promoted vigorously and simultaneously can a firm material and technical basis for communism be built and the thinking of people be remolded along communist lines. This is an absolute necessity for the successful construction of a communist society.

The period of transition from capitalism to communism may be shorter or longer in the developed and less developed capitalist countries. However, whatever the country concerned, the socialist state has to undertake this task of revolutionizing and working-classizing people in the transition period.

Only by waging a successful struggle to revolutionize and working-classize people can we uproot the poison of bourgeois ideology remaining in their minds and prevent the revival of capitalism. Moreover, imperialism still exists in the world and persists in its ideological and cultural infiltration so as to disintegrate the socialist countries from within. Under these conditions a working-class party and state cannot defend the socialist gains effectively unless they step up the ideological education of the working people.

An effective ideological education of the working people is a prerequisite to successful economic construction. The socialist economy can be consistently developed only by the conscious and positive efforts of the working people who have been freed from exploitation and oppression and have become masters of the country. Therefore, inspiring the revolutionary enthusiasm of the working people by strengthening their ideological education is a decisive factor in the vigorous promotion of socialist economic construction.

Since the survivals of capitalist ideology in the minds of people remain, if the socialist state fails to strengthen the ideological education of the working people, they may become selfish people who hate to work, yearn for a life of idleness and are interested only in money and pleasure. This would preclude the possibility of accelerating economic construction aimed at laying the material and technical foundations of communism and might even nullify the achievements gained in the building of socialism and communism.

Certain people are advancing the theory that when the socialist economy reaches a certain stage of development, its rate of growth drops gradually. This is but a sophistry put forward to justify the fact that the rate of economic construction is slow and the economy marks time because the working people are not educated in a revolutionary way and, consequently, they lose revolutionary activity and loaf about instead of working hard.

Our experience shows clearly that if the working people are encouraged through an intensified ideological revolution to display collective heroism and creative initiative, a socialist society can always develop its economy at a high rate. In the last few years our country has suffered a great deal from a shortage of electric power because of continued drought. Because the supply of coking coal from other countries has been insufficient, we have had great difficulty in normalizing industrial production. We had a shortage of manpower and, moreover, we had to channel considerable forces to strengthen the nation's defense capacities in the tense situation fraught with the threat of another war because of incessant U.S. imperialist provocations, including the *Pueblo* incident. In spite of such difficult and complex problems, our Party intensified political work among the working people and aroused their revolutionary enthusiasm, so that it succeeded in overcoming all difficulties in economic construction and developing the economy at a high annual rate.

From our historical experience in the socialist revolution and in building socialism, we have drawn the conclusion that if we are to build a communist society we should carry on not only economic construction but also the struggle for the revolutionization of people, that is, the struggle to take the material and ideological fortresses simultaneously.

It is an indispensable requirement of the building of communism to revolutionize and working-classize the people by intensifying the ideological revolution. Therefore, we must necessarily give first place to the revolutionization and working-classization of the students in school education. This must be the basic principle of socialist pedagogy.

It is our task now to perfect socialist pedagogy in conformity with this basic principle. This cannot be done through the efforts of one or two individuals only. All educational workers should put their heads together and solve the problem one by one.

Nobody has ever advanced a perfect theory on socialist pedagogy. And no country has provided a model of socialist pedagogy which we can follow. Never again can we introduce in our country a hodgepodge pedagogy having no clear demarcation between socialism and capitalism. Moreover, we should not try to copy from the outworn feudal and capitalist theories and methods of education. The pedagogy of an exploiter society was formed for the purpose of defending the exploiting system and so we have nothing to borrow from it. We must reject it entirely and create a new socialist pedagogy.

We must perfect socialist pedagogy in an original manner solely on the basis of Marxist-Leninist principles and our experiences of revolution and construction.

In his work *Principles of Communism* Engels suggested, as educational measures to be carried out by the working class after the seizure of power, that all children from the age when they no longer need motherly care should be educated in state establishments at state expense, and that education should be combined with factory work. Just as we develop the theory of building communism by enlarging on Lenin's idea that communism is Soviet power plus electrification of the whole country, so we must correctly understand Engels' idea and enlarge on it to develop socialist pedagogy.

Engels' idea concerning the education of the rising generation may be construed as meaning that they should be educated collectively in state establishments to prevent the old idea of their parents from exerting influence on them and that they should be given useful knowledge for the building of communism by combining education with productive labor. But Engels did not answer the question as to what kind of subjects and ideas should be taught to children when bringing them up in state establishments at state expense.

If we are to revolutionize and working-classize the new generation and train them to be staunch revolutionaries and true Communists, we must not only bring them up in state establishments but also have a theory and methods of teaching to educate them in communism. However many creches, kindergartens and schools the state may build to institute compulsory education, it will be impossible to revolutionize and working-classize the children and their upbringing at state expense will prove futile, unless we give them a correct ideological education.

Compulsory nine-year technical education is now in effect

and compulsory ten-year education will soon be introduced. When compulsory ten-year education becomes universal, all children will go to kindergarten for two years after leaving creche, and then will receive compulsory ten-year education at primary and secondary schools. This means our children will live collectively in state educational establishments for twelve years from kindergarten onwards. If, in this period, the educational establishments provide a good communist ideological and cultural education for the children, they will at least have shaped the framework of a communist world outlook, even if they do not attain perfection. If they are continually educated and seasoned through the organizational life of the League of Socialist Working Youth at colleges, in the People's Army or in factories for five or six years after secondary school, they can be equipped perfectly with a revolutionary world outlook. Then the revolutionization and working-classization of the whole of society will proceed successfully.

Our country now has every condition for bringing up the new generation in communism. What the educators have to do is to thoroughly apply in their work the principles of socialist pedagogy set forth by our Party.

In order to bring up the new generation as ardent revolutionaries and true Communists by applying the principles of socialist pedagogy, we must first educate and train them to have faith in communism.

Faith in communism is one of the lofty spiritual traits of Communists. They firmly believe in the victory of communism, the highest ideal of mankind and devote all their energies to the struggle for its realization.

As everyone knows, it is a law of historical development that capitalism will give way to communism. The length of the period of communist construction may differ in various countries according to their specific conditions. But there can be no doubt that communism will arrive ultimately in all countries. Nevertheless, communism cannot come of its own accord without struggle. In order to hasten the fall of capitalism and step up the building of communism, everyone must be firmly convinced of the victory of communism, and fight for it devotedly. To this end, it is particularly important to educate the new generation in such a way as to inspire them with faith in communism. Only when the new generation have unswerving faith in communism can they take over and continue the building of communism where we have left off.

The communism we are aspiring to is scientific communism. Therefore, our faith in communism has nothing to do with the religious doctrine which preaches that after death men may enter the "Kingdom of Heaven" or "Paradise." Throughout the ages people have yearned for a society where they could work and live together in comfort. The ancients knew that there were exploitation and oppression, speculation and jealousy, poverty and sorrow in this world, but they did not know that they could remove such social evils and build a society where all would live in happiness. So they gave ear to the doctrines of Christianity or Buddhism which said that they could enjoy happiness only if they entered the "Kingdom of Heaven" or "Paradise" after death.

But there is no such "Kingdom of Heaven" or "Paradise." Modern science and technology have undoubtedly proved that the "Kingdom of Heaven" and "Paradise" do not exist. In our age men frequently make flights into space, and they find no such "blessed lands" however far they go into orbit. That a dead man could enter the "Kingdom of Heaven" or "Paradise" implies that he could enjoy happiness after death. But how can a dead man enjoy happiness?

If people want to abolish misery and suffering and live happily, they have to abolish the exploiter society and build a communist society where they can work according to their abilities and receive according to their needs. Only then can man's centuries-old dream—a society of genuine happiness— come true in this land.

Some people now say that it will take several hundred years to build communism. This is tantamount to asserting that the building of communism is infeasible in our times and that communism can be built only after the death of our contemporaries. We must not foster such ideas in the minds of people. If a communist society were to appear in several hundred years' time, people would lose faith in communism and would not fight actively for its triumph.

It may indeed take a long time to complete the building of communism, but this is not a matter of the distant future. Whether or not we build communism at an early date depends entirely on how we fight for it. If the entire people unite and fight efficiently, they can build a communist society more quickly.

We can build a communist society quickly, but not at once. We must implement communist policies gradually, one by one, as the conditions for them arise. If we carry out communist policies one by one, without putting off till tomorrow whatever can be done today, a communist society will ultimately be built.

The free medical service introduced in our country is a communist measure. Previously our people could not afford to go to a hospital when they were ill, but today, under the system of free medical care, all of them can get medical treatment in hospitals without paying even a penny. This system still has some shortcomings, though; we are short of doctors, medicines and medical facilities, and so fail to give the people enough medical assistance. When we do produce various kinds of medicines and medical appliances in large quantities by further developing industry and when we train more doctors, we can do away with such shortcomings and bring the advantages of the free medical service into full play. By implementing such communist policies one by one and consolidating their achievements, we can build a communist society in our country so that all people can live happily.

Therefore, while we convince the students of the doom of capitalism and the victory of socialism and communism, we must teach them how to build communism after the overthrow of capitalism. We must see to it that our younger generation work energetically to build socialism and communism with faith in communism.

Furthermore, we must teach the students to hate the landlord and capitalist classes, and the exploiter system.

Today we are living in an age of fierce class struggle. The landlord and capitalist classes are making desperate attempts to save themselves from imminent doom, and are challenging socialism. It is therefore necessary to completely crush the resistance of the exploiter classes in order to consolidate the socialist system and successfully build socialism and communism.

Since we are now living in an age of class struggle and revolution, it is most important to educate the rising generation to hate the landlord and capitalist classes and the exploiter system. If we do not educate our young people along these lines, they will lose sight of the class enemies and, lapsing into a pacifist frame of mind, will be reluctant to make revolution and, in the end, may become degenerate. Then not only will it be impossible to build socialism and communism successfully but even the revolutionary gains we have already won may be endangered.

In our school education, therefore, stress should be laid on driving home to the students the true face of the landlord and capitalist classes as exploiters and their malevolence, the corruption of capitalist society and the falsity of bourgeois democracy. And it must be made known to them correctly that in capitalist society the toiling masses, including the working class, are not treated as human beings and they get nothing but poverty and sorrow for their backbreaking labor.

The students must be well acquainted, in particular, with the reactionary and corrupt nature of south Korean society. At present, the middle classes of south Korea, to say nothing of the workers and peasants, curse south Korean society and say, "The rich get ever richer and the poor get ever poorer." This means that in south Korea while the wealthy become still more wealthy, the poor become more and more poverty-stricken as the days go by. In fact, south Korea has now turned into a land of darkness where all democratic liberties and rights have been trampled, and the misery of the people there is beyond description owing to the colonial plunder by the U.S. imperialists and to the ruthless exploitation by the landlords and the comprador capitalists.

We must fully inform the new generation of the true nature of capitalist society and the reactionary character of south Korean society, thereby inculcating in them a fierce hatred for the landlord and capitalist classes and for the exploiter system and inducing them to fight against them resolutely.

At the same time, the superiority of socialism to capitalism must be fully explained to the students.

Socialist society is incomparably superior to capitalist society. In a socialist society the masses of the people are masters of the country. Everybody studies and works to his heart's content and enjoys a happy life, free from exploitation and oppression. Also, in a socialist society the distinctions between heavy and light labor, between agricultural and industrial labor, and between physical and mental labor will disappear gradually; so all working people can enjoy a more affluent and cultured life while working more easily. Only when school children are well acquainted with this superiority of socialist society, can they be brought up to be ardent revolutionaries who work actively to consolidate the socialist system and build socialism and communism.

When explaining to the younger generation the superiority of socialism over capitalism, it is important to show them the contrast between the northern and the southern half of the Republic.

Today the people in the northern half of the Republic are not worried about food, clothing and housing. Even when our working people fall ill and stay away from work, they receive rice and are provided with all the necessary living conditions by the state. Although our people cannot afford to dress as attractively as capitalists now, none of them is poorly clothed, and no one is homeless. People in the northern half of the Republic are not only free from anxiety about food, clothing and housing, but send their sons and daughters to school, to college and university free of charge.

But the south Korean people today are not provided with living conditions and are suffering from cold and hunger. If they fail to earn their bread one day, they have to starve the next; when they fall ill they cannot afford to buy medicine; and they are not in a position to send their children to school. Some time ago a south Korean paper reported that a woman who had been anxious about being unable to raise the money for her children's school fees killed her little ones and herself.

The realities of north and south Korea, which form a sharp contrast, demonstrate the overwhelming superiority of the socialist system in the north over the social system in the south. All foreign visitors speak about the superiority of the socialist system in the northern half of the Republic. On returning home many of them wrote articles praising the socialist system in the northern half of the Republic.

The puppet clique in south Korea are now greatly alarmed to see that the socialist system in the north is being consolidated and that its superiority is becoming increasingly apparent. They are making frantic efforts to prevent the socialist system from influencing the south Korean people. At present, delegates of the Red Cross organizations of north and south Korea are meeting at Panmunjom to discuss relief for our fellow countrymen who are separated in the two halves of the country. The south Korean side refuses to accept our just proposal to put on the agenda of the full-scale meeting the question of seeking families, relations and friends torn apart in north and south and enabling them to travel freely between the two zones. This is because the south Korean rulers are well aware that if free travel is allowed between north and south and people in the southern half come to the northern half of the Republic and see for themselves the superiority of the socialist system, they would fight more courageously for the reunification of the country. The puppet clique of south Korea now claim that should free travel between north and south be allowed, south Korea would turn "Red." This clearly shows how afraid they are lest the socialist system in the northern half of the Republic should influence the south Korean people.

The south Korean puppet clique have recently proclaimed a "state of emergency" on the plea of an alleged "threat of invasion from the north;" their real aim is to frustrate the contacts and negotiations between north and south, and suppress the south Korean people's ever-increasing yearning for the northern half of the Republic and peaceful reunification. In addition to the "state of emergency," they are daily rigging up a variety of evil fascist laws. To top it all, in defiance of the objections of the opposition parties and the public at large, they met together at 3 o'clock this morning like cat burglars and manufactured an unprecedented evil fascist law, the "special law on measures for national security."

This maneuver is nothing but a last-ditch struggle of the dying. No matter how frantically they may try with vociferous maneuvering of fascist suppression, the puppet clique in south Korea will never be able to stifle the yearning of the south Korean people for the northern half of the Republic; nor can they halt our people's struggle for the peaceful reunification of the country.

By acquainting the students with the totally different realities of north and south Korea, we must make them realize ever clearer the superiority of the socialist system in the northern half of the Republic. When the pupils and students clearly see the superiority of the socialist system established in the northern half of the Republic, they will jealously defend the socialist system and fight more resolutely for the victory of the great cause of socialism and communism.

Educating the new generation to be industrious is important in bringing them up as staunch builders of communism.

Communism can be built successfully only when all members of society love work and participate conscientiously in labor activities. If we do not inculcate in the rising generation a love for labor, we cannot build socialism and communism successfully.

As society advances and life becomes more affluent, we must work better. It will not do to try to lead an idle life. It would be wrong to think that one could live idle in a communist society. Communism does not mean a society where people can live without working. True, in a communist society the people's living standards will be the highest possible and work will become very easy. But even then everybody will have to work, for without working he cannot live well.

Labor is necessary for one's health as well. People should always do suitable work if only to be healthy and live long.

In future we must teach all students to regard labor as most sacred and honorable and to love work, to observe labor discipline voluntarily and to acquire working habits.

When cultivating in the students a communist attitude toward labor, an effective method is to point to living examples of devoted Communists who sincerely love labor. Our country now boasts of countless true and diligent Communists. Their examples can exert a great educative influence on the students.

I think the story of the "communist uncle" from the village of Chaegyong-ri which has already been reported in Rodong Sinmun will provide good educative material for the students. The old man had lived his life in Rajin. His son graduated from the University and taught at Kim Chaek Polytechnical Institute after the war. He brought his father to Pyongyang to live with him. One day the old man opened the window of his room in the apartment house in Pyongyang and looked out over the streets at the cranes moving to and fro, the new buildings springing up in many places and the young people working briskly and singing. On seeing this busy scene, the old man decided that though old he must go back to the countryside again and work. That was how he came to Chaegyong-ri to become a cooperative farmer again. When we went to Chaegyong-ri once, we met this old man. He was working better than anybody else on the cooperative farm. On the evening of that day I attended a meeting of the cooperative farmers, where I found him to be an active speaker. Under such a good social system as ours, he said, people must work hard, and must not shun work. And he strongly criticized those who did not take their work seriously.

I was told that his daughter-in-law in Pyongyang once came to see him. The mother-in-law had offered to give her some rice to help her out. When the old man came to know this, he scolded his wife and daughter-in-law, saying, "We are now living under such a good system; the state supplies us with enough rice to live on. What do you need more for? You must not take the rice with you; I'm going to put it aside for some families whose breadwinners were killed in war or are now on active service."

We can say that this grandfather is not only devoted wholeheartedly to labor but also is deeply convinced of the superiority of the socialist system by his own life experience. He is aware of his duty to further consolidate this system with his labor.

The mother of Comrade Ma Dong Hui, whom you know well, is also communist-minded. She is a bereaved member of a revolutionary family, who has given her son and daughter, her daughter-in-law and her husband to the revolution. She is close to 90, yet she finds it against her conscience to sit idle and remain under the Party's care. She is living alone and working diligently despite the Party's advice to have home help.

Not long ago we called on the mother of Comrade Ma Dong Hui. We advised her again to have someone to cook for her at least because she was now so old and cooking was too hard for her. To this she replied, "I am ready to do anything you say, dear Premier, except this. I am sorry that I am now old and living at the state expense without serving the country in any way; how can I ever allow myself to have a much-needed work hand just to look after my house?" As there was no use arguing with her, we appointed a nurse to live with her and help her at night, while going to work in the daytime.

Though old, Comrade Ma Dong Hui's mother is outstanding in the castor silk raising movement started by the Women's Union. She sows the whole of her garden with the castor-oil plants to provide feed for the silkworms raised by the Women's Union.

I think besides these people there are numerous unsung heroes among our working people today who are devoting all their energies and talents to the building of socialism. We must seek out many such good examples and educate the students more actively on these. All our children and youth must work and live with a communist attitude toward labor, no matter when and where and whether they are engaged in physical or mental labor.

In bringing up the new generation to be staunch builders of communism it is also important to educate them to take loving care of the common property of the state and society.

The state and social property in a socialist society is owned in common by the people. Our properties such as factories, schools and hospitals are all precious assets in making the country rich and strong and in assuring a happy life for the people. It is therefore the sacred duty of all the working people in a socialist society to spare and treasure the common property of the state and society. The better we manage state and social property and the more carefully we use it, the richer and stronger will the country become and the faster will the living standards of the people rise.

But, instead of taking care of the common property, some of our workers manage it carelessly and waste a great deal of it.

Workers in the building industry are using thick steel rods and pipes where thin ones would do; they handle cement carelessly, leaving it to be blown away by the wind and uncovered in the rain. The structural steel and cement wasted in this way at the construction sites alone are enormous. Much cloth is also wasted. Few of the garments now turned out at our clothing factories are well-tailored and elegant. It is tantamount to wasting cloth to make ill-fitting clothes out of nice fabrics.

We are still unable to supply the people with enough fish; it is not that our catch is small. We catch hundreds of thousands of tons of fish a year, sometimes 16,000 tons of *myongtae* a day. But our workers fail to preserve the fish well and transport it in good time, thus spoiling a large part of it. That is why we still fail to supply the people with sufficient fish.

We have expended a large amount of manpower and funds to build schools for rearing the successors to our revolution. But the schools are left neglected and are wasted.

If state and social property is mismanaged and wasted like this, the living standards of the people cannot be raised quickly, nor can a socialist and communist society be built successfully no matter how much is built and produced. Although we now have solid economic assets, we are not yet able to improve our well-being. This is because our workers are negligent of the state's economic life and waste a great deal of property; they lack the spirit of public service and of caring for and treasuring state and social property.

In order to do away with malpractices that lead to a waste of state and social property, it is necessary to educate people from childhood in the spirit of economizing and treasuring this property. We must strengthen the ideological education of the students, so that they take loving care of the common property of the state and society.

To continue. We must educate the students in the spirit of collectivism.

Collectivism constitutes the basis of social life under socialism and communism. In a socialist and communist society the interests of the collective and society involve those of every working man and woman; they are identical with those of the working people themselves. It is therefore an essential requirement of socialist and communist society that all people should work helping each other under the slogan of "One for all and all for one."

In order to equip the students with the collectivist spirit, they must first be awakened to the fact that the force of the collective is greater than the force of individuals, that collective heroism is superior to individual heroism and that the organizational or collective life is more important than the private life of individuals. The students should be encouraged from childhood to reject individualism and selfishness, to love the organization and the collective, and devote themselves to society and the people, to the Party and the revolution.

And it must be made clear to the students that the aim of their education and their scientific and technological studies is to serve the country and the people. As everyone knows, in a capitalist society science and technology are geared to the enjoyment of individuals and to the interests of the capitalist class, but in a socialist society they serve the interests of the working class and the entire people. In other words, in a socialist society science and technology do not serve lucrative ends or individual pleasure, but the cause of freeing the working people from heavy, arduous work, of enriching and strengthening the country, and improving the people's living standards.

In former times, it was thought by some that though they themselves were uneducated and were engaged in arduous farm work, their sons should be educated somehow or other to earn a comfortable living as sub-county office clerks or school teachers. I think rather elderly comrades present at this conference must have been influenced by this idea.

We must not instill such ideas in the minds of the rising generation. We must not bring them up to be people who would serve the capitalist should the latter ask them to or who would sell out anywhere for money. In our society today, science and technology that do not serve the interests of the revolution and the working class are of no use. We must encourage the students to clearly understand the aim and significance of scientific and technological studies in a socialist society, so that they may dedicate all their learning and talents to the cause of the Party and the revolution, to the welfare of the working class and the entire people.

Furthermore, in order to mold the new generation into true Communists we must educate them to discard the way of life belonging to the old society and to work and live according to the new, socialist way of life.

We still have many remnants of the old life in our private life and in various spheres of social life. Such practices as giving extravagant feasts on festive occasions and burning incense at funeral services are all manifestations of the old way of life. These senseless formalities and ostentatious and old customs are unnecessary for us who are now building socialism.

In order to build socialism and communism successfully, we must get rid of the way of life inherited from the old society in all social spheres and establish a new way of life consistent with socialist society. The old way of life cannot be abolished at once by force, but it can be eliminated gradually through patient education and struggle.

In abolishing the old way of life and establishing a socialist way of life it is important to educate the rising generation to live and work along socialist lines. If the whole of the rising generation live and act according to socialist standards and rules of conduct in keeping with the inherent nature of our society, every aspect of the old way of life will be ultimately eliminated and the socialist way of life will prevail in all spheres of society. Our schools, therefore, must in every respect teach their pupils to live and work in the socialist way of life.

To thoroughly apply the principles of socialist pedagogy to educational work, a child psychology befitting socialist society must be created and pupils educated according to it.

Child psychology is of great importance for school education. Only a schoolmaster who knows well the mental state of the pupils can educate them properly. Children are better educated in kindergartens and schools than at home because the teachers train them in a way best suited to their psychological peculiarities.

Child psychology must be elaborated on to educate the schoolchildren in a way suitable to their mentality. The child psychology of bourgeois society cannot be adopted in our socialist education today without certain changes.

Some people maintain that child psychology is the same in any society because the mentality of children is the same whatever the social system. This is clearly incorrect.

A child's mentality, too, is closely affected by its social environment. In feudal society the juvenile mentality reflects the social environment of that society; the same is the case in capitalist society. So the mentality of children growing up in a capitalist society and in a socialist society cannot be identical. These days we frequently meet children who have just been repatriated from capitalist society. Young as they are, they think money almighty and claim their own share of money even among brothers. This is something alien to the children growing up in our country today. The young repatriates from capitalist society have this mentality not because their parents brought them up in that way, but because in the society where they were born and bred—a capitalist society based on individualism—money is everything.

Because the mentality of juveniles in capitalist society differs from that in socialist society, child psychology is naturally different.

Yet the textbooks on child psychology now being used in

teacher training schools cannot be regarded as completely socialist-oriented. They contain many remnants of the child psychology of the old society. Educational workers must get together and examine these textbooks, eliminate the bourgeois and revisionist elements still found in them, and create a child psychology entirely oriented on socialism.

In order to apply the principles of socialist pedagogy comprehensively in educational work, teachers must be revolutionized and working-classized.

Unless the teachers directly in charge of educational work are revolutionized and working-classized, they cannot carry through the Party's educational policy; and unless they are Communists themselves, they will not be able to make their pupils into Communists. The revolutionization and working-classization of the teachers is an important guarantee for the thorough implementation of the Party's education policy and of the principles of socialist pedagogy in education.

The revolutionization and working-classization of the intellectuals, including the teachers, acquires still greater importance since theirs is mainly mental labor. By saying that theirs is mental labor I do not mean, of course, that they have an easy job. To give a lecture, standing for hours on end and writing on the blackboard, is very hard work. Intellectuals engaged in mental work, however, are not tempered through collective labor for production like workers, and so they lack the working-class spirit of devoting all one's efforts to the good of the collective and society. That is why our Party attaches great importance to the queston of revolutionizing and working-classizing intellectuals, including the teachers.

The revolutionization and working-classization of intellectuals does not necessarily imply that they must work in factories. The point is to uproot the remnants of old ideas from their minds and firmly equip them with the communist spirit of diligence and selfless work for the Party and the revolution, for society and the collective.

An important way of revolutionizing and working-classizing the teachers is by strengthening revolutionary organizational life. This alone will make it possible to eradicate the old ideas remaining in the minds of people and continue to temper them politically and ideologically. We should further strengthen the organizational life of the teachers in Party and working people's organizations, and thus lead them to wage an intense struggle against all kinds of unhealthy thoughts and temper themselves untiringly.

In order to revolutionize and working-classize teachers we must also establish a proper reorientation system for them and educate them tirelessly. In particular, we should strengthen the system of an annual one-month course and make the course compulsory for all teachers however busy they may be. While attending the course they must combine study with ideological struggle.

It is important for the revolutionization and working-classization of the teachers to build up adequately the teacher training centers such as normal and teachers' colleges.

These teacher training centers are what one might call "seedbeds" for rearing successors to our revolution. Only when the teacher training institutions educate their students proficiently can they turn out revolutionized and working-classized teachers, without whom we cannot bring up our pupils and students to be ardent revolutionaries and Communists.

In the past our authorities did not pay great attention to the training of teachers and failed to build up the teacher training centers. Educational workers ought to have selected and admitted capable boys and girls to the normal, teachers' and kindergarten teachers' colleges. Instead, they selected and admitted the capable ones to the University and other institutions of higher learning, and enrolled the remainder in teacher training colleges. It is indeed important to build up the University. But it is no less important to build up the normal, teachers' or kindergarten teachers' colleges. These colleges train teachers who are to educate successors to our revolution. From now on, we should select and admit to these colleges those with a stronger feeling of loyalty to the Party and a stronger revolutionary spirit.

In the meantime, we must reinforce the teaching staff in the sphere of teacher training with people who have a strong Party spirit and working-class spirit and allegiance to the people. There is no need to dismiss all the present teachers on the ground of building up the teaching staff in this sphere with people devoted to the Party. We must make them Communists by educating, revolutionizing and working-classizing them in every possible way.

In order to improve teacher training we must revise the textbooks. Educational workers should examine all the textbooks and eliminate everything in them that is contrary to the principles of socialist pedagogy. On this basis, all the colleges training teachers should give a revolutionary education to the students, using textbooks that conform to the working-class principle, and teach them the scientific, communist theory and methods of education.

We must further intensify Party guidance to the training of teachers. Party organizations at all levels should supervise and give day-to-day guidance to this work. In particular, the Science and Education Department of the Party Central Committee and the education departments of the provincial Party committees should correctly guide and assist in building up the teaching staffs and student bodies in the sphere of teacher training and in examining the textbooks.

An important goal in the field of education today is to carry out with credit the task of training a large contingent of technicians and specialists, a large army of intellectuals for the country—a task put forward by the Fifth Congress of the Party.

During the Six-Year Plan we must more than double the number of technicians and specialists as compared with now, thus bringing it to 1,000,000. Without expanding their ranks to more than 1,000,000 in the near future, we cannot properly run the national economy equipped with modern technology; nor can we successfully fulfill the tasks of the technical and cultural revolutions. The demand everywhere in our country today is for technicians and specialists.

We are planning to transform the village clinics into hospitals. If we are to convert a village clinic into a hospital, we will need at least one doctor or assistant doctor for internal medicine, surgery, pediatrics and obstetrics respectively. Hence, nearly 20,000 doctors will be needed to turn all the village clinics of our country into hospitals. It will also need a large number of doctors to open more modern hospitals in cities.

We are planning to introduce compulsory ten-year education in the near future. To do so, we must have many more teachers.

The technical revolution in the countryside and highly intensive farm production call for large numbers of technicians and specialists in mechanics, electric power, chemistry and biology. We must have nearly 20,000 technicians and specialists in order to assign only four of them to each cooperative farm.

We also intend to build many new large modern factories in the Six-Year Plan period. In order to run these factories properly in the future, we also need numerous technicians and specialists. And many more are required for the expansion and further development of the existing factories and enterprises.

As you see, we need a great many technicians and specialists. So we shall have to train as many as 500,000 intellectuals in the next few years. True, this is not an easy job to undertake within a short time. But if our authorities adhere to the Party's policy of training a large army of intellectuals and work energetically for its realization, the task will be quite feasible.

In order to create a large army of intellectuals for the country, it is essential, first of all, to improve and stimulate the work of the existing institutes of higher learning and higher technical schools and set up more colleges. Along with this, we must open a large number of factory colleges and factory higher technical schools to enroll worker-students and increase the correspondence and evening courses of universities and colleges.

If we are to establish new institutes of higher learning and increase various types of colleges and higher technical schools for worker-students, we need large numbers of teachers. While training more teachers in the sphere of education, we must see to it that working technicians and specialists take up teaching duties and lecture and teach the classes at colleges and higher technical schools and ensure production at the same time.

In order to train a large army of intellectuals, adequate study facilities must be provided for students and working people. More schools should be built through a mass movement, laboratories should be well equipped, and textbooks and reference books published in large quantities.

Libraries should be set up everywhere, including towns and workers' districts, and the students and working people should be encouraged to make full use of them. We are still unable to provide enough textbooks and reference books for all students and working people. So we must set up many libraries and see that they are used. If we open a well-equipped library in

Huichon, for example, and stock it with sufficient textbooks and reference books, the students and working people, including young workers, of the city will be able to study without being inconvenienced.

Efficient organizational work is needed to successfully fulfill these tasks which are essential for the creation of a large army of intellectuals. If we neglect organizational work and fail to make strenuous efforts, we will not be able to succeed in creating a large army of intellectuals in the Six-Year Plan period. All Party organizations and educators must organize work down to the last detail so that we attain the goal of increasing the number of technicians and specialists to more than 1,000,000.

To continue, educational workers must strive to carry out the Party's policy of introducing compulsory ten-year education.

Our Party is planning to introduce compulsory ten-year schooling in the future. The aim is to give a higher secondary general education to the rising generation. If all young people acquire a higher level of general knowledge, they will be able to perform their duties with credit when they go to work in factories or serve in the People's Army, and they will find it easier to enter college. Those who have received a higher secondary general education will find it quite possible to cover the whole college program by self-teaching even if they are unable to attend college.

At present compulsory nine-year technical education is in force in our country, and compulsory ten-year education means giving pupils one more year at school. We are going to introduce compulsory ten-year education by lowering the age at which children are admitted to school by one year, to six.

When the Party first suggested this, some voiced the opinion that if the children were too young, it would be hard to teach them. This, however, is the view of those who are unfamiliar with the specific features of children. It could be said that the mental development of a human being begins at the age of four or five. We can say this because people over fifty remember certain incidents in their lives when they were four or five.

Last year we tried teaching six-year-olds in some 40 schools, and reviewed the results in the autumn of this year. We drew the conclusion that if we prepare the children properly for primary school in their last months of the middle class of kindergarten, it will be quite possible to admit six-year-olds to school and teach them. What troubles us is that children whose homes are widely scattered in mountainous areas have to travel a long distance to school. They find it particularly difficult to go to school in the blizzards of winter. Therefore, branch schools have to be set up in the mountainous regions. If all join in building branch schools, just as the Women's Union did in the past when building mothers' schools, I think this problem, too, can be solved quite soon. Only one teacher is needed to teach in a branch school.

If we are to introduce compulsory ten-year education throughout the country, more schools should be built, large numbers of teachers trained, and the production of textbooks and school things increased. It is therefore impossible to put compulsory ten-year education into effect at once. Adhering to the principle of giving priority to urban communities, we should introduce it in over 20 percent of the whole country each year, thus completing the work by 1976.

Comrades,

The present meeting of educators has discussed an extremely important question relating to the thorough application of the principles of socialist pedagogy in educational work.

So far we have achieved great results in creating socialist pedagogy and applying it in educational work. But we cannot rest content with the present successes, for they are but elementary ones. In the future we must further elaborate and perfect socialist pedagogy and apply it comprehensively in education.

Those responsible for the first process of revolutionizing and working-classizing the whole of society are the teachers. They are bringing up the rising generation to be builders of communism equipped with a revolutionary world outlook and qualified in the respective fields of science and technology. They are thus contributing actively to the work of revolutionizing and working-classizing the whole society and conquering the ideological and material fortresses of communism. Therefore, teachers are not salary-earners but revolutionaries.

I hope that all of our teachers will keenly realize the import and honorable nature of their work and will strive to carry out with credit the responsible revolutionary assignments entrusted to them by the Party.

ON PRESENT POLITICAL
AND ECONOMIC POLICIES
OF THE DEMOCRATIC
PEOPLE'S REPUBLIC OF KOREA
AND SOME INTERNATIONAL PROBLEMS

Answers to the Questions Raised by Newsmen of the Japanese
Newspaper, *Yomiuri Shimbun, January 10, 1972*

It is my great pleasure to welcome you to our country.

Over the past years you have been friendly toward our country and have given great assistance to our citizens in Japan in their activities to defend their democratic, national rights and in their repatriation work.

You have also done much to improve relations between Korea and Japan.

We are grateful for this.

You have spoken a great deal about our on-the-spot guidance. We go to the masses to learn from them rather than to try to guide them.

We had been engaged in the revolutionary struggle in the past, and when we set about national building, we came up against many problems. In order to solve these problems we decided we should go to the masses, particularly the workers and peasants—the producers—and learn from them. That is why we often visit factories and villages and discuss issues with the workers, peasants and other working masses.

When a Marxist-Leninist party representing the interests of the working-class and working masses assumes power, it could become more and more subjective and commit bureaucratic errors. In order to avoid this, it must go to the masses. Especially when it is in a difficult situation, it should go deep among the masses and discuss all matters with them and take their advice.

The popular masses are our teachers. We always learn from them.

In the period of peaceful construction following liberation, during the Fatherland Liberation War and in the postwar years when we carried out the socialist revolution and socialist construction, we constantly went to the masses, with whom we sought ways out of the difficulties confronting us, and gained confidence and courage from them. We could quote many instances of this.

It is our steadfast belief that the key to success either in the revolutionary struggle or in the work of construction lies in unity between the Party and the masses.

Today we have hosts of unsung heroes in our factories and farm villages. They support the Party and propel the revolution and construction. Our Party informs the popular masses of its aims, synthesizes their creative opinions and, on this basis, formulates its lines and policies. Our Party's lines and policies, therefore, enjoy wholehearted popular support and all of them are carried out successfully by the united efforts of the Party and the masses.

Our Party always breathes with the masses of the people. We can say that this is the reason why our Party has become neither subjective nor misguided up to now. In the future, too, we will continue to strengthen the close ties with the masses to avoid committing subjective errors and further expand and develop existing successes.

I received your questions through the Central Committee of the Korean Journalists' Union.

They concern many problems in vast fields of activities.

For convenience's sake, I would like to classify them in groups according to their contents in order to give answers.

1. On the Juche Ideology

You asked me to explain the Juche ideology in detail.

I will give you a brief answer.

I think you will get a clearer idea of it if you read some of my books on the subject.

The Juche idea is the sole guiding idea of our Party and the guiding principle for all activities of the Democratic People's Republic of Korea. Taking the Juche idea as an unshakable guide in revolution and construction, we have firmly established Juche in all domains of our endeavors.

Establishing Juche means that the people approach the revolution and construction in their own country as masters. In other words, it means the embodiment of independent and creative spirits; the people must adopt an independent and creative stand to solve mainly by themselves all the problems arising from the revolutionary struggle and constructive work, in the context of their own country's actual conditions.

The revolution can neither be exported nor imported. Foreigners cannot carry out the revolution for us. The people are the masters of the revolution in each country, and the decisive factor of victory in this revolution is in the strength of the country itself.

Moreover, as the revolutionary movement of the working class and the popular masses forges ahead, many new problems, difficult and complex, arise.

Therefore, in order to carry out the revolution in each country, the people themselves, as masters of the revolution, must endeavor and fight, and through their own intelligence, judgment and efforts, solve all the problems that arise from the revolution and construction, in terms of the situation in their country. This is the only way to successfully carry out the revolution and construction.

Thus, the Juche idea demands that everyone make the revolution in his country the focal point of his thinking and revolutionary activity. Revolution and construction are carried on by people. For victory in the revolution, therefore, people must have a correct revolutionary world outlook, and it is important for them to have the readiness and ideas to accept responsibility as masters for the revolution and construction in their own country.

The Juche idea is based on these requirements of the revolution.

Establishing Juche was especially important for us. Long ago some people in our country developed flunkeyism toward great powers—the servile attitude of not believing in their own strength but worshipping others whether right or wrong and serving those powers. Even when the country was in danger, those who were infected by this attitude engaged in sectarian strife with the backing of their masters, looking to others for help instead of trying to meet the crises by relying firmly on their own people and their own efforts. As a result, our country was eventually ruined at the hands of others.

Flunkeyism toward great powers was not eliminated even later on and, accompanied by dogmatism, did great harm to the development of our revolution. The main reason for the collapse of the nationalist movement and the failure of the early communist movement in our country lay in flunkeyism and sectarianism resulting from it.

There are many such instances not only in our country but also in other countries. In some countries there appeared factionalists who failed to maintain a Juche-motivated stand in the national-liberation and communist movements following the ideological trends of foreign countries, greatly hampering the devleopment of revolution.

We learned from this the serious lesson that when a person takes to flunkeyism he becomes an idiot, when a nation takes to flunkeyism the country is ruined and when a party takes to flunkeyism it makes a mess of the revolution.

If one, captivated by flunkeyism, blindly follows others and acts as they do, he cannot find out the cause of an error he commits, nor the way to remedy it. But when one judges all matters for himself and solves them to suit the actual conditons of his own country, he will be able not only to conduct the revolution and construction successfully but will also be able to quickly find out the cause of an error and remedy it even if he is at fault.

In the light of this historical experience, the Korean revolutionaries were determined to definitively avoid sliding into flunkeyism in the revolutionary struggle and build a state independent and sovereign in the true sense of the words, on the basis of the Juche idea, when they would establish a new country in the future. This was the unanimous intention of the early Korean revolutionaries.

The establishment of Juche became increasingly important to us following the August 15 Liberation. Because of U.S. imperialist occupation of south Korea, our revolution became difficult and complex; the flunkeyist idea of worshipping, fearing and submitting to the U.S. took root in south Korea and illusions about Japanese militarism became widespread.

Viewing the establishment of Juche as the key to the destiny of the revolution and construction, we have struggled unyieldingly all the time against flunkeyism and dogmatism in order to firmly establish Juche. Through this historic battle, we achieved the complete spiritual emancipation of our people from the yoke of flunkeyist ideas which had corroded the spirit of national independence and creative wisdom for a long time. The Juche idea has been thoroughly embodied in all areas of the revolution and construction in our country.

Our people as well as the Party members and cadres arm themselves thoroughly with the Juche idea. They do not waver in the least, regardless of the winds that may blow in from other countries, and are not at all affected by these winds. The thoughts of our people are very sound.

You asked about the essential points of our Juche-based policy.

All our Party's internal and external policies are based on the Juche idea and proceed from it. Juche underlies our specific measures as well as all lines and policies, political, economic, cultural and military.

The Juche idea is embodied, first of all, in the lines of political independence, economic self-support and national self-defense.

Political independence is the prime criterion of any sovereign state. Only when a nation exercises its legitimate right to political self-determination, can it ensure the country's complete independence.

We have established and are establishing all our lines and policies independently on the Juche idea. We do not act on orders or instructions from any foreigners; neither do we copy nor imitate foreign ways. None of the policies determined and implemented by our Party since liberation have been copied. They were created by ourselves in accordance with the requirements of our revolution from the standpoint of Juche.

This does not mean that we do not refer at all to revolutionary movements of other countries and their experiences. We have objectively considered foreign ways and creatively applied the universal principles of Marxism-Leninism to suit our actual conditons from the Juche stand. That is why we have not committed errors and have been able to steer the revolution and construction along the right path.

From our Juche standpoint we have solved all issues entirely in accordance with the actual conditions of our country.

As an example, in order to lay the foundation for an independent national economy and to ensure rapid improvement in the impoverished lives of people in conditons of the severe ravages of war, we advanced our basic line of socialist economic construction, that of giving priority to the growth of heavy industry simultaneously with the development of light industry and agriculture. This is an original line arrived at by correctly reflecting the demands of our own economic development and through the creative interpretation of Marxist-Leninist theory.

After properly assessing our specific requirements, we also established a policy of agricultural cooperativization to reorganize the economic forms prior to technological reconstruction. We proposed the reorganization on socialist lines of the capitalist commerce and industry. These proposals were original and unknown in other countries. When our Party advanced this line and proposals, those who were infected with flunkeyism and dogmatism criticized them, saying, "No book has ever dealt with them," and "They had never been tried before." But the validity of the line and proposals has been proved by the fact that our country has become a socialist industrial state with a developed agriculture in a brief span of time.

With regard to our intelligentsia, we have also followed a policy different from that in other countries.

Despite their former wealth, the old intellectuals of our country have a national, revolutionary spirit, because they were subjected to national oppression and discrimination under the colonial rule of Japanese imperialism.

As for those intellectuals who were educated in the old way and worked in bourgeois or feudal society, if they wanted to work for the people and the development of the nation, we pursued the policy of developing the revolution together with them, educating and remolding them in the practice of revolution. Thus, they have been remolded as revolutionary intellectuals serving the revolutionary cause of the working class. They have already done a great deal and even now, are still working faithfully.

The Juche ideology is demonstrated in our unique line of simultaneously building up the nation's economy and defenses to increase both our economic and defense powers to meet the imperialist maneuvers for aggression and war, and also in our original line and policy of peaceful reunification of Korea by the Koreans themselves, following the expulsion of the U.S. imperialist aggressors from south Korea, and free from foreign interference.

That is why all our Party's policies are in accord with the actual conditions of our country and the aspirations of our people, and we are able to firmly maintain our political independence without indecision in adversity.

Economic self-support is the material basis of political independence. The country which depends economically on others cannot help depending on others politically.

This was why immediately after liberation we put forward the line of building an independent national economy and implemented it despite all difficulties.

To build an independent national economy by one's own efforts does not mean closing the door of one's country. While building an independent national economy under the banner of self-reliance, we have developed economic relations of mutual accommodation and cooperation with other countries on the principles of complete equality and mutual benefit.

Our struggle has borne good fruit, and as a result, we now have a comprehensively developed independent national economy equipped with modern technology. This firmly guarantees the political independence of the country.

National self-defense is the military guarantee for the country's political independence and economic self-support. As long as the world is divided into national states and imperialism remains on the globe, one cannot speak of independence and self-support if one has not the defense capacity to safeguard his country and people from foreign aggression.

By thoroughly implementing the military line of self-defense, we have built up an enormous defense capacity for smashing any provocation of the aggressors and firmly defending the country's security and the revolutionary gains.

With the thorough implementation of the principles of independence in politics, self-support in the economy and self-defense in guarding the nation, we have built the proud, powerful and reliable new socialist country that we aspired for. If we had not established Juche but bent instead with the wind and danced to the tune of others we could not hope for today's successes.

Some capitalist newspapers call a socialist country maintaining independence "national communism." Our Juche ideology has nothing in common with the "national communism" which the reactionaries are noisily talking about.

The Juche ideology is based on Marx's principle "Workers of all countries, unite!" and is in full accord with proletarian internationalism.

We make it a principle to maintain and defend independence on the Juche ideology and, at the same time, to strengthen internationalist unity and cooperation. The independence we advocate is by no means separated from proletarian internationalism. There can be no internationalism separated from independence, and vice versa. It does not befit a Communist to turn his back on proletarian internationalism under the pretext of maintaining independence. This means simply sliding into ethnocentrism.

We now maintain mutual relations with other countries on a completely equal and independent basis.

We neither intend to encroach upon the interests of other nations nor allow anyone to trample upon the rights and dignity of our nation. We are developing political and economic relations, on the principles of complete equality and mutual respect, with big and small countries which take a friendly attitude toward our country.

Independence, too, is a prerequisite to unity and cooperation among the socialist countries. In order to achieve genuine unity, all should abide strictly by the principle of independence. We now hold fast to our principles in the efforts to achieve unity and cohesion among the socialist countries.

Our principles are, firstly, to oppose imperialism; secondly, to support the national-liberation movement in colonies and the working-class movement in various countries; thirdly, to march on toward socialism and communism; and fourthly, to abide by the principles of noninterference in each other's internal affiars, mutual respect, equality and mutual benefit. It is our idea that even if differences exist, they should give way to these four principles to attain unity.

As regards our attitude toward the revolutionary struggle and democratic movement in other countries, we also abide strictly by the principles of independence and noninterference.

The party and people of each country know their national affairs better than anyone else. It is natural, therefore, that they should decide how to conduct the revolutionary movement in their country. All we have to do is support and encourage as best we can the just struggle of other peoples for national and social emancipation. We will not meddle in it or force our idea upon them. We do not mechanically follow the examples of others nor ask them to swallow ours whole.

The revolutionary and democratic movements now going on in many countries can develop successfully and emerge victorious only when the parties and people of those countries independently work out a correct guiding theory and scientific methods of struggle according to the actual conditions in their countries and put them into practice.

2. On Socialist Construction in Our Country and Central Tasks of the Six-Year Plan

As you know, the Fifth Congress of our Party summed up the successes in the fulfillment of the Seven-Year Plan and adopted the Six-Year Plan as another target of socialist construction.

Originally, the Seven-Year Plan was to be carried out between 1961 and 1967. But due to the tense situation around our country, its fulfillment was delayed. While our people were carrying out the Seven-Year Plan, the U.S. imperialists created the Caribbean crisis and escalated the war of aggression against the Vietnamese people, thus greatly increasing tension. Moreover, the U.S. imperialists perpetrated

grave military provocations against the northern half of the
Republic, while stepping up their new war preparations in
south Korea.

Under these conditions, we had to increase the country's
defense potential and fully prepare to cope with the enemy's
invasion.

Our Party advanced the new line of simultaneously building
up the economy and defenses, and in accordance with this line,
it reorganized the socialist construction program as a whole and
appropriated adequate funds for defense preparations. Consequently, it took us more time than originally planned to carry
out the Seven-Year National Economic Plan.

At that time, we directed considerable efforts toward
strengthening the defense forces and attained a state of
complete national defense, even though this impeded our
economic development and the betterment of the people's
living standards. That was how we were able to prevent the
U.S. imperialists from daring to attack us, though they
openly attempted armed invasion of the northern half of the
Republic by creating the *Pueblo* and EC-121 incidents.

Despite the difficult conditions we succeeded in carrying out
the Seven-Year Plan. Although it took us ten years to complete
the plan, our national economy nevertheless developed at a
very high tempo. In the past decade during the implementation
of the plan, our industrial production has grown at an average
annual rate of 12.8%.

This I think is a very high rate of development in comparison
with other countries, and our people are very proud of this
achievement.

Last year we embarked upon a new long-range project, the
Six-Year Plan.

This plan is a blueprint for making great strides in the
struggle to consolidate our socialist system even further and
achieve complete victory for socialism. It is a blueprint for
turning our socialist country into a richer and stronger
state—independent, self-supporting and self-defensive.

As was clarified in the report to the Fifth Party Congress, the
basic task of the Six-Year Plan in the field of socialist economic
construction is that of cementing the material and technical
foundations of socialism and freeing the working people from
arduous labor in all fields of the national economy. This will be

achieved through the consolidation and expansion of our successes in industrialization and the advance of the technical revolution onto a new and higher plane.

The main contents of the Six-Year Plan consist of three major objectives of the technical revolution.

The objectives advanced by our Party are, firstly, to vigorously propel the technical revolution in industrial branches to narrow down the distinction between heavy and light labor; secondly, to continue to accelerate the technical revolution in the countryside to reduce the difference between agricultural and industrial labor; and thirdly, to extend the technical revolution toward freeing women from the heavy burdens of household chores. Simply stated, the three major tasks of the technical revolution are dedicated revolutionary endeavors to free the working people from heavy and strenuous labor.

They express the requirements for our economic development following the realization of socialist industrialization, coupled with the earnest wishes of the working people.

Our Party decided that the production of machine tools was the key to the three major tasks of the technical revolution.

The technical revolution is precisely an engineering revolution. It requires adequate supplies of machine tools.

Therefore, last year—the first year of the Six-Year Plan—we concentrated our efforts on the production of machine tools. Heartily responding to the Party's call, our machine-tool factory workers, including those from the Huichon Machine-tool Plant, energetically struggled to increase production through improvements in equipment and extensive automation of production processes. As a result, our engineering industry surpassed the level of producing 30,000 machine tools in a single year.

We have already made a major breakthrough in the implementation of the three tasks of the technical revolution, and now have before us good prospects for the successful completion of the Six-Year Plan.

In order to carry out the three major tasks, we will persevere in the production of machine tools, increasing output and variety and improving their quality. We will also continue to increase the production of tractors and automobiles and turn out more of various farm machines. And for the continuous intensification of the technical revolution, we intend directing great efforts to the development of the electronics and automation industries.

We will also increase production of steel and nonferrous metals for the engineering industry, as well as for the electronics and automation industries.

Judging by our achievements in the past year and the fighting spirit of our working people, we are certain that the three tasks of the technical revolution will be successfully fulfilled in a short span of time.

During the Six-Year Plan our people's standard of living will also be further improved.

Today our people have no worries about food, clothing and housing, and are leading a decent egalitarian life.

During the Six-Year Plan we intend to take steps to raise even higher their standards of living. The most important task we have set ourselves in the improvement of living standards is that of eliminating as quickly as possible the difference in the standards of living of workers and peasants, and the difference between urban and rural living conditions.

To this end, we will develop the county centers enhancing their role as supply bases for the rural areas, introduce bus services in all rural villages and provide them with water supplies. We will also build houses for 300,000 families each year in both towns and the countryside, and will continue to develop public health services. We will raise the wages of workers and office employees as a whole and bring about a new upswing in the production of consumer goods, thereby significantly improving the general living standard of our working population.

Providing we work efficiently for a number of years, our people should be able to live as well as in any other nation.

During the Six-Year Plan, we intend also proceeding vigorously with the cultural revolution in parallel to the technical revolution.

During this period the number of technicians and specialists will be increased to more than one million, the working people's level of general knowledge and their technological skill as a whole will be raised, and science, literature, the arts and physical culture and sports will be further developed.

One of the important tasks in the cultural revolution during the same period will be the enforcement of compulsory ten-year education.

With the introduction in 1967 of compulsory nine-year technical education in our country, all children and youths between 7 and 16 have received free education at regular schools. The introduction of this compulsory education was a landmark in the development of public education and the construction of socialist culture in our country. As a result, all members of our young generation are growing into versatile and reliable men, possessing wide general knowledge and the basics of modern science and technology.

We are going to introduce compulsory ten-year schooling following the successes and experiences gained in the compulsory nine-year technical education, and further improve the educational work in accordance with our Party's socialist pedagogic principles.

The introduction of universal compulsory ten-year education will bring about big progress in improving school education and in developing science and technology in our country. Of course, it is by no means an easy task to introduce compulsory education over a ten-year period, and to do this, the state must invest considerable funds. But we have strength enough to carry it out and we are sparing nothing for the education of our future generations. Last year we introduced the ten-year plan on an experimental basis in certain schools, accumulated experiences and laid its foundation to some extent. We intend to introduce compulsory ten-year education on a full scale throughout the country within a few years, beginning this year.

It is of great importance in developing a socialist society to properly combine the politico-ideological unity of the people with the class struggle.

This is why our Party has always paid great attention to this aspect.

In the northern half of our country the exploitation of man by man ceased to exist and a socialist system came into being a long time ago. As a result, the correlations of the working people have become a comradely relationship of mutual assistance and cooperation, which has further strengthened the politico-ideological unity of the entire people.

This, of course, does not imply that the unity of the popular masses grows stronger by itself simply because of the establishment of the socialist system. Under this system there remain hostile elements, though insignificant, and there are also remnants of outdated ideas in the minds of the working people.

Therefore, in order to consolidate firm revolutionary ranks and successfully build socialism, we should properly combine our activities to strengthen the unity and solidarity of the people with the struggle against the subtle maneuvers of hostile elements.

Under socialism the basis of social relations is the alliance of the working class, peasantry and intelligentsia. However, if one forgets this fact and emphasizes or overestimates only the class struggle, he will commit a "Leftist" error. In that instance, one would tend to suspect people, treat the innocent as hostile elements and create in society an atmosphere of unrest.

On the other hand, under socialism there are also hostile elements and obsolete ideological hangovers, and a class struggle continues. If one does not remember this fact but only sees and absolutizes the politico-ideological unity of the people, he will commit a Rightist error. In this instance, vigilance against hostile elements could be dulled, the struggle against outdated ideas weakened and the capitalist way of life could become wide-spread.

Therefore, we guard against Right and "Left" deviations and skillfully combine the fight against hostile elements with the work of cementing unity and solidarity among the working people. This leads to a constant strengthening in the unity and cohesion of the masses.

In order to strengthen politico-ideological unity among the working people, we must revolutionize and working-classize the whole society by giving priority to the ideological revolution.

Only when priority is given to the ideological revolution can the historical task of revolutionizing and working-classizing the whole society be solved successfully, and the ideological and material fortresses in socialist and communist construction be occupied at an earlier date.

To revolutionize and working-classize the entire society amounts to a class struggle to remove all the outdated ideas and non-working-class elements from every facet of social life. But this is totally different from the former class struggle, and the form of this struggle is also different.

The task of revolutionizing and working-classizing people is that of remolding the working people in their fight for earlier and better construction of socialism and communism, and this arises from the need to introduce all working people to communist society. That is why our Party has conducted, and is conducting, the revolutionization and working-classization of the working people through explanation and persuasion, with the main emphasis on ideological education.

We have made tireless efforts in this direction among people from all walks of life on the principle of boldly trusting all those who wish to follow our Party and of winning them over to the side of revolution, even when their family origins, their backgrounds and their social and political careers are questionable.

Because we have conducted the struggle for revolutionizing and working-classizing the whole society along the right lines, our people's ideological and moral qualities have now undergone a radical change, and our society has been consolidated internally more than ever before.

The unity of our workers, cooperative farmers and working intellectuals has been further cemented, and all the working people make up a great, united Red family, helping and leading each other forward.

The process of building socialism and communism is a process of revolutionizing the workers, peasants, intellectuals and all the other members of society, and of obliterating all class distinctions through the transformation of the entire society on a working-class pattern.

The building of socialism and communism requires the elimination of differences between the working class and the peasantry in their working conditions through the developed productive forces and, at the same time, the gradual obliteration of distinctions in the thought and morality, cultural and technical levels of all members of society.

An important problem in this connection is the correct solution of the rural question.

Only when a socialist state ends the backwardness of the countryside through the final settlement of the rural question, can it completely eliminate the breeding grounds for reactionary bourgeois virus infiltrating from outside and the footholds for the remnants of the overthrown exploiting classes to engage in insidious maneuvers. And only by elevating cooperative property to the level of public property can we greatly develop the productive forces of agriculture, root out the elements of selfishness remaining in the minds of the peasants, and lead all the working people confidently along the road of collectivism to work with much voluntary enthusiasm for society and the people.

Our Party has actively promoted the technical, cultural and ideological revolutions in the rural areas along the lines outlined in the *Theses on the Socialist Rural Question in Our Country*. The Party is thus eliminating the technological lag of agriculture behind modern industry, the cultural backwardness of the villages in relation to advanced towns, and the ideological lag of the peasants behind the working class, the most revolutionary class. We are also continuously strengthening the working-class party's and state's guidance and assistance to the rural areas, and are steadily bringing cooperative property closer to public property, while organically welding the development of the two.

Thus, once class distinction between the working class and the peasantry is eliminated and cooperative property is turned into public property, the entire society will achieve complete political and ideological unity with the common ideology on the same socio-economic basis. We are striving to hasten the day when this will be realized.

3. On the Problem of the Reunification of Our Country

Today the general situation in our country is developing very favorably for the struggle of our people for the independent and peaceful reunification of the country.

The successes of socialist construction in the northern half of the country scored under the banner of the Juche idea further consolidate the political and economic basis for the independent reunification of the country, give great hope and confidence to the people of the southern half and vigorously rouse them to the struggle for peaceful reunification.

Lately, a tendency toward peaceful reunification is rapidly

expanding in south Korea and the struggle against fascist rule and for the democratization of society is gaining momentum as never before. The massive advance of the youth, students and people that has continued both before and after last year's puppet presidential "election" and brisk arguments about national reunification in public and political circles, indicate that demands for peaceful reunification against the present ruling system in south Korea are rising with an irresistible force.

As our policy for peaceful reunification enjoys the unanimous support not only of the Korean people but of the broad public opinion of the world, and the tendency toward peaceful reunification increases in south Korea, even the south Korean authorities who had previously rejected any contact between the north and the south were obliged, under the pressure of these trends, to attend the north-south Red Cross talks. I think that the preliminary talks between the north and south Red Cross organizations held at Panmunjom are belated and have a limited scope of problems under discussion, but they are very significant since Koreans themselves have come together to discuss the nation's internal affairs. It can be said that this is a step forward in our people's struggle for peacefully reunifying the divided country.

Our stand on the talks between the north and south Red Cross organizations is clear. We want to bring the talks to success by showing our utmost sincerity and thus rid our people as soon as possible of the sufferings due to the division and pave the way, using these talks as a stepping stone, to the peaceful reunification of our country.

But the stand of the south Korean authorities is quite the opposite. From the first day they were compelled to attend the talks, they dragged them out under this or that pretext and poured cold water on the growing tendency toward peaceful reunification, saying: "Don't get too excited," and "It is premature." Moreover, they claimed that we would soon "invade the south" as we had "already prepared for war," and they declared a "state of national emergency." They are presently trumping up various evil fascist laws to buttress this declaration and are deliberately aggravating the situation.

This type of maneuver by the south Korean puppet clique cannot be interpreted as otherwise than being designed to prolong their remaining days by detracting from the increasing trend toward peaceful reunification in south Korea, and by frustrating north-south contacts and negotiation to perpetuate national division. It is not an accident that certain reactionary ruling circles and government-controlled press in the U.S. and Japan say that the proclamation of the "state of emergency" in south Korea is not because of the threat of "southward aggression" but, rather, a political trick hatched due to the internal situation.

With such foolish tactics the south Korean rulers can solve nothing, much less deceive anyone.

It seems that alarmed by the rapid change of internal and external situations to their disadvantage, they are going on a rampage. But they need to cool their heads and think over matters calmly.

Now the times and situation have changed.

The situation today is different from that of the 1940s when the U.S. imperialists could divide our country into north and south, abusing the name of the "United Nations." The day has gone when they could rule the roost meddling in the affairs of other countries.

Now the U.S. imperialists and Japanese militarists can hardly deal with their own affairs.

We think the time has come when the south Korean rulers should give up their present anti-national stand—seeking a way out by turning their backs on their compatriots and clinging to the sleeves of the U.S. imperialist aggressors and calling in the Japanese aggressors.

If the south Korean rulers are to find a true way out, they should adopt a national stand, immediately renounce their absurd assertion to "build up strength" with the backing of outside forces to overpower north Korea by force and thereby attain "reunification by prevailing over communism." They should accept our fair and sincere proposals to reunify the country in a peaceful way through the joint efforts of the Korean people themselves.

You asked about our concrete program for the reunification of the country. Our program for national reunification is no different from the previous one. We have constantly maintained that the question of our country's reunification, an internal affair of our nation, should be solved not by the interference of outside forces but by the efforts of the Korean people themselves, and not by means of war, but in a peaceful way.

We reclarified the program for the independent, peaceful reunification of the country in the eight-point proposal for national salvation advanced at a session of the Supreme People's Assembly of the Democratic People's Republic of Korea held in April last year, in the speech made on August 6 last year and in this year's New Year Address. We will continue to make every effort in the future to realize this program.

A successful conclusion of the talks between the north and south Red Cross organizations, amid the great interest of the whole nation, will create a favorable atmosphere for the peaceful reunification of the country.

The south Korean authorities, talking about some sort of "stage," claim that this can be done and that not, and that only something should be done first and the other things deferred. These are delaying tactics and not the correct attitude for solving our problems.

If the north-south Red Cross talks yield good results and free traffic is realized between the families, relatives and friends presently divided, their sufferings will be lessened and, at the same time, frozen feelings between north and south will be thawed, thus deepening mutual understanding.

The removal of tension in our country is a matter of vital importance for the peaceful reunification of the country as well as for peace in Asia and the rest of the world.

In order to remove this tension, it is necessary, first of all, to replace the Korean Armistice Agreement with a peace agreement between north and south. We maintain that a peace agreement should be concluded between north and south and the armed forces of both sides be cut drastically following the prior withdrawal of U.S. imperialist aggressor troops from south Korea.

We have made it clear more than once that we have no intention of "invading the south." If the south Korean rulers have no intentions of "marching north for reunification," there should be no reason for them to refuse a north-south peace agreement. If they truly want peace in our country and peaceful reunification, they should consent to this peace agreement, instead of clamoring about fictitious "threats of southward aggression."

We advocate strengthening contacts and ties between north and south and holding mutual political negotiations to solve the question of national reunification.

Many problems arise in bringing about peaceful reunification putting an end to the tragedy of national division. All these problems can only be satisfactorily solved through direct political negotiations between north and south.

We are ready to negotiate with the Democratic Republican Party, the New Democratic Party, the Nationalist Party and all other political parties in south Korea at any time and at any agreed place. The south Korean authorities now say this and that even without meeting us. We do not feel that the rejection of negotiations while giving lip service to "peaceful reunification" is the proper attitude toward the peaceful settlement of the reunification question. For the peaceful solution of this issue the various political parties of both north and south Korea must hold active bilateral or multilateral negotiations to exchange political views on national reunification and find a reasonable way toward peaceful settlement.

We keep our door constantly open to anyone for north-south negotiations and contacts. If anyone, regardless of earlier crimes against the country and the people, sincerely repents his past and takes the road of patriotism for the peaceful reunification of our country, we will not ask about his past crimes but gladly negotiate with him on the question of national reunification.

If all Koreans unite and fight for the reunification of our country, we will be able to drive out the U.S. and Japanese aggressors, overcome the crisis of national ruin created in south Korea and undoubtedly achieve the peaceful reunification of the country. We are sure that although the question of Korean reunification is still complicated, there is nevertheless the prospect of an eventual peaceful solution in accordance with the will of our people and on the principle of national self-determination.

4. On Some International Problems

We are seeing in our time the decline of the strength of

imperialism while the forces of the people toward peace, democracy, national independence and socialism are gaining in scope and strength.

The U.S. imperialists, who sustained in the Korean war an ignominious defeat for the first time in their history, are incessantly being beaten and cornered everywhere in the world and keep going downhill.

The U.S. imperialists are now facing a grave crisis both internally and externally. In the U.S., the people's anti-war movement proceeds with great force and there is increasing antagonism among the ruling circles. The economy has fallen into chronic stagnation and U.S. international payments are constantly deteriorating. The U.S. imperialists sustain one defeat after another in Indochina and other parts of the world while being isolated from their satellite countries as well as from their imperialistic colleagues.

The U.S. imperialists oppressed and controlled others through nuclear blackmail and dollars, but their strength has now waned. Now that nuclear blackmail no longer works and the dollars in their pockets have run out, few countries toe U.S. imperialism's line. In order to get out of their difficulties, the U.S. imperialists have formulated the notorious "Nixon doctrine," which is aimed at making Asians fight Asians and the Middle East people fight each other. But nobody, except a stupid person such as Sato, would support this doctrine.

Under these conditions, the U.S. imperialists have again put up the "peace" signboard, and Nixon finds himself compelled to go on a tour of mendicant diplomacy with his hat in his hand.

But this does not mean that U.S. imperialism has been completely ruined or that its true colors have changed. U.S. imperialism remains the main force of imperialism and its aggressive nature has not changed in the least. Whenever the imperialists get into difficulties, they usually perpetrate crafty acts of aggression and war under the signboard of "peace."

Resorting to a double-dealing policy, the U.S. imperialists are now making more insidious attempts to invade other countries. The peoples of revolutionary and all fighting countries must therefore maintain their constant vigilance against the U.S. imperialist machinations for new aggression and war carried on behind the curtain of "peace," and firmly unite to wage a more vigorous struggle against these imperialists. This is the only way to defend peace and attain national independence and social progress.

The U.S. imperialists attach special importance to Japanese militarism in realizing the "Nixon doctrine" in Asia.

They have long followed the policy of using Japanese militarism as the "shock force" in their Asian aggression, and the Japanese militarists, availing themselves of this policy, have been maneuvering to achieve their own goals. The U.S.-Japan summit talks held a few days ago were in lower spirits than previous talks, but showed that the collusion and conspiracy between these two aggressive forces remains unchanged in their Asian aggression. In the "joint communique" issued after the talks, Nixon and Sato reaffirmed the notorious "U.S.-Japan security pact" and promised to "closely cooperate" with each other in Asian aggression under the pretext of "peace" and "stability."

Under the aegis and backing of U.S. imperialism, Japanese militarism has been revived and the Japanese militarists have developed into a dangerous force of aggression in Asia. This is a hard fact.

Following the imperialist pattern, the Japanese militarists, in invading other countries, are employing the methods of economically subordinating those countries through a massive influx of goods and capital. They also paralyzed their people's spirit of independence through intensified ideological and cultural infiltration, and even send in their armed forces of aggression on the pretext of protecting Japanese economic rights.

Our country is the first target of Japanese militarism in its overseas aggression program.

The Japanese militarists, in conspiracy and collaboration with the south Korean puppets, have now extended their black, aggressive hands deep into the political, economic, cultural and military fields of the southern half of our country. They have also worked out operation plans for invading our country, and other socialist countries of Asia, and are conducting successive war exercises. Sato has gone so far as to vociferate for a "preemptive attack" against our country.

Such being the case, to argue about whether Japanese militarism has been revived or not is out of date. The point is to oppose the aggressive machinations of revived Japanese militarism and struggle to check them.

The struggle of the Japanese people is very important in frustrating the aggressive scheme of the Japanese militarists. As I said formerly, the Japanese people are not as they were before. They are a people who have suffered the pains and evil aftereffect of the overseas aggression of militarism; they are an awakened people. They will not remain passive if the Japanese militarists dare try to unleash another war of aggression. The Japanese people themselves are now resolutely fighting for democracy, neutrality and peace against the militarist forces of aggression. This struggle brings great pressure to bear on the reactionary ruling circles of Japan.

Opinions are divided among the Japanese ruling circles about the launching of a war of aggression. There seem to be people who are opposed to war, because they feel that once a war breaks out the situation will become very difficult for them. This is because Japan is an island country and imports nearly all industrial raw materials. They also feel that the objects of their aggression will not be easy to deal with. In fact, Asia today is unlike the Asia of yesterday, and its outlook has radically changed.

If all the anti-war forces in Japan unite and the Asian peoples, including the Koreans and Chinese, fight in concert, the Japanese militarists will not dare start a war, however wildly they may want it, and their aggressive machination will be easily frustrated.

Asia is now the main arena of the anti-imperialist revolutionary struggle and the developments in Asia exert a very great influence upon the changing situation of the whole world.

The peoples of our country, other socialist countries and the fighting nations of Asia, are achieving brilliant victories in the revolutionary struggle against imperialism and in the building of a new society, despite manifold difficulties and trials.

The U.S. imperialists have pursued a policy of isolation and blockade against China for over 20 years. But China has not gone under. On the contrary, she has become a powerful socialist state and has grown and strengthened into a reliable anti-imperialist revolutionary force. The international prestige of the People's Republic of China increases daily.

The People's Republic of China was restored to its legitimate position in the United Nations with the support of many countries, whereas the Chiang Kai-shek clique was expelled from all the UN bodies. This was a great event in the international political arena. It was a great victory for the Chinese people and also a victory for the peoples of the world who strive for peace and progress.

Through their heroic struggle against the U.S. imperialist aggressors, the Vietnamese people have inflicted a crushing defeat upon the enemy and are greatly contributing to the world progressive people's cause of peace, national independence and socialism. The Vietnamese people are stepping up the fight to clear South Vietnam of the aggressive forces of U.S. imperialism and attain genuine independence and reunification of the country.

The Vietnam question should be solved on the basis of the four-point proposal for the peaceful settlement of the Vietnam question advanced by the Democratic Republic of Vietnam and the seven-point proposal made by the Provisional Revolutionary Government of the Republic of South Vietnam. If the U.S. imperialists persist in challenging the Vietnamese people, refusing to accept their just demands, they will face a more ignominious defeat. The Vietnamese people will certainly win final victory in their struggle, holding higher the revolutionary banner of anti-imperialism.

The Cambodian and Laotian peoples, who have already won great victories in the resistance struggle for national salvation against imperialism, are making constant powerful attacks on the U.S. imperialists and their puppet mercenaries and have driven them into an inextricable corner.

In Asia the U.S. imperialists are now living their last days.

The peoples of Korea, China, Vietnam, Cambodia, Laos and other Asian countries will unite firmly behind the banner of the anti-imperialist, anti-U.S. common struggle to completely eliminate imperialism and all forms of colonialism, and thus build a new, independent and prosperous Asia.

As you know, some changes have also taken place recently in the United Nations, reflecting a change in the balance between progressive and reactionary forces in the world.

It is becoming difficult for the U.S. imperialists to act as they please in the United Nations as in the past. This illustrates that the days are over when the U.S. imperialists could commit crimes at will, abusing the UN flag.

As you have indicated, regarding the question of the United Nations, many countries and broad world public opinion now call 1972 the "year of Korea." Of course, we must wait and see whether this year will be the "year of Korea" or not, but we think it is an expression of the world people's support and trust in our struggle for national dignity, reunification and independence.

As for our stand on the United Nations, the Democratic People's Republic of Korea has always respected the UN Charter and has never violated it.

It is the U.S. imperialists themselves who have wantonly violated the UN Charter and defamed the name of the United Nations. Each time they resorted to policies of aggression and war, the U.S. imperialists abused the UN flag. Particularly, they committed aggression on Korea under the UN mask and thus left a most disgraceful blot in UN history.

To be faithful to its sacred Charter, I think, the United Nations must rectify its past errors in connection with the Korean question.

The United Nations should revoke all "resolutions" on the "Korean question" fabricated illegally by the U.S. imperialists in the world body. Or, it may adopt a just policy in the future toward Korea to ensure that all the previous illegal "resolutions" are nullified.

The United Nations must take steps to effect the withdrawal of the aggressive forces of U.S. imperialism presently occupying south Korea under the "UN" authority, and dissolve its "Commission for the Unification and Rehabilitation of Korea," which is a tool of U.S. imperialism for its aggression in Korea. The United Nations must stop any further interference in the Korean question.

5. On the Problem of Relations Between Korea and Japan

Japan is a neighbor of ours. As you say, however, our two countries have now become "close yet distant neighbors." This cannot but be a very abnormal situation.

Historically speaking, our country was invaded by Japan, the latter being an aggressor on our country. But the aggressor was the Japanese imperialist, not the Japanese people. It is not a bad but a desirable development that the Democratic People's Republic of Korea and Japan, neighbors to each other, should establish normal relations.

Ever since its founding, the Democratic People's Republic of Korea has hoped to establish good-neighbor relations with Japan despite the differing social systems. This stand is based on the fair and aboveboard foreign policy of our Republic which establishes amicable relations with all countries that adopt a friendly attitude toward our country on the principles of equality and mutual benefit.

To our regret, however, the Japanese government has been unfriendly toward our country from the outset. Although several Cabinet changes have been made from Yoshida to Kishi, Ikeda and Sato, there has been no change in the Japanese government's hostile policy toward our country.

This hostile policy has become even more unscrupulous since Sato formed a Cabinet. The Japanese government has been making inroads into south Korea following the conclusion of the "ROK-Japan treaty" with the south Korean puppets and encourages them to oppose national reunification and seek a fratricidal war. Japanese Prime Minister Sato and his followers openly talk about involvement in a war against the DPRK and wantonly insult the Korean people.

It is entirely because of the Japanese government's hostile policy toward our country that good-neighbor relations have not yet been established between us.

Our stand on the relations between Korea and Japan is clear and constant. We hope even now to put an early end to this abnormal situation and establish normal relations between the two countries. We believe this is in the interest and in accord with the desire of our two peoples and also beneficial to peace in Asia and the world.

The Japanese government should, first of all, change its attitude toward our country in order to establish friendly relations, and thereafter diplomatic relations, between our countries.

Whether the Japanese Cabinet will be replaced is an internal affair, and we we will not meddle in the matter. The main point is the attitude of the Japanese government toward our country. Even if the Prime Minister of Japan is replaced, relations between our two countries cannot be improved as long as its policy toward us remains unchanged. If the Japanese government adopts a friendly attitude toward our country, all problems will be solved smoothly.

The Japanese government should change its incorrect policy to keep abreast with present trends. It must give up its hostile policy toward the Democratic People's Republic of Korea. It must also abrogate the "ROK-Japan treaty," stop its act of reinvading south Korea, renounce the folly of trying to pit Koreans against Koreans by abetting the south Korean puppets and so fish in troubled waters.

These days an extensive campaign is afoot among the Japanese people and progressive circles to establish good-neighbor relations with the DPRK. Sometime ago there came into being the "Dietmen's League for Promotion of Japan-Korea Friendship" comprising 234 Diet members from the ruling and opposition parties. Local assemblies have also adopted resolutions demanding the establishment of state relations with the DPRK. We consider this is a very good development and hope their struggle will bear fine fruit.

If the Korean and Japanese peoples wage a joint struggle successfully, it will be possible to establish diplomatic relations between our two countries. Once this is done, the policy the Japanese government has so far wrongly pursued toward our country will end. We think that friendly relations between the two countries can be developed even before the establishment of diplomatic relations. The present conditions suggest that it will take some time for Korea and Japan to establish diplomatic relations. Even before we establish diplomatic relations with Japan, we are ready to have as many visits of people as possible and conduct wide-scale trade and interchanges in the economic and cultural fields.

The friendly relations between Korea and Japan should on all accounts be established on the principle of reciprocity. Though there is presently some interchange between the two countries, it cannot but be unilateral in character, owing to the unfriendly attitude of the Japanese government. I wonder if the Japanese government is afraid of falling out of favor with either the U.S. or the south Korean puppets. It is clear that in these circumstances it is absolutely impossible to improve the relations between the two countries.

After all, the establishment of good-neighbor relations between Korea and Japan and its timing depend entirely on the attitude of the Japanese government, regardless of the concrete procedures for it.

As for the question of the 600,000 Koreans in Japan, it is, in essence, a matter which resulted from past colonial rule of the Japanese imperialists in our country. Korean citizens in Japan are not accorded the treatment due to foreigners, although it is a stark fact that today they have their own fatherland. This is attributable also to the unfriendly attitude of the Japanese government toward our country.

Korean citizens in Japan have waged a strenuous struggle to defend their democratic, national rights, overcoming many difficulties. In particular, they formed Chongryon (the General Association of Korean Residents in Japan), an organization of overseas nationals of the Democratic People's Republic of Korea. They have splendidly embodied the Juche idea in the movement of Koreans in Japan and, united closely around Comrade Chairman Han Dok Su, have made great successes in the struggle to defend their democratic, national rights, promote the peaceful reunification of the country and cement international solidarity with the Japanese and the progressive people of the world.

It is thanks to the active support and encouragement of the Japanese people, progressive political parties and social organizations, and individuals from all walks of life that the Korean citizens in Japan under the guidance of Chongryon have scored these successes despite various obstructive machinations by the Japanese government. We are very grateful for this support and take this opportunity to express through the *Yomiuri Shimbun* heartfelt thanks to our Japanese friends.

It is natural for the Korean citizens in Japan to defend their national rights and it accords with international law, too. Probably Japanese residing in other countries will also defend their rights, and will not waive them. This is the case with all nations.

Let me speak of the national education of Korean citizens in Japan.

As you know, a nation is characterized above all by community of its speech and letters. There can be no Korean nation separate from our spoken and written language. The Japanese government's persecution of the national education of Korean citizens in Japan, therefore, cannot be construed otherwise than as an act prompted by an impure political motive. We attach great importance to their national education and intend to continue our assistance, both material and moral, to this work in the future.

The reactionary circles of the Japanese government, hand in glove with the south Korean puppet clique, are now forcing the Koreans in Japan to apply for "permanent residence" and imposing "ROK nationality" upon them. They are ostensibly talking about "freedom" to choose nationality but, in fact, accord special "favors" to Koreans in Japan if the latter accept "ROK nationality," and bring unfair pressure to bear upon those who have the DPRK nationality.

It seems some Koreans in Japan, harassed by this, accept "ROK nationality." It leaves no doubt that although they are forced to change their nationality, they will give active support to the DPRK just as the south Korean people unanimously support us today.

The repatriation of Korean citizens in Japan which was suspended for some time, has been resumed in accordance with the agreement reached between the Red Cross organizations of Korea and Japan. It is a positive step not only in defending the national rights of Korean citizens in Japan, but also in developing friendly relations between the Korean and Japanese peoples. We hope that with the support of the Japanese people, this operation will continue in the future, so all Korean citizens in Japan who want to return home may do so.

It is also important to guarantee to Korean citizens in Japan the freedom of travel to and from their homeland, along with the right to repatriation. Among the Korean citizens in Japan there may be some who cannot return home right now because of this or that reason. Nevertheless, they must not be deprived of the right to travel to and from their homeland. Of the foreigners now living in Japan, only Korean citizens are denied freedom to visit their homeland. This unwarranted discriminatory step and violation of human rights must be discontinued at once. The repatriation ship plying between Chongjin and

Niigata should be allowed to carry not only those returning to their homeland, but also those who wish to visit their families, relatives and friends in Korea and then return to Japan.

We respect the opinions of Chongryon in defending the democratic, national rights of Korean citizens in Japan. We believe that the Japanese people, progressive political parties and social organizations as well as individuals from all walks of life will consult well with Chongryon in future and continue to give valuable support and encouragement to the just struggle of the Korean citizens in Japan.

ON SOME PROBLEMS OF OUR PARTY'S JUCHE IDEA AND THE GOVERNMENT OF THE REPUBLIC'S INTERNAL AND EXTERNAL POLICIES (Excerpt)

Answers to the Questions Raised by Journalists of the Japanese Newspaper, *Mainichi Shimbun, September 17, 1972*

I warmly welcome your visit to our country.

I have received your questionnaire through the Central Committee of the Journalists' Union of Korea.

Now, I would like to give brief answers to your questions.

1. Some Problems Involved in the Idea of Juche

You requested me to tell how the Juche idea originated.

In a nutshell, the idea of Juche means that the masters of the revolution and the work of construction are the masses of the people and that they are also the motive force of the revolution and the work of construction. In other words, one is responsible for one's own destiny and one has also the capacity for hewing out one's own destiny.

We are not the author of this idea. Every Marxist-Leninist has this idea. I have just laid a special emphasis on this idea.

How keenly the necessity of establishing Juche is felt and how much emphasis is laid on it may depend on people and the social and historical backgrounds of a country.

In the course of my struggle for the freedom and independence of our country I came to a firm conviction that we must and could work out our own destiny with our own efforts. Our struggle was hard and complex. We had to solve everything by ourselves and use our own heads to formulate the lines and methods of struggle as well.

Naturally, therefore, we met indescribable difficulties and had to pass through harsh trials. Through this, however, we obtained absolutely unique experience and lessons. We realized that the simple and ordinary working masses, if only they were brought to revolutionary awareness, could display a really great force and carry out the revolution by their own efforts in any adverse and arduous conditions.

Our situation was also extremely difficult right after liberation. We had had no experience of running the state or managing the economy. Our country was very backward, and it was divided into north and south. We could look nowhere for a ready-made solution to the problem of building a new country in this complex situation.

The first problem that confronted us was whether to take the road to capitalism or the road to socialism, so that we might quickly free ourselves from our wretched situation.

The road to capitalism meant preserving exploitation and oppression. This would not only prevent us from rousing the broad masses of the proletariat to the building of a new country, but would also involve the great danger of our country being again subordinated by another imperialist power. It was evident, therefore, that we could not follow the road to capitalism.

However, we could not take the road to socialism immediately. Socialism was what we needed. Subjective desire alone could not obtain it. We were faced with the immediate tasks of the democratic revolution which must be solved before going over to socialism. So we could not just imitate the socialist system.

From the outset we had to use our own brains to determine a political system that would serve the interests of the working class and other sectors of the working masses and that would be able to rally the broad masses of the people. We also had to determine the way to effect democratic social reforms that might suit the specific conditions of our country. Accordingly, for agrarian reform, we went to farm villages and stayed many days with the peasants, exploring ways and means that would suit our rural situation.

Our experience showed that endeavoring to solve our problems in this way to suit our actual conditions was much better than mechanically copying foreign ways. Our post-liberation struggle for the building of a new country validated our Juche idea and increased our faith in it.

Then, we waged the harsh three-year war against the U.S. imperialists, and our country was reduced to ashes. This rendered our task of building socialism very difficult.

The U.S. imperialists destroyed not only the dwelling houses and property of our workers and peasants but also the economy of the small and medium entrepreneurs and the rich peasants as well. During their socialist revolutions, other nations eliminated the capitalist and rich peasant classes by expropriating them, but we had no need to do so. Immediately after liberation we consistently pursued the policy of encouraging the economy of the small and medium entrepreneurs, who could fight side by side with the workers and the peasants against imperialism. Moreover, it was necessary for us to protect national capital as at that stage our industry was not fully developed. However, since the economy of the small and medium capitalists and the rich peasants was utterly destroyed by the war, our Government had no need to take the trouble of reviving it.

Now that everything had been ravaged by the war, there was little difference between the small and medium entrepreneurs and the urban craftsmen. Everyone became a proletarian, so to speak. They had to pool their efforts and go along the road to socialism. This was the only way for them to subsist. In order to shore up their completely devastated agriculture, the peasants, too, had to do the same.

Proceeding from the Marxist-Leninist proposition that co-operation, even when it is based on primitive techniques, is far superior to private farming and considering the actual fact that our peasants badly needed to work together to free themselves from their plight, we adopted an original method—boldly pushing ahead with the socialist transformation of agriculture before industrialization. As regards the small and medium entrepreneurs and rich peasants we also chose a unique way — drawing them into the cooperatives and remolding them on socialist lines because there was no necessity to expropriate them.

Again experience justified our Party's line of solving all problems in the interests of our people and in conformity with the specific conditions of our country without recourse to any ready-made formula or proposition.

Through this course we have been more deeply convinced that the correct stand and attitude to maintain in revolution and construction is to settle all problems in the interests of our people and in conformity with the specific conditions of our country, believing in and relying on our own strength with the consciousness as the masters of the revolution.

Our revolution has traversed and is traversing a very complicated and difficult road. Whenever we were confronted with difficulties and ordeals, we maintained the attitude of a master toward the revolution and thereby achieved glorious victories. This process made our conviction still more unshakable — a conviction that only by firmly relying on the Juche idea can one thoroughly adhere to the revolutionary stand of the working class and creatively apply Marxism-Leninism to the realities of one's country.

You asked me whether you may understand that the Juche idea is embodied as independence in politics, self-reliance in the economy and self-defense in national defense. Your understanding is quite correct.

Establishing Juche means taking the attitude of a master towards the revolution and construction. Since the masters of the revolution and construction are the masses of the people, they should take a responsible attitude of a master toward the revolution and construction. The attitude of a master finds expression in an independent and creative stand.

Revolution and construction are a work for the masses of the people, a work that has to be carried out by them alone. Therefore, the transformation of nature and society demands their independent position and creative activity.

Based on the interests of our people and on the interests of our revolution, our Party has always maintained a firm independent stand in mapping out all policies and lines through its own efforts and responsibly carrying out the revolution and construction on the principle of self-reliance. Our Party has always been able to win victories because it believed in the strength of the people and gave full play to their revolutionary zeal and creative activity, thus encouraging them to realize themselves all potentialities and reserves and solve all problems arising in the revolution and construction to suit our true realities.

Adhering to the stand of master in the revolution and construction and enhancing the role as master are integrated concepts with different aspects. You may say that the independent stand is concerned with defense of the rights of the master and discharging the responsibility as such, whereas the creative stand concerns the development of the role of the people, the masters, in remaking nature and reconstructing society. In other words, the independent stand is the fundamental stand which we must maintain in the revolution and construction, and the creative stand is the fundamental method that we must apply in transforming nature and society.

To adhere to the independent stand it is most important that we fully guarantee independence in politics.

Independence is what keeps man alive. If he loses independence in society, he cannot be called a man; he differs little from an animal. We might say that socio-political life is more valuable to a man than physical life. He is a social being. If he is forsaken by society and deprived of political independence, though he seems alive, he is virtually dead as a social human being. That is why the revolutionaries deem it far more honorable to die in the fight for freedom than to keep themselves alive in slavery.

Ignoring independence is tantamount to ignoring man himself. Who likes to live shackled to others? Why did people fight to overthrow the feudal system in former days and why are the working class fighting against the capitalist system today? Needless to say, working people wanted to extricate themselves from feudal slavery just as they want to free themselves from capitalist exploitation and oppression. We are fighting against imperialism in order to liberate our nation completely from its yoke and enable it to enjoy freedom as a sovereign nation. In a word, all the revolutionary struggles aim to attain freedom from either class or national subjugation; they are struggles of the people in defence of their independence. Our struggle for the building of socialism and communism, too, is, in the long run, to enable the people to extricate themselves from many forms of subjugation and lead independent and creative lives as masters of nature and society.

In order to become the master of its own destiny, a nation must have an independent government and firmly guarantee political independence. This is why the Juche idea should first be embodied as the principle of independence in politics.

To guarantee solid independence in politics, there must be a special guiding idea and a capacity for formulating all policies and lines solely in the interests of one's people and in conformity with the specific conditions of one's country, according to one's own judgment. The government that acts under pressure from or instructions of others cannot be called a genuine people's government responsible for the destiny of the people. A country with this sort of government cannot be regarded as an independent, sovereign state.

The principle of independence in politics demands complete equality and mutual respect among all nations. It opposes both subjugating others and being subjugated by others. A nation that subjugates others can never be free itself.

In strengthening the independence of the country, it is essential to strengthen self-reliance in the economy along with political independence. Without self-reliance in the economy, it is impossible to meet the people's growing material demands and materially guarantee them a real role as masters of the state and society. Economic dependence on others cannot guarantee political independence and without independent economic power, it is impossible to carry through the line of self-defense in national defense.

Self-defense and self-protection are intrinsic to the nature of man. A country must also have the means to defend itself. The line of self-defense in national defense is an essential requirement of an independent and sovereign state. While there are still imperialist aggressors, the state that has no defense power of its own to protect its sovereignty against the internal and external enemies is, in fact, not a fully independent and sovereign state.

Our Party's consistent line of independence in politics, self-reliance in the economy and self-defense in national defense has long since been proved correct and vital by our people through their revolutionary practices.

Next, I am going to say a few words about your question as to what we stress as an embodiment of the Juche idea in our present domestic policy.

Embodying the Juche idea means powerfully stepping up revolution and construction from an independent and creative stand.

The most urgent problem facing us at present in embodying the Juche idea in the Korean revolution is that of bringing about the independent, peaceful reunification of our country.

Our people have been fighting for a long time to rid themselves of the yoke of imperialism but our national sovereignty is still being trampled underfoot by foreign aggressors in one half of our territory. Nothing is more urgent for our people today than driving out foreign aggressors and establishing national sovereignty throughout our country.

The south Korean rulers have been hampering the independent, peaceful reunification of the country for nearly 30 years pursuing the policy of dependence on outside forces. Dependence on outside forces is the road to national ruin. This is a serious lesson our people have drawn for themselves from a long history of national suffering; it is also a reality we are now clearly perceiving through the misfortunes and pains of the south Korean people under the U.S. imperialist occupation. Our immediate task is to see that all the people in north and south Korea fight against outside forces in the spirit of independence and self-reliance and rise in the forceful struggle for the independent, peaceful reunification of the country. Achieving this reunification is the most important work in embodying the Juche idea in the Korean revolution today.

The central task before us now to implement the Juche idea in the northern half of the Republic is to free our people from tough labor by dynamically pushing ahead with the three major tasks of the technical revolution.

Our people, freed from exploitation and oppression, have now the important task of emancipating themselves from arduous work.

Labor holds the most important place in people's social life. Eliminating fundamental distinctions that exist in work conditions and freeing the people from tough labor will be of great significance in making their lives more independent and creative.

In order to emancipate the people from backbreaking labor, it is imperative to push ahead with the three major tasks of the technical revolution. The three tasks we propose are designed to narrow down the distinctions between heavy and light labor and between agricultural and industrial work and to free our women from the heavy burdens of household chores by fully developing techniques by our own efforts. When they are carried out completely, arduous labor in town and country will be largely removed and the class difference in work between the working class and the peasantry be eliminated.

We proposed the three major tasks of the technical revolution as our goal in emancipating our people from arduous labor; we did this instead of merely referring in general terms to the development of heavy industry or light industry. This clearly testifies to our Party's consistent standpoint that economic construction or technical revolution should not be designed for its own sake but should serve as the means to provide the people with fruitful lives as the masters of the state and society. Attaching the greatest importance to people in every respect and serving them—this is precisely the requirement of the Juche idea.

Next, you asked me to tell about the education of our youth and children based on the Juche idea.

We are greatly concerned with the education of youth and children. This is because they are the reserves of our revolution who must carry forward the revolution through coming generations. Moreover, there is no more important job than that of educating and training people for the progress of society.

It is true that with no material means people can neither live nor develop. In this sense, the economy constitutes the material foundation of social life. However, this is always planned for the benefit of people and would be meaningless without them. It is also the people who create the means of living and improve living conditions. Therefore, what is most important in the development of society is training people to be more dynamic; in order to powerfully push ahead with the revolution and construction, top priority should be given to the work with men, that is, to the work of remolding men.

The basis of the Juche idea is that man is the master of all things and the decisive factor in everything. Remaking nature and society is also for people and it is work done by them. Man is the most precious treasure in the world, and he is also the most powerful. All our work is for the people and its success depends on the way we work with them. Education is an important aspect of the work with men.

Education involves training people to be social beings fully prepared mentally, morally and physically. In order to become social beings, they should first have sound social consciousness. If the younger generation, who were born in this revolutionary era, are not armed with revolutionary ideas and if they are ignorant of science, technique or literature and art as the men in our era of socialist construction, they cannot be called social beings.

Only when people have an ideological and cultural background which they should possess as social beings, can they participate as masters in all aspects of social life and energetically accelerate the revolution and construction. This is why our Party always places greater emphasis on education than on any other work.

We regard as the core of education the implementation of the socialist pedagogical doctrine. Its basic principle lies in training people to be reliable revolutionary workers equipped with the ideology, knowledge and a strong physique that will enable them to take the role of master in the revolution and construction.

It is most important in training and educating people to remold their ideology in a revolutionary way. All human activity is determined by ideology. If a man is ideologically backward and morally degenerate, despite his excellent health, he cannot but be regarded as utterly useless and mentally disabled in our society. Therefore, our Party always directs its primary attention to remolding people's ideology in a revolutionary manner.

In the education of youth and children, we should give top priority to the work of training them in revolutionary ideas. If they hate work and do not serve the state and society, their knowledge and skills will be of no use however excellent they may be. They must be so equipped with socialist patriotism and a revolutionary world outlook as to work for their people and homeland instead of trying to get promoted or earn money; we should see to it that whatever they learn is useful and that all children and young people grow up into a new type of men with communist moral traits, who are eager to work, protect and take good care of state and social property, and take the lead in the revolution and construction. This is the fundamental requirement of socialist pedagogy.

Today we are making great efforts to enforce universal compulsory ten-year senior middle school education. When this has been effected, our rising generation will grow up as an able builder of socialism, equipped with the essentials of a revolutionary world outlook, with a basic knowledge of nature and society and more than one technical skill. This is of tremendous significance in revolutionizing and working-classizing the entire society and advancing our socialist construction.

You requested me to give a detailed explanation of the Juche idea. But there is no end to it. All the policies and lines of our Party emanate from the Juche idea and they embody this idea. The Juche idea is not a theory for theory's sake; it is the guiding idea of the revolution and construction in our country that we put forth on the basis of the experiences and lessons obtained through our complicated revolutionary struggles. In our country the Juche idea is a stern fact of history established in all aspects of social life. To have a deep understanding of the Juche idea, it is necessary to make a detailed study of our Party's policy and our country's reality.

TALK WITH THE MANAGING EDITOR OF THE JAPANESE POLITICO-THEORETICAL MAGAZINE SEKAI (Excerpt)

October 6, 1972

I am grateful to you for your visit to our country. I also extend my thanks to your director for the letter he has sent me. When you are back home, please convey my greetings to him.

You have addressed me a number of questions, and now I will make my comments.

You asked me when the Juche idea was formed and established.

On this question I am going to give you a general account as I did to the correspondents of the *Mainichi Shimbun*.

You asked if you may consider it right to say that the history of the Juche idea is the history of the Democratic People's Republic of Korea itself. I quite agree with you.

The Juche idea could be fully materialized in our country after the people assumed power. We can say that since then the struggle has been conducted to put the Juche idea into reality in all spheres of activity.

But as for the background of the emergence of the Juche idea, we came to form this idea in the course of a long revolutionary struggle waged through many turns and twists.

To illustrate how I came to form the Juche idea, I must mention two facts which I witnessed while I was still young. Of what I saw when I was still young, particularly when I was a student, there were two facts I thought most unjust.

One of them was the fact that the Communists and nationalists who professed themselves to be engaged in the national-liberation movement of Korea were divorced from the masses, a few top-level personalities simply playing with words and quarrelling, instead of arousing the masses to the actual revolutionary movement. It was essential to organize and mobilize all the masses to assure success in the revolutionary movement. But those people, isolated from the masses, only scrambled for hegemony and had "theoretical" arguments with each other, each claiming his own superiority. Their "theory" was not for the advancement of the revolution, but was a sophism that had nothing to do with the revolutionary work. So I wondered how they could ever bring the revolution to success merely by getting together and indulging in controversy all the time without developing a mass movement, and began to take a critical view of these phenomena.

The masters of the revolutionary struggle are the masses, and only when they rise will it be possible to win the struggle. Yet, a handful of leaders, divorced from the masses, were only talking nonsense. What was the use of it? We pondered seriously over it. Those people ought to have gone among the masses and awakened them so that the masses became masters in the revolutionary struggle. While a few persons of leadership indulged only in word play, no problem could be solved. This led us to attach great importance to Juche, to the viewpoint that the masses themselves were the main factor in solving all questions.

Another fact I faced was that there were many factions within the Korean communist movement at that time. I am not sure whether this was because of the mysticism of the communist movement or a scramble for power or flunkeyism. But our country had many factions then, such as the M-L group, the Tuesday group and the North Wind Association group. All these factions sent their representatives to the Communist

International in their efforts to obtain its recognition. If they conducted the communist movement well, they would be recognized without taking such troubles. However, they formed their own groups by ganging up three or five persons and busied themselves in gaining the recognition of the Communist International, instead of carrying out revolutionary movements. Each of the groups insisted that it was the only orthodox and genuine Marxist group. As a result, the Korean Communist Party was expelled from the Communist International in 1928, and was finally dissolved. We thought it a disgrace to the Korean nation. If one conducts the revolutionary movement well, one will be recognized by others without going to all the trouble of asking for their recognition. Is a Communist Party regarded as such only when it has obtained others' recognition? We need not get others' approval before starting our revolutionary movement. We carry it out if we want to. When we do so properly, what does it matter whether others give us approval or not? If only we make revolution well, others will naturally give us recognition. What is the need of bustling about to gain others' recognition?

These two factors—the serious factional strife in the Korean national-liberation and communist movements and the leadership divorced from the masses—strongly convinced us that we must not carry out our revolution in that way. We keenly felt that we must go among the masses and rely on them in our struggle, that we must solve our problems by our own efforts, and that if we worked well, others' recognition would be out of the question.

The two aspects as mentioned above had great impact on the development of my revolutionary thinking. From then on we emphasized that the populace are the masters of revolution, and accordingly, we must go among them and that if we step up the revolution of our own country with our own efforts in a responsible manner, whether or not recognized by others, we will naturally gain sympathy, recognition and assistance from other countries. We can say this was the starting point of our Juche idea.

As I said to the *Mainichi Shimbun* journalists the other day, the long revolutionary struggle deepened our conviction that the force of the masses is the main factor in the solution of all problems. We must solve all problems, relying on the force of the masses, and since revolution is a struggle of the masses to emancipate themselves, they must rise up in unity. It is on this basis that we carried out our revolutionary struggle.

We also thought that all problems had to be posed in accord with the masses' political awareness.

In 1936 we organized the Association for the Restoration of the Fatherland and advanced its Ten-Point Program. I will not refer to its details. At the time we presented a program for mass unity—that the whole nation must be banded together and all the populace must be united—a program to form an anti-imperialist, anti-feudal united front against the imperialists and traitors to the nation. This was a most appropriate slogan for our people at that time. After liberation, too, we based ourselves on this line in carrying out a number of policies.

Our fundamental problem was how to get more masses to participate in the revolutionary movement and the building of the country. In the early days after liberation we organized the Communist Party and the Young Communist League. Right after liberation, however, our country had a small working class, and only a few of its members were armed with communist ideology. In this situation, if we stuck to the slogans of the Communist Party or the Young Communist League, it might split the masses and young people into many groups. We took stock of the situation and realized that the formation of the Communist Party did not conform with the masses' preparedness. Therefore, we promptly reorganized it into the Workers' Party. We also took the initiative in transforming the Young Communist League into the Democratic Youth League that embraced young men and women of all strata.

The revolutionary movement and the construction of the country cannot be carried out by the efforts of a few Communists. They must be joined by many youths and progressives. Hence, we desisted from the narrow-minded position and reformed our organizations to meet the demands of the realities.

After the founding of the Democratic People's Republic of Korea we laid greater emphasis on the necessity to solve all problems by ourselves.

Our situation was completely different from that in other countries. Ours was the only Asian country where the people seized power right after World War II. At the time China was still carrying on her revolutionary struggle. Our country's situation was quite different also from that in the European countries. We have characteristic features as an Oriental people, as the Korean nation. Therefore, we could not copy European things mechanically. Of course, we should study and refer to some experiences gained in the European countries, but we could not follow them mechanically. Ours was a backward country that had suffered for a long time from the corrupt policies of feudal rulers and then remained a colony over 36 years. If our country was to rid itself of backwardness, it was essential to adopt lines and policies to suit Korean realities. So we had to solve all problems in a unique way. Objective realities demanded us to do so. In other words, realities demanded us to display independence and creativity. That is why we believed more firmly that we had to pursue all policies in conformity with our country's conditions and our people's demands.

You asked among other things what the biggest headache was in the formation of the Juche idea. This is a very interesting question. In my opinion, it also has two aspects.

What is most important in establishing the Juche idea is to do work with men well, because men decide everything. Success in the struggle to transform society and nature, in the last analysis, depends largely upon how to do work with men.

Work with men is extremely important. As I always say, Party work is work with men, so is the work of mass organizations. Economic activity, too, goes well only when work with men is done well. But this work was often done not properly but in an administrative manner, instead of educating and teaching men patiently. This was our greatest difficulty.

It is wrong to do work with men in an administrative manner. The administrative method of work is a bureaucratic work method. Revolution must not be made in an administrative way. We have not yet been able to rectify this completely.

We are continuously endeavoring within the Party to change Party work into work with men. But in some cases work with men is replaced by issuing instructions or decisions or by holding meetings. I think this is one of the major defects that have to be overcome. We are now making efforts to rectify it.

In order to establish the Juche idea, it is most important to remold men's ideology. With administrative methods it is impossible. If we issue instructions in an administrative manner, people do not accept them actually although they do on the surface. If we issue orders which are not to their liking, the masses do not accept them at heart; they just pretend to accept them. We insist on rooting out the administrative methods. We are making sure that both in economic and state affairs or in any other activity, political work is done ahead of all other work before appropriate tasks are given.

In personnel administration, we should educate cadres after their assignment. Only then can we prevent them from committing errors. Giving them no education after their assignment and dismissing them after they have committed mistakes is wrong. This shows the ignorance of work with men and the inability to do it.

Another main stumbling block to establishing the Juche idea is flunkeyism. Flunkeyism is an old idea that had been handed down over centuries in our country. The flunkeyists claim that their own things are all bad, that they have nothing which is useful and that everything foreign is good. They take such a nihilistic attitude to things of their own.

Of course, there are good as well as bad ones in things foreign, and we may learn from good things. We do not mean that we are chauvinistic because we are opposed to flunkeyism.

Of things foreign we must learn from good ones and cast aside bad ones. Even in this case, we must take them in such a way as to suit our taste. We must not try to eat those things that we do not like. Some Koreans had been so deeply infected with flunkeyism in the past that we had to wage a hard struggle to root it out.

At one time flunkeyism was expressed to a great extent in our country. Let me tell you just how flunkeyism was manifested in the realm of literature and arts.

It happened when flunkeyism and dogmatism were manifested to a great extent in our country. I visited a local army hospital during the war in order to ask after the wounded. There was a picture hung on the wall. It showed a Siberian landscape with a bear creeping around on the snow-covered ground under a giant pine tree. I asked the soldiers which place the picture showed. They said that the painting showed a bear crawling around in a forest but they did not know where the place was. Then I asked them if there were many bears in our forests. They said there were some but they were not typical Korean animals.

I asked the soldiers which they liked, this picture or a nice painting of our Mt. Kumgang-san. They answered that they preferred the latter. So I asked the chief of the political department of the unit why he had this sort of picture hung instead of that of our Mt. Kumgang-san, which the soldiers liked better. I was shocked to hear his answer. He said that he had to buy it because our picture dealers sold only such pictures.

The occasion gave us a great mental stimulant, and we thought that all this was because of flunkeyism. So we began to check how things were going on in the realm of arts at that time. Our examination showed that almost all of our artists were engaged in Western painting.

At that time our musical world had a very few national instruments. There were national instruments at some places, but they were exactly the same as used in old days. Some artists alleged that our national music was old and Western music was modern. This is actually the way they used to call them. So I gathered artists and asked them why they, the contemporaries, could not produce their own music although our ancestors had created theirs, why they regarded Western music as the sole modern music, why there was no modern national music and on what ground they defined that modern music was Western music; I asked them why Korean national music should be an old music and modern music be Western music and why we Koreans could not create modern music to suit our national taste. They could not answer my questions.

Furthermore, I asked our artists about the meaning of the word "realism" they used so often. They knew the word only, not its real meaning. So I told them that they should not swallow up things that way. Then I gave a definition of socialist realism in our country: national in form and socialist in content.

I told them that they must not label everything as socialist realism, and that it was meaningless to create music that could not be understood by the Korean people. I also said to the artists: "Of course, I am not against your singing only Italian and other European songs. But I wonder how many Koreans will like them. You have failed to create art for the masses. What's the use of making art for art's sake? Art should serve the people. Music should be nice to hear; it should bring joy to people; it should be understood and approved by them. But they say they don't understand your music. If you indulge in the old musical art under the pretense of reclaiming national music, our young peole will not like it. You must not take to restorationism either. If you do, you'll eventually be inclined to admire the West. We should never do that.''

Instead of trying to serve their nation and people, some people thought that if they introduced everything foreign, it would do since foreign things were all good. This was a great problem.

In our country flunkeyism found expression also in the fields of construction, industrial management and education.

Thus, flunkeyism was manifested a great deal in different realms in our country before and it was very difficult to overcome. We have fought flunkeyism over a long period of time.

As I have said, we have two major obstacles to overcome in establishing the Juche idea in our country. One is flunkeyism and the other is the administrative method in working with men. I think this will be overcome only through a prolonged struggle.

We are still striving to overcome them and I think we should continue to do so. We do not consider that they have now been surmounted completely. That is why we are still stressing that both Party work and the activities of the working people's organizations should not be conducted by the administrative method but should be converted into work with people. At the same time, we are emphasizing that all of us must serve our country and people and that we must not take nihilistic attitudes toward our own things, alleging that we have nothing which is useful, while approving and worshipping everything foreign. In a nutshell, we are going to eliminate the idea of relying on others without having faith in our own strength. This does not mean national communism. If revolution and work of construction are conducted well at each national unit, they will also be successful on a worldwide scale, won't they? Marx, Engels and Lenin also said that Marxism is not a dogma and it should be applied creatively.

In your next question, you asked if the Juche idea is a new philosophy on the correlation between the national task and the task of internationalist solidarity. That is an excessive praise.

In my opinion, true Marxists must be independent and creative. As for me, I have only emphasized this point.

I will not make lengthy remarks on this matter. I have already talked a lot about the problems related to the content of the Juche idea. Since I fully touched upon them in my answers to the questions raised by the Japanese *Mainichi* and *Yomiuri Shimbun* journalists, I believe you understand them. So I am not going to make any further statement in order to avoid repetition.

I have spoken about the problems that have arisen in translating the Juche idea into reality. There are many other problems, of course, but I concentrated on fundamental points today. This much for the problem of the Juche idea.

I will answer your question about our education.

We attach more importance to this problem than others. As I have just said, what is important in establishing our Juche idea is to work well with men. In order to do this work well, we should first carry out education well.

Educational activity is the beginning of work with men. That is why our Party and Government have put a lot of energy into this problem from the start.

In order for our country to extricate itself from backwardness and advance rapidly, all our people had to be given education. The goal of socialist and communist construction itself demands us to conduct education well. After all, the construction of socialism and communism aims at providing all people with abundant lives. For this purpose it is important not only to raise everybody's material standard of life but also to elevate his ideological and cultural levels.

The aim of revolution is to get all people to lead affluent lives. To do so, everybody must work well and, in order to work well, he must have his consciousness.

The development of people's consciousness should start from education. It is clear what great power can be displayed when everyone works consciously. I think if all people take a conscious part in the work of construction and revolutionary struggle, it will bring about great power and make everyone well-off more quickly.

Unless the people get educated well, there may emerge such persons who neglect the property of the state and society and destroy or eat it away. Then it will be useless however much we may build. Some people like to live idle, but if we do so, it will be impossible to make our people equally well-off.

Our Party holds that we must occupy the material and ideological fortresses on the way to communism. It will be wrong to capture the material fortress only without conquering the ideological fortress. Unless the ideological fortress is occupied, it is impossible to capture the material fortress. Therefore, we presented the slogan: "The whole country must study, the entire Party must study, and all the people must study." Under this slogan everybody is studying now.

In our country people over 40 are made to attend the working people's middle schools to attain the knowledge of middle school graduates; all people under 40 are at the level of middle school graduates or above since they have received compulsory secondary education.

In order to educate people, cadres must show a practical example. We have set up a system under which cadres study two hours every day. They also study every Saturday afternoon, and we have a system for them to study for one month a year. This is to reeducate cadres. Under this system our cadres study to raise their ideological, cultural and technological standards.

Education of youth and children is very important. To this end, we have introduced universal compulsory ten-year senior middle school education. We have a Korean saying: "A decade changes the appearance of mountains and rivers." I think ten years of proper education will enable all the rising generation to lay the foundation of revolutionary world outlook.

Our compulsory education differs from that in capitalist countries. We give free education to all students; we do not engage them in physical labor during schooling. The state law prohibits labor by boys and girls under 16 years of age. If our children do any labor, they plant flowers on roadsides or trees on hills. That's about all. This is organized by schools to develop their love for labor, and it cannot be called labor in the true sense of the word. Our children have formed the Greening Guards and Hygienic Guards, swatting flies, polishing window glasses and cleaning classrooms. All this is designed to get all children and youth to love labor.

In our country today approximately six million members of the rising generation are receiving education at state expense at kindergartens, primary schools, senior middle schools and higher specialized schools. This imposes a considerable burden on the state. The burden is heavy now, but the prospects are bright. It will bear fruit ten years later.

In the old society the intelligentsia was regarded as a social stratum. Of course, it still is in capitalist society. But the intelligentsia may disappear in the future. When all people become intellectuals, then there will be no intelligentsia. At present our country has 500,000 technicians and specialists. We are putting up a slogan: Let's train another 500,000 during the Six-Year Plan and build a huge army of one million technicians and specialists. This is a task proposed by our Party at its Fifth Congress.

Party organizations at all levels are now stepping up a struggle to hit this target. We are increasing the number of factory colleges, along with regular institutes of higher learning. At factory colleges our workers study by day or by night according to shifts. We are going to form a great army of intellectuals in this way. From the prospective viewpoint, when almost all of our people graduate from colleges in the future, there will be no separate social stratum such as the intelligentsia. They used to call the intelligentsia a wobbly circle or an opportunistic stratum but there will be no such problem in the future.

Our universal compulsory ten-year education is compulsory senior middle schooling. Through this we aim to give all our people perfect middle school education.

We started universal compulsory ten-year senior middle school education this year. We are planning to introduce it 20% every year so that it will be completely introduced in five years. We think this is possible. Of course, there may be some difference between localities. This compulsory education may be fully introduced in four years in some places and three or two years in other places. We mean that its introduction will be completed in five years on a nationwide scale. Some time ago I visited Mundok County. Its chief Party secretary told me that they would complete it in two years. I said I had no objection.

Once all the young people acquire perfect knowledge of middle school standard through compulsory senior middle school education, they will further their study with more facility. They may finish collegiate courses by studying for themselves or may continue to study at colleges. In my opinion, when they have received fundamental education, they will be able to acquire specialized knowledge without much difficulty.

Next, you asked me if we conduct a genious education, that is, a special education of those children who have remarkable talents. We are now conducting such an education, too. Fundamentally speaking I oppose the theory on genius education, because it is difficult to classify people as talented or untalented.

But, in actual fact, we cannot deny that there are some who have peculiar talents for specific realms. In the Students and Children's Palace there is a girl who plays the xylophone. Probably you have seen her play. I think she has a special talent. She is 11 or 12 years old but plays the xylophone excellently. There do exist some who have exceptional skill for certain fields like this girl. We do not ignore this fact. Those children of remarkable talent are sent to appropriate schools.

For example, our country has the Institute of Science. This institute enrolls fresh middle school graduates, whereas, as a rule, other institutes of higher learning admit those middle school graduates who have received recommendations after having worked at factories or finished their service in the army. We have this sort of system, too. There are similar systems in art and other fields. In some cases school teachers pick out some young people and recommend that for their brilliant talents it will be more beneficial to the state to give them special education than sending them to factories or to the army. Such young people are allowed to enter institutes of higher learning immediately after graduation.

Social organizations also have their own schools. The Women's Union runs the mothers' schools in the countryside. Both educated and uneducated women attend these schools. They were established with a view to giving appropriate education for women, teaching such subjects as on the question of the emancipation of women. The League of Socialist Working Youth, too, has schools for young people. Adult education is conducted in all parts of the country. Therefore, the Government has to offer a huge amount of funds for education. We are allotting almost all the state funds for education.

We are now studying socialist pedagogy. The most important

thing in socialist pedagogy is training people to work willingly, which is the fundamental question in socialist construction. If one is to work well, one should study and raise one's technological level. It is also important to educate all the people to acquire the habit of taking care of social property, since all the wealth belongs to the people in socialist society. In this way, we attach great importance to the question of educating all men to love labor and look after the people's property in socialist society.

Furthermore, we must educate people to value the collective life more than the life of individuals, although the latter is also important. We educate our people with these subjects.

We can see such practices as hating labor, loafing on the job and embezzling and wasting the state property even in those countries whose people have received a fair education for many years. In order to eliminate such practices, I think, people should be educated to love labor, take care of the people's property and value their organizations and collectives.

We have proposed a task of studying socialist pedagogy consisting of the above-mentioned and some other aspects and are gradually putting it into practice. Perhaps you have received a lecture on this matter from our comrades, so I will cut my comment short here.

Capitalist society cannot abolish the police system. The police system aims to keep public order. In other words, the police performs the function of arresting thieves, controlling the violation of traffic regulations, keeping watch to prevent the illegal felling of trees in the mountains, collecting fines and so on. In order to put an end to such practices in the future, people should have a high level of consciousness and everyone should take care not to trouble others.

Our country has no forest ranger. But no one fells trees at will. We can find no practice of reckless felling in our country. I think this is because the people are conscious.

Would it be a good thing to increase the police as property increases? Our country has no police. We have public security men to keep order, but they should disappear in the future. People must be led to do everything for themselves. Therefore, we must educate them well.

In addition, it is important to intensify organizational life so that people teach each other and correct each other's errors.

Since socialist pedagogy was introduced, improvements have
been made in many aspects in our country.

LET US FURTHER STRENGTHEN THE SOCIALIST SYSTEM OF OUR COUNTRY

Speech at the First Session of the Fifth Supreme People's Assembly of the Democratic People's Republic of Korea, *December 25, 1972*

Comrade Deputies,

The election to the Fifth Supreme People's Assembly of the Democratic People's Republic of Korea was held successfully at a time when all of our people were making a new great revolutionary upswing on all fronts of socialist construction, upholding the decision of the historic Fifth Congress of the Workers' Party of Korea, and when the whole nation was seething with a burning desire for independent, peaceful reunification.

All our citizens, with great pride and sense of honor as citizens of the DPRK, actively participated in the election and expressed their unreserved support for and profound trust in our Party and the Government of the Republic. This election strengthened our revolutionary power still more, consolidating the revolutionary base of the northern half of the Republic.

On behalf of the Central Committee of the Workers' Party of

Korea and the Government of the Republic, I would like to express warm thanks to the entire people for their unreserved support for and deep trust in our Party and the Government of the Republic manifested in the recent elections.

Comrades, twenty-four years have elapsed since the Korean people embarked on the creation of a new society and a new life under the banner of the Republic, with a genuine people's Constitution, the first of its kind in their history. In this period our people, under the wise leadership of the Workers' Party of Korea, have made great achievements in the socialist revolution and building of socialism. During these years there has really been a great transformation in this country and epoch-making changes have taken place in the political, economic and cultural spheres of our people's life.

Our realities today urgently demand the establishment of a new Socialist Constitution to consolidate legally the tremendous achievements of our people in the socialist revolution and building of socialism and to lay down the principles of the political, economic and cultural features of socialist society. Therefore, we have formed a Commission for the Drafting of the Socialist Constitution of the DPRK and have prepared a draft Socialist Constitution. The draft Socialist Constitution of the DPRK was discussed at a plenary meeting of the Central Committee of the Workers' Party of Korea and considered at the Central Committee of the Democratic Front for the Reunification of the Fatherland before it was submitted to the Supreme People's Assembly.

The adoption of the Socialist Constitution of the DPRK at the current session of the Supreme People's Assembly will be a historic event in our people's revolutionary struggle and work of construction.

1. The Struggle of the Government of the Republic for the Socialist Revolution and Building of Socialism

Comrades,

The socialist revolution is the most thoroughgoing social transformation in the history of mankind for the abolition of the exploitation of man by man once and for all and for opening up a new path of social progress.

If the working class and the Marxist-Leninist party that fight to liberate the masses of the people from exploitation and oppression and guarantee them a happy life are to fulfill their historic mission, they must lead the people in carrying out the socialist revolution. Only when the people who have extricated themselves from the colonial enslavement of imperialism take the road to socialism, can they be completely liberated from class exploitation and national oppression, and enjoy a free and happy life and achieve their country's sovereignty and independence and national prosperity.

In our country the socialist revolution began after the carrying out of the anti-imperialist, anti-feudal, democratic revolution in the northern half following liberation. It is a legitimate process of revolutionary development that the anti-imperialist, anti-feudal, democratic revolution led by the working class passes over to the socialist revolution.

After the anti-imperialist, anti-feudal, democratic revolution had been carried out, our country had a socialist economic sector consisting mainly of the state-run economy, alongside a small-commodity sector consisting of individual peasant economy in the countryside and urban handicraft economy, and a capitalist economic sector of capitalist trade and manufacturing in towns and the rich peasant economy in rural areas.

As long as the capitalist and small-commodity sectors were left intact, it was impossible to thoroughly eradicate the sources of exploitation and poverty, and completely free the productive forces of society from the shackles of old production relations, and speedily develop the nation's economy as a whole in a planned way. Therefore, in order to completely free our people from all sorts of exploitation and oppression and rapidly develop the country's productive forces, we had to carry out the socialist revolution upon the completion of the democratic revolution.

Furthermore, we had to do this in order to strengthen the unity and solidarity of the entire people based on the worker-peasant alliance on a new socialist foundation, wipe out the strongholds of the reactionaries and the breeding ground of old ideas, and reinforce the political basis of the revolution.

Our people thus entered the period of transition to socialism immediately following the democratic revolution. However, in the days of peaceful construction our socialist revolution was only partially started; it was still in the preparatory stage. Because of the war forced on us by the U.S. imperialists the socialist transformation in the northern half had to be interrupted temporarily, and our socialist revolution had to start virtually after the war.

The postwar socio-economic conditions in the northern half of the Republic urgently demanded a full-scale acceleration of the socialist revolution.

The war badly damaged the material and technological foundations of agriculture and brought extreme impoverishment not only to poor peasants but also to middle and rich peasants. After the war our countryside was very short of draught animals, farm implements and manpower, and there was also an acute shortage of food and clothing. Since agriculture was so severely damaged, the continuation of the individual peasant economy would have made it impossible to speedily restore the productive forces of agriculture and solve the postwar food problem that had become very serious. Unless the destroyed productive forces of agriculture were rapidly restored and the food problem solved promptly, there was the danger that the development of industry and the national economy in general would be held back and there would arise a serious disparity between industry, which was then being reconstructed and developed quickly in a planned way, and agriculture, which was being rehabilitated slowly. In addition, if the small peasant economy had been left intact, we would not have been able to rapidly improve the living conditions of our impoverished peasants and, in particular, to solve the problem of the poor peasants whose number had increased during the war. In a word, the limitations of the individual peasant economy in our country manifested themselves most strikingly in the postwar years and we could not allow this situation to exist any longer. The only way to overcome these limitations was to go over to a cooperative form of agriculture.

The war also greatly impoverished individual trade and manufacturing in towns. The capitalist traders and manufacturers suffered such severe losses that they were reduced to straitened circumstances just as the handicraftsmen and small merchants were. After the war the entrepreneurs and merchants were unable to recover their previous economic positions or eke out a living by themselves. The only way out for these impoverished entrepreneurs and merchants was to work collectively, pooling their efforts and funds with the assistance of the state, that is, to take the socialist path. It was not only the demand of our revolution but also an objective necessity arising from the conditions facing the capitalist traders and manufacturers, that they had to be led to follow the road to socialism after the war.

The full-scale stepping up of the socialist revolution after the war was also necessary in order to strengthen the revolutionary base of the northern half of the Republic. Only by continuing to accelerate the revolution in the north was it possible to turn it into a strong base to eventually guarantee national reunification and the nationwide victory of the revolution. Therefore, the continued and vigorous acceleration of the revolution in the northern half was not only the demand of the revolutionary development of the north itself but also the essential demand of the advancement of the Korean revolution as a whole.

On the basis of a scientific analysis of the revolutionary situation created in our country after the war, our Party considered the postwar period the most appropriate stage for the socialist revolution, and in its April 1955 Theses, set forth the policy of stepping up the socialist revolution full scale.

What is most important in transforming the old production relations in town and country and establishing the unchallenged predominance of socialist production relations is the cooperativization of the individual peasant economy.

In the light of the specific postwar situation in our country our Party and the Government of the Republic advanced a policy to transform the economic forms along socialist lines prior to the technological reform of agriculture, and vigorously launched an agricultural cooperative movement.

Since the socialist transformation of agriculture was urgently demanded by the revolution after the war, we could not postpone agricultural cooperativization simply because the economy had been damaged and our technological development was still at a low level. The decisive condition for agricultural cooperativization lies not in whether agriculture is equipped with modern technology but in whether this step is a vital demand of the peasants themselves, whether the revolutionary forces are prepared to carry it out. As Marxism-Leninism teaches us, even a collective economy that merely pools the peasants' land and farm implements can achieve an improvement in the economy that would, otherwise, be impossible in the individual small peasant economy, and, at the same time, can raise the productivity of labor several times. Thus, our Party waged a struggle to transform economic forms first in order to meet the urgent demand of social development, instead of waiting until industrialization was carried out. As a result, we were able to rapidly restore and develop the productive forces of agriculture severely damaged by the war and to dynamically push ahead with the technical revolution in the countryside in keeping with industrial development.

In guiding the agricultural cooperative movement, our Party and the Government of the Republic strictly observed the voluntary principle.

Our Party categorically rejected coercive methods in this movement and adopted a number of correct policies to induce the peasants to voluntarily join the cooperative economy.

An object lesson in the cooperative movement is the best way of persuading the peasants engaged in centuries-old methods of individual farming to join cooperative farming voluntarily. We intensified the ideological education of the peasants, and at the same time, established a pilot stage and strove to show them the advantages of the cooperative economy by practical examples.

Taking into consideration the fact that the land remained the private property of the peasants and that their property status and ideological awareness varied, we laid down three forms of agricultural cooperative economy and encouraged the peasants to choose the form they considered most appropriate for them. In pooling the peasants' means of production, we saw to it that according to their desire, draught animals and farm implements were pooled or were left under private ownership for a certain period while being used collectively, and when they were pooled, due compensation was made without fail. These measures taken by our Party helped the peasants of different strata to readily accept the policy of cooperativization and made it possible to prevent some deviations which, otherwise, might have appeared in the course of the cooperative movement.

In drawing the peasants of various strata into cooperative farming according to the voluntary principle, our Party followed the class policy of relying firmly on the poor peasants, strengthening the alliance with the middle peasants, and restricting and gradually remolding the rich peasants.

Our Party first organized a few agricultural cooperatives in each county on a trial basis with the poor peasants and the hard core of people in the countryside who had most actively supported agricultural cooperativization, consolidated them and, on this basis, developed the cooperative movement. Meanwhile, the poor peasants were encouraged to play the leading role in all the agricultural cooperatives. It also made sure that cooperatives were not organized exclusively with well-to-do peasants and that the rich peasants were not allowed to influence the work of the agricultural cooperatives. At the same time, it strictly guarded against the tendency to force the middle peasants into the cooperative economy or infringe upon their interests and so weaken the alliance with them, and demonstrated the superiority of the cooperative economy to the middle peasants through the competition between individual and cooperative farming. As for the rich peasants we did not expropriate and eliminate them but encouraged them to join cooperatives voluntarily, restricting their ability to exploit.

Throughout the period of the agricultural cooperative movement our Party and the Government of the Republic persistently carried out organizational and political work among the peasants, and, relying on socialist industry, gave enormous material and technical assistance in diverse forms to the agricultural cooperatives and helped them in terms of manpower. Such guidance and assistance played a decisive role both, in shoring up the weak agricultural cooperatives organized with poor peasants in the incipient stage to show their advantages over the individual economy, and in consolidating the cooperative economic system politically and economically.

Thanks to these intelligent and creative policies of our Party and the Government of the Republic, our agricultural cooperative movement proceeded quite smoothly and was victoriously completed in only four or five years.

To establish the unchallenged sway of socialist production relations in town and country, it is necessary to carry out a socialist reorganization of individual trade and manufacturing as well as agricultural cooperativization.

In the early days of the transition period, our Party began to set up handicraft cooperatives on a trial basis, and in the postwar period, energetically pushed this program forward, carrying it out successfully in a brief period.

In the socialist reorganization of individual trade and manufacturing, our Party and the Government of the Republic devoted special attention to the transformation of capitalist trade and manufacturing. Taking into account their characteristic features in our country, our Party adopted the line of remolding the capitalist traders and manufacturers along socialist lines, instead of expropriating them.

The national capitalists in colonial, semi-feudal society, though inconsistent, have some revolutionary spirit and are keenly interested in the anti-imperialist, anti-feudal, democratic revolution. In the light of such characteristics in these capitalists, we drew them over to the side of the revolution and together with them, carried out the national-liberation struggle and the democratic revolution. From the beginning our policy in regard to the national capitalists was not only to carry out the anti-imperialist, anti-feudal, democratic revolution together with them, but also to take them along with us to a socialist, communist society. Therefore, we could not expropriate the entrepreneurs and traders in the stage of socialist revolution just because the capitalist traders and manufacturers were the targets of the revolution. Moreover, we had no need to expropriate them because capitalist trade and manufacturing were totally destroyed in the war and the entrepreneurs and traders supported the Party's line of socialist revolution. And they had nothing, so we could not expropriate them.

Hence, our Party adopted the line of transforming capitalist trade and manufacturing along socialist lines and saw to it that capitalist traders and manufacturers were drawn into diverse forms of cooperative economy in strict observance of the voluntary principle as all requisite conditions for this were ripe after the war.

We first strengthened producers' cooperatives, formed of handicraftsmen, and then gradually drew entrepreneurs into the cooperative economy; we organized marketing cooperatives or production-and-marketing cooperatives with individual traders and progressively increased the proportion of production in those cooperatives so as to reorganize them into cooperatives entirely engaged in production. Under the Party's wise guidance, our socialist transformation of capitalist trade and manufacturing progressed at a very high rate and was completed in 1958 almost simultaneously with agricultural cooperativization.

With the successful accomplishment of the historic task of the socialist transformation of the old production relations in town and country, an advanced socialist system free from exploitation and oppression was established in the northern half of our country. The victory of the socialist system in the north opened up a broad path for the further promotion of socialist construction and the radical improvement of the people's material and cultural welfare.

Comrades, our Party and the Government of the Republic forcefully pushed forward the struggle for socialist construction relying on the triumphant socialist system.

In socialist construction our Party held fast to the principle of energetically carrying on both the work of laying the material and technological foundations for socialism and the work of educating and remolding people along communist lines, that is, the struggles to seize the material and ideological fortresses for the building of communism.

Socialist economic construction is one of the most important revolutionary tasks facing the party and state of the working class. Only when socialist economic construction is carried out successfully is it possible to attain a high level of development of the productive forces commensurate with a socialist society, to systematically improve the people's material and cultural standards, and to firmly secure the political independence and sovereignty of the country.

Our people's struggle for socialist economic construction went through three stages—the stage of postwar rehabilitation and construction, the stage of laying the basis of industrialization and the stage of completing industrialization. At every stage of socialist economic construction our Party and the Government of the Republic set forth correct lines and policies which suited our specific conditions and organized and mobilized all Party members and working people for a powerful struggle for their implementation.

Over the whole period of socialist economic construction our Party has consistently adhered to the basic line of socialist economic construction on giving priority to the growth of heavy industry simultaneously with the development of light industry and agriculture.

This basic line is a correct line built on an accurate analysis of the requirements of the law of our postwar economic development and our actual possibilities. It is also a creative application of the Marxist-Leninist theory on extended reproduction in conformity with our specific conditions; it is a correct line which renders it possible to guarantee the balances between different branches of the national economy and attain a high rate of production growth.

In implementing this line our Party and the Government of the Republic gave priority to the creation of heavy industry with the engineering industry at its core.

Our Party's line in the building of heavy industry was to create our own solid bases of heavy industry which would be able to produce at home most of the raw materials, fuel, power, machines and equipment needed for the development of the national economy by relying on the rich natural resources and sources of raw materials in our country. In order to build solid bases of heavy industry we rebuilt and expanded the existing factories in this field and, at the same time, built new industrial branches and a number of factories and other enterprises. In building heavy industry, we ensured that this industry was built not as an end in itself, but to more effectively serve the development of light industry and agriculture and the improvement of the people's living standards. This policy of our Party has enabled us to build a powerful heavy industry of our own with a comparatively small capital investment, thereby rapidly developing light industry and agriculture.

Today we have a powerful heavy industry with all its key branches, and its capacity has increased considerably. In particular, our engineering industry has made rapid progress. It has reached such a level that it is now able to produce different kinds of large and precision machines and the complete sets of equipment for modern factories.

Our Party and the Government of the Republic have directed

considerable effort to the growth of light industry as well.

In this regard, our Party pursued a policy of simultaneously developing large-scale, centrally run industries along with the medium- and small-scale local industries. Our Party and the Government of the Republic saw to it that large, modern factories of the centrally-run light industry were established, and at the same time, that many local industry factories were set up by extensively using local reserves and that the technological reconstruction of local industry was stepped up vigorously.

The policy of simultaneous development of the central and local industries has helped to rapidly increase the production of consumer goods with no major capital investment from the state, and to guarantee a high rate of development of the national economy as a whole by concentrating state funds on heavy and central light industries. The growth of local industry has also made it possible to purchase and process in season farm produce and side-line products of the peasants, rapidly raising their living standards and improving the supply of consumer goods for urban dwellers as well.

As a result of the successful implementation of our Party's policy in the development of light industry, large, modern factories of central light industry and thousands of local factories have now come into being, and their technological equipment has been improved to a marked extent. Our light industry has now grown into a firm base for the production of a variety of consumer goods, capable of meeting the working people's demands.

The rational distribution of the productive forces is of great importance for the further development of the national economy as a whole and for successfully carrying out the long-term program of socialist and communist construction.

In distributing the country's productive forces our Party and the Government of the Republic followed the principle of bringing factories and other enterprises closer to the sources of raw materials and the consumer areas, of guaranteeing the balanced development of different branches of the national economy and all regions of the country, and rapidly narrowing the difference between town and country. In rebuilding the national economy after the war, we, in accordance with this principle, located new factories and enterprises in different areas, while rebuilding many factories and enterprises where they already existed in order to guarantee the speeding up of rehabilitation and save funds. As a result, new industrial towns came into being all over the country, the integrated bases for industrial production were built in localities and the previous defects and irrationalities in the distribution of industries were completely eliminated.

The rational distribution of industries enabled us to effectively use our nation's natural resources and manpower to speed up socialist economic construction and proportionately develop all the areas of the country. It also helped to consolidate the worker-peasant alliance by strengthening the political, economic and cultural ties between the working class and the peasantry, to eliminate the backwardness of the countryside and drastically reduce the distinctions between town and country, and class difference between the workers and peasants, by increasing the assistance of industry to agriculture and the support of towns for the countryside. Moreover, it prevented excessive concentration of factories and population in a few cities as well as environmental pollution, which poses a great social problem in capitalist countries today.

One of the cardinal tasks in socialist economic construction is that of rapidly developing agriculture. Our Party and the Government of the Republic strove to consolidate the material and technological foundations of agriculture and increase its production while cooperativizing the individual peasant economy. In particular, we gave top priority to the ideological revolution in the countryside, in accordance with our Party's program of socialist rural construction, *Theses on the Socialist Rural Question in Our Country,* and, at the same time, vigorously carried out the technical and cultural revolutions.

Irrigation was a primary task in the technical revolution in our countryside. In the years that followed the armistice, the Government of the Republic implemented many irrigation projects in step with the agricultural cooperative movement and, with the completion of cooperativization, pushed ahead with the irrigation program in a nationwide movement. In our country the irrigation of paddy fields has now been completed and a large portion of non-paddy fields irrigated, and drainage projects have been completed in our major rice-producing areas. Thus our peasants' centuries-old desire to farm free from the threat of drought and floods has come true.

The Government of the Republic saw to it that many medium and small power stations were built side by side with large ones and thus carried out successfully the task of rural electrification. Every *ri* in this country now has electricity and every farmhouse has electric lights. In the countryside, electricity is used extensively not only for the cultural home lives of the peasants but also as a source of power for machines and heat in agricultural production.

The Government of the Republic has also devoted much effort to develop mechanization and encourage the use of chemicals in agriculture. Our Party and the Government of the Republic have guaranteed that tractors, trucks and different kinds of efficient farm machines, chemical fertilizers and agricultural chemicals were produced in large quantities for the countryside. As a result, the level of mechanization and chemicalization of agriculture has risen greatly and our peasants are gradually being freed from hard and backbreaking work.

Agricultural production has rapidly increased with the progress of the rural technical revolution. Our countryside where poverty and ignorance prevailed before, has now become a rich modern socialist countryside.

Training our own cadres was a matter of vital importance in this country which was once a backward colony. Immediately following liberation, our nation had very few cadres, and this was a serious drawback in running the state and building our economy and culture. Therefore, our Party and the Government of the Republic devoted great efforts to the training of our own cadres and, in particular, actively endeavored to train a large army of technicians capable of carrying out socialist construction which was proceeding full scale after the war. We developed a regular system of higher education along with various programs offering higher education for those who were on the job, and firmly established comprehensive cadre-training bases in the localities. Consequently, our country now has a large army of some 500,000 technicians and specialists. They are excellently managing state and economic organizations and cultural institutions, and modern factories, enterprises and cooperative farms.

Our people's struggle for the socialist revolution and the

building of socialism was carried on under the very difficult conditions of the enemy's ceaseless aggressive maneuvers. In order to defend the country and the people and safeguard the gains of the revolution in the face of the enemy's aggression, our Party and the Government of the Republic paid great attention to increasing our defense capabilities through the whole course of the revolution and construction work. In particular, we advanced the new line of simultaneously carrying on economic and defense construction in the light of intensified aggressive maneuvers by the U.S. imperialists. We reorganized the whole work of socialist construction in a revolutionary way and directed greater efforts to building up our defense capabilities. In order to perfect our national defense we diverted a large amount of manpower and material resources to this purpose, even though this to a certain extent proved detrimental to economic construction, and vigorously organized and mobilized the entire people for the implementation of the Party's military line. As a result, our People's Army has now grown to be an invincible revolutionary armed force; all our people have been armed and the whole country has been fortified. We can confidently say that we have defense capabilities powerful enough to repulse the invasion of any and all enemies, defend our country and people, and safeguard our revolutionary gains.

Educating and transforming people along communist lines is one of the most important tasks of socialist and communist construction.

Man is the master of nature and society and the main factor that decides everything. The masses of the people are masters of socialist society, and it is also they who are able to promote the revolution and construction work. Therefore, if we are to build socialism and communism, we must not only lay the country's firm material and technological foundations but also educate and remold people, the masters of society, along communist lines and bring their creative wisdom and revolutionary enthusiasm into full play.

Our Party and the Government of the Republic advanced a correct line and policy to educate and remold the people at every stage of the revolution and construction and worked hard to implement this. In the period of socialist revolution we strove to turn all members of society into socialist working people through a close linking of the transformation of economic forms with the remolding of people. After the triumph of the socialist system, we vigorously pushed forward the reeducation of the people along communist lines, on the basis of the line of revolutionizing and working-classizing the whole of society.

In educating and remolding people, our Party and the Government of the Republic have always adhered to the principle of raising the ideological preparedness, the sense of organization and the cultural level of the working class and of educating and remolding the peasants and intellectuals on the working-class model.

We increased the class awareness of the workers, first of all, by strengthening political and ideological work among them, constantly tempered them in actual production and waged an energetic struggle for the organizational and ideological consolidation of the ranks of the working class. This greatly increased the vanguard role of the working class in the revolution and construction, and strengthened their revolutionary influence on the working people. Our working class has now become the most advanced and revolutionary class that, instead of working for a few cents, works with full devotion for the prosperity and progress of the country and the freedom and happiness of the people. It is admirably discharging its duties as the leading class of the Korean revolution.

Our Party and the Government of the Republic also paid great attention to educating and remolding the peasantry, one of the main forces of the revolution. By intensifying the working-class guidance and assistance to the countryside we have accelerated the technical and cultural revolutions there and on the other hand, energetically pushed forward the ideological revolution. As a result, the peasants' level of ideological consciousness has risen markedly and they have adopted a revolutionary and communist way of life. As reliable builders of socialism our peasants are today faithfully working for society and the collective, and are striving to supply more food to the workers and all other working people and to turn out sufficient raw materials for light industry.

The working class which has assumed power should build up the ranks of intellectuals. This is essential for the rapid development of science and technology, literature and art and for the successful building of socialism and communism. In the whole course of the revolution and construction, our Party and the Government of the Republic have perseveringly carried on the education of intellectuals and, in particular, directed great efforts to the education and remolding of old intellectuals. With the implementation of the Party's policy on the education and remolding of our intellectuals, they have become transformed into socialist working intellectuals and are confidently advancing along the road indicated by the Party. Our intellectuals are working not for fame or glory but for the Party and the revolution, for the country and the people with all their knowledge and talents, and are fighting vigorously side by side with the workers and peasants in the same revolutionary ranks to consolidate and develop our socialist system.

The education and remolding of the working people are tasks designed to eliminate all outdated ideas remaining in their minds and overcome their old habits and arm them with the revolutionary ideas of the working class, communist ideology. Our Party and the Government of the Republic, therefore, have conducted the work of educating and remolding people by means of explanation and persuasion with the main emphasis on ideological education. We intensified the education of the working people in Party policy and, at the same time, patiently carried on communist education with class ideas as its main content, so that all the working people have been firmly armed with the advanced revolutionary ideas of the working class, communist ideology.

Strengthening revolutionary organizational life is one of the important ways to educate and remold people along communist lines. Our Party and the Government of the Republic have paid serious attention to encouraging all the working people to take an active part in organizational life, voluntarily observe organizational discipline and conduct their lives under the guidance and supervision of their organizations. In particular, we have carried on the ideological struggle by the method of criticism and have tempered the working people in a revolutionary spirit through the ideological struggle.

Our Party and the Government of the Republic closely combined practical activities with the work of educating and remolding people through the Chollima Workteam Movement, and guaranteed that this work became the work of the masses themselves.

With the successful progress of the education and remolding of the working people in a communist way, a great change has taken place in the political and ideological life of our people and our revolutionary ranks have been strengthened and developed into an invincible force.

Under our Party's wise guidance the Government of the Republic has achieved really great successes in the revolutionary struggle and work of construction in the past years. It has established the most advanced socialist system in this land where exploitation and oppression prevailed before, and converted our backward colonial agrarian country in a very short time into a socialist power with its solid independent national economy and enormous defense capacities. It has brought about a brilliant flowering and development of science and culture and achieved great success also in the work of revolutionizing and working-classizing the whole society. We have won great victories in the socialist revolution and building of socialism and risen to a new high peak which lies on our way to socialism and communism.

2. The Superiority of our Socialist System

Comrades,

The outstanding success achieved in all spheres of politics, economy and culture since the triumph of our socialist revolution is graphic evidence of the superiority and indestructible vitality of our socialist system.

Our socialist system is the most advanced social system where the working masses are masters of everything and where everything in society serves the working masses.

The working masses transform nature and society and make history. The creative labor and struggle of the working masses produce all the material riches of society and bring about social renovation and progress. That is why the working masses should become masters of society and enjoy all its material wealth.

Not in every society, however, are the working masses masters of their society. People's position in society is determined by whether or not they hold state power and the means of production in their hands. Only those who have both can be the masters of society.

In an exploiter society, the toiling masses are not the masters of society but victims of exploitation and oppression, suffering all sorts of humiliations and insults to their dignity, because they hold no state power and own no means of production. In capitalist society where money is everything, even the dignity of a man is determined by the amount of money he has; poor people are treated like commodities.

Only in socialist society can the working masses enjoy an independent and creative life as real masters of society. Today all our government policies are geared to the interests and happiness of the workers, peasants and other working people; all the wealth of society is dedicated to the promotion of their welfare. In our society the working masses are highly valued and they and their rights are most respected. Especially in this country the rising generation who represent the future of society are treasured more than anyone else; all attention is directed to bringing them up to be happy, free from the social evils inherent in an exploiter society.

The fact that the working masses in socialist society are the masters of society and that they and their rights are respected to the utmost is explained precisely by their being masters of state power and the means of production. This is the basis of all the advantages and indestructible vitality of the socialist system.

Our socialist system is a genuinely democratic system that guarantees in practice the political rights and liberties of the workers, peasants and other working people.

Regardless of sex, occupation, property status, education and party affiliation, all our working people have the right to elect and to be elected and are guaranteed all rights to and freedom of social and political activities such as speech, press, assembly and demonstration. The workers, peasants and other working people, who were formerly held in bondage without any rights, now directly participate in state administration and politics as masters of state power and conduct free social and political activities as members of political parties and social organizations. Our working people today enjoy a dignified and fruitful life with genuine political rights and liberties under the socialist system.

In contrast, in capitalist society where state power is in the hands of the small minority of exploiting classes, the working masses have no political rights or freedoms. The working people do not even have the most elementary right and freedom to express their political views, to say nothing of the right to participate in state power; they only have the obligation to obey the exploiting classes. The so-called liberties and rights loudly advertised by capitalists are confined exclusively to the rulers and exploiting classes to oppress and exploit the masses of the people; the "democracy" they advocate is nothing but a means of camouflage to cover up the dictatorship of the bourgeoisie.

The superiority of our socialist system also lies in the fact that the state takes full responsibility for the material and cultural well-being of the workers, peasants and other working people.

Providing an equally abundant life for the people and systematically improving their material and cultural standards is one of the intrinsic characteristics of the socialist system. In socialist society the state serves the interests of the people and is responsible for guaranteeing the material and cultural well-being of the working people, whereas the state in exploiter society serves as a tool of oppression and exploitation against the workers and peasants.

Today everyone of working age in our country is provided with a job by the state, according to his ability and aptitude, and is rewarded according to the quantity and quality of work done. The working people also benefit from labor protection, an eight-hour workday, paid holidays, and accommodation at holiday homes and sanatoria; they are provided with safe working conditions and adequate leisure time. In particular, the working mothers enjoy tremendous benefits from the state. Besides providing jobs for all who can work, our state also assumes responsibility for those who cannot work because of old age, injuries arising from work or ill health, and for old people and children who have no other means of support. Therefore, in our country no one roams about hunting for a job or resorts to begging; all our people, young and old, are leading a happy life under the care of the state and society.

All our working people are provided with adequate food, clothing and housing by the state. Everyone in this land is given the right to be fed the moment he is born; all children and students, from those in creches and kindergartens to students in colleges and universities, are supplied with clothing by the state. The state provides our workers and office employees with good living quarters, and the peasants also live in modern houses built by the state.

Universal free medical care has also been introduced in this country, so that all working people are free from worries about medical care. There are medical institutions and medical workers in both urban and rural areas, wherever people work and live. Through the section doctor system, an advanced system of medical service, the state looks after the health of the working people in a responsible way. Our mortality rate has now been reduced by half, and the average life span of the people increased by 26 years, compared with the pre-liberation years. Our people's age-old desire to eradicate all sorts of diseases has been realized only under our social system.

Everyone in this country is provided with adequate conditions for education and development. All our students, from primary school children to university students, now receive free education, and preschool children are happily growing up in creches and kindergartens at state and public expense. In particular, with the introduction of universal compulsory ten-year senior middle school education which gives ten years of schooling, plus one year of compulsory preschool training, our younger generation are receiving eleven years of excellent secondary general education provided by the state. This is virtually an eleven-year compulsory education, which means that the most advanced compulsory education in the world is given in this country.

The socialist state offers opportunities of learning also for the adults who were previously deprived of the right to study in the exploiter society and left far behind in terms of social culture. All our working people are learning to the best of their abilities in accordance with their desire and aptitude, in working people's middle schools, factory higher technical schools, factory colleges and other educational institutions where they study while on the job. Indeed, our country is a "land of education," a "land of learning" where all the people study at the expense of the state.

Although they do not live in luxury like the landlords and capitalists, all our people are now living an equally good life and studying according to their desires, without having to worry about jobs, food, clothing and housing. This clearly shows that our socialist system is a system truly for the workers, farmers and all the other people.

The socialist system is the best social system, not only providing the people with a happy life today but also promising them a brighter future. Since all the fruits of labor in socialist society are used for social progress and for improving the welfare of the working people, increasing social wealth brings an ever greater abundance and an ever higher level of cultural life to the people.

However, in capitalist society the handful of exploiters grow richer with each passing day, whereas the working people making up the overwhelming majority of the population become more and more impoverished and miserable. Capitalist society is a society where "the rich get ever richer and the poor get ever poorer," the gulf between the exploiting and the exploited classes growing daily wider; it is a living hell where the working masses are impoverished and starved.

All these facts make us take a great pride in our socialist system, a people's social system truly for the workers, peasants and working intellectuals.

In our country the economy, culture, science and technology are making steady rapid progress. This is one of the great advantages of our socialist system.

Socialist society provides every condition and possibility for the rapid and continuous development of the economy. In this society a planned and balanced economic development is guaranteed by the state through a planned mobilization and use of all the nation's manpower and material resources and through a coordinated control and guidance of production, distribution, accumulation, and consumption. Also in this society the working people display a high degree of revolutionary enthusiasm and creative initiative in their productive activities, since they work for their society and collective and for their own welfare as masters of the country.

As the functions of the state as an economic organizer increase and the ideological consciousness of the working people grows in our country, the economy develops steadily at a high rate. Our industrial production grew at a high rate—an annual average of 19.1% — throughout the period of industrialization from 1957 to 1970, and the difficult and complex task of socialist industrialization was creditably accomplished in a very short time, in only 14 years.

In socialist society literature and art flower brilliantly. The socialist system has placed not only state power and the means of production but also literature and art in the hands of the people, and thus opened up a highway for the development of literature and art and made them true literature and art which serve the working masses.

Today broad sections of our working people take an active part in literary and artistic activities and enjoy them to their hearts' content. Because of their popular and revolutionary character our literature and art develop into full bloom, enjoying the boundless love of the people.

It is one of the essential advantages of the socialist system that the politico-ideological unity of the masses of the people is strengthened and the relationship of comradely cooperation between the working people develops day by day.

Elimination of the exploiting classes and all sorts of exploiting systems has fundamentally changed the position and social status of the workers, peasants and working intellectuals. The establishment of the socialist system has made all our people socialist working people and wrought a radical change in their spiritual and moral qualities. Because of their common socio-economic status and their common goals and interests, our working class, cooperative farmers and working intellectuals are firmly united politically and ideologically and closely cooperate with each other as comrades.

In capitalist society which is built on rabid selfishness and where the law of the jungle prevails, fraud and swindling are rampant and people are antagonistic and hostile to each other, and it is a common practice for them to sacrifice others for their own fame and career, comfort and pleasure. In our society, however, all its members are imbued with true comradeship, respecting, trusting and cooperating with each other on the principle of collectivism. Our working people are fully displaying the fine communist spirit of moving ahead together, the informed teaching the less informed and the advanced leading the laggards forward.

Today our society has been turned into a great, harmonious Red family where the entire people are closely united as a political force; in this great family all are working and living filled with revolutionary ardor and optimism. The entire people are united politically and ideologically and working with revolutionary zeal. This is precisely the basis of the solidity of our society and the source of our indestructible strength.

Our socialist system is displaying its superiority and unbreakable vitality more fully with each passing day.

Through their own experience our people are convinced that only the socialist system can guarantee genuine liberties and rights to the working masses and provide them with a most bountiful and happy life; they regard it as the greatest honor and pleasure to live and make revolution under this system. The people in the northern half of the Republic will not yield to anyone our socialist system which they themselves have chosen and whose superiority and great vitality have all been unequivocally proved, and they are all aglow with a determination to fight on staunchly to consolidate and develop this system.

3. The Main Content of the Socialist Constitution of the Democratic People's Republic of Korea

Comrades,

The current session of the Supreme People's Assembly is going to adopt the Socialist Constitution of the DPRK with a view to consolidating the socialist system established in the northern half of the Republic and intensifying the struggle for the complete victory of socialism.

The new Socialist Constitution correctly reflects the achievements made in the socialist revolution and in building socialism in our country, defines the principles to govern activities in the political, economic and cultural fields in socialist society and the basic rights and duties of citizens, and stipulates the composition and functions of the state organs and the principles of their activities. Its purpose is to protect by law the socialist system and the dictatorship of the proletariat established in the northern half of the Republic and to serve the revolutionary cause of the working class.

The Socialist Constitution of the DPRK legislatively affirms the political victories and successes attained by our people in the revolutionary struggle in the past years and defines the character and functions of our state and the principles of its activity to meet the demand of our revolutionary development.

It proclaims the Democratic People's Republic of Korea an independent socialist state. In our country the socialist system has been established, the political and ideological unity of the entire people resting on the worker-peasant alliance led by the working class strengthened with this system as its basis and the historic task of socialist industrialization creditably accomplished. As a result, the Government of the Republic has been strengthened and developed into a socialist power on a new socialist basis and a firm political foundation.

The sovereignty of the DPRK belongs to the workers, peasants, soldiers and working intellectuals. The Supreme People's Assembly and local people's assemblies at all levels are composed of deputies representing the workers, peasants, soldiers and working intellectuals, and they manage and operate the state organs. Our state is a genuine state of the workers and peasants in which the working masses are the masters of the country and the entire people exercise power. Therefore, our state regards it as its supreme duty to protect the interests of the workers, peasants, soldiers and working intellectuals freed from exploitation and oppression forever.

The Government of our Republic which has inherited the glorious revolutionary traditions of our people is guided in its activity by the Juche idea which is a creative application of Marxism-Leninism to the conditions of our country, and strives to execute the lines and policies of the Workers' Party of Korea.

It is the fundamental revolutionary task of the Government of the Republic to attain the complete victory of socialism in the northern half, expel foreign forces on a nationwide scale and achieve the reunification and independence of the country on a democratic basis. For the successful implementation of this task we must, first of all, strengthen the functions and role of our Government to intensify the struggle against the hostile elements at home and abroad opposed to our socialist system, and powerfully accelerate the ideological revolution to revolutionize and working-classize all the members of society.

The Socialist Constitution makes it clear that in its activity the Government of our Republic must always carry through the class and mass lines, give priority to political work, work with people in all matters as required by the Chongsan-ri spirit and Chongsan-ri method to rouse the conscious enthusiasm of the masses, and persistently keep up the Chollima Movement, our

Party's general line in socialist construction, thus powerfully pushing ahead with both communist education and the remolding of the working people and economic construction.

It also clearly stipulates the duties of the armed forces of the DPRK and the national defense policy based on the principle of self-defense as well as the foreign policy of the Republic based on the principles of complete equality and independence, Marxism-Leninism and proletarian internationalism.

The Socialist Constitution of the DPRK legally affirms the achievements attained by our people in the building of an independent national economy and clarifies the principles governing our socio-economic life.

The socialist ownership of the means of production is the economic foundation of the DPRK. All the economic activities of our state and the socio-economic life of the working people are thoroughly based on the principles of socialism, and the nation's economy is steadily developing at a very high rate, on the basis of the socialist relations of production which have held undivided sway in town and country. The economic power of the DPRK is firmly guaranteed by the great superiority of socialist production relations and the solid foundations of an independent national economy.

Labor is one of the most important elements which form the basis of socio-economic life in socialist society. The Socialist Constitution gives a clear definition of the character of labor, the principles governing the working life of the toiling people and the socialist principle of distribution in our society.

Socialism and communism can be built only by the creative labor of working millions. It is a solemn duty and the greatest honor of the working people in socialist society to love labor and conscientiously participate in the communal labor for the building of socialism and communism. All our working people take part in labor and work for the sake of their country and people and for their own welfare, displaying conscious enthusiasm and creativity.

The fruits of labor in our country are allocated entirely for national prosperity and progress and the promotion of the well-being of the working people. It is an immutable socialist principle that all the working people work according to their ability and take their share according to the quantity and quality of work done. Our state regards the steady improvement of the people's material and cultural life as its primary duty, as the supreme principle guiding its activity.

The Socialist Constitution stipulates the socialist form of economic management and the principle of state guidance of the economy in our country.

The Taean work system, under which the economy is managed in a scientific and rational way on the basis of the collective strength of the producer masses, and the new system of agricultural guidance, under which agriculture is directed by industrial methods, are the best socialist forms of economic management, whose superiority has been clearly proved in practice. In addition, the unified and the detailed planning constitute the socialist system and method of planning, which make it possible to tighten the discipline of democratic centralism in economic management and ensure a high rate of growth in production and the balanced development of the national economy. The decisive guarantee for the successful building of the socialist economy is to give full scope to the superiority of the socialist economic management systems created by our Party and guide and manage the economy to meet the requirements of these systems.

The Socialist Constitution also sets forth the economic tasks of laying firmer material and technological foundations of socialism, emancipating the working people once and for all from heavy labor, gradually turning cooperative property into all-people's property and eliminating the differences between town and country and the class distinction between workers and peasants.

The Socialist Constitution of the DPRK, on the basis of the shining achievements made by our people in the development of culture, makes clear the direction to be taken in thoroughly carrying out the cultural · revolution and accelerating the building of a socialist national culture, as well as the principles that must be observed by the state in this sphere.

The basic aim of the cultural revolution in socialist society is to train all the working people to be competent builders of socialism and communism with a profound knowledge of nature and society and a high level of technology, and make our culture a true people's revolutionary culture which serves the socialist working people. To attain this aim of the cultural revolution, we must resolutely combat cultural infiltration by imperialism and any tendency to return to the past and rapidly develop education, science, literature and art and all other domains of socialist cultural construction on a sound basis.

The Socialist Constitution specifically explains the state's educational policy of carrying through the principles of socialist pedagogy in education and closely combining general education with technical education, and education with productive labor, as well as vital people's education programs such as the introduction of compulsory ten-year senior middle school education for all our young people under working age. The Constitution also elucidates our state's revolutionary policies to develop science, literature and art, physical culture and sports and the public health service.

The Socialist Constitution of the DPRK explicitly provides for the basic rights and duties of citizens in keeping with the intrinsic nature of socialist society. In this country where there is no exploitation or oppression and where social and individual interests are in full accord, the citizens' rights and duties are based on the collectivist principle of "One for all and all for one." The basic rights of citizens laid down in the Socialist Constitution are a legal confirmation of the democratic rights and liberties enjoyed by our people in their actual social life. The duties of citizens as stipulated in the Constitution are honorable duties that should be fulfilled by the people, as the masters of their country, in consolidating and developing the socialist system and in making their homeland richer and stronger.

The Socialist Constitution of the DPRK contains new provisions concerning the composition and functions of the state organs, and the principles of their activity to suit the actual conditions of revolutionary development.

The new state structure instituted under the Socialist Constitution will allow the workers, peasants, soldiers and working intellectuals to take a more active part in state affairs and state administration and enable state organs to serve the people's interests better and push ahead more vigorously with the revolutionary struggle and work of construction by improving their functions and role.

Our organs of power are composed of representatives of the workers, peasants, soldiers and working intellectuals; they protect the interests of the working people and fight for the people's freedom and welfare. The new state structure is built in such a way that the activities of administrative bodies are always supervised and controlled by the masses of the people. Under the new state structure, unlike the old one, the people's committees are separated from administrative bodies, and the former which are composed of representatives of the workers, peasants, soldiers and working intellectuals are to perform the function of exercising day-to-day supervision and control over the latter's activities, so that the functionaries of the administrative bodies are able to do away with bureaucracy in their work and serve the people better as their servants.

The Socialist Constitution defines the principle of democratic centralism as the basic principle of organization and activity for all state organs. Democratic centralism in their organization and activity makes it possible for them to carry out Party lines and policies in a coordinated way throughout the country and dynamically organize and mobilize the entire people for the struggle to build socialism and communism. Since they are based on democratic centralism, the organs of people's power are able to perform their functions and role satisfactorily as a powerful weapon for the building of socialism and communism.

The Socialist Constitution of the DPRK is a most popular constitution for the benefit of the workers, peasants, soldiers and working intellectuals. The new Constitution fully reflects their will and desire and thoroughly defends the working people's interests. Also, the new Constitution gives the entire people genuine freedoms and rights in all spheres of social life and legally guarantees all conditions to make them viable.

The Socialist Constitution of the DPRK is a most revolutionary constitution. Unlike those constitutions which refer mainly to the state structure, our Socialist Constitution, which lays down all the principles governing the political, economic and cultural activities in socialist society, will serve as a sharp weapon of the proletarian dictatorship to protect the policy of our Party and the Government of the Republic and firmly safeguard the gains of the socialist revolution, as a powerful means for giving a strong impetus to socialist economic construction and for revolutionizing and working-classizing the whole society by intensifying the ideological and cultural revolutions and establishing a socialist mode of life.

With the institution of the Socialist Constitution, the

Government of the Republic will have a new weapon of the proletarian dictatorship and our people will be provided with a dependable legal guarantee in the struggle to achieve the complete victory of socialism and the independent, peaceful reunification of the country. The coming into force of the Socialist Constitution in the northern half of the Republic will greatly encourage the people in south Korea who are fighting for the democratization of society and the country's independent, peaceful reunification.

With the Socialist Constitution coming into force a new change will take place in the political, economic and cultural life of our people and they will advance with redoubled vigor along the path of socialism and communism, deeply convinced of the justness of their cause.

4. Our Tasks in the Consolidation and Development of the Socialist System

Comrades,

The Government of the Democratic People's Republic of Korea and our people are confronted today with the historic task of consolidating and developing the socialist system and attaining the complete victory of socialism, by promoting the revolutionary struggle and construction work continuously and vigorously, on the basis of the brilliant achievements gained in building a new society.

In order to achieve the complete victory of socialism we must obliterate the distinctions between towns and the countryside and the class distinction between the workers and the peasants, reinforce the material and technical foundations of socialism, markedly improve the material and cultural standards of the people, smash the insidious maneuvers of hostile classes and do away with the corrosive influence of old ideas once and for all.

The struggle for the complete victory of socialism is a struggle for the final liquidation of the vestiges of the old society from all spheres of social life; it is a struggle to transform society on the pattern of the working class in all realms of economy and culture, ideology and morality. To attain the complete victory of socialism, therefore, the party and state of the working class must push ahead energetically with the struggle to occupy two fortresses, the material and ideological, on the way to the building of communism. We must continue to dynamically promote the technical, cultural and ideological revolutions to consolidate the socialist system and achieve the complete victory of socialism.

The basic goal of the technical revolution at the present stage is to successfully carry out its three major tasks advanced at the Fifth Congress of the Workers' Party of Korea.

These three tasks which aim to considerably narrow the disparity between heavy and light labor and between agricultural and industrial labor and free women from the heavy burden of household chores, are an honorable undertaking to guarantee the complete victory of socialism; they are a strategic task facing us in socialist construction after socialist industrialization. To fulfill these three major tasks is the basic way to release the working peole from arduous labor, provide them more fully with equal conditions of working life and step up the technological reconstruction of the national economy and the development of the productive forces. Furthermore, only when these tasks are carried out, will it be possible to satisfactorily solve the question of elevating the technical and cultural standards of the working people, remolding their ideological consciousness and eliminating the difference between town and countryside and the class distinction between workers and peasants.

Regarding the three major tasks of the technical revolution set forth by the Party as the central question in socialist economic construction at present, the Government of the Republic will strive for their successful implementation.

In order to diminish the distinction between heavy and light labor and eliminate work in excessive heat or under other harmful conditions, we must raise the general level of mechanization, semi-automation and full-scale automation where these arduous and harmful labor conditions exist. We must also introduce the comprehensive mechanization and chemicalization of agriculture in an all-round way to reduce the difference between agricultural and industrial labor. At the same time, in order to free our women from the heavy burden of household drudgery we must provide them with adequate conditions to do kitchen and other household work quickly and easily. In order to reach these three major targets a vigorous mass movement for technological innovation must be unfolded in all fields of the national economy, bringing about a fresh upsurge in production.

We must first direct great efforts to the development of the engineering industry and bring about a renovation in this branch.

The technical revolution is, in essence, a mechanical revolution. Machinery is the decisive means for alleviating the arduous labor of people, and the productive forces are also developed by the improvement of machinery. The successful carrying out of the three major tasks of the technical revolution depends, in the final analysis, on whether or not diverse types of modern machinery and equipment are satisfactorily produced through the rapid development of the engineering industry.

For the advancement of the engineering industry priority must be given to rapidly and steadily increasing the production of machine tools. True to the Party's call, the heroic workers in this industry have recently brought about an innovation in the production of machine tools and admirably attained the goal of 30,000-unit production per annum, thus opening up bright prospects for the victorious implementation of the three major tasks of the technical revolution. Workers in the engineering industry, not resting content with this victory, must strive to continuously increase the output of machine tools while consolidating the success achieved and, in particular, work hard to increase variety and raise quality.

A rapid increase in the production of tractors and trucks is urgently needed for the fulfillment of the three major tasks of the technical revolution and one of the most important tasks confronting the engineering industry. To successfully carry out the comprehensive mechanization of agriculture, our Party advanced a policy of providing 6-7 tractors and one truck for every 100 *chongbo* of fields in the near future. For the thorough implementation of this policy, the tractor- and truck-manufacturing centers must be expanded and reinforced and a fresh innovation be effected in their production. Thus, we should attain an annual production level of 30,000 tractors and 15,000-30,000 trucks in a year or two.

An important task now facing the engineering industry is to increase the production of heavy machines and ordered plants.

We must expand and consolidate the heavy-machine production centers to manufacture greater quantities of universal drilling machines, large bulldozers and excavators and other different types of heavy machines needed for the extractive industries and big projects to harness nature, as well as large ships, and an innovation must be brought about in the production of ordered plants.

In order to introduce semi-automation and complete automation extensively in all domains of the national economy we must rapidly develop the electronics and automation industries. Different kinds of automation elements, gauges and instruments must be mass-produced by making the best use of the existing foundation of electronics and automation industries and, at the same time, many small and medium branch factories must be built up to produce automation parts and automation gauges and instruments.

In order to develop the engineering industry at a fast tempo and fully guarantee huge construction work we must markedly increase the production of different kinds of iron and steel materials and nonferrous metals by concentrating our efforts on the advancement of the metal industry. Projects now under way to reconstruct and enlarge the Kim Chaek Iron Works, the Kangson Steel Plant and other metallurgical plants along up-to-date lines must be completed quickly to bring about a radical growth of production and, at the same time, a vigorous struggle must be waged to build another big modern metallurgical base. Along with this, the production of various nonferrous metals must be drastically augmented through the consolidation of their production centers and the maximum use of the production capacities of the smelters.

To give priority to the extractive and power industries is an important guarantee for the successful fulfillment of the three major tasks of the technical revolution and for swift progress in all realms of the national economy. In the extractive industries, geological prospecting must always be given priority and the level of mechanization and automation at coal and ore mines be elevated decisively through a dynamic technical innovation movement and consequently fresh innovations will be made in production. In the power industry, production should be raised to the maximum by taking good care of the equipment of the existing power stations and, simultaneously, the construction of new projects must be speeded up vigorously to hasten their commissioning.

An important task of the chemical industry is to further expand and consolidate the raw material base for light industry and steadily augment the production of chemical fertilizers and agricultural chemicals needed for the technical revolution in the countryside. The workers in the chemical industry have already registered great achievements in the struggle to fulfill the Six-Year Plan. In particular, the production of vinalon and vinyl chloride this year has already exceeded the level envisaged for the end of the Six-Year Plan. In the chemical industry we must work from now on to make better use of the existing production capacities and, at the same time, strive to create up-to-date chemical industrial centers. We must also normalize the production of ammonia through gasification and markedly raise the proportion of phosphatic and microelement fertilizers in the production of chemical fertilizers. In addition, we have to build up the paper-making centers to supply sufficient paper needed for both the universal compulsory ten-year senior middle school education and the cultural revolution.

We must carry out enormous construction work for the successful implementation of the three major tasks of the technical revolution and for further progress in the national economy. In capital construction we have to concentrate our efforts on major projects which are of decisive significance in the national economic development and the improvement of the people's living conditions, in accordance with our Party's policy of concentrated construction, and thus hasten their commissioning to the maximum.

We must exert efforts to develop the building-materials and timber industries, so that the demands for different construction materials are fully met.

The rapid development of light industry is highly important in radically improving the people's living standards and freeing women from the heavy burden of household chores. The Government of the Republic must direct great efforts to the development of the textile and garment industries and, in particular, strive to modernize the daily necessities and food-processing industries. In order to streamline these latter, the engineering industry must produce large quantities of varied single-purpose machines. We must modernize the daily necessities and food-processing industries as soon as possible through a mass campaign for one machine to make another and for one factory to build another, and thus effect a great change in the production of consumer goods and food.

The cardinal task in narrowing the distinctions between agricultural and industrial labor and freeing the peasants from arduous work is to effect an overall, comprehensive mechanization of agriculture. In farming, we have to radically raise the level of mechanization and, in particular, concentrate our efforts on the introduction of mechanization in intermediary areas, in keeping with the rapid growth of the output of tractors and trucks. We must successfully carry out the comprehensive mechanization of agriculture; this can be done by making maximum use of tractors through the reinforcements of tractor repair bases and tractor implement production centers and the extensive levelling and rezoning of fields. In addition, we must step up the chemicalization of agriculture and widely introduce advanced methods of farming and thus bring about a fresh upswing in agricultural production.

Transport plays a vital part in carrying out the three major tasks of the technical revolution. In this branch we must continually accelerate railway electrification and vigorously push forward the construction of new railway lines and harbors, so that the material and technical basis of transport is further strengthened. We must also improve the organization of transport and actively mechanize loading and unloading operations. In this way, we will fully cope with the increasing freight turnover.

The Government of the Republic must vigorously continue to push ahead with the cultural revolution alongside the technical revolution.

The urgent task facing us today in the development of culture is to train large numbers of technical personnel to meet the real demands of socialist construction, and considerably raise the working people's general cultural level and technical skills.

We must improve the work of colleges and higher specialized schools, build more institutions of higher learning and strengthen the work of night schools and correspondence courses. By doing this we must carry out without fail the decision of our Party's Fifth Congress on increasing the number of technicians and specialists to more than a million in the coming few years.

If we are to raise the working people's cultural level and technical skills we must achieve universal compulsory ten-year senior middle school education on a high qualitative level. In order to fully guarantee this the Government of the Republic must provide all the necessary material conditions and decisively improve teachers' training to produce good teachers in great numbers. In the field of education, we must thoroughly apply the principles of socialist pedagogy so as to train all our students to be dependable builders of socialism and communism, firmly armed with our Party's revolutionary ideology and equipped with ample knowledge, high morality and strong bodies.

In order to raise the general cultural and technical levels of the working people we must further develop the spare-time educational system which comprises the working people's middle school, factory higher technical school and other schools, thus enrolling all working people in some educational establishments, so they can study on a regular basis.

In this way, we will ensure that all working people attain the level of a senior middle school graduate and master more than one technical skill.

The Government of the Republic must pursue the ideological revolution vigorously and so achieve the revolutionization and working-classization of the whole of society in accordance with the Party's consistent policy.

What is most important in revolutionizing and working-classizing the whole of society is to equip the working people firmly with our Party's monolithic idea, the Juche idea. Our Party's Juche idea is the only correct guide to the successful carrying out of the Korean revolution. Only when the working people are firmly armed with this idea can they have a genuine revolutionary world outlook and worthily discharge the tasks assigned to them in the revolutionary struggle and construction work. We should intensify the education of the working people in our Party policies and the revolutionary traditions to arm them firmly with our Party's monolithic idea, the Juche idea, thereby training all of them to be true Red fighters of the Party, communist revolutionaries, who adhere to revolutionary principles under any adversity and carry through the Party's lines and policies.

We should intensify communist education, with class education as its main content, among the working people, while arming them with the Juche idea, so that all of them are firmly armed with working-class consciousness and collectivism, ardently cherish our socialist system and devotedly work for its consolidation and development.

Steady improvement of the material and cultural standards of the people is the supreme principle governing all activities of the Government of the Republic. As in the past, the Government of the Republic will continue to make every effort to raise the people's material and cultural standards.

We must firmly adhere to the principle of ensuring a proportionate improvement of all the working people's living conditions while systematically promoting the people's welfare. The Government of the Republic should make active efforts especially to rapidly eliminate distinctions between the workers and the peasants in their living standards and between the urban and the rural population in their living conditions, while improving the lives of the people as a whole, in accordance with the policy set forth at the Fifth Congress of our Party.

We must strengthen the organs of power and improve their functions and role in order to successfully implement the revolutionary tasks confronting us at present and consolidate and develop the socialist system.

To strengthen the government of the workers and peasants, which is a powerful weapon of the revolution and construction, is an important guarantee for winning the complete victory of socialism and accomplishing the historic cause of the working class. We must make untiring efforts to fortify the organs of power at all levels and raise their functions and role in the revolution and construction.

The organs of power from top to bottom must radically increase their role as defenders of the political rights and interests of the workers, peasants and other working people and as masters responsible for their lives. They must strive to champion the working people's political rights in every way, protect their lives and property and see to it that the people all live well. The organs of power at all levels must take in hand commerce, town administration, education, public health services and production and construction which are directly related to the people's life, and strengthen their leadership over them to provide better living conditions for the people. They should fully protect and take good care of state and communal property and resolutely fight against its misappropriation and wastage.

For our Government to be a genuine government of the workers and peasants which faithfully serves the interests of the revolution and the people, we must see to it that the monolithic ideological system of the Party is thoroughly established, above all, among the officials of the government bodies. The government officials at all levels must arm themselves more firmly with our Party's monolithic ideology, always base all their activities strictly on the Party's lines and policies, and defend and carry them through to the end under whatever difficult conditions. At the same time, they must constantly improve their method and style of work. Bureaucratism is one of the major defects that may often manifest itself in the method and style of work after the seizure of power by the working class. The government officials' bureaucratism stems from subjectivism as well as from the mistaken idea of equating their posts with old-time government offices. It divorces the Party from the masses and makes it impossible to successfully carry out revolutionary tasks. We must completely do away with the bureaucratic work method of the functionaries of government bodies and strictly adhere to the Chongsan-ri method which is our Party's revolutionary method of work.

The Government of the Republic must continue to exert great efforts to increase the nation's defense capabilities.

Since we are building socialism in direct confrontation with U.S. imperialism, the ringleader of world imperialism, we must not neglect the work of increasing the nation's defense capabilities even for a moment. The Government of the Republic must always be highly vigilant against the war policy and aggressive maneuvers of the imperialists and augment in every way the nation's defense capabilities in accordance with the revolutionary principle of self-defense. We must continue to thoroughly implement the Party's military line, the main content of which is to turn the entire army into an army of cadres, modernize it, arm the entire people and fortify the whole country, and make the nation's defenses impregnable so as to promptly crush any aggressive acts of the imperialists and firmly defend the security of the country and the people and our socialist gains.

In order to consolidate and develop the socialist system and hasten the final victory of our revolution, we must strengthen our solidarity with the revolutionary forces of the world while increasing our own revolutionary forces.

The principle invariably followed by the Democratic People's Republic of Korea in its foreign policy is to develop friendship and cooperation with all countries that are friendly toward our country, on the principles of equality and mutual benefit. In the future, too, we will hold fast to this principle in our foreign policy.

The Government of the Republic will do its best to achieve unity and cohesion of the socialist countries and promote friendship and cooperation with them on the principles of Marxism-Leninism and proletarian internationalism.

It will strive to expand and strengthen its diplomatic relations with the Asian, African and Latin American countries that are fighting for freedom and national independence and to establish and promote friendly relations with more countries. We will also endeavor to establish diplomatic as well as political, economic and cultural relations, on the five principles of peaceful coexistence, with those capitalist countries which wish to have good relations with our country and which pursue unbiased policies free of an aggressive nature toward the north and south of the Korean peninsula.

The consistent policy followed by the Government of the Republic in its external activity is to fight against the U.S.-led imperialists' policy of aggression and war and for world peace and security.

The U.S.-led imperialists are still pursuing their policy of aggression and war in a crafty manner under ostentatious slogans of "peace" and "negotiations." Holding aloft the revolutionary banner of anti-imperialist, anti-U.S. struggle, we will fight on resolutely to check and frustrate the imperialists' policy of aggression and war and defend the peace of the world. Furthermore, we will render active support and encouragement to the struggle of all peoples of the world against imperialism and make energetic efforts to strengthen solidarity with all the anti-imperialist forces.

The Government of the DPRK and the Korean people will

always stand firmly on the side of the peoples who are fighting for peace and democracy, national independence and socialism.

In the past period the Korean citizens in Japan have achieved tremendous successes in their struggle to defend their democratic, national rights, facilitate the independent, peaceful reunification of the homeland and strengthen the international solidarity with the Japanese people and other progressive peoples of the world.

In the future, too, they should continue to struggle resolutely to develop national education and achieve the right to return home and visit their country, united closely around Chongryon (the General Association of Korean Residents in Japan), under the unfurled banner of the Juche idea. They should also actively contribute to hastening the country's reunification, the supreme national task of our people, upholding our Party's policy of independent, peaceful reunification, and strengthen internationalist friendship with the Japanese people and other peoples of the world.

The Government of the DPRK regards it as its solemn duty to protect our nationals in Japan and all other Korean citizens abroad. The Government of the Republic will continue to fight staunchly against all unwarranted acts of infringement upon the interests and national rights of our overseas citizens, and do all it can to support and encourage their just struggle.

Comrade Deputies,

Our people have achieved great victories and successes in the struggle for the socialist revolution and socialist construction under the wise leadership of the Workers' Party of Korea, courageously overcoming manifold difficulties and harsh trials. All these brilliant victories and achievements testify to the correctness and indestructible vitality of our Party's Juche idea and demonstrate our people's inexhaustible might.

Our people are confronted today with the important task of achieving the complete victory of socialism in the northern half of the Republic and the independent, peaceful reunification of the country by promoting the revolution and construction. In order to carry out this task, we must continue our vigorous struggle with unusual energy and devotion, and push forward more quickly, overcoming all difficulties.

We must thoroughly embody the new Socialist Constitution, which we are going to adopt here, in all fields of state and social life, and more powerfully push forward the revolution and construction. All our citizens must voluntarily observe the Socialist Constitution and thus bring about a great change in the revolutionary struggle and work of construction.

Our revolutionary cause is a just one, and victory is definitely ours.

No force can block the way of the Korean people who are marching forward under our Party's leadership, with state power firmly in their hands.

Let us all unite closely around the Party Central Committee and the Government of the Republic and advance valiantly toward the bright future of socialism and communism, holding high the banner of Marxism-Leninism, the revolutionary banner of the Juche idea.

ON THE FIVE-POINT POLICY FOR NATIONAL REUNIFICATION

Speech at an Enlarged Meeting of the Political Committee of the Central Committee of the Workers' Party of Korea, June 25, 1973

In our speech two days ago, on June 23, we clarified internally and externally our new five-point policy for the independent, peaceful reunification of the country.

From the first day, our speech met with a big response at home and abroad. Not only the entire Korean people warmly support and hail this five-point policy of our Party and the Government of the Republic; the governments and peoples of many countries loudly voice their support for it. The Party and Government delegation of Czechoslovakia on a visit to our country expressed full support for our five-point policy upon its announcement and, in its wake, many countries manifested their stand in support of it. Many foreign newspapers, news agencies and radios are giving wide publicity to the five-point policy of our Party and the Government of the Republic for national reunification and in their many comments welcome it.

Our new five-point policy for national reunification is a positive step towards smashing the maneuver of the U.S. imperialists and south Korean authorities to perpetuate national division, which has reached a very grave stage, and toward expediting the independent, peaceful reunification of the country.

Even after publication of the North-South Joint Statement, U.S. imperialism and the south Korean authorities persisted in their maneuvering for national division.

In an attempt to rig up "two Koreas," the U.S. imperialists have kept instigating the south Korean authorities to divisive actions under cover of the north-south dialogue. Openly declaring that south Korea should take up a "position of strength" in the north-south dialogue, they have continuously shipped new military equipment to south Korea and staged aggressive war exercises without letup. The Japanese militarists, dancing to the tune of the U.S. imperialists, have also hampered the north-south dialogue and taken many actions against the reunification of our country. The U.S. imperialists and the Japanese militarists aim, in the final analysis, at keeping our country divided in two indefinitely, and making south Korea their permanent colony and commodity market.

Under the active manipulation of U.S. imperialism the south Korean authorities have adhered to the road of division, and not of reunification, flagrantly ignoring the agreed points of the North-South Joint Statement. Since publication of the joint statement the south Korean authorities have clung on ever more desperately to the foreign forces. Crying for "confrontation with dialogue" and "competition with dialogue," they turned down all our proposals to remove military confrontation and to enter into many-sided cooperation and interchange between north and south and ceaselessly perpetrated aggressive provocations to aggravate tension. They also kept raising "anti-communist" clamors and intensified the fascist suppression of the south Korean people. They uttered words about reunification, but in deeds they worked frantically on the "two Koreas" plot aimed at freezing and perpetuating the division.

The south Korean authorities who had pursued their "two Koreas" plot in every way under the wirepulling of US imperialism, finally issued a so-called "special statement" on the morning of June 23, openly proclaiming to the world their "policy" of perpetuating the country's division.

In the "special statement" the south Korean authorities declared, in short, that the north and the south should enter the UN separately while keeping our country divided. This anti-national assertion is simply intolerable. Should things turn out as the south Korean authorities desire, our nation will be split in two forever and the south Korean people will remain permanently colonial slaves of the U.S. imperialists.

This policy of perpetuating national division pursued by the south Korean authorities with the backing of US imperialism, has placed a grave obstacle in the way of national reunification. In order to remove that obstacle and promote the national cause of independent, peaceful reunification we should resolutely and promptly smash the treacherous declaration of the south Korean authorities and open up before the whole nation a broad perspective and a clear-cut way to national reunification. That was why on the afternoon of June 23, we set forth the five-point policy for national reunification as a new measure to save the nation.

Our five-point policy is: to remove military confrontation and lessen tensions between north and south, to realize many-sided cooperation and interchange between north and south, to convene a Great National Congress comprising representatives of people of all strata, political parties and social organizations from the north and south, to institute a north-south Confederation under the single nomenclature of Confederal Republic of Koryo, and to enter the UN under the single nomenclature— Confederal Republic of Koryo.

First of all, we maintain that military confrontation should be eliminated and tensions be removed between north and south in order to improve relations and accelerate the country's peaceful reunification.

To remove military confrontation and tensions between north and south is now the most urgent, vital problem in dispelling misunderstanding and distrust, and deepening mutual understanding and trust, creating an atmosphere of great national unity, improving north-south relations, and in achieving the country's peaceful reunification.

The military confrontation between north and south with their huge armed forces is in itself not only a major factor endangering peace in our country but also a source of misunderstanding and distrust.

The solution of this fundamental problem is a prerequisite for the removal of tensions and distrust between north and south, the creation of an atmosphere of trust, and the satisfactory settlement of all problems on the basis of mutual trust. It is unnatural to advocate peaceful reunification and hold a dialogue with a dagger in one's belt. Unless the dagger is laid on the table, it is impossible to create an atmosphere of mutual trust or find satisfactory solutions to any national reunification problems, big or small, including that of realizing cooperation and interchange between north and south.

Therefore, as the first step towards the peaceful reunification of the country, we have put before the south Korean authorities more than once this five-point proposal: cessation of the reinforcement of armies and the arms race, withdrawal of all foreign troops, reduction of armed forces and armaments, ending of the introduction of weapons from outside and conclusion of a peace agreement.

Nevertheless, the south Korean authorities insist that the solution of this urgent problem should be put off and that at the most, matters of secondary importance should be settled step by step at various stages. This means that they do not sincerely want to increase mutual trust and promote great national unity, but to maintain and freeze the country's division, leaving the raw wound of national partition unhealed.

If the south Korean authorities truly desire peaceful reunification and seek a practical solution of the reunification question, they must renounce this position and take the course of eliminating military confrontation.

Now we maintain that many-sided cooperation and interchange between north and south should be accomplished in the political, military, diplomatic, economic and cultural fields in order to improve north-south relations and expedite the country's reunification.

Many-sided cooperation and interchange are of tremendous importance in rejoining the severed bonds of the nation and providing preconditions for reunification. Only when such cooperation and interchange are realized, will it be possible to consolidate the peace agreement to be concluded between north and south.

The south Korean authorities propose in word that both sides "throw open" their societies to each other, but, in fact, they are afraid of tearing down any of the barriers between the two parts of the country and are resolutely opposed to their interchange and collaboration.

Instead of collaborating with their own fellow countrymen, the south Korean authorities now collude with forces outside and invite foreign monopoly capital without any limitation, thus reducing the south Korean economy completely to an appendage. They are even spoiling our beautiful land by bringing in polluting industries rejected as "rubbish" in foreign countries.

If the south Korean authorities have an ounce of national conscience, they should naturally strive to develop the economy in the interests of our nation through the joint exploitation of our country's natural resources and bring about national cooperation in all fields of activity.

We also maintain that the broad masses of people of all strata in the north and the south should be given an opportunity to participate in the nationwide patriotic work for national reunification in order to settle the question of the country's reunification in conformity with the will and demand of our people.

The north-south dialogue for national reunification should not be confined to the authorities of the two zones but be held on a national scale. That is why we have proposed convening a Great National Congress composed of representatives of the people from all walks of life—of workers, peasants, working intellectuals, youth and students and soldiers in the northern half, and of workers, peasants, student youth, intellectuals, military men, non-comprador capitalists and petty bourgeoisie in south Korea—and representatives of political parties and social organizations in the north and south, to comprehensively discuss at the congress and solve the question of the country's reunification.

We also maintain that a north-south Confederation should be instituted under a single national nomenclature in order to hasten the country's reunification.

Needless to say, there may be various ways of achieving the complete reunification of the country. Under the prevailing situation, we think that the most reasonable way of reunification is to convene a Great Natonal Congress and realize national unity, and, on this basis, institute the north-south Confederation, leaving the two existing systems in the north and the south as they are for the time being.

In the event of the-north-south Confederation being instituted, it would be good to name the state the Confederal Republic of Koryo after the united state of Koryo which once existed in our territory and was widely known in the world. This will be a good name for the country acceptable to both the north and the south.

The founding of the Confederal Republic of Koryo will open up the decisive phase in preventing national division, bringing about all-round contact and cooperation between north and south and hastening complete reunification.

Further, we maintain that our country should be prevented from being split into two Koreas permanently as a result of freezing the present national division and that north and south should also work together in the field of external activity.

At present we develop state relations with all countries friendly to our Republic on the principles of equality and mutual benefit. But we must resolutely oppose all machinations designed to make use of this in manufacturing two Koreas.

We consider that the north and the south should not enter the UN separately and that if they want to enter the UN before the country's reunification, they should do so as a single state under the name of the Confederal Republic of Koryo, at least after the Confederation is set up.

But apart from the question of admission to the UN, if the Korean question is brought up for discussion at the UN General Assembly, the representative of our Republic should as a matter of course take part in the discussion and have his say as one of the parties concerned.

Our people are homogenous and have lived with the same culture and the same language for ages, and they can never live separated in two.

If our recent five-point policy for national reunification is carried into effect, there will be a great turn in realizing the historic cause of peaceful reunification on the principles set out in the North-South Joint Statement, in compliance with the common desire of our people and the peoples of the world.

The announcement of the five-point policy has shown more distinctly who really opposes division and desires reunification, and who is against reunification and seeks division. The world's public has come to see clearly that the U.S. imperialists and the south Korean authorities are doggedly opposed to the reunification of our country and are working to keep Korea divided indefinitely in two, whereas our Party and the Government of the Republic are making positive efforts to prevent the permanent division of the nation and achieve reunification in conformity with the will and desire of the entire Korean people.

The announcement of our five-point policy has proved to be a telling blow at the separatists within and without. It has blighted the so-called "special statement" of the south Korean authorities right after its pronouncement and laid bare every underhanded plot and trick devised by the U.S. imperialists and their stooges under the slogan of "peaceful reunification."

There is no doubt that our five-point policy will be warmly supported and welcomed by the peoples of an increasing number of countries as the days go by, and that the "two Koreas" plot of the U.S. imperialists and the south Korean authorities will meet with strong protest and denunciation from the world's public.

Our five-point policy is a most fair and reasonable plan acceptable to all who truly love the country and the nation and wish the country's reunification. Its realization is the only way to achieve the independent, peaceful reunification of the country in conformity with the common desire and aspirations of the whole nation.

We should make every effort in the future to carry this policy into effect at the earliest date.

We should widely explain and propagate the five-point policy for national reunification among the entire people in north and south Korea and vigorously rouse them for the sacred struggle for the independent, peaceful reunification of the country.

We should also make it widely known abroad. Thus, we will give greater numbers of people throughout the world a clear understanding of the policy of our Party and the Government of the Republic for independent, peaceful reunification, and steadily increase the number of people who support and sympathize with our people's struggle for national reunification.

The five-point policy for national reunification and our people's revolutionary struggle for its realization are fully justified. Victory will surely go to a people who fight for a righteous cause under the banner of justice. Although at present big obstacles and difficulties lie in the way of our struggle for the independent, peaceful reunification of the country, the internal and external separatists' maneuvering for permanent division will be checked and frustrated and our historic cause of national reunification will certainly be achieved through the brave struggle of the people in north and south Korea with the active support and encouragement of the progressive people of the world.

TALK WITH THE EXECUTIVE DIRECTOR AND CHIEF EDITOR OF IWANAMI PUBLISHING HOUSE IN JAPAN

September 19, 1973

I am very happy, Mr. Midorikawa Toru, that you came to our country and joined us in celebrating the 25th anniversary of the founding of the Democratic People's Republic of Korea.

Your visit to our country is the expression of your deep love for and trust in the Korean people. I am glad to have another Japanese friend like you, and I thank you for your coming to our country.

I also feel grateful to your publishing house for its friendly and brotherly attitude in widely introducing all the achievements made by the DPRK and for many good things it has done for our country out of its sympathetic stand toward us. On your return home, I hope you will convey my best regards to the president and the staff of Iwanami.

Sometime ago, *Sekai* magazine published by Iwanami carried an article entitled *South Korea Today*. I read the whole text. It was very interesting. It offered us plenty of information.

Though we have much information of south Korea, the corruption of the south Korean authorities laid bare in your article infuriates us as Koreans.

It is quite reasonable that you should draw your pen to expose and criticize the crimes of the south Korean authorities and their corruption. By so doing, you are helping to raise the awareness of the Japanese and south Korean peoples and all the rest of people in the world and making a great contribution to strengthening friendship between the peoples of Korea and Japan. Moreover, through this work, you are playing an important role in disseminating progressive ideas throughout the world.

We know well that the editorial staff of *Sekai* magazine and the staff of Iwanami are making great efforts for world progress.

You asked about my impression on the 25th anniversary of the founding of the DPRK. Well, we have just held a plenary meeting of the Party Central Committee, and analyzed the achievements scored in the ideological, technical and cultural revolutions in the last 25 years after the founding of the Republic. Therefore, if I tell you about them, I think it would adequately answer your question. Since I cannot say in a limited time everything discussed for over a week at the plenary meeting, I will just touch briefly on major points.

The last plenary meeting of the Party Central Committee considered that our Party's lines and policies pursued since the founding of the Republic are most correct. Their correctness is conspicuous most recently when the international situation is rapidly changing and developing in a diversified way. Especially our Party's line of independence in politics, self-reliance in economy and self-defense in guarding the nation has been proved quite correct. All our achievements are thanks to the Juche idea consistently maintained by our Party and to the line of independence, self-reliance and self-defense which is the embodiment of this idea.

How correct is our Party's maintenance of the principle of political independence, economic self-reliance and national self-defense has now been corroborated more evidently than ever. At present many countries of the world want to follow the road to independence—in our opinion, not merely the nations of the third world but also those of the second world such as

Japan, Canada and France. We are inclined to think that it is the common aspiration of the people the world over. It is true that the reactionary forces are taking up the policy of following in the wake of great powers. However, almost all the peoples of the world, progressive forces and highly awakened public figures are demanding independence. I think the same is true of Japan, our close neighbor. The great majority of the people, progressive forces and most of the public figures in Japan, except a tiny handful of reactionaries, are all stressing and demanding independence.

As you see, our Party's line of independence has come into being at a time when people in all countries are aspiring for independence, and it is in full accord with the trends of the present time. In other words, it is coincident with the aspiration of the world people, though the independence line of our Party and the Government of the Republic was chosen by the Korean people themselves. Therefore, we can say that we are taking the same road with the progressive people of the world, in keeping with international trends.

This was clearly shown also at the Fourth Summit Conference of Non-Aligned Nations recently held in Algeria with the participation of the heads of states and governments and their representatives from more than 80 nations or more than 100 delegations. Our country was not represented at this conference. However, the conference condemned foreign interference in Korea's internal affairs and the plot to rig up "two Koreas." It adopted a resolution that an end must be put to all forms of foreign interference in Korea's domestic affairs and that the 28th session of the UN General Assembly must decide on the withdrawal of foreign troops occupying south Korea under the UN flag and on the dissolution of the "UN Commission for the Unification and Rehabilitation of Korea." The conference also resolved that Korea must be admitted to the UN after the complete reunification of Korea or after the institution of a north-south Confederation under a single name. We got this information during the last plenary meeting of the Party Central Committee and through this we have been convinced more firmly of the correctness of our Party's line and realized more clearly than ever that many peoples in the world are supporting us.

Not only the non-aligned nations but the peoples of Japan

and many other countries are backing our line of independence. This support and encouragement convinces our people more deeply of the justness of their struggle and inspires our struggle.

We have made great progress not only in the sphere of foreign activity but also in internal affairs.

Our people are united solidly with one mind and one purpose on the basis of the Juche idea. In our country today the tendency to flunkeyism handed down over many years has been eliminated and the firm politico-ideological unity of all people materialized on the basis of the Juche idea. If our Party had been captivated by flunkeyism and had not carved out its destiny with its own efforts, blindly following the policies of other countries, it would not have obtained this politico-ideological unity of all people nor achieved shining victories in the revolution and construction as today.

At the recent plenary meeting of the Party Central Committee we proudly analyzed that despite manifold hardships in its advance over the last 25 years after the founding of the Republic, our Party had been able to gain the brilliant successes as we are witnessing today because it had hewed out its way with its own efforts, using its own brains. We also estimated that the proud successes were possible because our Party's Juche idea and the line of independence, self-reliance and self-defense gripped the hearts of our people, and because all Party, all army and all people accepted and made them part of their own bodies.

Today all our working people are firmly equipped with the Juche idea and giving full play to their creative zeal to carry out their tasks with the attitude of masters. Our Republic has made all these successes in the last 25 years because those who had money donated their money, those with knowledge devoted their knowledge and those with techniques offered their techniques. In other words, they are the fruit of the struggle all our people have waged to overcome hardships by giving full play to their energy and talents. Needless to say, with a few persons' efforts and talents, it would have been impossible to turn our Republic in such a short span of time into a powerful socialist country which is prospering and developing today.

Not only workers and peasants but also the intellectuals who had been well-off before took part in the struggle for the prosperity and progress of the Republic, dedicating all their wisdom. Thanks to our Party's correct policy of intelligentsia, none of the old intellectuals who had joined our revolutionary ranks became a laggard. Many of them fought devotedly to carry through the lines and policies of the Party and the Government to the last moment of their days.

Our Republic has been able to enjoy the present prosperity and progress because all our people, ideologically united as one man, worked in this way with the attitude of masters in order to consolidate their government and make their country richer and stronger.

Much progress has also been made in the sphere of culture.

Right after liberation we began with the work of eradicating illiteracy. When I was Chairman of the Provisional People's Committee of North Korea, we discussed the pencil problem as the first item of the agenda for the committee. We did this immediately after liberation in order to educate our children and wipe out illiteracy, but now, we are considering how to make all the working people acquire a high level of cultural and intellectual attainments—the middle school graduate standard and above—and master at least one kind of technical skill.

Moreover, our Party trained large numbers of new intellectuals, at the same time reeducating the old intellectuals to be working intellectuals who serve the people. The result is that we have now more than 600,000 technicians and specialists. The Party has proposed the goal to increase their ranks to more than one million in the near future and is striving to attain it.

All these successes scored in the development of culture fully show how correct was our Party's cultural policy pursued over the last 25 years since the birth of the Republic and how rapidly the cultural revolution was going on in our country.

We have also made big headway in the economic field.

Of course, we received aids from the fraternal countries for our economic construction. This was not the main thing, however. Our Party persisted in relying on its own internal forces for economic construction.

Now we can say that we have succeeded in building a completely independent national economy. Our economy is not only able to stand firmly on its own feet but also has foundations to develop more rapidly in the future. Today our nation's economy is powerful enough to advance independently and confidently, unaffected by any worldwide economic fluctuations. This has been proved by reality.

At present we are discussing how to develop our economy more quickly. If there is any hardship in our economic development it may arise in the course of our rapid advancement. There is neither economic stagnation nor depression any more. It is a thing of the past now.

We can affirm with great pride and confidence that in the last 25 years following the founding of the Republic, we have made tremendous progress and successes throughout the ideological, cultural and economic realms.

Now our Party is appealing to the entire membership and the working people not to be complacent with the existing successes but to wage an uninterrupted struggle to consolidate them and make a fresh advance.

In order to consolidate the nation's economic foundation and capture the material fortress to satisfy the people's vital demands more fully, all the working people must continue to work hard, without getting intoxicated with the successes or indolent. If we do not strengthen the ideological education of the working people, they may get conceited and lax as they become better off. Therefore, we must guard against any tendency to indolence and selfishness which may be expressed among the working people as they become well-off and must induce all of them to work and live with the collectivist spirit under the slogan: "One for all and all for one." So the recent plenary meeting of the Party Central Committee laid great emphasis on the necessity of ideological struggle against the tendencies to self-conceit and slackness which may breed as cares and worries are removed from our lives, and called upon the whole Party to prevent such tendencies.

You asked me about how the Six-Year-Plan is being carried on in our country. Let me say a few words about it.

Today our workers and farmers have a high spirit to fulfill the Six-Year Plan ahead of time and the whole nation is striving to do so.

The three major tasks of the technical revolution are the crux of the Six-Year Plan. At the last plenary meeting of our Party Central Committee great emphasis was given to the necessity of dynamically carrying on the three major tasks of the technical revolution in order to fulfill the Six-Year Plan successfully.

We are now striving to narrow down the gap between heavy and light work and bring the former closer to the latter. Only when we quickly accomplish the tasks confronting us to diminish the differences between heavy and light work and liberate all the working people from backbreaking labor, can we fulfill the Six-Year Plan before the set time.

It is no easy job to completely eliminate the distinctions between heavy and light work. We intend to reduce their differences to a considerable extent in the near future. Now our country is making steady progress in lessening the differences between heavy and light work. We have already scored a big success in this respect.

In narrowing down these differences and freeing the working people from toilsome work the primary task is that of introducing technological innovations in the mining industry.

We must also put an end to heat-affected work in the realm of industry. What is important here is to introduce automation into production processes and then gradually switch over to telemechanics. Therefore, the Fifth Congress of our Party proposed the development of electronics as a major task in order to introduce automation satisfactorily.

All these problems are by no means simple ones. However, we are capable of solving them one by one.

If we are to fulfill our tasks of the technical revolution, we must study and invent many things for ourselves. We are now exerting much effort for this. In addition, we must also actively introduce foreign techniques. This is not contradictory to self-reliance. Some people regard self-reliance as doing everything entirely on one's own. This is not correct. Self-reliance means to rely on one's own efforts, instead of depending on others. As for the techniques already invented and developed by others we had better introduce them than start research on them by ourselves. In my opinion, adequately learning foreign techniques also conforms with self-reliance. It is wrong to keep the door shut, instead of learning from others. If we inspect technological branches in foreign countries and learn their techniques, we will advance more quickly.

I think most of the indices envisaged under the Six-Year Plan will be attained by 1975. However, we will have to strive continuously to develop our technology.

From now, we must exert much effort for heavy industry.

If we quickly complete construction projects for heavy industry, we will expedite the fulfillment of the tasks assigned to this field. But if we slow down the construction, the fulfillment of these tasks may be somewhat delayed. We are now pressing forward to fulfill the tasks of heavy industry under the Six-Year Plan by the end of 1975. But I am afraid some of the indices of heavy industry might not be achieved before the first half of 1976.

At present light industry is also going well. I think this industry will attain the major goals of the Six-Year Plan next year.

Our country is developing light industry in two directions. Namely, we are developing central and local industries. By developing central industries we mean to build and run the large-scale, modern light industry factories, and by local industries we mean to operate the small and medium-sized light industry factories in localities, using their raw materials.

In 1975 we will fulfill the tasks assigned to light industries, envisaged in the Six-Year Plan.

Now our working people are in high spirits to accomplish the Six-Year Plan ahead of schedule and we have also many favorable conditions. Formerly we traded only with socialist countries but at present, we have trade relations with many capitalist as well as newly independent countries. Particularly, we have closer trade relations with the newly independent nations in the third world.

Next, we are striving to diminish differences between agricultural and industrial work and bring the former closer to the latter. What is important here is to accomplish the tasks advanced in the *Theses on the Socialist Rural Question in Our Country*.

Next year we will mark the tenth anniversary of the announcement of the *Theses on the Socialist Rural Question in Our Country*. We are endeavoring to carry out the tasks put forth in the theses on the occasion of the tenth anniversary. I think that next year we will fulfill almost all the tasks of the theses except those of the ideological revolution.

We are foreseeing that the major tasks of the rural technical revolution proposed by the theses will be almost fulfilled next year.

The irrigation of land in our countryside has long since been completed and the electrification has also been splendidly materialized. We are now striving to complete mechanization.

The theses defines that the number of tractors in the countryside must be increased to 70,000-80,000 (in terms of 15 hp units). The workers at the tractor plants are battling to hit this target by next July.

In our country there are some 1,500,000 *chongbo* of cultivated land where machines are applicable. If 80,000 tractors are produced, we can supply five or six tractors per 100 *chongbo* of land. When 70,000-80,000 tractors are supplied to the countryside, we will have basically satisfied its demands for the machines.

The Six-Year Plan envisages the number of tractors per 100 *chongbo* of arable land to be augmented to six or seven. We think we will be able to attain this goal in 1975. The task of chemicalization of agriculture set forth in the theses will also be fulfilled next year. The theses on the rural question set it as a task to provide each *chongbo* with more than one ton of chemical fertilizer. This goal will be accomplished by the first half of next year. One ton of chemical fertilizer for each *chongbo* is not so bad. Next year the goal of supplying different agricultural chemicals will also be attained. Next year will thus see the fulfillment of the major tasks of the rural technical revolution put forth in the theses.

The prospect of grain production is also fine. As we have just seen in the farming villages, our country is expecting a bumper crop this year. Onchon County which we have just visited was one of the most backward counties before, but now its grain production increases every year. This county's grain production record was 53,000 tons. But they say it will harvest 70,000 tons this year. This county has the goal to produce 73,000 tons of grain under the Six-Year Plan. So, if it produces 3,000 tons more next year, the county will have fulfilled the Six-Year Plan. This is not a very hard job. If just a bit more is turned out at each *chongbo*, that will do. Our rural officials may rest content with the achievements we have made this year. That is why at the last plenary meeting of the Party Central Committee we warned them not to get self-complacent.

In all probability the agricultural goal of the Six-Year Plan will be attained next year. As a whole, our Six-Year Plan is being carried out satisfactorily.

Next, we are waging a struggle to liberate our women from the heavy burden of household chores. This struggle is also being conducted on a nationwide scale. Especially our women are striving to liberate themselves from the toil, displaying a high degree of creativity.

In the battle to free women from the heavy burden of household chores, many successes have already been made. Korean women had carried water jars on their heads over many centuries. But now, with the introduction of water service to many villages, they no longer carry water jars on their heads. When I talk with old women in the countryside, they say through tears of emotion that they had to carry water jars on their heads for so many years, but only in the era of the Workers' Party have they been relieved from this trouble. Indeed, carrying water jars on their heads was a very heavy burden for our women.

The introduction of water service has eliminated the practice of carrying water jars on the heads in the countryside and, moreover, enabled the villagers to drink purified water. The farmers are most delighted at the introduction of water service.

While lessening the women's burdensome work, we have also taken measures to lighten their burden of raising their children. Rearing children is a heavy burden to women. The state has built many nurseries and kindergartens in order to ease this burden.

The children looked after at nurseries and kindergartens are provided with lunch and snack there, though they have breakfast at home. Our women are deeply moved by this solicitude shown by the Party and the state. They say that since all these conditions are guaranteed, they never feel tired from their work.

If you talk with our comrades you will obtain more detailed information about the Six-Year Plan. We are sure that we can succeed in fulfilling this plan. Come again to our country when the Six-Year Plan is completed. You said in the car that in the DPRK one year makes an epoch. When the Six-Year Plan is over, the look of our country will change still further.

You asked about the questions of Korean reunification and the UN, so I will refer to the former in relation to the latter.

As far as the UN is concerned, its Charter is not bad in itself. However, the UN has so far been dominated by great powers; it has been under their control. Therefore, the UN has been unable to work in accordance with its Charter. The UN Charter has not been observed especially because the U.S. imperialists have indulged in power politics and wielded their baton in the United Nations.

But today many newly independent nations and progressive countries have become members of the UN. As I have said, the newly independent nations demand independence. Accordingly, among the UN member states there is an increasing demand that the UN be an organization to ensure every country independence.

If it is to be faithful to its Charter, the UN must be an organization that ensures independence to all countries alike, big or small. And yet we do not mean that the UN is no longer necessary. Many countries are still pinning great hopes on the United Nations.

Of course, should the UN continue to act contrary to its Charter, under the influence of great nations' power politics and their batons, it would lose the confidence of the world's people.

As the people of all countries are now beginning to see through the essence of the U.S. imperialist policies of aggression and neocolonialism, the prestige of U.S. imperialism is being gradually shaken. The baton wielded by it at the UN is also losing its force. At present, many countries are putting up a firm struggle, demanding the UN to act in the spirit of its Charter. In my opinion, the political awakening of the newly independent nations will be decisive to the future functioning of the United Nations.

Now, the south Korean authorities, U.S. imperialism and the Japanese government have been maneuvering toward the simultaneous admission of "two Koreas" to the UN. This is why the problem of admitting "two Koreas" to the UN has been placed on the agenda of the UN General Assembly for discussion this year.

Why have they advanced the proposal on the the simultaneous admission of "two Koreas" to the UN at a time when negotiations are going on between the north and south and no agreement has been reached as yet between the two sides?

This proposal lays bare the real intention of the U.S. imperialists and some of the Japanese reactionaries who have long since schemed to perpetuate the division of Korea. In other words, it fully reveals their ambitions toward Korea.

The proposal on the simultaneous admission of "two Koreas" to the UN is also aimed at forestalling the discussion at the UN General Assembly on the problem of the withdrawal of U.S. troops out of south Korea. This is the main purpose they are pursuing. They advanced this proposal in an attempt to arouse the world's interest in the problem of the simultaneous entry of "two Koreas" into the UN and divert its attention from the question of the withdrawal of U.S. troops from south Korea. The proposal is a trick to achieve this very purpose. In short, it is based on the scheme to keep U.S. troops in south Korea, as they are no longer able to find any excuse for this. In the last analysis, the proposal is designed to attract less attention of many nations at the UN General Assembly to the question of the withdrawal of U.S. troops from south Korea and keep them in south Korea under the UN signboard.

The U.S. imperialists, the Japanese reactionaries and the south Korean puppets also know that they cannot materialize the simultaneous entry of "two Koreas" into the UN. They cannot because one of the two agrees to the entry into the UN while the other disagrees.

However, the U.S. imperialists advanced the proposal on the simultaneous entry of "two Koreas" into the UN in an endeavor to cause polemics over this question and then equivocally skip over the question of the withdrawal of U.S. troops from south Korea. This is a mere conjury to hoodwink the world people. Deceptive tactics cannot last long before their eyes. If you see a juggler's trick more than once, you can fully grasp the secret.

This problem may create a sensation at the UN General Assembly this year. However, the substance of the matter is already being brought to light.

The Fourth Summit Conference of the Non-Aligned Nations held in Algeria declared that Korea should enter into the UN as one, not as two. In my opinion, the countries participating in the conference came to this conclusion because they had seen through the trick of the entry of "two Koreas" into the UN.

The simultaneous admission of "two Koreas" to the UN will never be beneficial to the Korean people. We will never recognize "two Koreas."

The American and the Japanese reactionaries and the south Korean authorities have stubbornly insisted on placing the simultaneous entry of "two Koreas" on the agenda of this year's session of the UN General Assembly also because it is going to consider the admission of East and West Germany to the UN. They want to take advantage of this. The U.S. imperialists are very cunning.

Ours is fundamentally different from the case of East and West Germany. Both of them want separation. Formerly Germany was an aggressor nation. As a result of war, it was divided into two; one became a worker-peasant state, and the other a monopoly-capitalist state. The maintenance of the worker-peasant state in East Germany will, in the long run, serve to weaken the strength of monopoly capital in West Germany. In addition, the adjacent European countries do not want Germany to reunite and become a strong militarist power. Because then Germany may reappear as a force of aggression.

But our case is quite different. We have never invaded any country. Our country was a colony before and then liberated. Our neighbors do not consider that our country would invade others when reunified. Neither the Chinese nor the Soviets nor the Japanese think so. For the Asian countries reunified Korea would be more beneficial than two Koreas antagonistic to each other. The Japanese people have this view, and so have the Chinese and Soviet peoples.

What is most important here is that the Korean people both in the north and south do not want the division of their country. Koreans are a homogenous nation which has a long history of a unified state. That is why they never want themselves to be divided.

It is only a handful of south Korea's reactionary forces, the pro-American reactionaries in Japan and the U.S. imperialists who want the partition of our country. The U.S. imperialists want this in order to keep south Korea as their military base.

Why should our country be divided when the overwhelming majority of nations want to see Korea reunified? We have had enough suffering of national division in the last 28 years. Why must we continue to have this suffering? We are resolutely opposed to the entry of "two Koreas" into the UN. We believe that the countries sympathetic toward us are also against it.

Now let me touch briefly on your question about how to form

the Confederal Republic of Koryo.

We proposed that the Confederation be named Confederal Republic of Koryo because once on our territory there existed a unified state named Koryo. It is a good name acceptable to both sides. If we named the confederal state the Democratic People's Republic of Korea or the "Republic of Korea," it would mean to force one side's demand on the other. For this reason we proposed naming it Confederal Republic of Koryo so that both the north and south may accept it on the principle of equality.

Our Confederation proposal is that a confederal state be formed, leaving the present social systems in the north and south as they are for the time being. So the main thing here is that the two sides trust each other and achieve great national unity.

In our opinion, it is necessary first to convene a Great National Congress and settle matters concerning the country's reunification through extensive consultations. This congress must discuss the question of eliminating military confrontation and removing tension between the north and south. In order to solve this question, it is necessary to take a number of measures already proposed by us, such as the reduction of armed forces of the north and south. This will create conditions for mutual trust and national amity between the two sides.

We also hold that there should be overall collaboration and interchange between the north and south in the political, economic, cultural and all other realms.

Despite the institutional differences between the north and south there are many problems on which we can work together now. Both sides can jointly exploit the mineral resources and make use of the results of scientific and technological researches. Overall collaboration is realizable in many other fields.

If the north and south materialize all-round collaboration and interchange in different spheres, conditions will be created for the two sides to understand and trust each other in this course, and as the time goes by, their mutual understanding will deepen. Then the two sides will be able to have a correct understanding of each other's system, and this will help remove the fear still entertained by some south Koreans for the socialist system in the northern half of the Republic. Further, if, through the north-south collaboration, right is distinguished from wrong, the latter eliminated and the former encouraged, favorable conditions will be created-for achieving great national unity.

Since ours is a single nation which has lived with the same culture and the same language through many centuries, we will understand each other quickly once the north and south collaborate.

All we are doing today is for the benefit of our nation. We have done nothing which conflicts with the interests of our nation. We have never sold our national interests. We are always doing all we can to protect and safeguard our nation's interests.

Quite contrary to this, the south Korean authorities are selling our national interests. We cannot tolerate it.

Should they collaborate with us the south Korean authorities can solve many problems without selling the interests of the nation. Let me cite an example. At present they are exporting huge manpower, including nurses and miners. Instead of this, if they collaborate with us, they will be able to solve their problems of livelihood.

We are proposing to institute the north-south Confederation on the basis of the mutual understanding between the two sides and of the great national unity through these different measures.

At present the south Korean people are criticizing their authorities for their excessive irregularities and corruptions. The south Korean authorities are apprehensive lest these misdeeds should be brought to light once they collaborate with us. We have repeatedly made clear that if the south Korean authorities frankly admit their crimes against the country and people and desist from treacheries, their past crimes will be condoned. If they assure that they will not commit irregularities and corruptions any more, we will not be particular about their past doings. However, if the south Korean authorities continue to indulge in them, they will inevitably be criticized and condemned not only by the people in south Korea but by the whole Korean people.

Since the detailed measures for the formation of the Confederal Republic of Koryo have to be decided upon through consultations between the north and south, I cannot make any further remarks.

And as regards your question about the North-South Coordination Commission, I have nothing to say because the Premier of the Administration Council dwelt on it in detail in his report made at the central meeting to celebrate the 25th anniversary of the founding of the Republic. The views he expressed were not his own but our Party Central Committee's.

Our position is that the north and south must continue to promote contact and dialogue, instead of keeping the door closed. The matter depends entirely on the attitude of the south Korean authorities. We have to wait and see how they will react.

Now, I would like to refer to the relations between our country and Japan.

As we have stated on a number of occasions, the normalization of state relations between our country and Japan is entirely up to the Japanese government's attitude.

At present, we are not so much concerned about the normalization of state relations between our country and Japan. The normalized relationship will not settle all problems arising between our country and Japan. We cannot say that once the Japanese embassy is set up in Pyongyang or our embassy in Tokyo, everything will have been settled with regard to the relations between our country and Japan.

What is important in improving the relations between our country and Japan is that the two countries should deepen their mutual understanding and, especially, that the Japanese government should stop its hostile policy toward our country. Our country and Japan do not properly understand each other. In our opinion, the two countries should first have a better understanding of each other.

You said that the visit of our Mansudae Art Troupe to Japan had given a great help to increasing mutual understanding between the two countries. I thank you for this estimation.

While our Mansudae Art Troupe was staying in Japan, the political parties, social organizations, individual figures of different strata and the mass of people expressed their active support for our people. They showed hospitality to our artistes, as their friends and comrades, and firmly supported our people's struggle to reunify the country. It means that our two peoples have a very amicable relationship. We have an old saying: A good neighbor is better than a cousin. I wonder whether you have a similar Japanese proverb.

We believe that despite their different social systems, our country and Japan can have good-neighbor relations and further cement friendship and solidarity between their peoples. If the Japanese government has no objection, from now on, we will make arrangements for more visits to Japan, similar to the Mansudae Art Troupe's. This will help develop the friendly relations between the Korean and Japanese peoples.

ANSWERS TO QUESTIONS PUT BY THE CHIEF EDITOR OF THE YUGOSLAV NEWSPAPER VECERNJE NOVOSTI

February 22, 1974

Question: *Yugoslavia knows well and supports the consistent efforts of the Government of the Democratic People's Republic of Korea for the country's independent and peaceful reunification.*

Would you please tell me of the present political situation in the context of the dialogue between the north and south and of the prospect of Korean reunification?

Answer: As you know, as a result of the persevering efforts of our Party and the Government of the Republic for the country's independent and peaceful reunification, the dialogue started between the north and the south of Korea and in July 1972 the North-South Joint Statement was made public with the three principles of independence, peaceful reunification and great national unity as its keynote.

After the announcement of the North-South Joint Statement

the Government of our Republic put forward a number of specific and reasonable proposals to translate it into practice and made all sincere efforts for the successful progress of the dialogue. However, owing to the maneuvers of the splittists within and without, the north-south dialogue has been deadlocked and great difficulties and obstacles have been laid in the way of the reunification of the fatherland.

Even after the announcement of the North-South Joint Statement the south Korean authorities, instigated by the U.S. intensified war preparations and fascist repression, more stubbornly sticking to the policy of dependence on outside forces in total contravention of the principles clarified in the statement. Then, in June last year, they made public the so-called "special statement," declaring to the world a "policy" to perpetuate the division of the nation.

At the UN General Assembly last year the U.S. and Japanese reactionaries and the south Korean authorities put forward a proposal for simultaneous UN membership for "two Koreas" and employed every conceivable trick to force it through. But this scheme was completely frustrated by the just struggle of the socialist countries, non-aligned states and many other countries of the world which support our Party's policy of independent and peaceful reunification. The UN General Assembly expressed full support to the three principles of national reunification laid down in the North-South Joint Statement and adopted a resolution on the dissolution of the "United Nations Commission for the Unification and Rehabilitation of Korea," a U.S. instrument for aggression and interference in another's internal affairs. This is a great victory for the policy of our Party and the Government of the Republic for independent and peaceful reunification and a staggering defeat for those who seek the permanent division of Korea.

The south Korean authorities' maneuvers to perpetuate the division of the nation at the instigation of the imperialist forces have caused national indignation of the entire Korean people who aspire for the reunification of the fatherland and have inevitably roused them to the struggle against the splittists within and without.

Harsh as fascist repression is today, the south Korean student youth and personages of all strata are valiantly fighting to bring about the democratization of south Korean society, save the country and the people and reunify the fatherland.

We put forward the five-point proposition: to remove the military confrontation and ease the tension between the north and the south, to materialize many-sided collaboration and exchange between the north and the south, to convoke a Great National Congress comprising representatives of people of all strata, political parties and social organizations in the north and the south, to institute a north-south Confederation under the single name of the Confederal Republic of Koryo and to enter the UN under the single name—the Confederal Republic of Koryo. This is an epochal save-the-nation plan aimed at preventing the division of the nation and reunifying the fatherland.

The only obstacle to the solution of the question of our country's reunification today is the maneuvers of the splittists within and without to keep our nation indefinitely divided. If the question of our country's reunification is to be solved smoothly, an end must be put first to the "two Koreas" plot of the U.S. and Japanese reactionaries and their interference in Korea's domestic affairs and the south Korean authorities must renounce the policy of dependence on outside forces and honestly observe the principles of the North-South Joint Statement. The south Korean authorities must discontinue their fascist repression of the south Korean people who demand democracy and the country's independent and peaceful reunification and open the way for representatives of all parties, groupings and people of all strata in south Korea to participate directly in the solution of the question of reunification. Only then will the dialogue between the north and the south make a smooth progress and the solution of the question of the country's reunification be facilitated quickly.

Because of foreign interference we are now going through turns and twists in the solution of the question of the country's reunification. However, we will definitively win the cause of national reunification through an indefatigable united struggle of all the north and south Korean people with the active support and encouragement of the progressive people the world over.

Availing myself of this opportunity, I would like to express my deep thanks to the Government of the Socialist Federal Republic of Yugoslavia and the Yugoslav people for their active support to the DPRK Government's policy for independent and peaceful reunification and to the Korean people's struggle to put it into effect.

Question: *We know well that the Korean people have converted their country into a powerful socialist industrial state by registering great achievements in the socialist construction of the country.*

Would you please tell us what are the motive force and basic factor of these achievements?

Answer: All victories and successes we have gained in the socialist revolution and socialist construction have been possible thanks to the correct leadership of the Workers' Party of Korea, the unbreakable unity of the Party and the masses of the people and the high revolutionary enthusiasm and creative struggle of our people.

Our Party takes the Juche idea as the immovable guideline in leading the revolutionary struggle and the work of construction. At each stage of revolutionary development, basing ourselves on the Juche position, we worked out a line and policy to conform to the specific conditions of our country and strove to carry our revolution through to completion by our own efforts, refusing to depend on others.

Because we established Juche and relied on our own efforts, we have been able to lead our revolution along the most straight path, surmounting manifold difficulties and trials.

Each time we encountered difficulties and trials in the course of the revolutionary struggle and the work of construction, we placed trust in the masses of the people and consulted them and pulled through the difficulties and trials facing us by bringing their strength and wisdom into play.

As we strengthened political work among the working people and firmly armed them with the Juche idea, they took the Party's policies to heart and dedicated all their strength and wisdom to the struggle to carry them out.

Today all the workers, cooperative farmers and working intellectuals of our country are firmly united around the Party with one ideology and purpose. They are working and living, full of revolutionary passion and optimism.

The entire people are firmly rallied and welded around the Party politically and ideologically and are working with revolutionary enthusiasm and creative initiative. Herein lie the sources of our invincibility and the solid guarantee for all victories.

Our Party will continue to develop the revolution and construction uninterruptedly at a high tempo by more firmly uniting the masses of the people around itself and giving full rein to their inexhaustible creativity.

Question: *Yugoslavia supports the position of the DPRK Government which is striving to liquidate the consequences of imperialist interference in Korea's domestic affairs and force the U.S. troops to withdraw from south Korea in order to achieve the independent and peaceful reunification of the country.*

Friendship and bilateral cooperation between the DPRK and the SFRY are now developing successfully in all spheres. But it seems that much still remains to be done in this regard.

What is your opinion about the prospects of further development of friendship and cooperation between the Korean and Yugoslav peoples?

Answer: Today the relations of friendship and cooperation between the DPRK and the SFRY are developing more and more excellently. Between our two countries visits and contacts are becoming frequent and liaison and cooperation are increasing in all spheres. We are satisfied with the ever-strengthening bonds of friendship between the Parties, governments and peoples of the two countries. You said that much still remains to be done for the development of friendly relations between Korea and Yugoslavia, and we also think so.

From now, the Government of our Republic will make every possible effort to further expand and develop the relations of friendship and cooperation with the Socialist Federal Republic of Yugoslavia in many fields of politics, economy and culture.

I express the firm belief that the friendly relations between Korea and Yugoslavia will continue to develop favorably on the principle of Marxism-Leninism and on the principles of complete equality, independence, mutual respect and noninterference in each other's internal affairs.

At the same time, I sincerely wish greater successes to the

fraternal Yugoslav people who are struggling for the prosperity
and progress of their country under the leadership of the Yugoslav League of Communists.

Question: *Yugoslavia, an active member of the non-alignment movement, and other non-aligned nations hold the idea
that international problems cannot be solved by a group of nations or by great powers and that they must become a matter of
concern for the entire international community. This idea and
practice based on it must prevail in international relations.*

*Peace is indivisible and nations, both big and small, should
participate on an equal footing in guaranteeing it.*

*This is what was pointed out in the resolutions of the Fourth
Conference of Non-Aligned States. The countries of the non-
aligned world are taking this stand as regards the Middle East
crisis and other international events of urgency.*

*In this connection, we shall be grateful if you will tell us your
opinion about the activities of the non-aligned states and the
results of the Fourth Conference of Non-Aligned States held in
Algiers.*

Answer: The activities of non-aligned states have had a great
influence on the struggle against all forms of aggression and
interference, subjugation and inequality and for the achievement of peace and a fair settlement of international issues.

It is very good that the forces of non-aligned states are growing and their role is increasing.

It has now become an irresistible trend of the times that imperialism is going downhill and many countries of the world
claim complete equality in international relations and advance
along the road to independence.

The activities of the non-aligned states are powerful, for they
reflect this trend of the present time.

The Fourth Summit Conference of Non-Aligned States held
in Algeria last year was an event of epochal significance in the
struggle of the peoples of the third world against imperialism,
colonialism, old and new, and racism and for national liberation
and sovereignty, peace and social progress.

The conference convincingly demonstrated the firm unity of
the peoples of the third world and made a great contribution to
the further promotion of the national-liberation movement and

preservation and consolidation of world peace.

Special mention must be made of the fact that the Fourth Summit Conference of Non-Aligned States unanimously adopted a resolution on the termination of all forms of foreign interference in Korea's internal affairs, the withdrawal of foreign troops occupying south Korea under the UN flag, the dissolution of the "UNCURK" and the admission of Korea to the UN under a single state name, either after the country's complete reunification or after the institution of a Confederation. This was a forceful encouragement to our people battling for national reunification and a hard blow to the imperialists and their lackeys bent on obstructing the reunification of Korea and perpetuating its division.

The Korean people highly estimate the results of the Fourth Summit Conference of Non-Aligned States and express heartfelt gratitude to all the countries for their sincere efforts for the adoption of the resolution on the Korean question at the conference and for their manifestation of active support and encouragement for our cause of independent and peaceful reunification.

For their common plight in the past when they were maltreated and oppressed and for their common struggle of today against imperialism and colonialism and for the creation of a new life, the Korean people are closely united with the peoples of the third world and actively support and encourage the latter's national-liberation movement and revolutionary struggle. The Korean people will, in the future, too, always remain firmly welded with the peoples of the third world in the common cause of peace and democracy, national independence and social progress, holding aloft the revolutionary banner of anti-imperialist struggle.

Question: *The imperialist forces of aggression are openly interfering in the internal affairs of Asian countries, constantly threatening peace in this part of the world.*

What should be done to turn Asia into a secure continent and what is the prerequisite?

What are the most fundamental features of the recent political developments on the Asian continent?

Answer: What is characteristic of the recent development of

the Asian situation is that the struggle of peoples against imperialist aggression and intervention and for national independence and the independent development of the countries is being intensified as never before, while the imperialists' maneuvers for aggression and intervention in this region are going into total bankruptcy.

The overwhelming majority of the Asian peoples have already cast off the yoke of colonial slavery and won national independence and are fighting vigorously against imperialist aggression and intervention under the banner of anti-imperialism and independence.

The U.S. imperialists are running up against the powerful resistance of peoples everywhere in Asia and are being chased out.

However, this never means that the imperialists have been completely destroyed in Asia or will no longer commit a crime of aggression.

Stepping up its maneuvers toward aggression and intervention against the Asian countries, the U.S. is craftily working to attain its aggressive aim by means of making Asians fight Asians in accordance with the notorious "Nixon doctrine."

In order to prevent a new war and remove tension in Asia and turn it into a continent of peace, it is necessary, above all, to drive the U.S. imperialists off all parts of Asia and bar them from suppressing the national-liberation movement of peoples in this region and interfering in the internal affairs of other countries.

At the same time, the expansion of Japanese militarism revived under the aegis of the U.S. and its ambition for overseas aggression must be thwarted and frustrated.

The Asian people know well from historical experience that only through their own struggle can they repulse imperialist aggression and intervention and achieve national independence and the security of their countries.

All the progressive people of Asia will certainly build a new Asia, peaceful and prosperous, in the future by keeping up the persistent struggle against all maneuvers of the imperialists for aggression and intervention, rallied close under the banner of anti-imperialism and independence.

THE PEOPLES OF THE THIRD WORLD WHO ADVANCE UNDER THE UPLIFTED BANNER OF INDEPENDENCE WILL CERTAINLY WIN THEIR REVOLUTIONARY CAUSE

Speech at the Pyongyang Mass Rally to Welcome Houari Boumedienne, President of the Council of Revolution and Chairman of the Council of Ministers of the Algerian Democratic and People's Republic, *March 4, 1974*

Your Excellency esteemed President Houari Boumedienne,
Esteemed guests from Algeria,
Dear comrades and friends,

The people of all strata in Pyongyang city have gathered here today, overjoyed to meet the Algerian friends, goodwill envoys who have come from the far-off African continent.

First, in the name of the Central Committee of the Workers' Party of Korea, the Government of the Democratic People's Republic of Korea and the Korean people, I would like again to warmly welcome the visit to our country by Your Excellency Houari Boumedienne, President of the Council of Revolution and Chairman of the Council of Ministers of the Algerian Democratic and People's Republic and your party.

Allow me also to send, through you, the warm, fraternal greetings of the Korean people to the heroic Algerian people.

The current visit to our country by Your Excellency President

Houari Boumedienne, the outstanding leader of the Algerian revolution, a prominent anti-imperialist fighter of the third world and our most intimate friend, strikingly demonstrates the militant friendship and solidarity firmly established between the peoples of Korea and Algeria and constitutes an epochal event which strengthens and develops them to a new, higher stage.

Our people cherish particularly friendly sentiments toward the Algerian people and hold in high esteem Your Excellency Houari Boumedienne, the leader of the Algerian revolution, for the community of their past struggles, the armed struggles against imperialism which culminated in the attainment of national liberation and independence, and for the identity of their present struggles to accelerate the building of a new society along an independent path after independence.

The friendship between the peoples of Korea and Algeria is a genuine friendship between revolutionary comrades-in-arms forged long ago in the flames of fierce struggle against foreign imperialist aggressors. This friendship is also an embodiment of the militant friendship between the brotherly peoples in Asia and Africa fighting against all forms of aggression and subjugation and for defending their Juche-based stand and sovereignty.

Though geographically far away from the Algerian people, our people always follow with deep interest their struggle to build a new life.

Through our present meeting with the Algerian friends, we have come to acquaint ourselves better with the wonderful successes achieved in building a new society by the Algerian people who won national independence through their heroic armed struggle.

A people who have cut off the chains of imperialism, colonialism and become the master of the country can, indeed, work miracles.

The Algerian people, under the correct leadership of the Council of Revolution headed by Your Excellency President Houari Boumedienne, their outstanding leader, have carried out important socio-economic transformations under the militant slogan of self-reliance. In Algeria, factories, enterprises and companies formerly owned by foreign imperialist monopolies have been nationalized; the foundations of an independent national economy are being firmly laid; the look of the countryside is also being changed radically; and education and culture are developing on new lines.

All the changes that have taken place in Algeria in only a little more than ten years after independence are the precious fruition of the firm determination and vigorous labor efforts of the Algerian people to build a rich and strong, sovereign and independent state through the mobilization of their own strength and resources.

We admire the big successes made by the Algerian people in the industrial, agrarian and cultural revolutions now under way, and rejoice over their successes as our own.

It is very good that the Algerian people are fighting dynamically under the motto of the three revolutions, industrial, agrarian and cultural. This shows that they are playing the role of a pioneer in hewing the road to progress as the people of a fledgling independent state.

Now the Algerian people are fighting to carry out the Second Four-Year Plan with a visible prospect of the stage of building a modern state based on socialist economy in a few years to come.

The Algerian Democratic and People's Republic has carried through the just line of developing an independent national economy, with the result that she can now carry out her independent lines and policies, not wavering under any pressure in the international arena.

The progressive people throughout the world highly esteem the positive role played by the Algerian Democratic and People's Republic in achieving the unity of the peoples of the third world, holding fast to the revolutionary principle in the anti-imperialist, anti-colonialist struggle and pursuing a policy of non-alignment in the external spheres.

The Algerian Government and people are resolutely struggling against the U.S. imperialists and the Israeli Zionists backed by them and for the restoration of the legitimate rights of the Palestinian people and the dignity of the Arab peoples.

The Algerian people are also giving support, both material and moral, to the national liberation struggle of the African peoples and making a great contribution to the anti-imperialist revolutionary movement of the oppressed peoples the world over.

Historical experience shows that if newly independent peoples are to defend the gains of revolution and attain the prosperity of their countries and nations, they should destroy the old colonial ruling machine and set up a new, progressive social system, smash the subversive machinations of the foreign imperialists and domestic reactionary forces and deprive them of their economic footholds, and build an independent national economy and national culture.

The wonderful reality achieved in Algeria thanks to the energetic activities of Your Excellency President Houari Boumedienne affords a good example to confirm this truth.

We are very happy to have such brave and revolutionary comrades-in-arms as the Algerian people on the African continent.

We sincerely hope that the brotherly Algerian people who are advancing toward socialism under the uplifted banner of anti-imperialism and independence will gain still greater successes in their future struggle.

Comrades and friends,

Today it is an irresistible trend of the times that the world's people are taking the path to independence.

Hundreds of millions of people in Asia, Africa and Latin America have courageously risen in a sacred liberation struggle, firmly taking their destiny in their hands, and are dynamically forging ahead along the path to independence and self-support in order to consolidate and develop the national independence and gains of revolution they have already won.

Independence is each nation's right; no nation wants to be subjugated by anybody or to allow its dignity to be trampled underfoot. Independence is a prerequisite for national welfare and honor and a nation with an independent spirit alone can achieve genuine independence and prosperity.

The exploited and oppressed peoples who had groaned for a long time under imperialist, colonialist tyranny have bravely fought for freedom, liberation and national independence. As a result, ours is now changing into an era in which the oppressed and maltreated peoples are taking their place on the stage of history as masters, whereas the imperialists are destined to fall like the setting sun.

The historic Fourth Summit Conference of Non-Aligned States held in Algeria last year mirrored this very fundamental change in the development of our time and furnished vivid proof of the powerful influence being exerted by the third world upon the present development of international relations.

Resorting to more crafty double-dealing tactics in an attempt to find a way to save themselves from their doom, the imperialists headed by U.S. imperialism are trying to swallow up small nations one by one while improving their relations with big countries, and maneuvering to make Asians fight among themselves in Asia, Africans fight among themselves in Africa and Latin Americans fight among themselves in Latin America.

However, neither war of aggression and armed suppression nor double-dealing tactics and neocolonialist policy can save the imperialists from their doom or check the trend of today when the world's people are following the road to independence.

This is well proved by the fact that the imperialists suffered one ignominious defeat after another everywhere in Asia, Africa and Latin America including Korea and Algeria, Vietnam and Cuba.

During the Middle East War in October last year the Arab countries dealt heavy blows at U.S. imperialism and the Israeli Zionists, with more united efforts than ever before.

The Arab nations have taken a resolute action: laying an embargo on the export of oil to the imperialists supporting the Israeli aggressors. This has driven the Western world into an economic crisis which is getting out of hand.

The just struggle of the Arab peoples including the Palestinian people against the Israeli aggressors is enlisting the support and sympathy of the peoples the world over.

The Arab peoples will continue to fight resolutely until they completely liberate their occupied territory and restore the legitimate rights of the Palestinian people and will certainly win final victory in this struggle.

Ever mounting among the peoples of the third world today is a struggle to destroy the economic foothold of the imperialist monopolies and regain the usurped natural resources of their countries not only for defending political sovereignty but also achieving economic independence.

On the African continent a widespread struggle is being fought to wipe out the remnants of colonialism in accordance with the joint resolution of the Organization of African Unity; in many Southeast Asian countries a mass struggle is being waged against the U.S. policy of reducing those countries to military bases and the economic aggression by Japan; and in Latin American countries a struggle is being intensified against the U.S. domination and control and for defending national sovereignty, natural resources and territorial waters.

Sometime ago Your Excellency Houari Boumedienne, as Chairman of the Summit Conference of Non-Aligned States, proposed to convene a special session of the UN General Assembly aimed to settle the problems of international economic relations including those of fuel and raw materials. This is an important measure to correctly settle those problems, which have so far involved the sacrifice of the interests of the third world peoples, on the principles of complete equality and independence.

The Islamic Summit Conference held sometime ago in Lahore, Pakistan, demonstrated once again the unshakable resolve of the peoples of the third world to advance, taking their destiny into their own hands.

The time has gone, never to return, when the imperialists could freely oppress and plunder the peoples of the third world and bargain about and decide on their destiny behind the scene.

At present the imperialist world is undergoing the most acute economic fluctuation after the Second World War and is writhing in greater agony, faced with a general crisis. Now it is the oppressed people who have a say on the world scene.

We are convinced that the peoples of all countries, small or poor, in Asia, Africa, Latin America and the rest of the world can defeat imperialism and achieve the final victory of the revolution if they, in firm unity, administer hard blows at and bring pressure to bear upon it everywhere giving it no breathing space.

To secure victory for the cause of peace and democracy, national independence and socialism and to build independent, prosperous and new Asia, Africa and Latin America, the Korean people will, in the future, too, actively support and encourage the anti-imperialist revolutionary struggle and the national-liberation struggle of the fighting Indochinese and Arab peoples and the rest of the tri-continental peoples and all other peoples of the world and strengthen militant solidarity with them in every way.

Comrades and friends,

The Korean people have waged a protracted struggle to accomplish their cause of national liberation.

We have been able to lead the revolution and construction along a straight road to victory, because we have pursued independent lines and policies with the Juche idea as our guiding principle ever since the days of the anti-Japanese armed struggle.

Even under the difficult conditions after liberation in which their country was divided into the north and the south and they came to directly stand opposed to U.S. imperialism, the chieftain of world reaction, our people established Juche and worked out their salvation by their own efforts under the leadership of the Workers' Party of Korea. This enabled them to creditably carry out the democratic revolution, the socialist revolution and the historic task of socialist industrialization in a short span of time and turn their one-time backward country into a socialist industrial state with solid foundations of an independent national economy.

Today in our country the whole Party, the whole country and the entire people are launching themselves into the grand socialist construction for fulfilling the huge tasks of the Six-Year Plan ahead of schedule and scaling a new higher peak of socialism and the entire working people are effecting a great revolutionary upsurge in the Chollima advance on all fronts, holding high the banner of the three revolutions, ideological, technical and cultural.

The steady development of the economy at a high rate in our country at a time when the Western capitalist world is being severely shaken, driven into an acute economic crisis previously unknown, demonstrates with added proof the great vitality of our Party's line of building an independent national economy and the superiority of the socialist system of our country.

In the struggle for the achievement of the country's reunification, the long-cherished desire of our nation, too, we have maintained consistently the independent stand: our national problem must be solved by ourselves, resolutely rejecting the attempts to rely on outside forces.

Today the Korean question, after all, boils down to the question of whether reunification or division, whether one Korea or two Koreas.

The entire Korean people unanimously aspire to the reunification of their country.

But the great powers want the division of our country. To divide and rule is an old method of imperialism.

The U.S. imperialists and the Japanese militarists seek the permanent division of Korea, the former to reduce south Korea to their permanent colonial military base and the latter to take hold of south Korea as their permanent commodity market.

Big obstacles are still lying in the way of the reunification of our country even after the publication of the July 4 North-South Joint Statement, owing to the U. S. and Japanese reactionaries' maneuvers of intervention and their stooges' country-selling, treacherous acts.

These days the nation-splitting machinations of the south Korean rulers and their acts of provocation against the northern half of the Republic have reached a more intolerable extent.

The south Korean rulers are intensifying their fascist suppression of the south Korean people as never before, arresting and imprisoning at random the south Korean youths and students and conscientious intellectuals and even religious figures because they have demanded peaceful reunification, and are turning the whole of south Korea into a horrible prison.

In an effort to cover up these criminal acts of theirs and divert the attention of the people elsewhere, the south Korean rulers have committed such premeditated military provocations as spy ship infiltration in the West Sea and, capitalizing on it, are raising a wholesale clamor about the "threat of aggression from the north" and deliberately increasing tensions between the north and the south.

It must not be overlooked here that the U.S. imperialists, in step with the provocations of the south Korean bellicose elements, have sent repeatedly high-speed, high-altitude reconnaissance planes into the air space of the northern half of the Republic to commit espionage acts and have openly declared that they would further increase military aid to south Korea.

All these abnormal developments in our country show that the splittists within and without are, in fact, leading the north-south relationship back to where it was before the announcement of the North-South Joint Statement and driving the situation to the brink of war.

It has become clearer now who in Korea is grinding the sword of aggression under the cloak of "peace" and who is seeking the perpetuation of split under the cloak of "reunification."

Those who love the country and the nation should not tolerate the maneuvers of the U. S. and Japanese reactionaries to convert south Korea into a permanent colony, but compel the U.S. troops out of south Korea, forestall the infiltration of the Japanese militarists and actively turn out to build a sovereign, reunified and independent Korea.

What is the use of holding the north-south dialogue, if our nation is to live divided? The north-south dialogue must be conducted for the purpose of achieving the reunification.

If the south Korean authorities really want the reunification, they should retract the "special statement" of June last year advocating the membership of two Koreas for the United Nations and approach the talks for reunification in conformity with the interests of the whole nation.

And they should not come forward with such a proposal as a "non-aggression pact" devoid of any guarantee for peace, but accept our proposal for concluding a peace agreement.

The so-called "non-aggression pact" suggested by the south Korean authorities sometime ago is merely designed to flout the nation with the question of reunification.

As is generally known to the world, it is not the south Korean authorities but the U.S. commander acting as "UN commander" who holds the commanding power over the south Korean armed forces and it is also the U. S. imperialists who have their grip on guns, rifles and all other means of war. Under these conditions it is utterly ridiculous for the empty-handed south Korean rulers to propose us to conclude a "non-aggression pact," leaving the U. S. imperialist aggressor forces to stay in south Korea. Their proposal is not worth discussing at all.

In view of the fact that the south Korean authorities still persist in splitting machinations, we can hardly believe that they came out to the dialogue in good faith to achieve reunification.

That is why we think that for its peaceful solution the question of reunification of the country should not be discussed only between the authorities of the north and the south but be referred to the entire nation for discussion.

In this connection, we propose once again to convene a Great National Congress or a North-South Political Consultative Meeting participated in by the representatives of all political parties and social organizations and personages of all strata in the north and south, apart from the existing North-South Coordination Commission. This is the only way for realizing the reunification of Korea.

The question of Korea's reunification should be settled by the Koreans themselves; this cannot be solved by any big powers or any other countries.

The present situation urgently demands that we further intensify the struggle against the splittists in order to prevent the division of the country and realize the peaceful reunification of the country. This is a struggle to decide whether to save or betray the nation.

If the south Korean authorities reject the independent and peaceful reunification of the country and attempt to frabricate two Koreas, persistently clinging to the policy of dependence upon outside forces, they will meet their destruction, leaving behind them the indelible disgrace as traitors.

The south Korean people are now fighting courageously for freedom and democratic rights and the independent and peaceful reunification of the country, not yielding to the harsh fascist suppression by the south Korean rulers.

The struggle of the south Korean people is a patriotic struggle for saving the country and the nation and reunifying the fatherland and a just struggle directly related to the vital interests of the nation. That is why our Party and the Government of our Republic will always actively support the revolutionary struggle of the south Korean people with might and main.

Our support to the revolutionary struggle of the south Korean people is by no means an "interference in another's internal affairs," but it is for solving by ourselves the internal affairs of our nation. As one and the same nation, we regard it as our natural duty to support the revolutionary struggle of the south Korean people.

In order to remove the tensions and prevent war in Korea, the U. S. imperialists and the Japanese militarists should not protect the present south Korean authorities who are indulging in fascist repression and war provocation maneuvers but desist from their interference in the internal affairs of our country.

As an important link in the worldwide anti-imperialist national-liberation struggle, our people's struggle for national reunification enjoys ever greater support and sympathy in the international arena.

The Fourth Summit Conference of Non-Aligned States held in Algeria last year adopted with unanimous approval a resolution fully conforming to our five-point proposition of national reunification. This is convincing proof that our people's struggle for national reunification enjoys full support of the progressive people all over the world.

In keeping with this world trend the UN General Assembly last year rejected the proposal of the U.S. and the south Korean authorities for the entry of "two Koreas" into the United Nations designed for the perpetuation of the division of Korea and adopted a decision on dissolving the "United Nations Commission for the Unification and Rehabilitation of Korea," the U.S. imperialists' tool of aggression. This is a great victory for our people and a common victory for the world peace-loving people.

We voice our conviction that in the future, too, the peoples of socialist countries and all the progressive people throughout the world including the Asian, African and Latin American peoples will render active support to the just struggle of our people for the peaceful reunification of the fatherland and will deal a collective blow both at the wild ambition of the imperialists to split our nation, a single nation, into two forever and at their stooges' country-selling, treacherous acts.

The Algerian Democratic and People's Republic has made positive efforts for the victory of the righteous struggle of our people in the international arena, always regarding our cause as its own, and, especially, extended great support to us at the Summit Conference of Non-Aligned States and the 28th Session of the United Nations General Assembly. Our people will always remember this.

Allow me to take this opportunity to express once again our deep thanks to Your Excellency President Houari Boumedienne and the Algerian Government and people for the unstinted support and encouragement they extend to the policy of our

Party and the Government of our Republic for the independent and peaceful reunification of the country and the struggle of our people for its implementation.

The militant solidarity and the relations of fraternal friendship and cooperation between the Korean and Algerian peoples will be brought to overall efflorescence and development in all fields, political, economic and cultural, in the future. The friendship and mutual cooperation between Korea and Algeria are of important significance not only for defense of the sovereignty and independence of the two countries but also for the growth of the anti-imperialist, revolutionary forces as a whole.

Both the Korean people and the Algerian people will always fight shoulder to shoulder for the victory of the anti-imperialist common cause, as comrades-in-arms and brothers who have glorious revolutionary traditions and hold aloft the banner of independence.

Long live the indestructible militant friendship and solidarity between the Korean and Algerian peoples!

Long live the solidarity among the progressive peoples of Asia, Africa and Latin America and the rest of the world!

Long live the Algerian Democratic and People's Republic headed by Your Excellency President Houari Boumedienne!